CFA Institute

CW01677914

PORTFOLIO MANAGEMENT

CFA® Program Curriculum

2026 • LEVEL I • VOLUME 9

WILEY

ISBN 978-1-961409-91-0

May 2025

Please visit our website at
www.WileyGlobalFinance.com.

WILEY

CONTENTS

How to Use the CFA Program Curriculum

The CFA® Program exams measure your mastery of the core knowledge, skills, and abilities required to succeed as an investment professional. These core competencies are the basis for the Candidate Body of Knowledge (CBOK™). The CBOK consists of four components:

- A broad outline that lists the major CFA Program topic areas (www.cfainstitute.org/programs/cfa/curriculum/cbok/cbok)
- Topic area weights that indicate the relative exam weightings of the top-level topic areas (www.cfainstitute.org/en/programs/cfa/curriculum)
- Learning outcome statements (LOS) that tell you the specific knowledge, skills, and abilities you should gain from each curriculum topic area. You will find these statements at the start of each learning module and lesson. We encourage you to review the information about the LOS on our website (www.cfainstitute.org/programs/cfa/curriculum/study-sessions), including the descriptions of LOS "command words" on the candidate resources page at www.cfainstitute.org/-/media/documents/support/programs/cfa-and-cipm-los-command-words.ashx.
- The CFA Program curriculum that candidates receive access to upon exam registration.

Therefore, the key to your success on the CFA exams is studying and understanding the CBOK. You can learn more about the CBOK on our website: www.cfainstitute.org/programs/cfa/curriculum/cbok.

The curriculum, including the practice questions, is the basis for all exam questions. The curriculum is selected/developed specifically to provide candidates with the knowledge, skills, and abilities reflected in the CBOK.

CFA INSTITUTE LEARNING ECOSYSTEM (LES)

Your exam registration fee includes access to the CFA Institute Learning Ecosystem (LES). This digital learning platform provides access to all the curriculum content and practice questions. The LES is organized as a series of learning modules consisting of short online lessons and associated practice questions. This tool is your source for all study materials, including practice questions and mock exams. The LES is the primary method by which CFA Institute delivers your curriculum experience. Here, you will find additional practice questions to test your knowledge, including some interactive questions.

DESIGNING YOUR PERSONAL STUDY PROGRAM

An orderly, systematic approach to exam preparation is critical. You should dedicate a consistent block of time every week to reading and studying. Review the LOS both before and after you study curriculum content to ensure you can demonstrate the knowledge, skills, and abilities described by the LOS and the assigned learning module. Use the LOS as a self-check to track your progress and highlight areas of weakness for later review.

Successful candidates report an average of more than 300 hours preparing for each exam. Your preparation time will vary based on your prior education and experience, and you will likely spend more time on some topics than on others.

ERRATA

The curriculum development process is rigorous and involves multiple rounds of reviews by content experts. Despite our efforts to produce a curriculum that is free of errors, we must make corrections in some instances. Curriculum errata are periodically updated and posted by exam level and test date on the Curriculum Errata webpage (www.cfainstitute.org/en/programs/submit-errata). If you believe you have found an error in the curriculum, you can submit your concerns through our curriculum errata reporting process found at the bottom of the Curriculum Errata webpage.

OTHER FEEDBACK

Please send any comments or suggestions to info@cfainstitute.org, and we will review your feedback thoughtfully.

Portfolio Management

LEARNING MODULE

1

Portfolio Risk and Return: Part I

by Vijay Singal, PhD, CFA.

Vijay Singal, PhD, CFA, is at Virginia Tech (USA).

LEARNING OUTCOMES

Mastery	The candidate should be able to:
☐	describe characteristics of the major asset classes that investors consider in forming portfolios
☐	explain risk aversion and its implications for portfolio selection
☐	explain the selection of an optimal portfolio, given an investor's utility (or risk aversion) and the capital allocation line
☐	calculate and interpret the mean, variance, and covariance (or correlation) of asset returns based on historical data
☐	calculate and interpret portfolio standard deviation
☐	describe the effect on a portfolio's risk of investing in assets that are less than perfectly correlated
☐	describe and interpret the minimum-variance and efficient frontiers of risky assets and the global minimum-variance portfolio

INTRODUCTION

1

Construction of an optimal portfolio is an important objective for an investor. In this reading, we will explore the process of examining the risk and return characteristics of individual assets, creating all possible portfolios, selecting the most efficient portfolios, and ultimately choosing the optimal portfolio tailored to the individual in question.

During the process of constructing the optimal portfolio, several factors and investment characteristics are considered. The most important of those factors are risk and return of the individual assets under consideration. Correlations among individual assets along with risk and return are important determinants of portfolio risk. Creating a portfolio for an investor requires an understanding of the risk profile of the investor. Although we will not discuss the process of determining risk aversion for individuals or institutional investors, it is necessary to obtain such information for making an informed decision. In this reading, we will explain the broad types of investors and how their risk–return preferences can be formalized to select the optimal portfolio from among the infinite portfolios contained in the investment opportunity set.

The reading is organized as follows: Sections 2–3 discuss the investment characteristics of assets. Sections 4–6 discuss risk aversion and how indifference curves, which incorporate individual preferences, can be constructed. The indifference curves are then applied to the selection of an optimal portfolio using two risky assets. Sections 7–9 provide an understanding and computation of portfolio risk. The role of correlation and diversification of portfolio risk are examined in detail. Sections 10–12 begins with the risky assets available to investors and constructs a large number of risky portfolios. It illustrates the process of narrowing the choices to an efficient set of risky portfolios before identifying the optimal risky portfolio. The risky portfolio is combined with investor risk preferences to generate the investor's optimal portfolio. A summary concludes this reading.

2 HISTORICAL RETURN AND RISK

☐ describe characteristics of the major asset classes that investors consider in forming portfolios

Before examining historical data, it is useful to distinguish between the historical mean return and expected return, which are very different concepts but easy to confuse. Historical return is what was actually earned in the *past*, whereas expected return is what an investor anticipates to earn in the *future*.

Expected return is the nominal return that would cause the marginal investor to invest in an asset based on the real risk-free interest rate (r_{rF}), expected inflation [$E(\pi)$], and expected risk premium for the risk of the asset [$E(RP)$]. The real risk-free interest rate is expected to be positive as compensation for postponing consumption. Similarly, the risk premium is expected to be positive in most cases.[1] The expected inflation rate is generally positive, except when the economy is in a deflationary state and prices are falling. Thus, expected return is generally positive. The relationship between the expected return and the real risk-free interest rate, inflation rate, and risk premium can be expressed by the following equation:

$$1 + E(R) = (1 + r_{rF}) \times [1 + E(\pi)] \times [1 + E(RP)]$$

The historical mean return for investment in a particular asset, however, is obtained from the actual return that was earned by an investor. Because the investment is risky, there is no guarantee that the actual return will be equal to the expected return. In fact, it is very unlikely that the two returns are equal for a specific time period being considered. Given a long enough period of time, we can *expect* that the future (expected) return will equal the average historical return. Unfortunately, we do not know how long that period is—10 years, 50 years, or 100 years. As a practical matter, we often assume that the historical mean return is an adequate representation of the expected return, although this assumption may not be accurate. For example, Exhibit 1 shows that the historical equity returns in the last eight years (2010–2017) for large US company stocks were positive whereas the actual return was negative the prior decade, but nearly always positive historically. Nonetheless, longer-term returns

1 There are exceptions when an asset reduces overall risk of a portfolio. We will consider those exceptions in Section 9.

(1926–2017) were positive and could be consistent with expected return. Though it is unknown if the historical mean returns accurately represent expected returns, it is an assumption that is commonly made.

Exhibit 1: Risk and Return for US Asset Classes by Decade (%)

		1930s	1940s	1950s	1960s	1970s	1980s	1990s	2000s	2010s*	1926–2017
Large company stocks	Return	−0.1	9.2	19.4	7.8	5.9	17.6	18.2	−1.0	13.9	10.2
	Risk	41.6	17.5	14.1	13.1	17.2	19.4	15.9	16.3	13.6	19.8
Small company stocks	Return	1.4	20.7	16.9	15.5	11.5	15.8	15.1	6.3	14.8	12.1
	Risk	78.6	34.5	14.4	21.5	30.8	22.5	20.2	26.1	19.4	31.7
Long-term corporate bonds	Return	6.9	2.7	1	1.7	6.2	13	8.4	7.7	8.3	6.1
	Risk	5.3	1.8	4.4	4.9	8.7	14.1	6.9	11.7	8.8	8.3
Long-term government bonds	Return	4.9	3.2	−0.1	1.4	5.5	12.6	8.8	7.7	6.8	5.5
	Risk	5.3	2.8	4.6	6	8.7	16	8.9	12.4	10.8	9.9
Treasury bills	Return	0.6	0.4	1.9	3.9	6.3	8.9	4.9	2.8	0.2	3.4
	Risk	0.2	0.1	0.2	0.4	0.6	0.9	0.4	0.6	0.1	3.1
Inflation	Return	−2.0	5.4	2.2	2.5	7.4	5.1	2.9	2.5	1.7	2.9
	Risk	2.5	3.1	1.2	0.7	1.2	1.3	0.7	1.6	1.1	4.0

* *Through 31 December 2017*
Note: Returns are measured as annualized geometric mean returns.
Risk is measured by annualizing monthly standard deviations.
Source: 2018 SBBI Yearbook (Exhibits 1.2,1.3, 2.3 and 6.2).

Going forward, be sure to distinguish between expected return and historical mean return. We will alert the reader whenever historical returns are used to estimate expected returns.

Nominal Returns of Major US Asset Classes

We focus on three major asset categories in Exhibit 1: stocks, bonds, and T-bills. The mean nominal returns for US asset classes are reported decade by decade since the 1930s. The total for the 1926–2017 period is in the last column. All returns are annual geometric mean returns. Large company stocks had an overall annual return of 10.2 percent during the 92-year period. The return was negative in the 1930s and 2000s, and positive in all remaining decades. The 1950s and 1990s were the best decades for large company stocks. Small company stocks fared even better. The nominal return was never negative for any decade, and had double-digit growth in all decades except two, leading to an overall 92-year annual return of 12.1 percent.

Long-term corporate bonds and long-term government bonds earned overall returns of 6.1 percent and 5.5 percent, respectively. The corporate bonds did not have a single negative decade, although government bonds recorded a negative return in the 1950s when stocks were doing extremely well. Bonds also had some excellent decades, earning double-digit returns in the 1980s and 2000s.

Treasury bills (short-term government securities) did not earn a negative return in any decade. In fact, Treasury bills earned a negative return only in 1938 (−0.02 percent) when the inflation rate was −2.78 percent. Consistently positive returns for Treasury bills are not surprising because nominal interest rates are almost never negative and the Treasury bills suffer from little interest rate or inflation risk. Since the Great Depression, there has been no deflation in any decade, although inflation rates were highly negative in 1930 (–6.03 percent), 1931 (–9.52 percent), and 1932 (–10.30 percent). Conversely, inflation rates were very high in the late 1970s and early 1980s, reaching 13.31 percent in 1979. Inflation rates have been largely range bound between 1 and 3 percent from 1991 to 2017. Overall, the inflation rate was 2.9 percent for the 92-year period.

Real Returns of Major US Asset Classes

Because annual inflation rates can vary greatly, from –10.30 percent to +13.31 percent in the last 92 years, comparisons across various time periods are difficult and misleading using nominal returns. Therefore, it is more effective to rely on real returns. Real returns on stocks, bonds, and T-bills are reported from 1900 in Exhibit 2 and Exhibit 3.

Exhibit 2: Cumulative Returns on US Asset Classes in Real Terms, 1900–2017

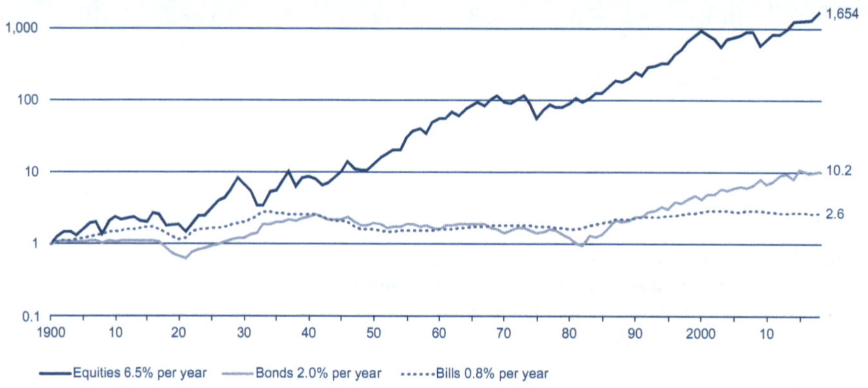

Source: E. Dimson, P. Marsh, and M. Staunton, *Credit Suisse Global Investment Returns Yearbook 2018*, Credit Suisse Research Institute (February 2018). This chart is updated annually and can be found at https://www.credit-suisse.com/media/assets/corporate/docs/about-us/media/media-release/2018/02/giry-summary-2018.pdf.

Exhibit 2 shows that $1 would have grown to $1,654 if invested in stocks, to only $10.20 if invested in bonds, and to $2.60 if invested in T-bills. The difference in growth among the three asset categories is huge, although the difference in real returns does not seem that large: 6.5 percent per year for equities compared with 2.0 percent per year for bonds. This difference represents the effect of compounding over a 118-year period.

Exhibit 3 reports real rates of return. As we discussed earlier and as shown in the table, geometric mean is never greater than the arithmetic mean. Our analysis of returns focuses on the geometric mean because it is a more accurate representation of returns for multiple holding periods than the arithmetic mean. We observe that the real returns for stocks are higher than the real returns for bonds.

Exhibit 3: Real Returns and Risk Premiums for Asset Classes (1900–2017)

		United States			World			World excluding United States		
	Asset	*GM* (%)	*AM* (%)	*SD* (%)	*GM* (%)	*AM* (%)	*SD* (%)	*GM* (%)	*AM* (%)	*SD* (%)
Real Returns	Equities	6.5	8.4	20.0	5.2	6.6	17.4	4.5	6.2	18.9
	Bonds	2.0	2.5	10.4	2.0	2.5	11.0	1.7	2.7	14.4
Premiums	Equities vs. bonds	4.4	6.5	20.7	3.2	4.4	15.3	2.8	3.8	14.4

Note: All returns are in percent per annum measured in US$. GM = geometric mean, AM = arithmetic mean, SD = standard deviation.
"World" consists of 21 developed countries: Australia, Austria, Belgium, Canada, Denmark, Finland, France, Germany, Ireland, Italy, Japan, the Netherlands, New Zealand, Norway, Portugal, South Africa, Spain, Sweden, Switzerland, United Kingdom, and the United States. Weighting is by each country's relative market capitalization size. See source for details of calculations.
Source: Credit Suisse Global Investment Returns Sourcebook, 2018.

Nominal and Real Returns of Asset Classes in Major Countries

Along with US returns, real returns of major asset classes for a 21-country world and the world excluding the United States are also presented in Exhibit 3. Equity returns are weighted by each country's GDP before 1968 because of a lack of reliable market capitalization data. Returns are weighted by a country's market capitalization beginning with 1968. Similarly, bond returns are defined by a 21-country bond index, except GDP is used to create the weights because equity market capitalization weighting is inappropriate for a bond index and bond market capitalizations were not readily available.

The real geometric mean return for the world stock index over the last 117 years was 5.2 percent, and bonds had a real geometric mean return of 2.0 percent. The real geometric mean return for the world excluding the United States were 4.5 percent for stocks and 1.7 percent for bonds. For both stocks and bonds, the United States earned higher returns than the world excluding the United States. Similarly, real returns for stocks and bonds in the United States were higher than the real returns for rest of the world.

Risk of Major Asset Classes

Risk for major asset classes in the United States is reported for 1926–2017 in Exhibit 1, and the risk for major asset classes for the United States, the world, and the world excluding the United States are reported for 1900–2017 in Exhibit 3. Exhibit 1 shows that US small company stocks had the highest risk, 31.7 percent, followed by US large company stocks, 19.8 percent. Long-term government bonds and long-term corporate bonds had lower risk at 9.9 percent and 8.3 percent, with Treasury bills having the lowest risk at about 3.1 percent.

Exhibit 3 shows that the risk for world stocks is 17.4 percent and for world bonds is 11.0 percent. The world excluding the United States has risks of 18.9 percent for stocks and 14.4 percent for bonds. The effect of diversification is apparent when world risk is compared with US risk and world excluding US risk. Although the risk of US stocks is 20.0 percent and the risk of world excluding US stocks is 18.9 percent, the combination gives a risk of only 17.4 percent for world stocks.

Risk–Return Trade-off

The expression "risk–return trade-off" refers to the positive relationship between expected risk and return. In other words, a higher return is not possible to attain in **efficient markets** and over long periods of time without accepting higher risk. Expected returns should be greater for assets with greater risk.

The historical data presented above show the risk–return trade-off. Exhibit 1 shows for the United States that small company stocks had higher risk and higher return than large company stocks. Large company stocks had higher returns and higher risk than both long-term corporate bonds and government bonds. Bonds had higher returns and higher risk than Treasury bills. Uncharacteristically, however, long-term government bonds had higher total risk than long-term corporate bonds, although the returns of corporate bonds were slightly higher. These factors do not mean that long-term government bonds had greater default risk, just that they were more variable than corporate bonds during this historic period.

Exhibit 3 reveals that the risk and return for stocks were the highest of the asset classes, and the risk and return for bonds were lower than stocks for the United States, the world, and the world excluding the United States.

Another way of looking at the risk–return trade-off is to focus on the **risk premium**, which is the extra return investors can expect for assuming additional risk, after accounting for the risk-free interest rate. The nominal risk premium is the nominal risky return minus the nominal risk-free rate (which includes both compensation for expected inflation and the real risk-free interest rate). The real risk premium is the real risky return minus the real risk-free rate. Worldwide equity risk premiums reported at the bottom of Exhibit 3 show that equities outperformed bonds. Investors in equities earned a higher return than investors in bonds because of the higher risk in equities.

A more dramatic representation of the risk–return trade-off is shown in Exhibit 2, which shows the cumulative returns of US asset classes in real terms. The line representing T-bills is much less volatile than the other lines. Adjusted for inflation, the average real return on T-bills was 0.8 percent per year. The line representing bonds is more volatile than the line for T-bills but less volatile than the line representing stocks. The total return for equities including dividends and capital gains shows how $1 invested at the beginning of 1900 grows to $1,654, generating an annualized return of 6.5 percent in real terms.

Over long periods of time, we observe that higher risk does result in higher mean returns. Thus, it is reasonable to claim that, over the long term, market prices reward higher risk with higher returns, which is a characteristic of a risk-averse investor, a topic that we discuss in Section 4.

3 OTHER INVESTMENT CHARACTERISTICS

☐ describe characteristics of the major asset classes that investors consider in forming portfolios

In evaluating investments using only the mean (expected return) and variance (risk), we are implicitly making two important assumptions: 1) that the returns are normally distributed and can be fully characterized by their means and variances and 2) that markets are not only informationally efficient but that they are also operationally efficient. To the extent that these assumptions are violated, we need to consider additional investment characteristics. These are discussed below.

Distributional Characteristics

As explained in an earlier reading, a **normal distribution** has three main characteristics: its mean and median are equal; it is completely defined by two parameters, mean and variance; and it is symmetric around its mean with:

- 68 percent of the observations within $\pm 1\sigma$ of the mean,
- 95 percent of the observations within $\pm 2\sigma$ of the mean, and
- 99 percent of the observations within $\pm 3\sigma$ of the mean.

Using only mean and variance would be appropriate to evaluate investments if returns were distributed normally. Returns, however, are not normally distributed; deviations from normality occur both because the returns are skewed, which means they are not symmetric around the mean, and because the probability of extreme events is significantly greater than what a normal distribution would suggest. The latter deviation is referred to as kurtosis or fat tails in a return distribution. The next sections discuss these deviations more in-depth.

Skewness

Skewness refers to asymmetry of the return distribution, that is, returns are not symmetric around the mean. A distribution is said to be left skewed or negatively skewed if most of the distribution is concentrated to the right, and right skewed or positively skewed if most is concentrated to the left. Exhibit 4 shows a typical representation of negative and positive skewness, whereas Exhibit 5 demonstrates the negative skewness of stock returns by plotting a histogram of US large company stock returns for 1926–2017.

Exhibit 4: Skewness

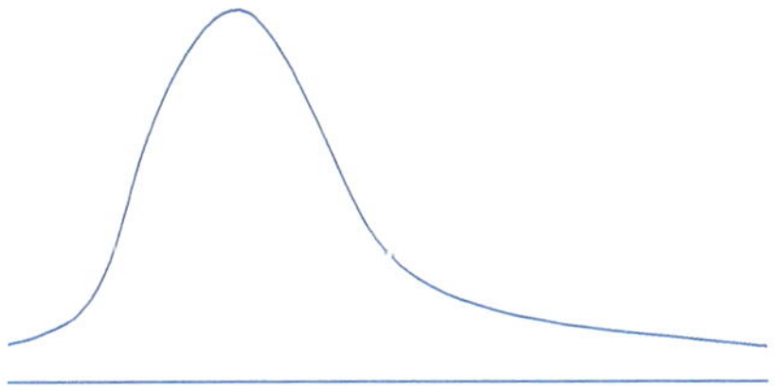

Distribution Skewed to the Right (Positively Skewed)

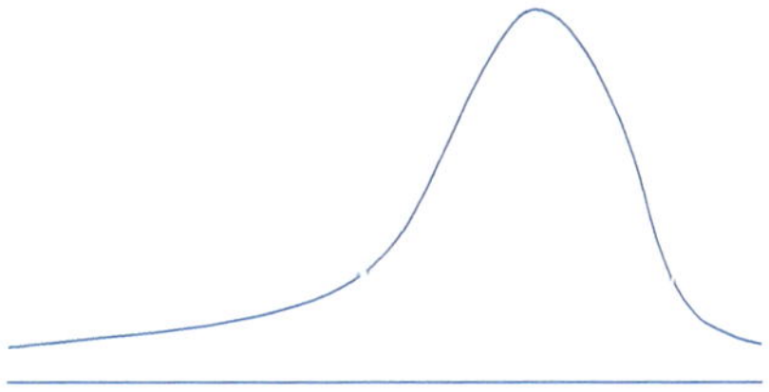

Distribution Skewed to the Left (Negatively Skewed)

Source: Reprinted from *Fixed Income Readings for the Chartered Financial Analyst® Program.* Copyright CFA Institute.

Exhibit 5: Histogram of US Large Company Stock Returns, 1926–2017 (Percent)

						2016				
						2014				
						2012				
						2010				
					2015	2006	2017			
					2011	2004	2009	2013		
				2000	2007	1988	2003	1997		
				1990	2005	1986	1999	1995		
				1981	1994	1979	1998	1991		
				1977	1993	1972	1996	1989		
				1969	1992	1971	1983	1985		
				1962	1987	1968	1982	1980		
				1953	1984	1965	1976	1975		
				1946	1978	1964	1967	1955		
			2001	1940	1970	1959	1963	1950		
			1973	1939	1960	1952	1961	1945		
		2002	1966	1934	1956	1949	1951	1938	1958	
	2008	1974	1957	1932	1948	1944	1943	1936	1935	1954
1931	1937	1939	1941	1929	1947	1926	1942	1927	1928	1933

–60 –50 –40 –30 –20 –10 0 10 20 30 40 50 60 70

Source: 2018 SBBI Yearbook (Appendix A1)

Kurtosis

Kurtosis refers to fat tails or higher than normal probabilities for extreme returns and has the effect of increasing an asset's risk that is not captured in a mean–variance framework, as illustrated in Exhibit 6. Investors try to evaluate the effect of kurtosis by using such statistical techniques as value at risk (VaR) and conditional tail expectations.[2] Several market participants note that the probability and the magnitude of extreme events is underappreciated and was a primary contributing factor to the financial crisis of 2008.[3] The higher probability of extreme negative outcomes among stock returns can also be observed in Exhibit 5.

2 Value at risk is a money measure of the minimum losses expected on a portfolio during a specified time period at a given level of probability. It is commonly used to measure the losses a portfolio can suffer under normal market conditions. For example, if a portfolio's one-day 10 percent VaR is £200,000, it implies that there is a 10 percent probability that the value of the portfolio will decrease by more than £200,000 over a single one-day period (under normal market conditions). This probability implies that the portfolio will experience a loss of at least £200,000 on one out of every ten days.

3 For example, see Bogle (2008) and Taleb (2007).

Exhibit 6: Kurtosis

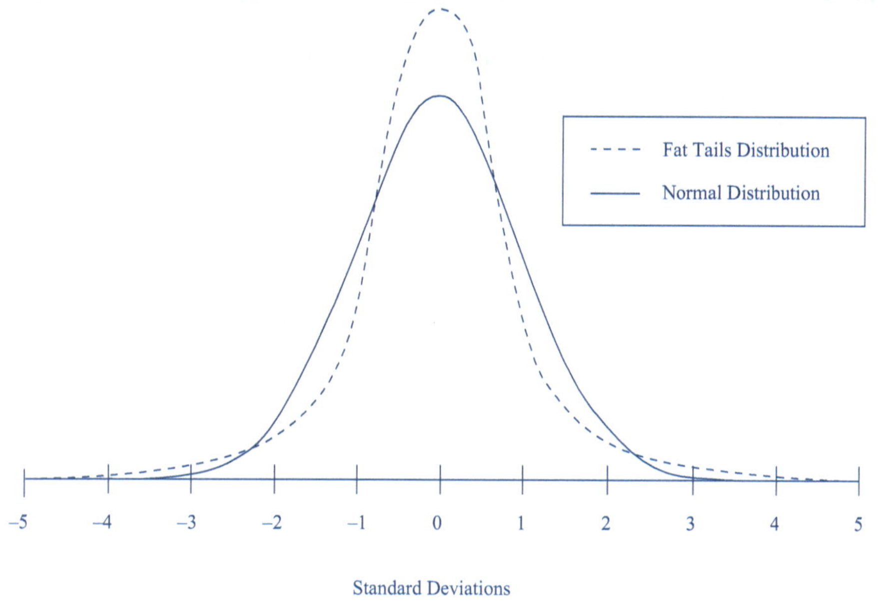

Source: Reprinted from *Fixed Income Readings for the Chartered Financial Analyst® Program.* Copyright CFA Institute.

Market Characteristics

In the previous analysis, we implicitly assumed that markets are both informationally and operationally efficient. Although informational efficiency of markets is a topic beyond the purview of this reading, we should highlight certain operational limitations of the market that affect the choice of investments. One such limitation is **liquidity**.

The cost of trading has three main components—brokerage commission, bid–ask spread, and price impact. Liquidity affects the latter two. Stocks with low liquidity can have wide bid–ask spreads. The bid–ask spread, which is the difference between the buying price and the selling price, is incurred as a cost of trading a security. The larger the bid–ask spread, the higher the cost of trading. If a $100 stock has a spread of 10 cents, the bid–ask spread is only 0.1 percent ($0.10/$100). On the other hand, if a $10 stock has a spread of 10 cents, the bid–ask spread is 1 percent. Clearly, the $10 stock is more expensive to trade and an investor will need to earn 0.9 percent extra to make up the higher cost of trading relative to the $100 stock.

Liquidity also has implications for the price impact of trade. Price impact refers to how the price moves in response to an order in the market. Small orders usually have little impact, especially for liquid stocks. For example, an order to buy 100 shares of a $100 stock with a spread of 1 cent may have no effect on the price. On the other hand, an order to buy 100,000 shares may have a significant impact on the price as the buyer has to induce more and more stockholders to tender their shares. The extent of the price impact depends on the liquidity of the stock. A stock that trades millions of shares a day may be less affected than a stock that trades only a few hundred thousand shares a day. Investors, especially institutional investors managing large sums of money, must keep the liquidity of a stock in mind when making investment decisions.

Liquidity is a bigger concern in emerging markets than in developed markets because of the smaller volume of trading in those markets. Similarly, liquidity is a more important concern in corporate bond markets and especially for bonds of lower credit quality than in equity markets because an individual corporate bond issue may not trade for several days or weeks. This certainly became apparent during the global financial crisis.

There are other market-related characteristics that affect investment decisions because they might instill greater confidence in the security or might affect the costs of doing business. These include analyst coverage, availability of information, firm size, etc. These characteristics about companies and financial markets are essential components of investment decision making.

4 RISK AVERSION AND PORTFOLIO SELECTION

☐ explain risk aversion and its implications for portfolio selection

As we have seen, stocks, bonds, and T-bills provide different levels of returns and have different levels of risk. Although investment in equities may be appropriate for one investor, another investor may not be inclined to accept the risk that accompanies a share of stock and may prefer to hold more cash. In the last section, we considered investment characteristics of assets in understanding their risk and return. In this section, we consider the characteristics of investors, both individual and institutional, in an attempt to pair the right kind of investors with the right kind of investments.

First, we discuss risk aversion and utility theory. Later we discuss their implications for portfolio selection.

The Concept of Risk Aversion

The concept of **risk aversion** is related to the behavior of individuals under uncertainty. Assume that an individual is offered two alternatives: one where he will get £50 for sure and the other is a gamble with a 50 percent chance that he gets £100 and 50 percent chance that he gets nothing. The expected value in both cases is £50, one with certainty and the other with uncertainty. What will an investor choose? There are three possibilities: an investor chooses the gamble, the investor chooses £50 with certainty, or the investor is indifferent. Let us consider each in turn. However, please understand that this is only a representative example, and a single choice does not determine the risk aversion of an investor.

Risk Seeking

If an investor chooses the gamble, then the investor is said to be risk loving or risk seeking. The gamble has an uncertain outcome, but with the same expected value as the guaranteed outcome. Thus, an investor choosing the gamble means that the investor gets extra "utility" from the uncertainty associated with the gamble. How much is that extra utility worth? Would the investor be willing to accept a smaller expected value because he gets extra utility from risk? Indeed, risk seekers will accept less return because of the risk that accompanies the gamble. For example, a risk seeker may choose a gamble with an expected value of £45 in preference to a guaranteed outcome of £50.

There is a little bit of gambling instinct in many of us. People buy lottery tickets although the expected value is less than the money they pay to buy it. Or people gamble at casinos with the full knowledge that the expected return is negative, a characteristic of risk seekers. These or any other isolated actions, however, cannot be taken at face value except for compulsive gamblers.

Risk Neutral

If an investor is indifferent about the gamble or the guaranteed outcome, then the investor may be risk neutral. Risk neutrality means that the investor cares only about return and not about risk, so higher return investments are more desirable even if they come with higher risk. Many investors may exhibit characteristics of risk neutrality when the investment at stake is an insignificant part of their wealth. For example, a billionaire may be indifferent about choosing the gamble or a £50 guaranteed outcome.

Risk Averse

If an investor chooses the guaranteed outcome, he/she is said to be **risk averse** because the investor does not want to take the chance of not getting anything at all. Depending on the level of aversion to risk, an investor may be willing to accept a guaranteed outcome of £45 instead of a gamble with an expected value of £50.

In general, investors are likely to shy away from risky investments for a lower, but guaranteed return. That is why they want to minimize their risk for the same amount of return, and maximize their return for the same amount of risk. The risk–return trade-off discussed earlier is an indicator of risk aversion. A risk-neutral investor would maximize return irrespective of risk and a risk-seeking investor would maximize both risk and return.

Data presented in the last section illustrate the historically positive relationship between risk and return, which demonstrates that market prices were based on transactions and investments by risk-averse investors and reflect risk aversion. Therefore, for all practical purposes and for our future discussion, we will assume that the representative investor is a risk-averse investor. This assumption is the standard approach taken in the investment industry globally.

Risk Tolerance

Risk tolerance refers to the amount of risk an investor can tolerate to achieve an investment goal. The higher the risk tolerance, the greater is the willingness to take risk. Thus, risk tolerance is negatively related to risk aversion.

UTILITY THEORY AND INDIFFERENCE CURVES 5

☐ explain risk aversion and its implications for portfolio selection

Continuing with our previous example, a risk-averse investor would rank the guaranteed outcome of £50 higher than the uncertain outcome with an expected value of £50. We can say that the utility that an investor or an individual derives from the guaranteed outcome of £50 is greater than the utility or satisfaction or happiness he/she derives from the alternative. In general terms, utility is a measure of relative satisfaction from consumption of various goods and services or in the case of investments, the satisfaction that an investor derives from a portfolio.

Because individuals are different in their preferences, all risk-averse individuals may not rank investment alternatives in the same manner. Consider the £50 gamble again. All risk-averse individuals will rank the guaranteed outcome of £50 higher than the gamble. What if the guaranteed outcome is only £40? Some risk-averse investors might consider £40 inadequate, others might accept it, and still others may now be indifferent about the uncertain £50 and the certain £40.

A simple implementation of utility theory allows us to quantify the rankings of investment choices using risk and return. There are several assumptions about individual behavior that we make in the definition of utility given in the equation below. We assume that investors are risk averse. They always prefer more to less (greater return to lesser return). They are able to rank different portfolios in the order of their preference and that the rankings are internally consistent. If an individual prefers X to Y and Y to Z, then he/she must prefer X to Z. This property implies that the indifference curves (see Exhibit 7) for the same individual can never touch or intersect. An example of a utility function is given below

$$U = E(r) - \frac{1}{2}A\sigma^2$$

where, U is the utility of an investment, $E(r)$ is the expected return, and σ^2 is the variance of the investment.

In the above equation, A is a measure of risk aversion, which is measured as the marginal reward that an investor requires to accept additional risk. More risk-averse investors require greater compensation for accepting additional risk. Thus, A is higher for more risk-averse individuals. As was mentioned previously, a risk-neutral investor would maximize return irrespective of risk and a risk-seeking investor would maximize both risk and return.

We can draw several conclusions from the utility function. First, utility is unbounded on both sides. It can be highly positive or highly negative. Second, higher return contributes to higher utility. Third, higher variance reduces the utility but the reduction in utility gets amplified by the risk aversion coefficient, A. Utility can always be increased, albeit marginally, by getting higher return or lower risk. Fourth, utility does not indicate or measure satisfaction itself—it can be useful only in ranking various investments. For example, a portfolio with a utility of 4 is not necessarily two times better than a portfolio with a utility of 2. The portfolio with a utility of 4 could increase our happiness 10 times or just marginally. But we do prefer a portfolio with a utility of 4 to a portfolio with a utility of 2. Utility cannot be compared among individuals or investors because it is a very personal concept. From a societal point of view, by the same argument, utility cannot be summed among individuals.

Let us explore the utility function further. The risk aversion coefficient, A, is greater than zero for a risk-averse investor. So any increase in risk reduces his/her utility. The risk aversion coefficient for a risk-neutral investor is 0, and changes in risk do not affect his/her utility. For a risk lover, the risk aversion coefficient is negative, creating an inverse situation so that additional risk contributes to an increase in his/her utility. Note that a risk-free asset ($\sigma^2 = 0$) generates the same utility for all individuals.

Indifference Curves

An **indifference curve** plots the combinations of risk–return pairs that an investor would accept to maintain a given level of utility (i.e., the investor is indifferent about the combinations on any one curve because they would provide the same level of overall utility). Indifference curves are thus defined in terms of a trade-off between expected rate of return and variance of the rate of return. Because an infinite number of combinations of risk and return can generate the same utility for the same investor, indifference curves are continuous at all points.

Exhibit 7: Indifference Curves for Risk-Averse Investors

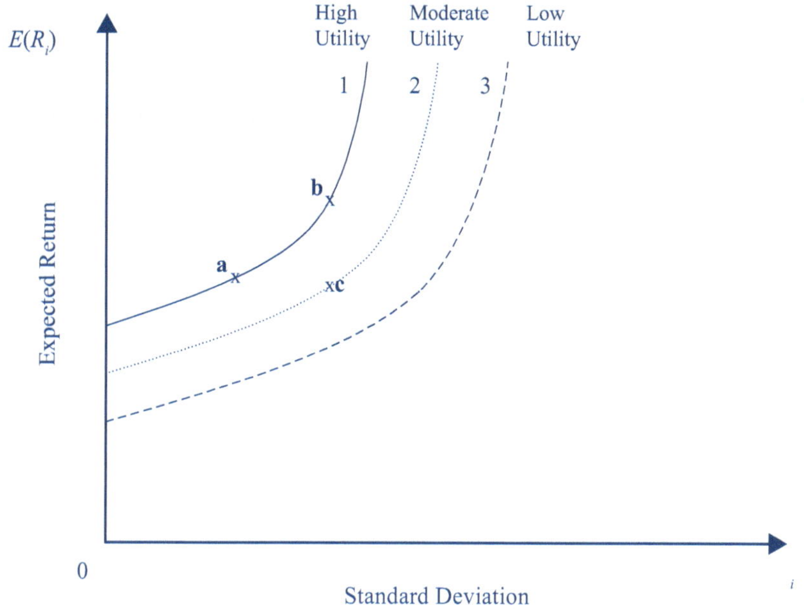

A set of indifference curves is plotted in Exhibit 7. By definition, all points on any one of the three curves have the same utility. An investor does not care whether he/she is at Point **a** or Point **b** on indifference Curve 1. Point **a** has lower risk and lower return than Point **b**, but the utility of both points is the same because the higher return at Point **b** is offset by the higher risk.

Like Curve 1, all points on Curve 2 have the same utility and an investor is indifferent about where he/she is on Curve 2. Now compare Point **c** with Point **b**. Point **c** has the same risk but significantly lower return than Point **b**, which means that the utility at Point **c** is less than the utility at Point **b**. Given that all points on Curve 1 have the same utility and all points on Curve 2 have the same utility and Point **b** has higher utility than Point **c**, Curve 1 has higher utility than Curve 2. Therefore, a risk-averse investor with indifference Curves 1 and 2 will prefer Curve 1 to Curve 2. The utility of a risk-averse investor always increases as you move northwest—higher return with lower risk. Because all investors prefer more utility to less, investors want to move northwest to the indifference curve with the highest utility.

The indifference curve for risk-averse investors runs from the southwest to the northeast because of the risk–return trade-off. If risk increases (going east) then it must be compensated by higher return (going north) to generate the same utility. The indifference curves are convex because of diminishing marginal utility of return (or wealth). As risk increases, an investor needs greater return to compensate for higher risk at an increasing rate (i.e., the curve gets steeper). The upward-sloping convex indifference curve has a slope coefficient closely related to the risk aversion coefficient. The greater the slope, the higher is the risk aversion of the investor as a greater increment in return is required to accept a given increase in risk.

Indifference curves for investors with different levels of risk aversion are plotted in Exhibit 8. The most risk-averse investor has an indifference curve with the greatest slope. As volatility increases, this investor demands increasingly higher returns to compensate for risk. The least risk-averse investor has an indifference curve with the least slope and so the demand for higher return as risk increases is not as acute as for the more risk-averse investor. The risk-loving investor's indifference curve, however, exhibits a negative slope, implying that the risk-lover is happy to substitute risk for return. For a risk lover, the utility increases both with higher risk and higher return. Finally, the indifference curves of risk-neutral investors are horizontal because the utility is invariant with risk.

Exhibit 8: Indifference Curves for Various Types of Investors

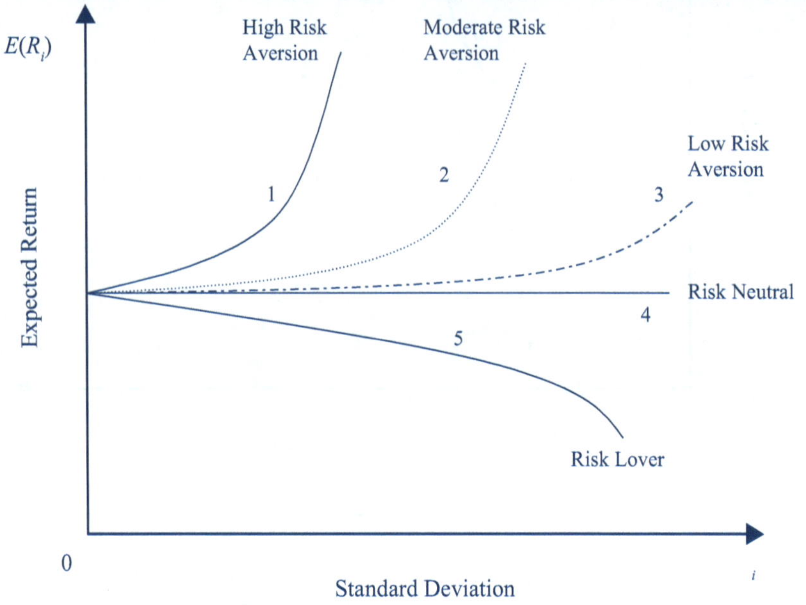

In the remaining parts of this reading, all investors are assumed to be risk averse unless stated otherwise.

EXAMPLE 1

Comparing a Gamble with a Guaranteed Outcome

Assume that you are given an investment with an expected return of 10 percent and a risk (standard deviation) of 20 percent, and your risk aversion coefficient is 3.

1. What is your utility of this investment?

   Solution:

   $U = 0.10 - 0.5 \times 3 \times 0.20^2 = 0.04.$

2. What must be the minimum risk-free return you should earn to get the same utility?

   Solution:

   A risk-free return's σ is zero, so the second term disappears. To get the same utility (0.04), the risk-free return must be at least 4 percent. Thus, in your mind, a risky return of 10 percent is equivalent to a risk-free return or a guaranteed outcome of 4 percent.

EXAMPLE 2

Computation of Utility

Based on investment information given below and the utility formula $U = E(r) - 0.5A\sigma^2$, answer the following questions. Returns and standard deviations are both expressed as percent per year. When using the utility formula, however, returns and standard deviations must be expressed in decimals.

Investment	Expected Return $E(r)$	Standard Deviation σ
1	12%	30%
2	15	35
3	21	40
4	24	45

1. Which investment will a risk-averse investor with a risk aversion coefficient of 4 choose, and which investment will a risk-averse investor with a risk aversion coefficient of 2 choose?

   Solution:

   The utility for risk-averse investors with $A = 4$ and $A = 2$ for each of the four investments are shown in the following table. Complete calculations for Investment 1 with $A = 4$ are as follows: $U = 0.12 - 0.5 \times 4 \times 0.30^2 = -0.06$.

Investment	Expected Return $E(r)$	Standard Deviation σ	Utility $A = 4$	Utility $A = 2$
1	12%	30%	−0.0600	0.0300
2	15	35	−0.0950	0.0275
3	21	40	−0.1100	0.0500
4	24	45	−0.1650	0.0375

   The risk-averse investor with a risk aversion coefficient of 4 should choose Investment 1. The risk-averse investor with a risk aversion coefficient of 2 should choose Investment 3.

2. Which investment will a risk-neutral investor choose?

   Solution:

   A risk-neutral investor cares only about return. In other words, his risk aversion coefficient is 0. Therefore, a risk-neutral investor will choose Investment 4 because it has the highest return.

3. Which investment will a risk-loving investor choose?

   Solution:

   A risk-loving investor likes both higher risk and higher return. In other words, his risk aversion coefficient is negative. Therefore, a risk-loving investor will choose Investment 4 because it has the highest return and highest risk among the four investments.

6 APPLICATION OF UTILITY THEORY TO PORTFOLIO SELECTION

- [ ] explain risk aversion and its implications for portfolio selection
- [ ] explain the selection of an optimal portfolio, given an investor's utility (or risk aversion) and the capital allocation line

The simplest application of utility theory and risk aversion is to a portfolio of two assets, a risk-free asset and a risky asset. The risk-free asset has zero risk and a return of R_f. The risky asset has a risk of σ_i (> 0) and an expected return of $E(R_i)$. Because the risky asset has risk that is greater than that of the risk-free asset, the expected return from the risky asset will be greater than the return from the risk-free asset, that is, $E(R_i) > R_f$.

We can construct a portfolio of these two assets with a portfolio expected return, $E(R_p)$, and portfolio risk, σ_p, based on the formulas provided below. In the equations given below, w_1 is the weight in the risk-free asset and $(1 – w_1)$ is the weight in the risky asset. Because $\sigma_f = 0$ for the risk-free asset, the first and third terms in the formula for variance are zero leaving only the second term. We arrive at the last equation by taking the square root of both sides, which shows the expression for standard deviation for a portfolio of two assets when one asset is the risk-free asset:

$$E(R_p) = w_1 R_f + (1 - w_1)E(R_i)$$

$$\sigma_p^2 = w_1^2\sigma_f^2 + (1 - w_1)^2\sigma_i^2 + 2w_1(1 - w_1)\rho_{12}\sigma_f\sigma_i = (1 - w_1)^2\sigma_i^2$$

$$\sigma_p = (1 - w_1)\sigma_i$$

The two-asset portfolio is drawn in Exhibit 9 by varying w_1 from 0 percent to 100 percent. The portfolio standard deviation is on the horizontal axis and the portfolio return is on the vertical axis. If only these two assets are available in the economy and the risky asset represents the market, the line in Exhibit 9 is called the **capital allocation line**. The capital allocation line represents the portfolios available to an investor. The equation for this line can be derived from the above two equations by rewriting the second equation as $w_1 = 1 - \frac{\sigma_p}{\sigma_i}$. Substituting the value of w_1 in the equation for expected return, we get the following equation for the capital allocation line:

$$E(R_p) = \left(1 - \frac{\sigma_p}{\sigma_i}\right) R_f + \frac{\sigma_p}{\sigma_i}E(R_i)$$

This equation can be rewritten in a more usable form:

$$E(R_p) = R_f + \frac{(E(R_i) - R_f)}{\sigma_i}\sigma_p$$

The capital allocation line has an intercept of R_f, and a slope of $\frac{(E(R_i) - R_f)}{\sigma_i}$, which is the additional required return for every increment in risk, and is sometimes referred to as the market price of risk.

Exhibit 9: Capital Allocation Line with Two Assets

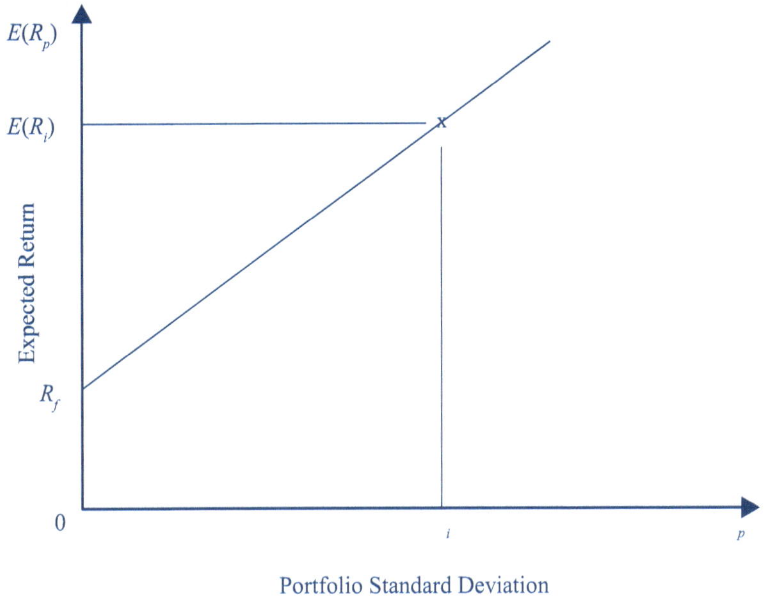

Because the equation is linear, the plot of the capital allocation line is a straight line. The line begins with the risk-free asset as the leftmost point with zero risk and a risk-free return, R_f. At that point, the portfolio consists of only the risk-free asset. If 100 percent is invested in the portfolio of all risky assets, however, we have a return of $E(R_i)$ with a risk of σ_i.

We can move further along the line in pursuit of higher returns by borrowing at the risk-free rate and investing the borrowed money in the portfolio of all risky assets. If 50 percent is borrowed at the risk-free rate, then $w_1 = -0.50$ and 150 percent is placed in the risky asset, giving a return $= 1.50E(R_i) - 0.50R_f$, which is $> E(R_i)$ because $E(R_i) > R_f$.

The line plotted in Exhibit 9 is comprised of an unlimited number of risk–return pairs or portfolios. Which *one* of these portfolios should be chosen by an investor? The answer lies in combining indifference curves from utility theory with the capital allocation line from portfolio theory. Utility theory gives us the utility function or the indifference curves for an individual, as in Exhibit 9, and the capital allocation line gives us the set of feasible investments. Overlaying each individual's indifference curves on the capital allocation line will provide us with the optimal portfolio for that investor. Exhibit 10 illustrates this process of portfolio selection.

Exhibit 10: Portfolio Selection

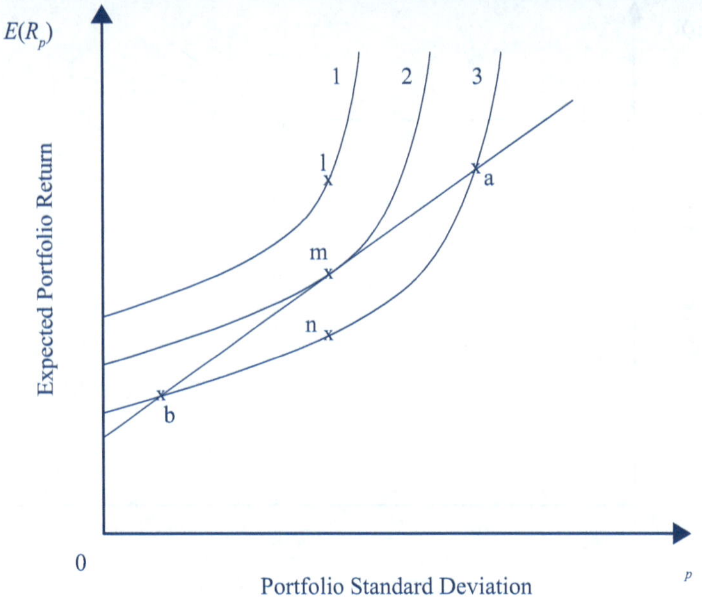

The capital allocation line consists of the set of feasible portfolios. Points under the capital allocation line may be attainable but are not preferred by any investor because the investor can get a higher return for the same risk by moving up to the capital allocation line. Points above the capital allocation line are desirable but not achievable with available assets.

Three indifference curves for the same individual are also shown in Exhibit 10. Curve 1 is above the capital allocation line, Curve 2 is tangential to the line, and Curve 3 intersects the line at two points. Curve 1 has the highest utility and Curve 3 has the lowest utility. Because Curve 1 lies completely above the capital allocation line, points on Curve 1 are not achievable with the available assets on the capital allocation line. Curve 3 intersects the capital allocation line at two Points, **a** and **b**. The investor is able to invest at either Point **a** or **b** to derive the risk–return trade-off and utility associated with Curve 3. Comparing points with the same risk, observe that Point **n** on Curve 3 has the same risk as Point **m** on Curve 2, yet Point **m** has the higher expected return. Therefore, all investors will choose Curve 2 instead of Curve 3. Curve 2 is tangential to the capital allocation line at Point **m**. Point **m** is on the capital allocation line and investable. Point **m** and the utility associated with Curve 2 is the best that the investor can do because he/she cannot move to a higher utility indifference curve. Thus, we have been able to select the optimal portfolio for the investor with indifference Curves 1, 2, and 3. Point **m**, the optimal portfolio for one investor, may not be optimal for another investor. We can follow the same process, however, for finding the optimal portfolio for other investors: the optimal portfolio is the point of tangency between the capital allocation line and the indifference curve for that investor. In other words, the optimal portfolio maximizes the return per unit of risk (as it is on the capital allocation line), and it simultaneously supplies the investor with the most satisfaction (utility).

As an illustration, Exhibit 11 shows two indifference curves for two different investors: Kelly with a risk aversion coefficient of 2 and Jane with a risk aversion coefficient of 4. The indifference curve for Kelly is to the right of the indifference curve for Jane because Kelly is less risk averse than Jane and can accept a higher amount of risk, i.e. has a higher tolerance for risk. Accordingly, their optimal portfolios are different:

Point **k** is the optimal portfolio for Kelly and Point **j** is the optimal portfolio for Jane. In addition, for the same return, the slope of Jane's curve is higher than Kelly's suggesting that Jane needs greater incremental return as compensation for accepting an additional amount of risk compared with Kelly.

Exhibit 11: Portfolio Selection for Two Investors with Various Levels of Risk Aversion

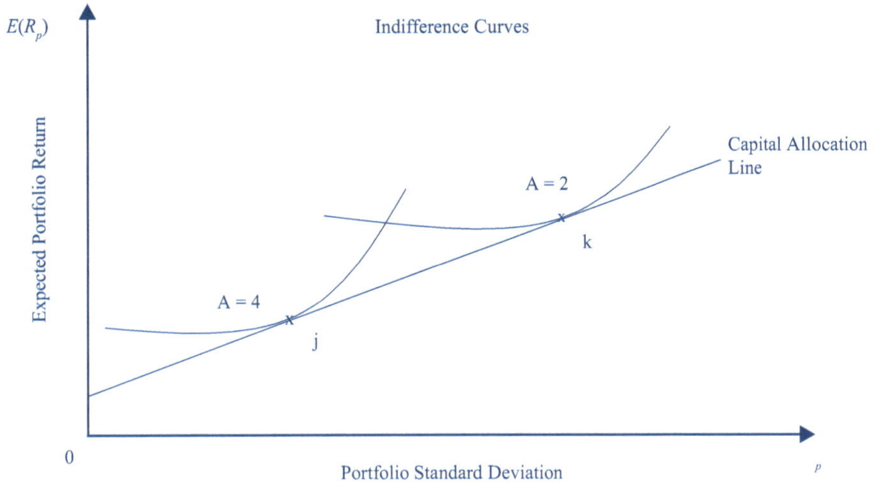

PORTFOLIO RISK & PORTFOLIO OF TWO RISKY ASSETS

7

- ☐ calculate and interpret the mean, variance, and covariance (or correlation) of asset returns based on historical data
- ☐ calculate and interpret portfolio standard deviation
- ☐ describe the effect on a portfolio's risk of investing in assets that are less than perfectly correlated

We have seen before that investors are risk averse and demand a higher return for a riskier investment. Therefore, ways of controlling portfolio risk without affecting return are valuable. As a precursor to managing risk, this section explains and analyzes the components of portfolio risk. In particular, it examines and describes how a portfolio consisting of assets with low correlations have the potential of reducing risk without necessarily reducing return.

Portfolio of Two Risky Assets

The return and risk of a portfolio of two assets was introduced in Sections 2–3 of this reading. In this section, we briefly review the computation of return and extend the concept of portfolio risk and its components.

Portfolio Return

When several individual assets are combined into a portfolio, we can compute the portfolio return as a weighted average of the returns in the portfolio. The portfolio return is simply a weighted average of the returns of the individual investments, or assets. If Asset 1 has a return of 20 percent and constitutes 25 percent of the portfolio's investment, then the contribution to the portfolio return is 5 percent (= 25% of 20%). In general, if Asset i has a return of R_i and has a weight of w_i in the portfolio, then the portfolio return, R_P, is given as:

$$R_P = \sum_{i=1}^{N} w_i R_i, \quad \sum_{i=1}^{N} w_i = 1$$

Note that the weights must add up to 1 because the assets in a portfolio, including cash, must account for 100 percent of the investment. Also, note that these are single period returns, so there are no cash flows during the period and the weights remain constant.

When two individual assets are combined in a portfolio, we can compute the portfolio return as a weighted average of the returns of the two assets. Consider Assets 1 and 2 with weights of 25 percent and 75 percent in a portfolio. If their returns are 20 percent and 5 percent, the weighted average return = (0.25 × 20%) + (0.75 × 5%) = 8.75%. More generally, the portfolio return can be written as below, where R_p is return of the portfolio, w_1 and w_2 are the weights of the two assets, and R_1, R_2 are returns on the two assets:

$$R_p = w_1 R_1 + (1 - w_1) R_2$$

Portfolio Risk

Like a portfolio's return, we can calculate a portfolio's variance. Although the return of a portfolio is simply a weighted average of the returns of each security, this is not the case with the standard deviation of a portfolio (unless all securities are perfectly correlated—that is, correlation equals one). Variance can be expressed more generally for N securities in a portfolio using the notation from the portfolio return calculation above:

$$\sum_{i=1}^{N} w_i = 1$$

$$\sigma_P^2 = \text{Var}(R_P) = \text{Var}\left(\sum_{i=1}^{N} w_i R_i\right)$$

Note that the weights must add up to 1. The right side of the equation is the variance of the weighted average returns of individual securities. Weight is a constant, but the returns are variables whose variance is shown by Var(R_i). We can rewrite the equation as shown next. Because the covariance of an asset with itself is the variance of the asset, we can separate the variances from the covariances in the second equation:

$$\sigma_P^2 = \sum_{i,j=1}^{N} w_i w_j \text{Cov}(R_i, R_j)$$

$$\sigma_P^2 = \sum_{i=1}^{N} w_i^2 \text{Var}(R_i) + \sum_{i,j=1, i \neq j}^{N} w_i w_j \text{Cov}(R_i, R_j)$$

Cov(R_i,R_j) is the covariance of returns, R_i and R_j, and can be expressed as the product of the correlation between the two returns ($\rho_{1,2}$) and the standard deviations of the two assets. Thus, Cov(R_i,R_j) = $\rho_{ij}\sigma_i\sigma_j$.

For a two asset portfolio, the expression for portfolio variance simplifies to the following using covariance and then using correlation:

$$\sigma_P^2 = w_1^2\sigma_1^2 + w_2^2\sigma_2^2 + 2w_1w_2\text{Cov}(R_1, R_2)$$
$$\sigma_P^2 = w_1^2\sigma_1^2 + w_2^2\sigma_2^2 + 2w_1w_2\rho_{12}\sigma_1\sigma_2$$

The standard deviation of a two asset portfolio is given by the square root of the portfolio's variance:

$$\sigma_P = \sqrt{w_1^2\sigma_1^2 + w_2^2\sigma_2^2 + 2w_1w_2\text{Cov}(R_1, R_2)}$$

or,

$$\sigma_P = \sqrt{w_1^2\sigma_1^2 + w_2^2\sigma_2^2 + 2w_1w_2\rho_{12}\sigma_1\sigma_2}$$

EXAMPLE 3

Return and Risk of a Two-Asset Portfolio

1. Assume that as a US investor, you decide to hold a portfolio with 80 percent invested in the S&P 500 US stock index and the remaining 20 percent in the MSCI Emerging Markets index. The expected return is 9.93 percent for the S&P 500 and 18.20 percent for the Emerging Markets index. The risk (standard deviation) is 16.21 percent for the S&P 500 and 33.11 percent for the Emerging Markets index. What will be the portfolio's expected return and risk given that the covariance between the S&P 500 and the Emerging Markets index is 0.5 percent or 0.0050? Note that units for covariance and variance are written as $\%^2$ when not expressed as a fraction. These are units of measure like squared feet and the numbers themselves are not actually squared.

Solution:

Portfolio return, $R_P = w_1R_1 + (1 - w_1), R_2 = (0.80 \times 0.0993) + (0.20 \times 0.1820)$ $= 0.1158$

$= 11.58\%$.

$$\text{Portfolio risk} = \sigma_P = \sqrt{w_1^2\sigma_1^2 + w_2^2\sigma_2^2 + 2w_1w_2Cov(R_1, R_2)}$$

$$\sigma_p^2 = w_{US}^2\sigma_{US}^2 + w_{EM}^2\sigma_{EM}^2 + 2w_{US}w_{EM}Cov_{US,EM}$$
$$\sigma_p^2 = (0.80^2 \times 0.1621^2) + (0.20^2 \times 0.3311^2)$$
$$+ (2 \times 0.80 \times 0.20 \times 0.0050)$$
$$\sigma_p^2 = 0.01682 + 0.00439 + 0.00160 = 0.02281$$
$$\sigma_p = 0.15103 = 15.10\%$$

The portfolio's expected return is 11.58 percent and the portfolio's risk is 15.10 percent. Look at this example closely. It shows that we can take the portfolio of a US investor invested only in the S&P 500, combine it with a *riskier* portfolio consisting of emerging markets securities, and the return of the US investor increases from 9.93 percent to 11.58 percent while the risk of the portfolio actually falls from 16.21 percent to 15.10 percent. Exhibit 12 depicts how the combination of the two assets results in a superior risk–return trade-off. Not only does the investor get a higher return, but he also gets it at a lower risk. That is the power of diversification as you will see later in this reading.

Exhibit 12: Combination of Two Assets

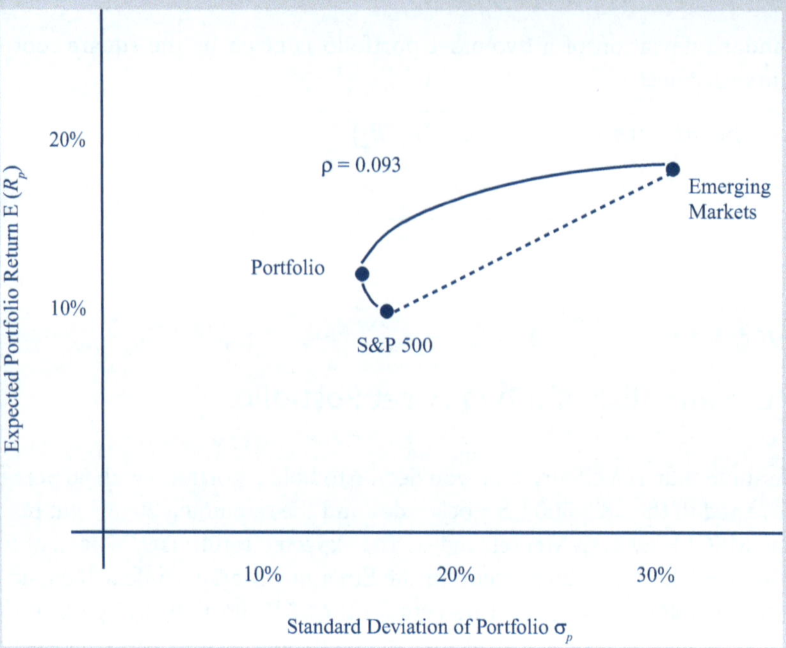

Covariance and Correlation

The **covariance** in the formula for portfolio standard deviation can be expanded as $\text{Cov}(R_1,R_2) = \rho_{12}\sigma_1\sigma_2$ where ρ_{12} is the correlation between returns, R_1, R_2. Although covariance is important, it is difficult to interpret because it is unbounded on both sides. It is easier to understand the **correlation coefficient** (ρ_{12}), which is bounded but provides similar information.

Correlation is a measure of the consistency or tendency for two investments to act in a similar way. The correlation coefficient, ρ_{12}, can be positive or negative and ranges from −1 to +1. Consider three different values of the correlation coefficient:

- $\rho_{12} = +1$: Returns of the two assets are perfectly *positively* correlated. Assets 1 and 2 move together 100 percent of the time.
- $\rho_{12} = -1$: Returns of the two assets are perfectly *negatively* correlated. Assets 1 and 2 move in opposite directions 100 percent of the time.
- $\rho_{12} = 0$: Returns of the two assets are *uncorrelated*. Movement of Asset 1 provides no prediction regarding the movement of Asset 2.

The correlation coefficient between two assets determines the effect on portfolio risk when the two assets are combined. To see how this works, consider two different values of ρ_{12}. You will find that portfolio risk is unaffected when the two assets are perfectly correlated ($\rho_{12} = +1$). In other words, the portfolio's standard deviation is simply a weighted average of the standard deviations of the two assets and as such a portfolio's risk is unchanged with the addition of assets with the same risk parameters. Portfolio risk falls, however, when the two assets are not perfectly correlated ($\rho_{12} <$ +1). Sufficiently low values of the correlation coefficient can make the portfolio riskless under certain conditions.

First, let $\rho_{12} = +1$

$$\sigma_p^2 = w_1^2\sigma_1^2 + w_2^2\sigma_2^2 + 2w_1w_2\rho_{12}\sigma_1\sigma_2 = w_1^2\sigma_1^2 + w_2^2\sigma_2^2 + 2w_1w_2\sigma_1\sigma_2$$
$$= (w_1\sigma_1 + w_2\sigma_2)^2$$
$$\sigma_p = w_1\sigma_1 + w_2\sigma_2$$

The first set of terms on the right side of the first equation contain the usual terms for portfolio variance. Because the correlation coefficient is equal to +1, the right side can be rewritten as a perfect square. The third row shows that portfolio risk is a weighted average of the risks of the individual assets' risks. We showed earlier that the portfolio return is a weighted average of the assets' returns. Because both risk and return are just weighted averages of the two assets in the portfolio there is no reduction in risk when $\rho_{12} = +1$.

Now let $\rho_{12} < +1$

The above analysis showed that portfolio risk is a weighted average of asset risks when $\rho_{12} = +1$. When $\rho_{12} < +1$, the portfolio risk is less than the weighted average of the individual assets' risks.

To show this, we begin by reproducing the general formula for portfolio risk, which is expressed by the terms to the left of the "<" sign below. The term to the right of "<" shows the portfolio risk when $\rho_{12} = +1$:

$$\sigma_p = \sqrt{w_1^2\sigma_1^2 + w_2^2\sigma_2^2 + 2w_1w_2\rho_{12}\sigma_1\sigma_2} < \sqrt{w_1^2\sigma_1^2 + w_2^2\sigma_2^2 + 2w_1w_2\sigma_1\sigma_2}$$
$$= (w_1\sigma_1 + w_2\sigma_2)$$
$$\sigma_p < (w_1\sigma_1 + w_2\sigma_2)$$

The left side is smaller than the right side because the correlation coefficient on the left side for the new portfolio is <1. Thus, the portfolio risk is less than the weighted average of risks while the portfolio return is still a weighted average of returns.

As you can see, we have achieved diversification by combining two assets that are not perfectly correlated. For an extreme case in which $\rho_{12} = -1$ (that is, the two asset returns move in opposite directions), the portfolio can be made risk free.

EXAMPLE 4

Effect of Correlation on Portfolio Risk

Two stocks have the same return and risk (standard deviation): 10 percent return with 20 percent risk. You form a portfolio with 50 percent each of Stock 1 and Stock 2 to examine the effect of correlation on risk.

1. Calculate the portfolio return and risk if the correlation is 1.0.

   Solution:

   $R_1 = R_2 = 10\% = 0.10$; $\sigma_1 = \sigma_2 = 20\% = 0.20$; $w_1 = w_2 = 50\% = 0.50$. Case 1: $\rho_{12} = +1$

   $$R_p = w_1R_1 + w_2R_2$$
   $$R_p = (0.5 \times 0.1) + (0.5 \times 0.1) = 0.10 = 10\%$$
   $$\sigma_p^2 = w_1^2\sigma_1^2 + w_2^2\sigma_2^2 + 2w_1w_2\sigma_1\sigma_2\rho_{12}$$
   $$\sigma_p^2 = (0.5^2 \times 0.2^2) + (0.5^2 \times 0.2^2) + (2 \times 0.5 \times 0.5 \times 0.2 \times 0.2 \times 1) = 0.04$$
   $$\sigma_p = \sqrt{0.04} = 0.20 = 20\%$$

   This equation demonstrates the earlier point that with a correlation of 1.0 the risk of the portfolio is the same as the risk of the individual assets.

2. Calculate the portfolio return and risk if the correlation is 0.0.

Solution:

$$\rho_{12} = 0$$
$$R_p = w_1 R_1 + w_2 R_2 = 0.10 = 10\%$$
$$\sigma_p^2 = w_1^2 \sigma_1^2 + w_2^2 \sigma_2^2 + 2 w_1 w_2 \sigma_1 \sigma_2 \rho_{12}$$
$$\sigma_p^2 = (0.5^2 \times 0.2^2) + (0.5^2 \times 0.2^2) + (2 \times 0.5 \times 0.5 \times 0.2 \times 0.2 \times 0) = 0.02$$
$$\sigma_p = \sqrt{0.02} = 0.14 = 14\%$$

This equation demonstrates the earlier point that, when assets have correlations of less than 1.0, they can be combined in a portfolio that has less risk than either of the assets individually.

3. Calculate the portfolio return and risk if the correlation is –1.0.

Solution:

$$\rho_{12} = -1$$
$$R_p = w_1 R_1 + w_2 R_2 = 0.10 = 10\%$$
$$\sigma_p^2 = w_1^2 \sigma_1^2 + w_2^2 \sigma_2^2 + 2 w_1 w_2 \sigma_1 \sigma_2 \rho_{12}$$
$$\sigma_p^2 = (0.5^2 \times 0.2^2) + (0.5^2 \times 0.2^2) + (2 \times 0.5 \times 0.5 \times 0.2 \times 0.2 \times -1) = 0$$
$$\sigma_p = 0\%$$

This equation demonstrates the earlier point that, if the correlation of assets is low enough, in this case 100 percent negative correlation or –1.00 (exactly inversely related), a portfolio can be designed that eliminates risk. The individual assets retain their risk characteristics, but the portfolio is risk free.

4. Compare the return and risk of portfolios with different correlations.

Solution:

The expected return is 10 percent in all three cases; however, the returns will be more volatile in Case 1 and least volatile in Case 3. In the first case, there is no diversification of risk (same risk as before of 20 percent) and the return remains the same. In the second case, with a correlation coefficient of 0, we have achieved diversification of risk (risk is now 14 percent instead of 20 percent), again with the same return. In the third case with a correlation coefficient of –1, the portfolio is risk free, although we continue to get the same return of 10 percent. This example shows the power of diversification that we expand on further in Section 9.

Relationship between Portfolio Risk and Return

The previous example illustrated the effect of correlation on portfolio risk while keeping the weights in the two assets equal and unchanged. In this section, we consider how portfolio risk and return vary with different portfolio weights and different correlations.

Asset 1 has an annual return of 7 percent and annualized risk of 12 percent, whereas Asset 2 has an annual return of 15 percent and annualized risk of 25 percent. The relationship is tabulated in Exhibit 13 for the two assets and graphically represented in Exhibit 14.

Exhibit 13: Relationship between Risk and Return

Weight in Asset 1 (%)	Portfolio Return	Portfolio Risk with Correlation of			
		1.0	0.5	0.2	−1.0
0	15.0	25.0	25.0	25.0	25.0
10	14.2	23.7	23.1	22.8	21.3
20	13.4	22.4	21.3	20.6	17.6
30	12.6	21.1	19.6	18.6	13.9
40	11.8	19.8	17.9	16.6	10.2
50	11.0	18.5	16.3	14.9	6.5
60	10.2	17.2	15.0	13.4	2.8
70	9.4	15.9	13.8	12.3	0.9
80	8.6	14.6	12.9	11.7	4.6
90	7.8	13.3	12.2	11.6	8.3
100	7.0	12.0	12.0	12.0	12.0

Exhibit 14: Relationship between Risk and Return

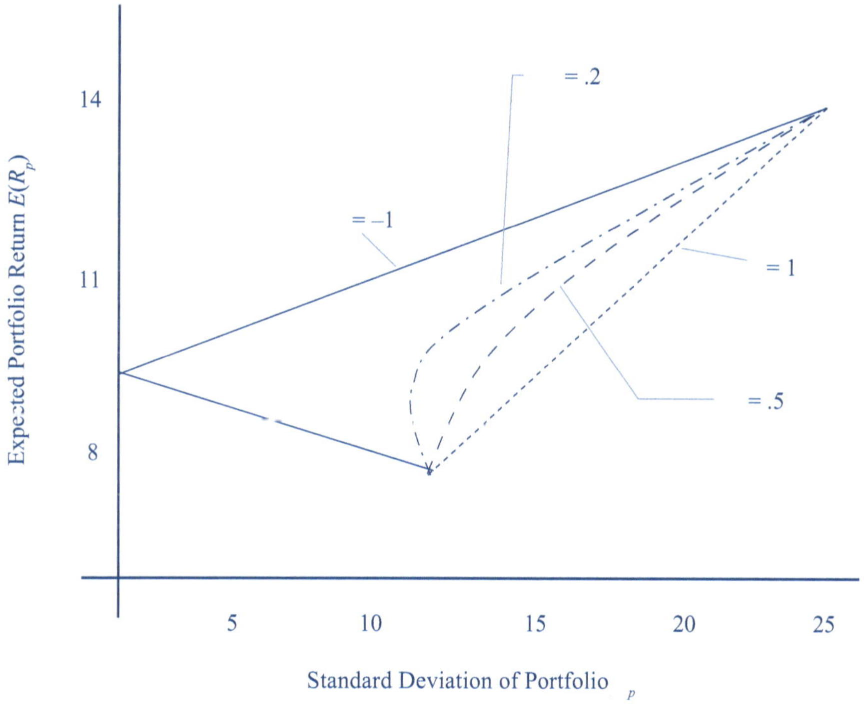

The table shows the portfolio return and risk for four correlation coefficients ranging from +1.0 to −1.0 and 11 weights ranging from 0 percent to 100 percent. The portfolio return and risk are 15 percent and 25 percent, respectively, when 0 percent is invested in Asset 1, versus 7 percent and 12 percent when 100 percent is invested in Asset 1. The portfolio return varies with weights but is unaffected by the correlation coefficient.

Portfolio risk becomes smaller with each successive decrease in the correlation coefficient, with the smallest risk when $\rho_{12} = -1$. The graph in Exhibit 14 shows that the risk–return relationship is a straight line when $\rho_{12} = +1$. As the correlation falls, the risk becomes smaller and smaller as in the table. The curvilinear nature of a portfolio of assets is recognizable in all investment opportunity sets (except at the extremes where $\rho_{12} = -1$ or $+1$).

EXAMPLE 5

Portfolio of Two Assets

Assume you are a UK investor holding a portfolio invested 60% in UK large-capitalization equities (as proxied by the FTSE 100 Index) and 40% in local medium-duration Treasury bonds ("gilts"). The expected return on the FTSE 100 is 5.5% and on the medium-duration gilts it is 0.7%. The risk (standard deviation of returns) is 13.2% and 4.2%, respectively. The correlation between the two assets is −0.01.

The expected return of this portfolio is

$$R_p = w_1 \times R_1 + (1 - w_1) \times R_2 = 0.6 \times 0.055 + 0.4 \times 0.07 = 0.0358 \approx 3.6\%.$$

The risk of this portfolio is

$$\sigma_p = \sqrt{w_1^2\sigma_1^2 + w_2^2\sigma_2^2 + 2 \times w_1 w_2 \times \rho \times \sigma_1\sigma_2}.$$

$$\sigma_p = \sqrt{(0.6^2 \times 0.132^2) + (0.4^2 \times 0.042^2) + 2 \times 0.6 \times 0.4 \times -0.01 \times 0.132 \times 0.042}.$$

$$\sigma_p = 0.0808 \approx 8.1\%$$

You notice that compared with US Treasury bonds, the expected return on gilts is lower and the risk of gilts is higher. US Treasury bonds have an expected return for a US-based investor of 1.5% and a risk of 4.0%. You wonder whether replacing the gilts in your portfolio with US Treasury bonds ("Treasuries") would improve the risk and return profile of your portfolio.

1. Do the given risk and return assumptions for US Treasury bonds allow you as a UK-based investor to calculate the expected return and risk of your portfolio with US Treasury bonds replacing UK gilts?

   Solution:

   No. The expected return and risk for Treasuries apply to a US investor, who invests in US dollars. To calculate expected return and risk in sterling for a UK-based portfolio of FTSE 100 equities and US Treasuries, one needs to take into account the exchange rate between the US dollar and UK pound sterling. This exchange rate has a volatility (risk) of its own, and a return expectation for the GBP/USD exchange rate has to be specified.

   For the purpose of calculating the return and risk of a foreign asset in a domestic investor's portfolio, the foreign asset can be seen as a "portfolio" of two assets. The return of a foreign asset in domestic (i.e., non-foreign) currency can be decomposed into a local currency return component and an exchange rate component:

   $$R_D = (1 + R_{lc}) \times (1 + R_{FX}) - 1$$

   Because the portfolio is fully exposed to the movement in both the asset's value in local currency and the currency exchange rate, the foreign currency and the asset each have a 100% portfolio weight. Note that the exchange rate must be specified as domestic currency/foreign currency to convert the foreign currency return into the investor's domestic currency. The risk can be calculated as follows:

$$\sigma_D = \sqrt{w_1^2 \sigma_{lc}^2 + w_2^2 \sigma_{FX}^2 + 2 \times w_1 w_2 \times \rho \times \sigma_{lc} \sigma_{FX}}$$
$$= \sqrt{\sigma_{lc}^2 + \sigma_{FX}^2 + 2 \times \rho \times \sigma_{lc} \times \sigma_{FX}}.$$

Assume in what follows that the risk (measured as expected standard deviation) of the GBP/USD currency exchange rate is 9.0% and the returns on Treasuries have a correlation with the GBP/USD exchange rate of 0.33. Assume also that you have no forecast for the future value of the USD/GBP exchange rate, and hence assume a 0% return.

2. What would be the expected risk of US Treasuries to you as a UK investor?

Solution:

$$\sigma_D = \sqrt{\sigma_{lc}^2 + \sigma_{FX}^2 + 2 \times \rho \times \sigma_{lc} \times \sigma_{FX}}$$
$$= \sqrt{0.040^2 + 0.090^2 + 2 \times 0.33 \times 0.040 + 0.090}.$$

$$\sigma_D = 0.110 = 11.0\%.$$

The correlations between the FTSE 100, US Treasuries, and the USD/GBP exchange rate are as depicted in the following correlation matrix.

	FTSE 100	US Treasuries	GBP/USD
FTSE 100	1.00	–0.32	–0.06
US Treasuries	–0.32	1.00	0.33
GBP/USD	–0.06	0.33	1.00

3. What would be the expected return and risk for your portfolio if you replace the UK gilts with US Treasuries?

Solution:

The expected return is the weighted average of the expected returns in British pound sterling (GBP) of UK large-capitalization equities and of US Treasuries. Recall that the return of a foreign asset in domestic currency consists of a foreign currency component and an asset component. All expected returns can be found above.

$$R_p = w_1 \times R_1 + (1 - w_1) \times [(1 + R_{lc}) \times (1 + R_{FX}) - 1].$$

$$R_p = 0.6 \times 0.055 + 0.4 \times [(1 + 0.015) \times (1 + 0.0) - 1] = 0.039 = 3.9\%.$$

Calculation of the risk of the portfolio involves a slightly more complicated formula. Recall that the risk of a two-asset portfolio depends on the risk and the weights of the individual assets and the co-movements between the two. For a three-asset portfolio (an equity portion, a foreign fixed-income portion, and the associated foreign currency exposure), the calculation is essentially the same, however there are three pairs of co-movements between assets, rather than one.

The formula for the standard deviation of a three-asset portfolio is therefore

$$\sigma_p = \sqrt{w_1^2 \sigma_1^2 + w_2^2 \sigma_2^2 + w_3^2 \sigma_3^2 + 2\rho_{1,2} w_1 w_2 \sigma_1 \sigma_2 + 2\rho_{1,3} w_1 w_3 \sigma_1 \sigma_3 + 2\rho_{2,3} w_2 w_3 \sigma_2 \sigma_3}.$$

The portfolio weight of the foreign currency exposure is equal to the portfolio weight of the US Treasuries.

Using the information provided above, we can calculate the risk of the portfolio with UK large-capitalization equities and US Treasuries as follows:

$\sigma_p = (0.6^2 \times 0.132^2 + 0.4^2 \times 0.040^2 + 0.4^2 \times 0.090^2 + 2 \times -0.32 \times 0.6 \times 0.4 \times 0.132 \times 0.040 + 2 \times -0.06 \times 0.6 \times 0.4 \times 0.132 \times 0.090 + 2 \times 0.33 \times 0.4 \times 0.4 \times 0.040 \times 0.090)^{1/2}$.

$\sigma_p = 0.0841 \approx 8.4\%$.

Compared to the UK equity/gilt portfolio, the UK equity/US Treasury portfolio has a higher expected return, because the UK gilts were replaced with an asset with superior return expectations. The risk of the new portfolio, however, is slightly higher despite the lower risk in local currency terms of US Treasuries compared to gilts. Owning US Treasuries as a non-US investor means being exposed to exchange rate risk, which should be considered when evaluating the risk profile.

8 PORTFOLIO OF MANY RISKY ASSETS

- ☐ calculate and interpret portfolio standard deviation
- ☐ describe the effect on a portfolio's risk of investing in assets that are less than perfectly correlated

In the previous section, we discussed how the correlation between two assets can affect the risk of a portfolio and the smaller the correlation the lower is the risk. The above analysis can be extended to a portfolio with many risky assets (N). Recall the previous equations for portfolio return and variance:

$$E(R_p) = \sum_{i=1}^{N} w_i E(R_i), \quad \sigma_P^2 = \left(\sum_{i=1}^{N} w_i^2 \sigma_i^2 + \sum_{i,j=1, i \neq j}^{N} w_i w_j \text{Cov}(i,j)\right), \quad \sum_{i=1}^{N} w_i = 1$$

To examine how a portfolio with many risky assets works and the ways in which we can reduce the risk of a portfolio, assume that the portfolio has equal weights ($1/N$) for all N assets. In addition, assume that $\bar{\sigma}^2$ and $\overline{\text{Cov}}$ are the average variance and average covariance. Given equal weights and average variance/covariance, we can rewrite the portfolio variance as below (intermediate steps are omitted to focus on the main result):

$$\sigma_P^2 = \left(\sum_{i=1}^{N} w_i^2 \sigma_i^2 + \sum_{i,j=1, i \neq j}^{N} w_i w_j \text{Cov}(i,j)\right)$$

$$\sigma_P^2 = \frac{\bar{\sigma}^2}{N} + \frac{(N-1)}{N}\overline{\text{Cov}}$$

The equation in the second line shows that as N becomes large, the first term on the right side with the denominator of N becomes smaller and smaller, implying that the contribution of one asset's variance to portfolio variance gradually becomes negligible. The second term, however, approaches the average covariance as N increases. It is reasonable to say that for portfolios with a large number of assets, covariance among the assets accounts for almost all of the portfolio's risk.

Importance of Correlation in a Portfolio of Many Assets

The analysis becomes more instructive and interesting if we assume that all assets in the portfolio have the same variance and the same correlation among assets. In that case, the portfolio risk can then be rewritten as:

$$\sigma_p = \sqrt{\frac{\sigma^2}{N} + \frac{(N-1)}{N}\rho\sigma^2}$$

The first term under the root sign becomes negligible as the number of assets in the portfolio increases leaving the second term (correlation) as the main determining factor for portfolio risk. If the assets are unrelated to one another, the portfolio can have close to zero risk. In the next section, we review these concepts to learn how portfolios can be diversified.

THE POWER OF DIVERSIFICATION 9

- ☐ describe characteristics of the major asset classes that investors consider in forming portfolios
- ☐ describe the effect on a portfolio's risk of investing in assets that are less than perfectly correlated

Diversification is one of the most important and powerful concepts in investments. Because investors are risk averse, they are interested in reducing risk preferably without reducing return. In other cases, investors may accept a lower return if it will reduce the chance of catastrophic losses. In previous sections of this reading, you learned the importance of correlation and covariance in managing risk. This section applies those concepts to explore ways for risk diversification. We begin with a simple but intuitive example.

EXAMPLE 6

Diversification with Rain and Shine

Assume a company Beachwear rents beach equipment. The annual return from the company's operations is 20 percent in years with many sunny days but falls to 0 percent in rainy years with few sunny days. The probabilities of a sunny year and a rainy year are equal at 50 percent. Thus, the average return is 10 percent, with a 50 percent chance of 20 percent return and a 50 percent chance of 0 percent return. Because Beachwear can earn a return of 20 percent or 0 percent, its average return of 10 percent is risky.

You are excited about investing in Beachwear but do not like the risk. Having heard about diversification, you decide to add another business to the portfolio to reduce your investment risk.

- There is a snack shop on the beach that sells all the healthy food you like. You estimate that the annual return from the Snackshop is also 20 percent in years with many sunny days and 0 percent in other years. As with the Beachwear shop, the average return is 10 percent.

You decide to invest 50 percent each in Snackshop and Beachwear. The average return is still 10 percent, with 50 percent of 10 percent from Snackshop and 50 percent of 10 percent from Beachwear. In a sunny year, you would earn 20 percent (= 50% of 20% from Beachwear + 50% of 20% from Snackshop). In a rainy year, you would earn 0 percent (=50% of 0% from Beachwear + 50% of 0% from Snackshop). The results are tabulated in Exhibit 15.

Exhibit 15

Type	Company	Percent Invested	Return in Sunny Year (%)	Return in Rainy Year (%)	Average Return (%)
Single stock	Beachwear	100	20	0	10
Single stock	Snackshop	100	20	0	10
Portfolio of two stocks	Beachwear	50	20	0	10
	Snackshop	50	20	0	10
	Total	100	20	0	10

These results seem counterintuitive. You thought that by adding another business you would be able to diversify and reduce your risk, but the risk is exactly the same as before. What went wrong? Note that both businesses do well when it is sunny and both businesses do poorly when it rains. The correlation between the two businesses is +1.0. No reduction in risk occurs when the correlation is +1.0.

- To reduce risk, you must consider a business that does well in a rainy year. You find a company that rents DVDs. DVDrental company is similar to the Beachwear company, except that its annual return is 20 percent in a rainy year and 0 percent in a sunny year, with an average return of 10 percent. DVDrental's 10 percent return is also risky just like Beachwear's return.

If you invest 50 percent each in DVDrental and Beachwear, then the average return is still 10 percent, with 50 percent of 10 percent from DVDrental and 50 percent of 10 percent from Beachwear. In a sunny year, you would earn 10 percent (= 50% of 20% from Beachwear + 50% of 0% from DVDrental). In a rainy year also, you would earn 10 percent (=50% of 0% from Beachwear + 50% of 20% from DVDrental). You have no risk because you earn 10 percent in both sunny and rainy years. Thus, by adding DVDrental to Beachwear, you have reduced (eliminated) your risk without affecting your return. The results are tabulated in Exhibit 16.

Exhibit 16

Type	Company	Percent Invested	Return in Sunny Year (%)	Return in Rainy Year (%)	Average Return (%)
Single stock	Beachwear	100	20	0	10
Single stock	DVDrental	100	0	20	10
Portfolio of two stocks	Beachwear	50	20	0	10
	DVDrental	50	0	20	10
	Total	100	10	10	10

In this case, the two businesses have a correlation of −1.0. When two businesses with a correlation of −1.0 are combined, risk can always be reduced to zero.

Correlation and Risk Diversification

Correlation is the key in diversification of risk. Notice that the returns from Beachwear and DVDrental always go in the opposite direction. If one of them does well, the other does not. Therefore, adding assets that do not behave like other assets in your portfolio is good and can reduce risk. The two companies in the above example have a correlation of −1.0.

Even when we expand the portfolio to many assets, correlation among assets remains the primary determinant of portfolio risk. Lower correlations are associated with lower risk. Unfortunately, most assets have high positive correlations. The challenge in diversifying risk is to find assets that have a correlation that is much lower than +1.0.

Historical Risk and Correlation

When we previously discussed asset returns, we were careful to distinguish between historical or past returns and expected or future returns because historical returns may not be a good indicator of future returns. Returns may be highly positive in one period and highly negative in another period depending on the risk of that asset. Exhibit 1 showed that returns for large US company stocks were high in the 1990s but were very low in the 2000s.

Risk for an asset class, however, does not usually change dramatically from one period to the next. Stocks have been risky even in periods of low returns. T-bills are always less risky even when they earn high returns. From Exhibit 1, we can see that risk has typically not varied much from one decade to the next, except that risk for bonds has been much higher in recent decades when compared with earlier decades. Therefore, it is not unreasonable to assume that historical risk can work as a good proxy for future risk.

As with risk, correlations are quite stable among assets of the same country. Intercountry correlations, however, have been on the rise in the last few decades as a result of globalization and the liberalization of many economies. A correlation above 0.90 is considered high because the assets do not provide much opportunity for diversification of risk Low correlations—generally less than 0.50—are desirable for portfolio diversification.

Historical Correlation among Asset Classes

Correlations among major US asset classes and international stocks are reported in Exhibit 17 for 1970–2017. The highest correlation is between US large company stocks and US small company stocks at about 70 percent, whereas the correlation between US large company stocks and international stocks is approximately 66 percent. Although these are the highest correlations, they still provide diversification benefits because the correlations are less than 100 percent. The correlation between international stocks and US small company stocks is lower, at 50 percent. The lowest correlations are between stocks and bonds, with some correlations being negative, such as that between US small company stocks and US long-term government bonds. Similarly, the correlation between T-bills and stocks is close to zero.[4]

Exhibit 17: Correlation Among US Assets and International Stocks (1970–2017)

Series	International Stocks	US Large Company Stocks	US Small Company Stocks	US Long-Term Corporate Bonds	US Long-Term Treasury Bonds	US T-Bills	US Inflation
International stocks	1.00						
US large company stocks	0.66	1.00					
US small company stocks	0.50	0.72	1.00				
US long-term corporate bonds	0.02	0.23	0.06	1.00			
US long-term Treasury bonds	−0.13	0.01	−0.15	0.89	1.00		
US T-bills	0.01	0.04	0.02	0.05	0.09	1.00	
US inflation	−0.06	−0.11	0.04	−0.32	−0.26	0.69	1.00

Source: 2018 SBBI Yearbook (Exhibit 12.13).

The low correlations between stocks and bonds are attractive for portfolio diversification. Similarly, including international securities in a portfolio can also control portfolio risk. It is not surprising that most diversified portfolios of investors contain domestic stocks, domestic bonds, foreign stocks, foreign bonds, real estate, cash, and other asset classes.

Avenues for Diversification

The reason for diversification is simple. By constructing a portfolio with assets that do not move together, you create a portfolio that reduces the ups and downs in the short term but continues to grow steadily in the long term. Diversification thus makes a portfolio more resilient to gyrations in financial markets.

We describe a number of approaches for diversification, some of which have been discussed previously and some of which might seem too obvious. Diversification, however, is such an important part of investing that it cannot be emphasized enough, especially when we continue to meet and see many investors who are not properly diversified.

- *Diversify with asset classes.* Correlations among major asset classes[5] are not usually high, as can be observed from the few US asset classes listed in Exhibit 17. Correlations for other asset classes and other countries are also typically low, which provides investors the opportunity to benefit from diversifying among many asset classes to achieve the biggest benefit from diversification. A partial list of asset classes includes domestic large caps, domestic small caps, growth stocks, value stocks, domestic corporate bonds, long-term domestic government bonds, domestic Treasury bills (cash),

4 In any short period, T-bills are riskless and uncorrelated with other asset classes. For example, a 3-month US Treasury bill is redeemable at its face value upon maturity irrespective of what happens to other assets. When we consider multiple periods, however, returns on T-bills may be related to other asset classes because short-term interest rates vary depending on the strength of the economy and outlook for inflation.

5 Major asset classes are distinguished from sub-classes, such as US value stocks and US growth stocks.

emerging market stocks, emerging market bonds, developed market stocks (i.e., developed markets excluding domestic market), developed market bonds, real estate, and gold and other commodities. In addition, industries and sectors are used to diversify portfolios. For example, energy stocks may not be well correlated with health care stocks. The exact proportions in which these assets should be included in a portfolio depend on the risk, return, and correlation characteristics of each and the home country of the investor.

- *Diversify with index funds.* Diversifying among asset classes can become costly for small portfolios because of the number of securities required. For example, creating diversified exposure to a single category, such as a domestic large company asset class, may require a group of at least 30 stocks. Exposure to 10 asset classes may require 300 securities, which can be expensive to trade and track. Instead, it may be effective to use exchange-traded funds or mutual funds that track the respective indexes, which could bring down the costs associated with building a well-diversified portfolio. Therefore, many investors should consider index mutual funds as an investment vehicle as opposed to individual securities.
- *Diversification among countries.* Countries are different because of industry focus, economic policy, and political climate. The US economy produces many financial and technical services and invests a significant amount in innovative research. The Chinese and Indian economies, however, are focused on manufacturing. Countries in the European Union are vibrant democracies whereas East Asian countries are experimenting with democracy. Thus, financial returns in one country over time are not likely to be highly correlated with returns in another country. Country returns may also be different because of different currencies. In other words, the return on a foreign investment may be different when translated to the home country's currency. Because currency returns are uncorrelated with stock returns, they may help reduce the risk of investing in a foreign country even when that country, in isolation, is a very risky emerging market from an equity investment point of view. Investment in foreign countries is an essential part of a well-diversified portfolio.
- *Diversify by* not *owning your employer's stock.* Companies encourage their employees to invest in company stock through employee stock plans and retirement plans. You should evaluate investing in your company, however, just as you would evaluate any other investment. In addition, you should consider the nonfinancial investments that you have made, especially the human capital you have invested in your company. Because you work for your employer, you are already heavily invested in it—your earnings depend on your employer. The level of your earnings, whether your compensation improves or whether you get a promotion, depends on how well your employer performs. If a competitor drives your employer out of the market, you will be out of a job. Additional investments in your employer will concentrate your wealth in one asset even more so and make you less diversified.
- *Evaluate each asset before adding to a portfolio.* Every time you add a security or an asset class to the portfolio, recognize that there is a cost associated with diversification. There is a cost of trading an asset as well as the cost of tracking a larger portfolio. In some cases, the securities or assets may have different names but belong to an asset class in which you already have

sufficient exposure. A general rule to evaluate whether a new asset should be included to an existing portfolio is based on the following risk–return trade-off relationship:

$$E(R_{new}) = R_f + \frac{\sigma_{new}\rho_{new,p}}{\sigma_p} \times \left[E(R_p) - R_f\right]$$

where *E(R)* is the return from the asset, R_f is the return on the risk-free asset, σ is the standard deviation, ρ is the correlation coefficient, and the subscripts *new* and *p* refer to the new stock and existing portfolio. If the new asset's risk-adjusted return benefits the portfolio, then the asset should be included. The condition can be rewritten using the Sharpe ratio on both sides of the equation as:

$$\frac{E(R_{new}) - R_f}{\sigma_{new}} > \frac{E(R_p) - R_f}{\sigma_p} \times \rho_{new,p}$$

If the Sharpe ratio of the new asset is greater than the Sharpe ratio of the current portfolio times the correlation coefficient, it is beneficial to add the new asset.

- *Buy insurance for risky portfolios.* It may come as a surprise, but insurance is an investment asset—just a different kind of asset. Insurance has a negative correlation with your assets and is thus very valuable. Insurance gives you a positive return when your assets lose value, but pays nothing if your assets maintain their value. Over time, insurance generates a negative average return. Many individuals, however, are willing to accept a small negative return because insurance reduces their exposure to an extreme loss. In general, it is reasonable to add an investment with a negative return if that investment significantly reduces risk (an example of a classic case of the risk–return trade-off).

  Alternatively, investments with negative correlations also exist. Historically, gold has a negative correlation with stocks; however, the expected return is usually small and sometimes even negative. Investors often include gold and other commodities in their portfolios as a way of reducing their overall portfolio risk, including currency risk and inflation risk.

  Buying put options is another way of reducing risk. Because put options pay when the underlying asset falls in value (negative correlation), they can protect an investor's portfolio against catastrophic losses. Of course, put options cost money, and the expected return is zero or marginally negative.

10 EFFICIENT FRONTIER: INVESTMENT OPPORTUNITY SET & MINIMUM VARIANCE PORTFOLIOS

- ☐ describe the effect on a portfolio's risk of investing in assets that are less than perfectly correlated
- ☐ describe and interpret the minimum-variance and efficient frontiers of risky assets and the global minimum-variance portfolio

In this section, we formalize the effect of diversification and expand the set of investments to include all available risky assets in a mean–variance framework. The addition of a risk-free asset generates an optimal risky portfolio and the capital allocation line. We can then derive an investor's optimal portfolio by overlaying the capital allocation line with the indifference curves of investors.

Investment Opportunity Set

If two assets are perfectly correlated, the risk–return opportunity set is represented by a straight line connecting those two assets. The line contains portfolios formed by changing the weight of each asset invested in the portfolio. This correlation was depicted by the straight line (with $\rho = 1$) in Exhibit 14. If the two assets are not perfectly correlated, the portfolio's risk is less than the weighted average risk of the components, and the portfolio formed from the two assets bulges on the left as shown by curves with the correlation coefficient (ρ) less than 1.0 in Exhibit 14. All of the points connecting the two assets are achievable (or feasible). The addition of new assets to this portfolio creates more and more portfolios that are either a linear combination of the existing portfolio and the new asset or a curvilinear combination, depending on the correlation between the existing portfolio and the new asset.

As the number of available assets increases, the number of possible combinations increases rapidly. When all investable assets are considered, and there are hundreds and thousands of them, we can construct an opportunity set of investments. The opportunity set will ordinarily span all points within a frontier because it is also possible to reach every possible point within that curve by judiciously creating a portfolio from the investable assets.

We begin with individual investable assets and gradually form portfolios that can be plotted to form a curve as shown in Exhibit 18. All points on the curve and points to the right of the curve are attainable by a combination of one or more of the investable assets. This set of points is called the investment opportunity set. Initially, the opportunity set consists of domestic assets only and is labeled as such in Exhibit 18.

Exhibit 18: Investment Opportunity Set

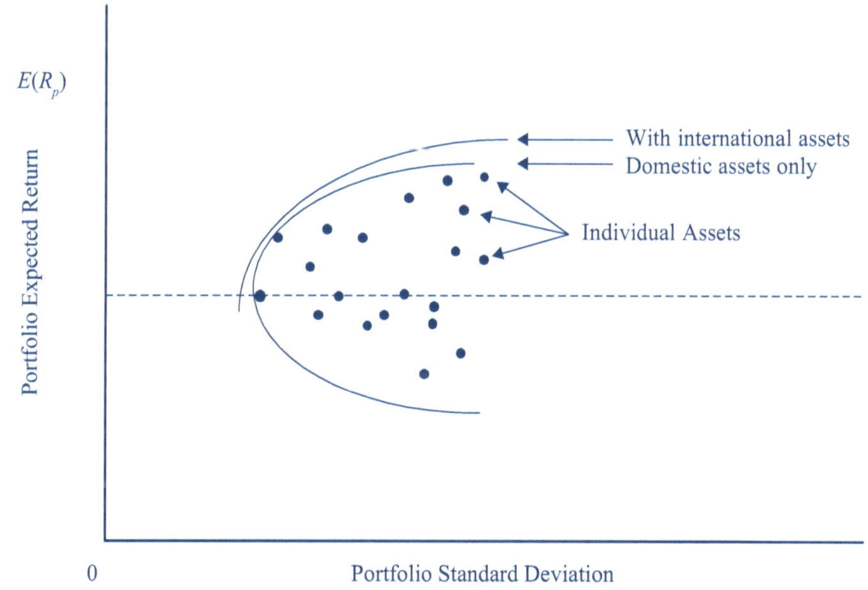

Addition of Asset Classes

Exhibit 18 shows the effect of adding a new asset class, such as international assets. As long as the new asset class is not perfectly correlated with the existing asset class, the investment opportunity set will expand out further to the northwest, providing a superior risk–return trade-off.

The investment opportunity set with international assets dominates the opportunity set that includes only domestic assets. Adding other asset classes will have the same impact on the opportunity set. Thus, we should continue to add asset classes until they do not further improve the risk–return trade-off. The benefits of diversification can be fully captured in this way in the construction of the investment opportunity set, and eventually in the selection of the optimal portfolio.

In the discussion that follows in this section, we will assume that *all* investable assets available to an investor are included in the investment opportunity set and no special attention needs to be paid to new asset classes or new investment opportunities.

Minimum-Variance Portfolios

The investment opportunity set consisting of all available investable sets is shown in Exhibit 19. There are a large number of portfolios available for investment, but we must choose a single optimal portfolio. In this subsection, we begin the selection process by narrowing the choice to fewer portfolios.

Exhibit 19: Minimum-Variance Frontier

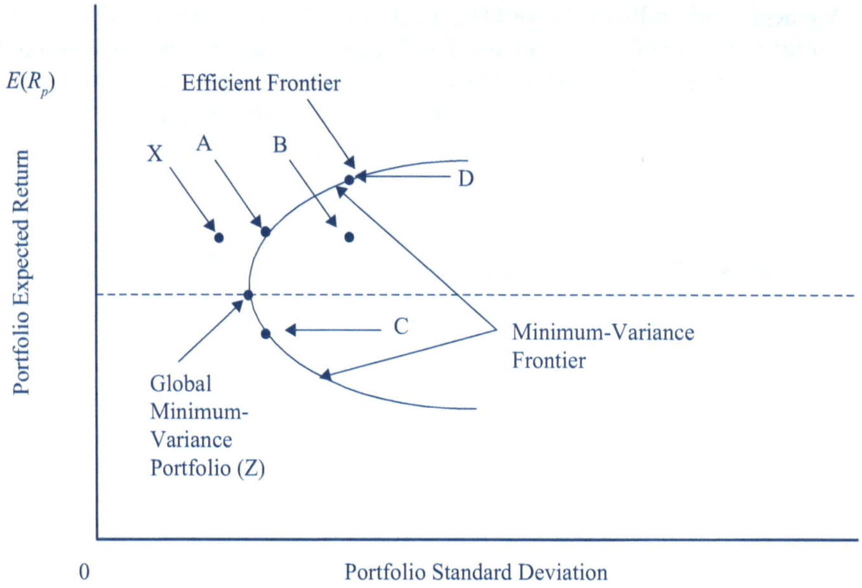

Minimum-Variance Frontier

Risk-averse investors seek to minimize risk for a given return. Consider Points A, B, and X in Exhibit 19 and assume that they are on the same horizontal line by construction. Thus, the three points have the same expected return, $E(R_1)$, as do all other points on the imaginary line connecting A, B, and X. Given a choice, an investor will choose the point with the minimum risk, which is Point X. Point X, however, is unattainable because it does not lie within the investment opportunity set. Thus, the minimum risk that we can attain for $E(R_1)$ is at Point A. Point B and all points to the right of Point A are feasible but they have higher risk. Therefore, a risk-averse investor will choose only Point A in preference to any other portfolio with the same return.

Similarly, Point C is the minimum variance point for the return earned at C. Points to the right of C have higher risk. We can extend the above analysis to all possible returns. In all cases, we find that the **minimum-variance portfolio** is the one that lies on the solid curve drawn in Exhibit 19. The entire collection of these minimum-variance portfolios is referred to as the minimum-variance frontier. The minimum-variance frontier defines the smaller set of portfolios in which investors would want to invest. Note that no risk-averse investor will choose to invest in a portfolio to the right of the minimum-variance frontier because a portfolio on the minimum-variance frontier can give the same return but at a lower risk.

Global Minimum-Variance Portfolio

The left-most point on the minimum-variance frontier is the portfolio with the minimum variance among all portfolios of risky assets, and is referred to as the **global minimum-variance portfolio**. An investor cannot hold a portfolio consisting of *risky* assets that has less risk than that of the global minimum-variance portfolio. Note the emphasis on "risky" assets. Later, the introduction of a risk-free asset will allow us to relax this constraint.

Efficient Frontier of Risky Assets

The minimum-variance frontier gives us portfolios with the minimum variance for a given return. However, investors also want to maximize return for a given risk. Observe Points A and C on the minimum-variance frontier shown in Exhibit 19. Both of them have the same risk. Given a choice, an investor will choose Portfolio A because it has a higher return. No one will choose Portfolio C. The same analysis applies to all points on the minimum-variance frontier that lie below the global minimum-variance portfolio. Thus, portfolios on the curve below the global minimum-variance portfolio and to the right of the global minimum-variance portfolio are not beneficial and are inefficient portfolios for an investor.

The curve that lies above and to the right of the global minimum-variance portfolio is referred to as the **Markowitz efficient frontier** because it contains all portfolios of risky assets that rational, risk-averse investors will choose.

An important observation that is often ignored is the slope at various points on the efficient frontier. As we move right from the global minimum-variance portfolio (Point Z) in Exhibit 19, there is an increase in risk with a concurrent increase in return. The increase in return with every unit increase in risk, however, keeps decreasing as we move from left to the right because the slope continues to decrease. The slope at Point D is less than the slope at Point A, which is less than the slope at Point Z. The increase in return by moving from Point Z to Point A is the same as the increase in return by moving from Point A to Point D. It can be seen that the additional risk in moving from Point A to Point D is 3 to 4 times more than the additional risk in moving from Point Z to Point A. Thus, investors obtain decreasing increases in returns as they assume more risk.

11 EFFICIENT FRONTIER: A RISK-FREE ASSET AND MANY RISKY ASSETS

☐ explain the selection of an optimal portfolio, given an investor's utility (or risk aversion) and the capital allocation line

Until now, we have only considered risky assets in which the return is risky or uncertain. Most investors, however, have access to a risk-free asset, most notably from securities issued by the government. The addition of a risk-free asset makes the investment opportunity set much richer than the investment opportunity set consisting only of risky assets.

Capital Allocation Line and Optimal Risky Portfolio

By definition, a risk-free asset has zero risk so it must lie on the y-axis in a mean-variance graph. A risk-free asset with a return of R_f is plotted in Exhibit 20. This asset can now be combined with a portfolio of risky assets. The combination of a risk-free asset with a portfolio of risky assets is a straight line, such as in Section 6 (see Exhibit 9). Unlike in Section 6, however, we have many risky portfolios to choose from instead of a single risky portfolio.

Exhibit 20: Optimal Risky Portfolio

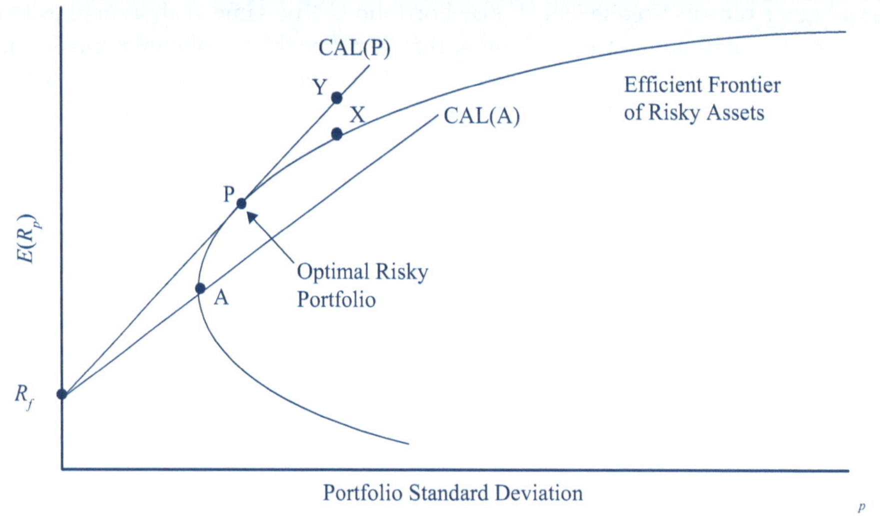

All portfolios on the efficient frontier are candidates for being combined with the risk-free asset. Two combinations are shown in Exhibit 20: one between the risk-free asset and efficient Portfolio A and the other between the risk-free asset and efficient Portfolio P. Comparing capital allocation line A and capital allocation line P reveals that there is a point on CAL(P) with a higher return and same risk for each point on CAL(A). In other words, the portfolios on CAL(P) dominate the portfolios on CAL(A). Therefore, an investor will choose CAL(P) over CAL(A). We would like to move further northwest to achieve even better portfolios. None of those portfolios, however, is attainable because they are above the efficient frontier.

What about other points on the efficient frontier? For example, Point X is on the efficient frontier and has the highest return of all risky portfolios for its risk. However, Point Y on CAL(P), achievable by leveraging Portfolio P as seen in Section 6, lies above Point X and has the same risk but higher return. In the same way, we can observe that not only does CAL(P) dominate CAL(A) but it also dominates the Markowitz efficient frontier of risky assets.

CAL(P) is the optimal capital allocation line and Portfolio P is the optimal risky portfolio. Thus, with the addition of the risk-free asset, we are able to narrow our selection of risky portfolios to a single optimal risky portfolio, P, which is at the tangent of CAL(P) and the efficient frontier of risky assets.

The Two-Fund Separation Theorem

The **two-fund separation theorem** states that all investors regardless of taste, risk preferences, and initial wealth will hold a combination of two portfolios or funds: a risk-free asset and an optimal portfolio of risky assets.[6]

The separation theorem allows us to divide an investor's investment problem into two distinct steps: the investment decision and the financing decision. In the first step, as in the previous analysis, the investor identifies the optimal risky portfolio. The optimal risky portfolio is selected from numerous risky portfolios without considering the investor's preferences. The investment decision at this step is based on the optimal risky portfolio's (a single portfolio) return, risk, and correlations.

The capital allocation line connects the optimal risky portfolio and the risk-free asset. All optimal investor portfolios must be on this line. Each investor's optimal portfolio on the CAL(P) is determined in the second step. Considering each individual investor's risk preference, using indifference curves, determines the investor's allocation to the risk-free asset (lending) and to the optimal risky portfolio. Portfolios beyond the optimal risky portfolio are obtained by borrowing at the risk-free rate (i.e., buying on margin). Therefore, the individual investor's risk preference determines the amount of financing (i.e., lending to the government instead of investing in the optimal risky portfolio or borrowing to purchase additional amounts of the optimal risky portfolio).

EXAMPLE 7

Choosing the Right Portfolio

In Exhibit 21, the risk and return of the points marked are as follows:

Point	Return (%)	Risk (%)	Point (%)	Return (%)	Risk (%)
A	15	10	B	11	10
C	15	30	D	25	30
F	4	0	G (gold)	10	30
P	16	17			

6 In the next reading, you will learn that the optimal portfolio of risky assets is the market portfolio.

Exhibit 21

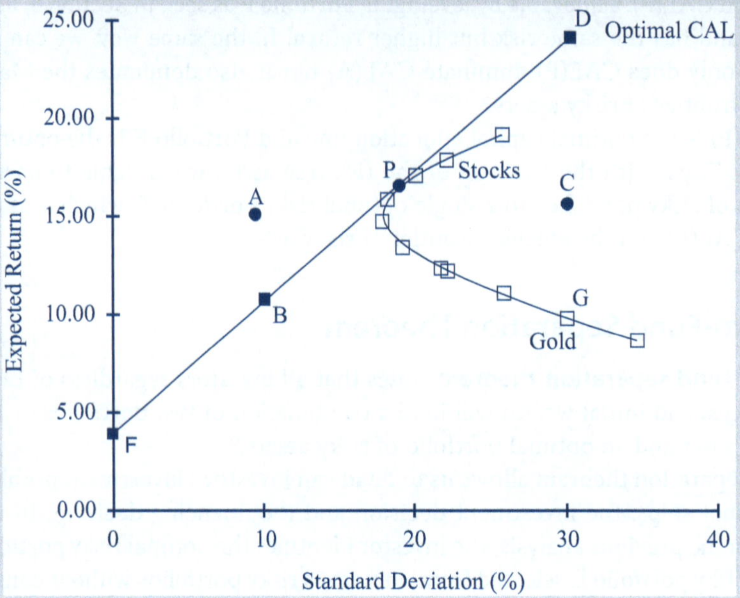

Answer the following questions with reference to the points plotted on Exhibit 21 and explain your answers. The investor is choosing one portfolio based on the graph.

1. Which of the above points is not achievable?

   Solution:

   Portfolio A is not attainable because it lies outside the feasible set and not on the capital allocation line.

2. Which of these portfolios will not be chosen by a rational, risk-averse investor?

   Solution:

   Portfolios G and C will not be chosen because D provides higher return for the same risk. G and C are the only investable points that do not lie on the capital allocation line.

3. Which of these portfolios is most suitable for a risk-neutral investor?

   Solution:

   Portfolio D is most suitable because a risk-neutral investor cares only about return and portfolio D provides the highest return. A = 0 in the utility formula.

4. Gold is on the inefficient part of the feasible set. Nonetheless, gold is owned by many rational investors as part of a larger portfolio. Why?

   Solution:

   Gold may be owned as part of a portfolio (not as *the* portfolio) because gold has low or negative correlation with many risky assets, such as stocks. Being part of a portfolio can thus reduce overall risk even though its standalone risk is high and return is low. Note that gold's price is not stable—its return is very risky (30 percent). Even risk seekers will choose D over G, which has the same risk but higher return.

5. What is the utility of an investor at point P with a risk aversion coefficient of 3?

Solution:

$U = E(r) - 0.5A\sigma^2 = 0.16 - 0.5 \times 3 \times 0.0289 = 0.1167 = 11.67\%.$

EFFICIENT FRONTIER: OPTIMAL INVESTOR PORTFOLIO

12

- [ ] explain the selection of an optimal portfolio, given an investor's utility (or risk aversion) and the capital allocation line

The CAL(P) in Exhibit 22 contains the best possible portfolios available to investors. Each of those portfolios is a linear combination of the risk-free asset and the optimal risky portfolio. Among the available portfolios, the selection of each investor's optimal portfolio depends on the risk preferences of an investor. In Sections 4–6, we discussed that the individual investor's risk preferences are incorporated into their indifference curves. These can be used to select the optimal portfolio.

Exhibit 22 shows an indifference curve that is tangent to the capital allocation line, CAL(P). Indifference curves with higher utility than this one lie above the capital allocation line, so their portfolios are not achievable. Indifference curves that lie below this one are not preferred because they have lower utility. Thus, the optimal portfolio for the investor with this indifference curve is portfolio C on CAL(P), which is tangent to the indifference curve.

Exhibit 22: Optimal Investor Portfolio

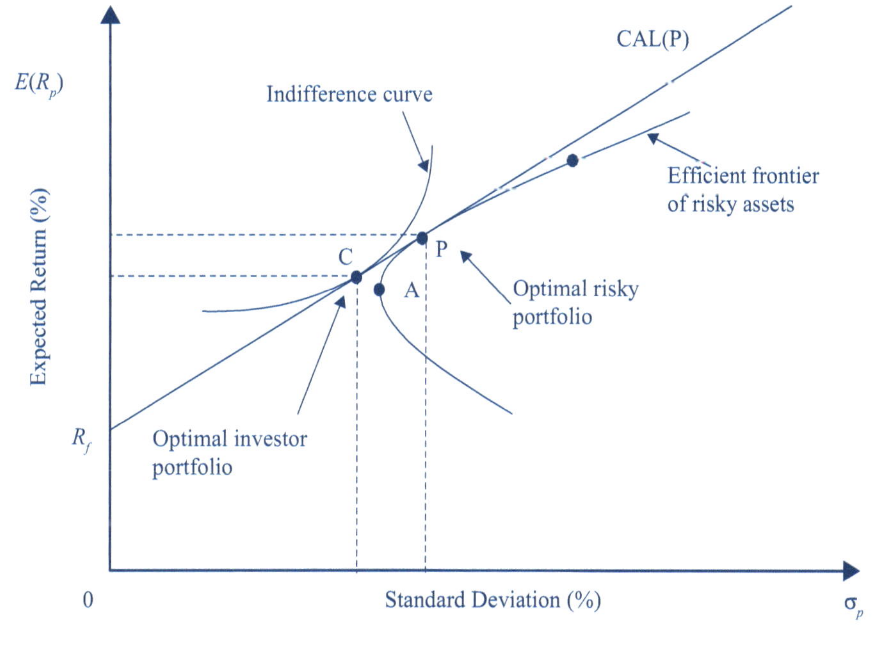

EXAMPLE 8

Comprehensive Example on Portfolio Selection

This comprehensive example reviews many concepts learned in this reading. The example begins with simple information about available assets and builds an optimal investor portfolio for the Lohrmanns.

Suppose the Lohrmanns can invest in only two risky assets, A and B. The expected return and standard deviation for asset A are 20 percent and 50 percent, and the expected return and standard deviation for asset B are 15 percent and 33 percent. The two assets have zero correlation with one another.

1. Calculate portfolio expected return and portfolio risk (standard deviation) if an investor invests 10 percent in A and the remaining 90 percent in B.

Solution:

The subscript "*rp*" means risky portfolio.

$$R_{rp} = [0.10 \times 20\%] + [(1 - 0.10) \times 15\%] = 0.155 = 15.50\%$$

$$\sigma_{rp} = \sqrt{w_A^2\sigma_A^2 + w_B^2\sigma_B^2 + 2w_Aw_B\rho_{AB}\sigma_A\sigma_B}$$

$$= \sqrt{(0.10^2 \times 0.50^2) + (0.90^2 \times 0.33^2) + (2 \times 0.10 \times 0.90 \times 0.0 \times 0.50 \times 0.33)}$$

$$= 0.3012 = 30.12\%$$

Note that the correlation coefficient is 0, so the last term for standard deviation is zero.

2. Generalize the above calculations for portfolio return and risk by assuming an investment of w_A in Asset A and an investment of $(1 - w_A)$ in Asset B.

Solution:

$$R_{rp} = w_A \times 20\% + (1 - w_A) \times 15\% = 0.05w_A + 0.15$$

$$\sigma_{rp} = \sqrt{w_A^2 \times 0.5^2 + (1 - w_A)^2 \times 0.33^2} = \sqrt{0.25w_A^2 + 0.1089(1 - 2w_A + w_A^2)}$$

$$= \sqrt{0.3589w_A^2 - 0.2178w_A + 0.1089}$$

The investment opportunity set can be constructed by using different weights in the expressions for $E(R_{rp})$ and σ_{rp} in Part 1 of this example. Exhibit 23 shows the combination of Assets A and B.

Exhibit 23

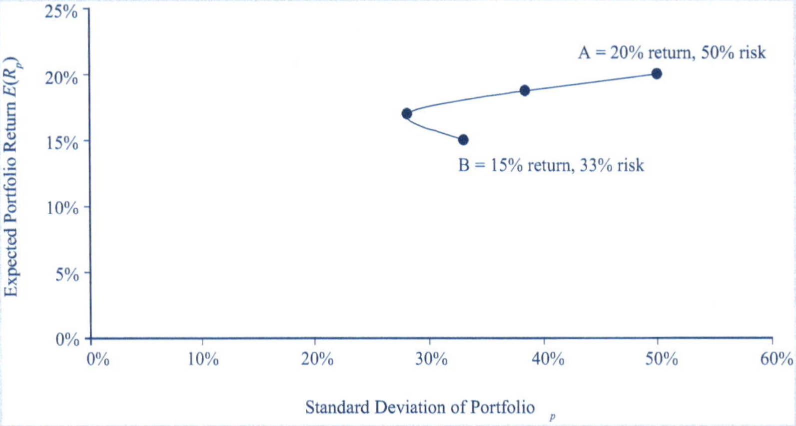

3. Now introduce a risk-free asset with a return of 3 percent. Write an equation for the capital allocation line in terms of w_A that will connect the risk-free asset to the portfolio of risky assets. (Hint: use the equation in Section 6 and substitute the expressions for a risky portfolio's risk and return from Part 2 above).

   Solution:

   The equation of the line connecting the risk-free asset to the portfolio of risky assets is given below (see Section 6), where the subscript "*rp*" refers to the risky portfolio instead of "*i*," and the subscript "*p*" refers to the new portfolio of two risky assets and one risk-free asset.

$$E(R_p) = R_f + \frac{E(R_i) - R_f}{\sigma_i}\sigma_p,$$

   Rewritten as

$$E(R_p) = R_f + \frac{E(R_{rp}) - R_f}{\sigma_{rp}}\sigma_p$$

$$= 0.03 + \frac{0.05\,w_A + 0.15 - 0.03}{\sqrt{0.3589\,w_A^2 - 0.2178\,w_A + 0.1089}}\sigma_p$$

$$= 0.03 + \frac{0.05\,w_A + 0.12}{\sqrt{0.3589\,w_A^2 - 0.2178\,w_A + 0.1089}}\sigma_p$$

   The capital allocation line is the line that has the maximum slope because it is tangent to the curve formed by portfolios of the two risky assets. Exhibit 24 shows the capital allocation line based on a risk-free asset added to the group of assets.

Exhibit 24

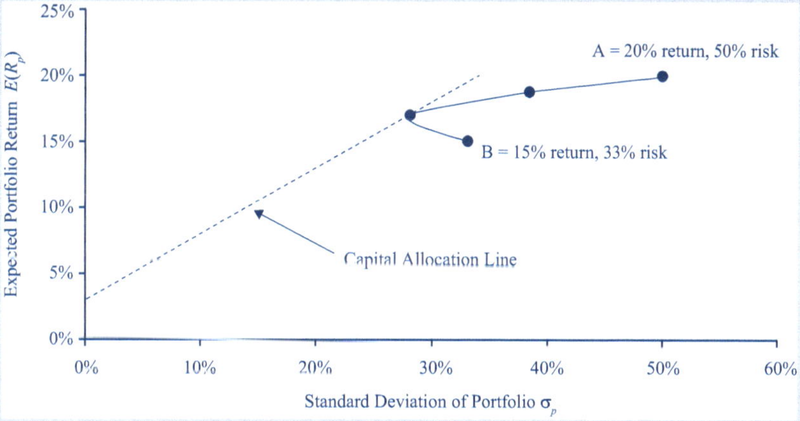

4. The slope of the capital allocation line is maximized when the weight in Asset A is 38.20 percent.[7] What is the equation for the capital allocation line using w_A of 38.20 percent?

   Solution:

   By substituting 38.20 percent for w_A in the equation in Part 3, we get $E(R_p) = 0.03 + 0.4978\sigma_p$ as the capital allocation line.

7 You can maximize

$$\frac{0.05\,w_A + 0.12}{\sqrt{0.3589\,w_A^2 - 0.2178\,w_A + 0.1089}}$$

by taking the first derivative of the slope with respect to w_A and setting it to 0.

5. Having created the capital allocation line, we turn to the Lohrmanns. What is the standard deviation of a portfolio that gives a 20 percent return and is on the capital allocation line? How does this portfolio compare with asset A?

Solution:

Solve the equation for the capital allocation line to get the standard deviation: $0.20 = 0.03 + 0.4978\sigma_p$. $\sigma_p = 34.2\%$. The portfolio with a 20 percent return has the same return as Asset A but a lower standard deviation, 34.2 percent instead of 50.0 percent.

6. What is the risk of portfolios with returns of 3 percent, 9 percent, 15 percent, and 20 percent?

Solution:

You can find the risk of the portfolio using the equation for the capital allocation line: $E(R_p) = 0.03 + 0.4978\sigma_p$.
For a portfolio with a return of 15 percent, write $0.15 = 0.03 + 0.4978\sigma_p$. Solving for σ_p gives 24.1 percent. You can similarly calculate risks of other portfolios with the given returns.
The risk of the portfolio for a return of 3 percent is 0.0 percent, for a return of 9 percent is 12.1 percent, for a return of 15 percent is 24.1 percent, and for a return of 20 percent is 34.2 percent. The points are plotted in Exhibit 25.

Exhibit 25

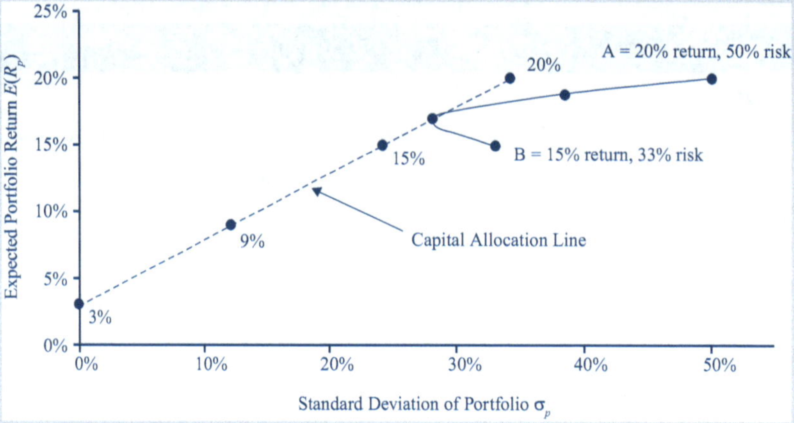

7. What is the utility that the Lohrmanns derive from a portfolio with a return of 3 percent, 9 percent, 15 percent, and 20 percent? The risk aversion coefficient for the Lohrmanns is 2.5.

Solution:

To find the utility, use the utility formula with a risk aversion coefficient of 2.5:

$$\text{Utility} = E(R_p) - 0.5 \times 2.5\sigma_p^2$$

$$\text{Utility (3\%)} = 0.0300$$

$$\text{Utility (9\%)} = 0.09 - 0.5 \times 2.5 \times 0.121^2 = +0.0717$$

$$\text{Utility (15\%)} = 0.15 - 0.5 \times 2.5 \times 0.241^2 = +0.0774$$

$$\text{Utility (20\%)} = 0.20 - 0.5 \times 2.5 \times 0.341^2 = +0.0546$$

Based on the above information, the Lohrmanns choose a portfolio with a return of 15 percent and a standard deviation of 24.1 percent because it has the highest utility: 0.0774. Finally, Exhibit 26 shows the indifference curve that is tangent to the capital allocation line to generate Lohrmanns' optimal investor portfolio.

Exhibit 26

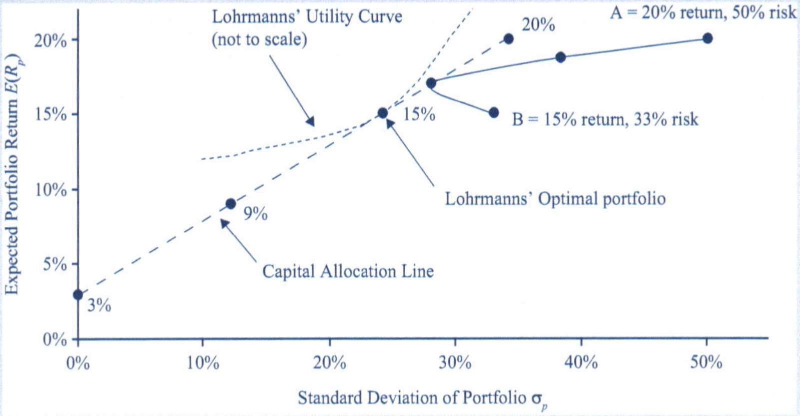

Investor Preferences and Optimal Portfolios

The location of an optimal investor portfolio depends on the investor's risk preferences. A highly risk-averse investor may invest a large proportion, even 100 percent, of his/her assets in the risk-free asset. The optimal portfolio in this investor's case will be located close to the y-axis. A less risk-averse investor, however, may invest a large portion of his/her wealth in the optimal risky asset. The optimal portfolio in this investor's case will lie closer to Point P in Exhibit 22.

Some less risk-averse investors (i.e., with a high risk tolerance) may wish to accept even more risk because of the chance of higher return. Such an investor may borrow money to invest more in the risky portfolio. If the investor borrows 25 percent of his wealth, he/she can invest 125 percent in the optimal risky portfolio. The optimal investor portfolio for such an investor will lie to the right of Point P on the capital allocation line.

Thus, moving from the risk-free asset along the capital allocation line, we encounter investors who are willing to accept more risk. At Point P, the investor is 100 percent invested in the optimal risky portfolio. Beyond Point P, the investor accepts even more risk by borrowing money and investing in the optimal risky portfolio.

Note that we are able to accommodate all types of investors with just two portfolios: the risk-free asset and the optimal risky portfolio. Exhibit 22 is also an illustration of the two-fund separation theorem. Portfolio P is the optimal risky portfolio that is selected without regard to investor preferences. The optimal investor portfolio is selected on the capital allocation line by overlaying the indifference curves that incorporate investor preferences.

SUMMARY

This reading provides a description and computation of investment characteristics, such as risk and return, that investors use in evaluating assets for investment. This was followed by sections about portfolio construction, selection of an optimal risky portfolio, and an understanding of risk aversion and indifference curves. Finally, the tangency point of the indifference curves with the capital allocation line allows identification of the optimal investor portfolio. Key concepts covered in the reading include the following:

- Holding period return is most appropriate for a single, predefined holding period.
- Multiperiod returns can be aggregated in many ways. Each return computation has special applications for evaluating investments.
- Risk-averse investors make investment decisions based on the risk–return trade-off, maximizing return for the same risk, and minimizing risk for the same return. They may be concerned, however, by deviations from a normal return distribution and from assumptions of financial markets' operational efficiency.
- Investors are risk averse, and historical data confirm that financial markets price assets for risk-averse investors.
- The risk of a two-asset portfolio is dependent on the proportions of each asset, their standard deviations and the correlation (or covariance) between the assets' returns. As the number of assets in a portfolio increases, the correlation among asset risks becomes a more important determinant of portfolio risk.
- Combining assets with low correlations reduces portfolio risk.
- The two-fund separation theorem allows us to separate decision making into two steps. In the first step, the optimal risky portfolio and the capital allocation line are identified, which are the same for all investors. In the second step, investor risk preferences enable us to find a unique optimal investor portfolio for each investor.
- The addition of a risk-free asset creates portfolios that are dominant to portfolios of risky assets in all cases except for the optimal risky portfolio.

By successfully understanding the content of this reading, you should be comfortable calculating an investor's optimal portfolio given the investor's risk preferences and universe of investable assets available.

REFERENCES

2009 Ibbotson Stocks, Bonds, Bills, and Inflation (SBBI) Classic Yearbook. 2009. Chicago, IL: Morningstar.

Bogle, John C. 2008. "Black Monday and Black Swans." *Financial Analysts Journal* 64, vol. , no. 2: 30–40. 10.2469/faj.v64.n2.9

Dimson, Elroy, Paul Marsh, and Mike Staunton. 2009. *Credit Suisse Global Investment Returns Sourcebook. 2009.* Zurich, Switzerland: Credit Suisse Research Institute.

Taleb, Nassim N. 2007. *The Black Swan: The Impact of the Highly Improbable*. New York: Random House Inc.

PRACTICE PROBLEMS

1. With respect to trading costs, liquidity is *least likely* to impact the:

   A. stock price.

   B. bid–ask spreads.

   C. brokerage commissions.

2. Evidence of risk aversion is *best* illustrated by a risk–return relationship that is:

   A. negative.

   B. neutral.

   C. positive.

3. With respect to risk-averse investors, a risk-free asset will generate a numerical utility that is:

   A. the same for all individuals.

   B. positive for risk-averse investors.

   C. equal to zero for risk seeking investors.

4. With respect to utility theory, the most risk-averse investor will have an indifference curve with the:

   A. most convexity.

   B. smallest intercept value.

   C. greatest slope coefficient.

5. With respect to an investor's utility function expressed as: $U = E(r) - \frac{1}{2}A\sigma^2$, which of the following values for the measure for risk aversion has the *least* amount of risk aversion?

   A. −4.

   B. 0.

   C. 4.

The following information relates to questions 6-7

A financial planner has created the following data to illustrate the application of utility theory to portfolio selection:

Investment	Expected Return (%)	Expected Standard Deviation (%)
1	18	2
2	19	8
3	20	15
4	18	30

6. A risk-neutral investor is *most likely* to choose:

   A. Investment 1.

   B. Investment 2.

   C. Investment 3.

7. If an investor's utility function is expressed as $U = E(r) - \frac{1}{2}A\sigma^2$ and the measure for risk aversion has a value of −2, the risk-seeking investor is *most likely* to choose:

   A. Investment 2.

   B. Investment 3.

   C. Investment 4.

---

8. If an investor's utility function is expressed as $U = E(r) - \frac{1}{2}A\sigma^2$ and the measure for risk aversion has a value of 2, the risk-averse investor is *most likely* to choose:

   A. Investment 1.

   B. Investment 2.

   C. Investment 3.

9. If an investor's utility function is expressed as $U = E(r) - \frac{1}{2}A\sigma^2$ and the measure for risk aversion has a value of 4, the risk-averse investor is *most likely* to choose:

   A. Investment 1.

   B. Investment 2.

   C. Investment 3.

10. With respect to the mean–variance portfolio theory, the capital allocation line, CAL, is the combination of the risk-free asset and a portfolio of all:

    A. risky assets.

    B. equity securities.

    C. feasible investments.

11. Two individual investors with different levels of risk aversion will have optimal portfolios that are:

    A. below the capital allocation line.

B. on the capital allocation line.

C. above the capital allocation line.

12. With respect to capital market theory, which of the following asset characteristics is *least likely* to impact the variance of an investor's equally weighted portfolio?

A. Return on the asset.

B. Standard deviation of the asset.

C. Covariances of the asset with the other assets in the portfolio.

13. A portfolio manager creates the following portfolio:

Security	Security Weight (%)	Expected Standard Deviation (%)
1	30	20
2	70	12

If the correlation of returns between the two securities is 0.40, the expected standard deviation of the portfolio is *closest* to:

A. 10.7%.

B. 11.3%.

C. 12.1%.

14. A portfolio manager creates the following portfolio:

Security	Security Weight (%)	Expected Standard Deviation (%)
1	30	20
2	70	12

If the covariance of returns between the two securities is −0.0240, the expected standard deviation of the portfolio is *closest* to:

A. 2.4%.

B. 7.5%.

C. 9.2%.

The following information relates to questions 15-16

A portfolio manager creates the following portfolio:

Security	Security Weight (%)	Expected Standard Deviation (%)
1	30	20
2	70	12

15. If the standard deviation of the portfolio is 14.40%, the correlation between the two securities is equal to:

    A. -1.0.

    B. 0.0.

    C. 1.0.

16. If the standard deviation of the portfolio is 14.40%, the covariance between the two securities is equal to:

    A. 0.0006.

    B. 0.0240.

    C. 1.0000.

The following information relates to questions 17-19

A portfolio manager creates the following portfolio:

Security	Expected Annual Return (%)	Expected Standard Deviation (%)
1	16	20
2	12	20

17. If the portfolio of the two securities has an expected return of 15%, the proportion invested in Security 1 is:

    A. 25%.

    B. 50%.

    C. 75%.

18. If the correlation of returns between the two securities is −0.15, the expected standard deviation of an equal-weighted portfolio is *closest* to:

    A. 13.04%.

    B. 13.60%.

    C. 13.87%.

19. If the two securities are uncorrelated, the expected standard deviation of an

equal-weighted portfolio is *closest* to:

A. 14.00%.

B. 14.14%.

C. 20.00%.

The following information relates to questions 20-21

An analyst has made the following return projections for each of three possible outcomes with an equal likelihood of occurrence:

Asset	Outcome 1 (%)	Outcome 2 (%)	Outcome 3 (%)	Expected Return (%)
1	12	0	6	6
2	12	6	0	6
3	0	6	12	6

20. If the analyst constructs two-asset portfolios that are equally-weighted, which pair of assets has the *lowest* expected standard deviation?

A. Asset 1 and Asset 2.

B. Asset 1 and Asset 3.

C. Asset 2 and Asset 3.

21. If the analyst constructs two-asset portfolios that are equally weighted, which pair of assets provides the *least* amount of risk reduction?

A. Asset 1 and Asset 2.

B. Asset 1 and Asset 3.

C. Asset 2 and Asset 3.

22. As the number of assets in an equally-weighted portfolio increases, the contribution of each individual asset's variance to the volatility of the portfolio:

A. increases.

B. decreases.

C. remains the same.

23. With respect to an equally weighted portfolio made up of a large number of assets, which of the following contributes the *most* to the volatility of the portfolio?

A. Average variance of the individual assets.

B. Standard deviation of the individual assets.

C. Average covariance between all pairs of assets.

24. The correlation between assets in a two-asset portfolio increases during a market decline. If there is no change in the proportion of each asset held in the portfolio or the expected standard deviation of the individual assets, the volatility of the portfolio is *most likely* to:

   A. increase.

   B. decrease.

   C. remain the same.

25. Which of the following statements is *least* accurate? The efficient frontier is the set of all attainable risky assets with the:

   A. highest expected return for a given level of risk.

   B. lowest amount of risk for a given level of return.

   C. highest expected return relative to the risk-free rate.

26. The portfolio on the minimum-variance frontier with the lowest standard deviation is:

   A. unattainable.

   B. the optimal risky portfolio.

   C. the global minimum-variance portfolio.

27. The set of portfolios on the minimum-variance frontier that dominates all sets of portfolios below the global minimum-variance portfolio is the:

   A. capital allocation line.

   B. Markowitz efficient frontier.

   C. set of optimal risky portfolios.

28. The dominant capital allocation line is the combination of the risk-free asset and the:

   A. optimal risky portfolio.

   B. levered portfolio of risky assets.

   C. global minimum-variance portfolio.

29. Compared to the efficient frontier of risky assets, the dominant capital allocation line has higher rates of return for levels of risk greater than the optimal risky portfolio because of the investor's ability to:

   A. lend at the risk-free rate.

   B. borrow at the risk-free rate.

   C. purchase the risk-free asset.

30. With respect to the mean–variance theory, the optimal portfolio is determined by each individual investor's:

   A. risk-free rate.

B. borrowing rate.

C. risk preference.

SOLUTIONS

1. C is correct. Brokerage commissions are negotiated with the brokerage firm. A security's liquidity impacts the operational efficiency of trading costs. Specifically, liquidity impacts the bid–ask spread and can impact the stock price (if the ability to sell the stock is impaired by the uncertainty associated with being able to sell the stock).

2. C is correct. Historical data over long periods of time indicate that there exists a positive risk–return relationship, which is a reflection of an investor's risk aversion.

3. A is correct. A risk-free asset has a variance of zero and is not dependent on whether the investor is risk neutral, risk seeking or risk averse. That is, given that the utility function of an investment is expressed as $U = E(r) - \frac{1}{2}A\sigma^2$, where A is the measure of risk aversion, then the sign of A is irrelevant if the variance is zero (like that of a risk-free asset).

4. C is correct. The most risk-averse investor has the indifference curve with the greatest slope.

5. A is correct. A negative value in the given utility function indicates that the investor is a risk seeker.

6. C is correct. Investment 3 has the highest rate of return. Risk is irrelevant to a risk-neutral investor, who would have a measure of risk aversion equal to 0. Given the utility function, the risk-neutral investor would obtain the greatest amount of utility from Investment 3.

Investment	Expected Return (%)	Expected Standard Deviation (%)	Utility $A = 0$
1	18	2	0.1800
2	19	8	0.1900
3	20	15	0.2000
4	18	30	0.1800

7. C is correct. Investment 4 provides the highest utility value (0.2700) for a risk-seeking investor, who has a measure of risk aversion equal to −2.

Investment	Expected Return (%)	Expected Standard Deviation (%)	Utility $A = -2$
1	18	2	0.1804
2	19	8	0.1964
3	20	15	0.2225
4	18	30	0.2700

8. B is correct. Investment 2 provides the highest utility value (0.1836) for a risk-averse investor who has a measure of risk aversion equal to 2.

Investment	Expected Return (%)	Expected Standard Deviation (%)	Utility $A = 2$
1	18	2	0.1796
2	19	8	0.1836
3	20	15	0.1775
4	18	30	0.0900

9. A is correct. Investment 1 provides the highest utility value (0.1792) for a risk-averse investor who has a measure of risk aversion equal to 4.

Investment	Expected Return (%)	Expected Standard Deviation (%)	Utility $A = 4$
1	18	2	0.1792
2	19	8	0.1772
3	20	15	0.1550
4	18	30	0.0000

10. A is correct. The CAL is the combination of the risk-free asset with zero risk and the portfolio of all risky assets that provides for the set of feasible investments. Allowing for borrowing at the risk-free rate and investing in the portfolio of all risky assets provides for attainable portfolios that dominate risky assets below the CAL.

11. B is correct. The CAL represents the set of all feasible investments. Each investor's indifference curve determines the optimal combination of the risk-free asset and the portfolio of all risky assets, which must lie on the CAL.

12. A is correct. The asset's returns are not used to calculate the portfolio's variance [only the assets' weights, standard deviations (or variances), and covariances (or correlations) are used].

13. C is correct.

$$\sigma_{port} = \sqrt{w_1^2\sigma_1^2 + w_2^2\sigma_2^2 + 2w_1w_2\rho_{1,2}\sigma_1\sigma_2}$$
$$= \sqrt{(0.3)^2(20\%)^2 + (0.7)^2(12\%)^2 + 2(0.3)(0.7)(0.40)(20\%)(12\%)}$$
$$= (0.3600\% + 0.7056\% + 0.4032\%)^{0.5} = (1.4688\%)^{0.5} = 12.11\%$$

14. A is correct.

$$\sigma_{port} = \sqrt{w_1^2\sigma_1^2 + w_2^2\sigma_2^2 + 2w_1w_2Cov(R_1R_2)}$$
$$= \sqrt{(0.3)^2(20\%)^2 + (0.7)^2(12\%)^2 + 2(0.3)(0.7)(-0.0240)}$$
$$= (0.3600\% + 0.7056\% - 1.008\%)^{0.5} = (0.0576\%)^{0.5} = 2.40\%$$

15. C is correct. A portfolio standard deviation of 14.40% is the weighted average, which is possible only if the correlation between the securities is equal to 1.0.

16. B is correct. A portfolio standard deviation of 14.40% is the weighted average, which is possible only if the correlation between the securities is equal to 1.0. If the correlation coefficient is equal to 1.0, then the covariance must equal 0.0240, calculated as: $Cov(R_1,R_2) = \rho_{12}\sigma_1\sigma_2 = (1.0)(20\%)(12\%) = 2.40\% = 0.0240$.

17. C is correct.

$$R_p = w_1 \times R_1 + (1 - w_1) \times R_2$$
$$R_p = w_1 \times 16\% + (1 - w_1) \times 12\%$$
$$15\% = 0.75(16\%) + 0.25(12\%)$$

18. A is correct.

$$\sigma_{port} = \sqrt{w_1^2\sigma_1^2 + w_2^2\sigma_2^2 + 2w_1w_2\rho_{1,2}\sigma_1\sigma_2}$$
$$= \sqrt{(0.5)^2(20\%)^2 + (0.5)^2(20\%)^2 + 2(0.5)(0.5)(-0.15)(20\%)(20\%)}$$
$$= (1.0000\% + 1.0000\% - 0.3000\%)^{0.5} = (1.7000\%)^{0.5} = 13.04\%$$

19. B is correct.

$$\sigma_{port} = \sqrt{w_1^2\sigma_1^2 + w_2^2\sigma_2^2 + 2w_1w_2\rho_{1,2}\sigma_1\sigma_2}$$
$$= \sqrt{(0.5)^2(20\%)^2 + (0.5)^2(20\%)^2 + 2(0.5)(0.5)(0.00)(20\%)(20\%)}$$
$$= (1.0000\% + 1.0000\% - 0.0000\%)^{0.5} = (2.0000\%)^{0.5} = 14.14\%$$

20. C is correct. An equally weighted portfolio of Asset 2 and Asset 3 will have the lowest portfolio standard deviation, because for each outcome, the portfolio has the same expected return (they are perfectly negatively correlated).

21. A is correct. An equally weighted portfolio of Asset 1 and Asset 2 has the highest level of volatility of the three pairs. All three pairs have the same expected return; however, the portfolio of Asset 1 and Asset 2 provides the least amount of risk reduction.

22. B is correct. The contribution of each individual asset's variance (or standard deviation) to the portfolio's volatility decreases as the number of assets in the equally weighted portfolio increases. The contribution of the co-movement measures between the assets increases (i.e., covariance and correlation) as the number of assets in the equally weighted portfolio increases. The following equation for the variance of an equally weighted portfolio illustrates these points: $\sigma_p^2 = \frac{\bar{\sigma}^2}{N} + \frac{N-1}{N}\overline{COV} = \frac{\bar{\sigma}^2}{N} + \frac{N-1}{N}\bar{\rho}\ \bar{\sigma}^2.$

23. C is correct. The co-movement measures between the assets increases (i.e., covariance and correlation) as the number of assets in the equally weighted portfolio increases. The contribution of each individual asset's variance (or standard deviation) to the portfolio's volatility decreases as the number of assets in the equally weighted portfolio increases. The following equation for the variance of an equally weighted portfolio illustrates these points:

$$\sigma_p^2 = \frac{\bar{\sigma}^2}{N} + \frac{N-1}{N}\overline{COV} = \frac{\bar{\sigma}^2}{N} + \frac{N-1}{N}\bar{\rho}\ \bar{\sigma}^2.$$

24. A is correct. Higher correlations will produce less diversification benefits provided that the other components of the portfolio standard deviation do not change (i.e., the weights and standard deviations of the individual assets).

25. C is correct. The efficient frontier does not account for the risk-free rate. The efficient frontier is the set of all attainable risky assets with the highest expected return for a given level of risk or the lowest amount of risk for a given level of return.

26. C is correct. The global minimum-variance portfolio is the portfolio on the minimum-variance frontier with the lowest standard deviation. Although

the portfolio is attainable, when the risk-free asset is considered, the global minimum-variance portfolio is not the optimal risky portfolio.

27. B is correct. The Markowitz efficient frontier has higher rates of return for a given level of risk. With respect to the minimum-variance portfolio, the Markowitz efficient frontier is the set of portfolios above the global minimum-variance portfolio that dominates the portfolios below the global minimum-variance portfolio.

28. A is correct. The use of leverage and the combination of a risk-free asset and the optimal risky asset will dominate the efficient frontier of risky assets (the Markowitz efficient frontier).

29. B is correct. The CAL dominates the efficient frontier at all points except for the optimal risky portfolio. The ability of the investor to purchase additional amounts of the optimal risky portfolio by borrowing (i.e., buying on margin) at the risk-free rate makes higher rates of return for levels of risk greater than the optimal risky asset possible.

30. C is correct. Each individual investor's optimal mix of the risk-free asset and the optimal risky asset is determined by the investor's risk preference.

LEARNING MODULE

2

Portfolio Risk and Return: Part II

by Vijay Singal, PhD, CFA.

Vijay Singal, PhD, CFA, is at Virginia Tech (USA).

LEARNING OUTCOMES

Mastery	The candidate should be able to:
☐	describe the implications of combining a risk-free asset with a portfolio of risky assets
☐	explain the capital allocation line (CAL) and the capital market line (CML)
☐	explain systematic and nonsystematic risk, including why an investor should not expect to receive additional return for bearing nonsystematic risk
☐	explain return generating models (including the market model) and their uses
☐	calculate and interpret beta
☐	explain the capital asset pricing model (CAPM), including its assumptions, and the security market line (SML)
☐	calculate and interpret the expected return of an asset using the CAPM
☐	describe and demonstrate applications of the CAPM and the SML
☐	calculate and interpret the Sharpe ratio, Treynor ratio, M^2, and Jensen's alpha

INTRODUCTION

1

Our objective in this reading is to identify the optimal risky portfolio for all investors by using the capital asset pricing model (CAPM). The foundation of this reading is the computation of risk and return of a portfolio and the role that correlation plays in diversifying portfolio risk and arriving at the efficient frontier. The efficient frontier and the capital allocation line consist of portfolios that are generally acceptable to all investors. By combining an investor's individual indifference curves with the market-determined capital allocation line, we are able to illustrate that the only optimal risky portfolio for an investor is the portfolio of all risky assets (i.e., the market).

Additionally, we discuss the capital market line, a special case of the capital allocation line that is used for passive investor portfolios. We also differentiate between systematic and nonsystematic risk, and explain why investors are compensated for bearing systematic risk but receive no compensation for bearing nonsystematic risk. We discuss in detail the CAPM, which is a simple model for estimating asset returns based only on the asset's systematic risk. Finally, we illustrate how the CAPM allows security selection to build an optimal portfolio for an investor by changing the asset mix beyond a passive market portfolio.

The reading is organized as follows. In Section 2, we discuss the consequences of combining a risk-free asset with the market portfolio and provide an interpretation of the capital market line. Section 3 decomposes total risk into systematic and nonsystematic risk and discusses the characteristics of and differences between the two kinds of risk. We also introduce return-generating models, including the single-index model, and illustrate the calculation of beta. In Section 4, we introduce the capital asset pricing model and the security market line. Our focus on the CAPM does not suggest that the CAPM is the only viable asset pricing model. Although the CAPM is an excellent starting point, more advanced readings expand on these discussions and extend the analysis to other models that account for multiple explanatory factors. Section 5 covers several post-CAPM developments in theory. Section 6 covers measures for evaluating the performance of a portfolio which take account of risk. Section 7 covers some applications of the CAPM in portfolio construction. A summary and practice problems conclude the reading.

2 CAPITAL MARKET THEORY: RISK-FREE AND RISKY ASSETS

- ☐ describe the implications of combining a risk-free asset with a portfolio of risky assets
- ☐ explain the capital allocation line (CAL) and the capital market line (CML)

You have learned how to combine a risk-free asset with one risky asset and with many risky assets to create a capital allocation line. In this section, we will expand our discussion of multiple risky assets and consider a special case of the capital allocation line, called the capital market line. While discussing the capital market line, we will define the market and its role in passive portfolio management. Using these concepts, we will illustrate how leveraged portfolios can enhance both risk and return.

Portfolio of Risk-Free and Risky Assets

Although investors desire an asset that produces the highest return and carries the lowest risk, such an asset does not exist. As the risk–return capital market theory illustrates, one must assume higher risk in order to earn a higher return. We can improve an investor's portfolio, however, by expanding the opportunity set of risky assets because this allows the investor to choose a superior mix of assets.

Similarly, an investor's portfolio improves if a risk-free asset is added to the mix. In other words, a combination of the risk-free asset and a risky asset can result in a better risk–return trade-off than an investment in only one type of asset because the risk-free asset has zero correlation with the risky asset. The combination is called the **capital allocation line** (and is depicted in Exhibit 2). Superimposing an investor's indifference curves on the capital allocation line will lead to the optimal investor portfolio.

Investors with different levels of risk aversion will choose different portfolios. Highly risk-averse investors choose to invest most of their wealth in the risk-free asset and earn low returns because they are not willing to assume higher levels of risk. Less risk-averse investors, in contrast, invest more of their wealth in the risky asset, which is expected to yield a higher return. Obviously, the higher return cannot come without higher risk, but the less risk-averse investor is willing to accept the additional risk.

Combining a Risk-Free Asset with a Portfolio of Risky Assets

We can extend the analysis of one risky asset to a portfolio of risky assets. For convenience, assume that the portfolio contains all available risky assets (N), although an investor may not wish to include all of these assets in the portfolio because of the investor's specific preferences. If an asset is not included in the portfolio, its weight will be zero. The risk–return characteristics of a portfolio of N risky assets are given by the following equations:

$$E\left(R_p\right) = \sum_{i=1}^{N} w_i E\left(R_i\right)$$

$$\sigma_p^2 = \left(\sum_{i=1,j=1}^{N} w_i w_j \text{Cov}\left(i,j\right)\right), \text{ and } \sum_{i=1}^{N} w_i = 1$$

The expected return on the portfolio, $E(R_p)$, is the weighted average of the expected returns of individual assets, where w_i is the fractional weight in asset i and R_i is the expected return of asset i. The risk of the portfolio (σ_p), however, depends on the weights of the individual assets, the risk of the individual assets, and their interrelationships. The **covariance** between assets i and j, Cov(i,j), is a statistical measure of the interrelationship between each pair of assets in the portfolio and can be expressed as follows, where ρ_{ij} is the **correlation** between assets i and j and σ_i is the risk of asset i:

$$\text{Cov}(i,j) = \rho_{ij}\sigma_i\sigma_j$$

Note from the equation below that the correlation of an asset with itself is 1; therefore:

$$\text{Cov}(i,i) = \rho_{ii}\sigma_i\sigma_i = \sigma_i^2$$

By substituting the above expressions for covariance, we can rewrite the portfolio variance equation as

$$\sigma_p^2 = \left(\sum_{i=1}^{N} w_i^2\sigma_i^2 + \sum_{i,j=1,i\neq j}^{N} w_i w_j \rho_{ij}\sigma_i\sigma_j\right)$$

The suggestion that portfolios have lower risk than the assets they contain may seem counterintuitive. These portfolios can be constructed, however, as long as the assets in the portfolio are not perfectly correlated. As an illustration of the effect of asset weights on portfolio characteristics, consider a simple two-asset portfolio with zero weights in all other assets. Assume that Asset 1 has a return of 10 percent and a standard deviation (risk) of 20 percent. Asset 2 has a return of 5 percent and a standard deviation (risk) of 10 percent. Furthermore, the correlation between the two assets is zero. Exhibit 1 shows risks and returns for Portfolio X with a weight of 25 percent in Asset 1 and 75 percent in Asset 2, Portfolio Y with a weight of 50 percent in each of the two assets, and Portfolio Z with a weight of 75 percent in Asset 1 and 25 percent in Asset 2.

Exhibit 1: Portfolio Risk and Return

Portfolio	Weight in Asset 1 (%)	Weight in Asset 2 (%)	Portfolio Return (%)	Portfolio Standard Deviation (%)
X	25.0	75.0	6.25	9.01
Y	50.0	50.0	7.50	11.18
Z	75.0	25.0	8.75	15.21
Return	10.0	5.0		
Standard deviation	20.0	10.0		
Correlation between Assets 1 and 2		0.0		

From this example we observe that the three portfolios are quite different in terms of their risk and return. Portfolio X has a 6.25 percent return and only 9.01 percent standard deviation, whereas the standard deviation of Portfolio Z is more than two-thirds higher (15.21 percent), although the return is only slightly more than one-third higher (8.75 percent). These portfolios may become even more dissimilar as other assets are added to the mix.

Consider three portfolios of risky assets, A, B, and C, as in Exhibit 2, that may have been presented to a representative investor by three different investment advisers. Each portfolio is combined with the risk-free asset to create three capital allocation lines, CAL(A), CAL(B), and CAL(C). The exhibit shows that Portfolio C is superior to the other two portfolios because it has a greater expected return for any given level of risk. As a result, an investor will choose the portfolio that lies on the capital allocation line for Portfolio C. The combination of the risk-free asset and the risky Portfolio C that is selected for an investor depends on the investor's degree of risk aversion.

Exhibit 2: Risk-Free Asset and Portfolio of Risky Assets

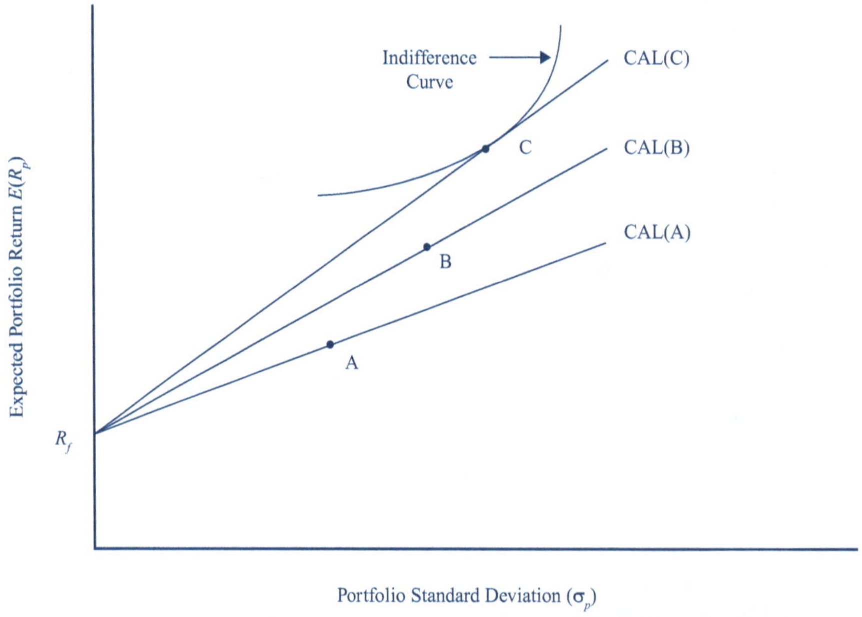

Does a Unique Optimal Risky Portfolio Exist?

We assume that all investors have the same economic expectation and thus have the same expectations of prices, cash flows, and other investment characteristics. This assumption is referred to as **homogeneity of expectations**. Given these investment characteristics, everyone goes through the same calculations and should arrive at the same optimal risky portfolio. Therefore, assuming homogeneous expectations, only one optimal portfolio exists. If investors have different expectations, however, they might arrive at different optimal risky portfolios. To illustrate, we begin with an expression for the price of an asset:

$$P = \sum_{t=0}^{T} \frac{\mathrm{CF}_t}{(1 + r_t)^t}$$

where CF_t is the cash flow at the end of period t and r_t is the discount rate or the required rate of return for that asset for period t. Period t refers to all periods beginning from now until the asset ceases to exist at the end of time T. Because the current time is the end of period 0, which is the same as the beginning of period 1, there are $(T + 1)$ cash flows and $(T + 1)$ required rates of return. These conditions are based on the assumption that a cash flow, such as an initial investment, can occur now (t = 0). Ordinarily, however, CF_0 is zero.

We use the formula for the price of an asset to estimate the intrinsic value of an asset. Assume that the asset we are valuing is a share of Siemens AG which trades on Xetra. In the case of corporate stock, there is no expiration date, so T could be extremely large, meaning we will need to estimate a large number of cash flows and rates of return. Fortunately, the denominator reduces the importance of distant cash flows, so it may be sufficient to estimate, say, 20 annual cash flows and 20 rates of returns. How much will Siemens earn next year and the year after next? What will the product markets Siemens operates in look like in five years' time? Different analysts and investors will have their own estimates that may be quite different from one another. Also, as we delve further into the future, more serious issues in estimating future revenue, expenses, and growth rates arise. Therefore, to assume that cash flow estimates for Siemens will vary among these investors is reasonable. In addition to the numerator (cash flows), it is also necessary to estimate the denominator, the required rates of return. We know that riskier companies will require higher returns because risk and return are positively correlated. Siemens stock is riskier than a risk-free asset, but by how much? And what should the compensation for that additional risk be? Again, it is evident that different analysts will view the riskiness of Siemens differently and, therefore, arrive at different required rates of return.

Siemens closed at €111.84 on Xetra on 31 August 2018. The traded price represents the value that a marginal investor attaches to a share of Siemens, say, corresponding to Analyst A's expectation. Analyst B may think that the price should be €95, however, and Analyst C may think that the price should be €125. Given a price of €111.84, the expected returns of Siemens are quite different for the three analysts. Analyst B, who believes the price should be €95, concludes that Siemens is overvalued and may assign a weight of zero to Siemens in the recommended portfolio even though the market capitalization of Siemens was in excess of €100 billion as of the date of the quotation. In contrast, Analyst C, with a valuation of €125, thinks Siemens is undervalued and may significantly overweight Siemens in a portfolio.

Our discussion illustrates that analysts can arrive at different valuations that necessitate the assignment of different asset weights in a portfolio. Given the existence of many asset classes and numerous assets in each asset class, one can visualize that each investor will have his or her own optimal risky portfolio depending on his or her assumptions underlying the valuation computations. Therefore, market participants will have their own and possibly different optimal risky portfolios.

If investors have different valuations of assets, then the construction of a unique optimal risky portfolio is not possible. If we make a simplifying assumption of homogeneity in investor expectations, we will have a single optimal risky portfolio as previously mentioned. Even if investors have different expectations, market prices are a proxy of what the marginal, informed investor expects, and the market portfolio becomes the base case, the benchmark, or the reference portfolio that other portfolios can be judged against. For Siemens, the market price was €111.84 per share and the market capitalization was about €108 billion. In constructing the market portfolio, Siemens's weight in the market portfolio will be equal to its market value divided by the value of all other assets included in the market portfolio.

3 CAPITAL MARKET THEORY: THE CAPITAL MARKET LINE

- [ ] explain the capital allocation line (CAL) and the capital market line (CML)

In the previous section, we discussed how the risk-free asset could be combined with a risky portfolio to create a capital allocation line (CAL). In this section, we discuss a specific CAL that uses the market portfolio as the optimal risky portfolio and is known as the capital market line. We also discuss the significance of the market portfolio and applications of the capital market line (CML).

Passive and Active Portfolios

In the above subsection, we hypothesized three possible valuations for each share of Siemens: €95, €111.84, and €125. Which one is correct?

If the market is an **informationally efficient market**, the price in the market, €111.84, is an unbiased estimate of all future discounted cash flows (recall the formula for the price of an asset). In other words, the price aggregates and reflects all information that is publicly available, and investors cannot expect to earn a return that is greater than the required rate of return for that asset. If, however, the price reflects all publicly available information and there is no way to outperform the market, then there is little point in investing time and money in evaluating Siemens to arrive at your price using your own estimates of cash flows and rates of return.

In that case, a simple and convenient approach to investing is to rely on the prices set by the market. Portfolios that are based on the assumption of unbiased market prices are referred to as passive portfolios. Passive portfolios most commonly replicate and track market indexes, which are passively constructed on the basis of market prices and market capitalizations. Examples of market indexes are the S&P 500 Index, the Nikkei 300, and the CAC 40. Passive portfolios based on market indexes are called index funds and generally have low costs because no significant effort is expended in valuing securities that are included in an index.

In contrast to passive investors' reliance on market prices and index funds, active investors may not rely on market valuations. They have more confidence in their own ability to estimate cash flows, growth rates, and discount rates. Based on these estimates, they value assets and determine whether an asset is fairly valued. In an actively managed portfolio, assets that are undervalued, or have a chance of offering above-normal returns, will have a positive weight (i.e., overweight compared to the market weight in the benchmark index), whereas other assets will have a zero weight, or even a negative weight if short selling is permitted (i.e., some assets will be underweighted compared with the market weight in the benchmark index). (**Short selling** is a transaction in which borrowed securities are sold with the intention to repurchase them at a lower price at a later date and return them to the lender.) This style of investing is called active investment management, and the portfolios are referred to as active portfolios. Most open-end mutual funds and hedge funds practice active investment management, and most analysts believe that active investing adds value. Whether these analysts are right or wrong is the subject of continuing debate.

What Is the "Market"?

In the previous discussion, we referred to the "market" on numerous occasions without actually defining the market. The optimal risky portfolio and the capital market line depend on the definition of the market. So what is the market?

Theoretically, the market includes all risky assets or anything that has value, which includes stocks, bonds, real estate, and even human capital. Not all assets are tradable, however, and not all tradable assets are investable. For example, the Taj Mahal in India is an asset but is not a tradable asset. Similarly, human capital is an asset that is not tradable. Moreover, assets may be tradable but not investable because of restrictions placed on certain kinds of investors. For example, all stocks listed on the Shanghai Stock Exchange are tradable. However, whereas Class A shares are listed in RMB and open to domestic investors and qualified foreign investors, Class B shares are listed in USD and open to foreign investors and domestic investors holding foreign currency dealing accounts.

If we consider all stocks, bonds, real estate assets, commodities, etc., probably hundreds of thousands of assets are tradable and investable. The "market" should contain as many assets as possible; we emphasize the word "possible" because it is not practical to include all assets in a single risky portfolio. Even though advancements in technology and interconnected markets have made it much easier to span the major equity markets, we are still not able to easily invest in other kinds of assets like bonds and real estate except in the most developed countries.

For the rest of this reading, we will define the "market" quite narrowly because it is practical and convenient to do so. Typically, a local or regional stock market index is used as a proxy for the market because of active trading in stocks and because a local or regional market is most visible to the local investors. For our purposes, we will use the S&P 500 Index as the market's proxy. The S&P 500 is commonly used by analysts as a benchmark for market performance throughout the United States. It contains 500 of the largest stocks that are domiciled in the United States, and these stocks are weighted by their market capitalization (price times the number of outstanding shares).

As of mid-2018, the stocks in the S&P 500 account for approximately 80 percent of the total equity market capitalization in the United States, and because the US stock markets represent about 40 percent of the world markets, the S&P 500 represents roughly 32 percent of worldwide publicly traded equity. Our definition of the market does not include non-US stock markets, bond markets, real estate, and many other asset classes, and therefore, "market" return and the "market" risk premium refer to US equity return and the US equity risk premium, respectively. The use of this proxy, however, is sufficient for our discussion, and is relatively easy to expand to include other tradable assets.

The Capital Market Line (CML)

A capital allocation line includes all possible combinations of the risk-free asset and an investor's optimal risky portfolio. The **capital market line** is a special case of the capital allocation line, where the risky portfolio is the market portfolio. The risk-free asset is a debt security with no default risk, no inflation risk, no liquidity risk, no interest rate risk, and no risk of any other kind. US Treasury bills are usually used as a proxy of the risk-free return, R_f.

The S&P 500 is a proxy of the market portfolio, which is the optimal risky portfolio. Therefore, the expected return on the risky portfolio is the expected market return, expressed as $E(R_m)$. The capital market line is shown in Exhibit 3, where the standard deviation (σ_p), or total risk, is on the x-axis and expected portfolio return, $E(R_p)$, is on the y-axis. Graphically, the market portfolio is the point on the Markowitz efficient frontier where a line from the risk-free asset is tangent to the Markowitz efficient frontier. All points on the interior of the Markowitz efficient frontier are inefficient portfolios in that they provide the same level of return with a higher level of risk or a lower level of return with the same amount of risk. When plotted together, the point at which the CML is tangent to the Markowitz efficient frontier is the optimal combination of risky assets, on the basis of market prices and market capitalizations. The optimal risky portfolio is the market portfolio.

Exhibit 3: Capital Market Line

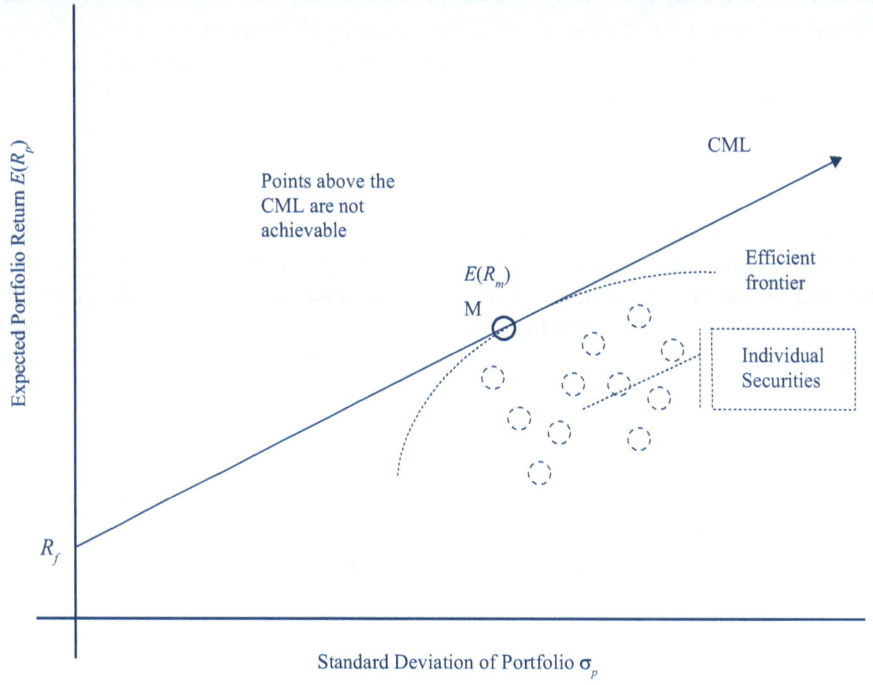

The CML's intercept on the y-axis is the risk-free return (R_f) because that is the return associated with zero risk. The CML passes through the point represented by the market return, $E(R_m)$. With respect to capital market theory, any point above the CML is not achievable and any point below the CML is dominated by and inferior to any point on the CML.

Note that we identify the CML and CAL as lines even though they are a combination of two assets. Unlike a combination of two risky assets, which is usually not a straight line, a combination of the risk-free asset and a risky portfolio is a straight line, as illustrated below by computing the combination's risk and return.

Risk and return characteristics of the portfolio represented by the CML can be computed by using the return and risk expressions for a two-asset portfolio:

$$E(R_p) = w_1 R_f + (1 - w_1)E(R_m),$$

and

$$\sigma_p = \sqrt{w_1^2 \sigma_f^2 + (1 - w_1)^2 \sigma_m^2 + 2 w_1 (1 - w_1) \operatorname{Cov}(R_f, R_m)}$$

The proportion invested in the risk-free asset is given by w_1, and the balance is invested in the market portfolio, $(1 - w_1)$. The risk of the risk-free asset is given by σ_f, the risk of the market is given by σ_m, the risk of the portfolio is given by σ_p, and the covariance between the risk-free asset and the market portfolio is represented by $\operatorname{Cov}(R_f, R_m)$.

By definition, the standard deviation of the risk-free asset is zero. Because its risk is zero, the risk-free asset does not co-vary or move with any other asset. Therefore, its covariance with all other assets, including the market portfolio, is zero, making the first and third terms under the square root sign zero. As a result, the portfolio return and portfolio standard deviation can be simplified and rewritten as:

$$E(R_p) = w_1 R_f + (1 - w_1) E(R_m),$$

and

$$\sigma_p = (1 - w_1)\sigma_m$$

By substitution, we can express $E(R_p)$ in terms of σ_p. Substituting for w_1, we get:

$$E(R_p) = R_f + \left(\frac{E(R_m) - R_f}{\sigma_m}\right) \times \sigma_p$$

Note that the expression is in the form of a line, $y = a + bx$. The y-intercept is the risk-free rate, and the slope of the line referred to as the market price of risk is $[E(R_m) - R_f]/\sigma_m$. The CML has a positive slope because the market's risky return is larger than the risk-free return. As the amount of the total investment devoted to the market increases—that is, as we move up the line—both standard deviation (risk) and expected return increase.

EXAMPLE 1

Risk and Return on the CML

Mr. Miles is a first time investor and wants to build a portfolio using only US T-bills and an index fund that closely tracks the S&P 500 Index. The T-bills have a return of 5 percent. The S&P 500 has a standard deviation of 20 percent and an expected return of 15 percent.

1. Draw the CML and mark the points where the investment in the market is 0 percent, 25 percent, 75 percent, and 100 percent.

Solution:

We calculate the equation for the CML as $E(R_p) = 5\% + 0.50 \times \sigma_p$ by substituting the given information into the general CML equation. The intercept of the line is 5 percent, and its slope is 0.50. We can draw the CML by arbitrarily taking any two points on the line that satisfy the above equation.

Alternatively, the CML can be drawn by connecting the risk-free return of 5 percent on the y-axis with the market portfolio at (20 percent, 15 percent). The CML is shown in Exhibit 4.

Exhibit 4: Risk and Return on the CML

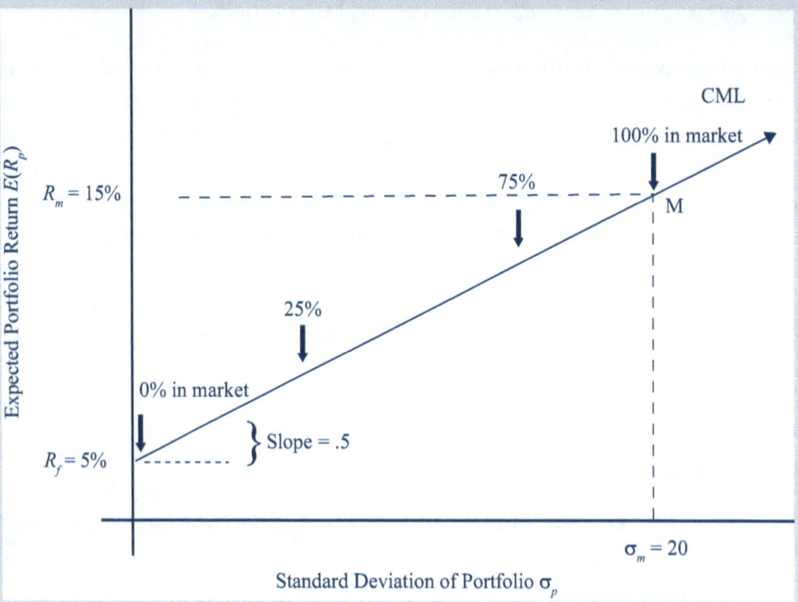

2. Mr. Miles is also interested in determining the exact risk and return at each point.

Solution:

Return with 0 percent invested in the market
= 5 percent, which is the risk-free return.

Standard deviation with 0 percent invested in the market
= 0 percent because T-bills are not risky.

Return with 25 percent invested in the market = (0.75 × 5%) + (0.25 × 15%)
= 7.5%.

Standard deviation with 25 percent invested in the market = 0.25 × 20% = 5%.

Return with 75 percent invested in the market = (0.25 × 5%) + (0.75 × 15%)
= 12.50%.

Standard deviation with 75 percent invested in the market = 0.75 × 20% = 15%.

Return with 100 percent invested in the market
= 15 percent, which is the return on the S&P 500.

Standard deviation with 100 percent invested in the market
= 20 percent, which is the risk of the S&P 500.

CAPITAL MARKET THEORY: CML - LEVERAGED PORTFOLIOS

4

☐ explain the capital allocation line (CAL) and the capital market line (CML)

In the previous example, Mr. Miles evaluated an investment of between 0 percent and 100 percent in the market and the balance in T-bills. The line connecting R_f and M (market portfolio) in Exhibit 4 illustrates these portfolios with their respective levels of investment. At R_f, an investor is investing all of his or her wealth into risk-free securities, which is equivalent to lending 100 percent at the risk-free rate. At Point M he or she is holding the market portfolio and not lending any money at the risk-free rate. The combinations of the risk-free asset and the market portfolio, which may be achieved by the points between these two limits, are termed "lending" portfolios. In effect, the investor is lending part of his or her wealth at the risk-free rate.

If Mr. Miles is willing to take more risk, he may be able to move to the right of the market portfolio (Point M in Exhibit 4) by borrowing money and purchasing more of Portfolio M. Assume that he is able to borrow money at the same risk-free rate of interest, R_f, at which he can invest. He can then supplement his available wealth with borrowed money and construct a borrowing portfolio. If the straight line joining R_f and M is extended to the right of Point M, this extended section of the line represents borrowing portfolios. As one moves further to the right of Point M, an increasing amount of borrowed money is being invested in the market. This means that there is *negative* investment in the risk-free asset, which is referred to as a *leveraged position* in the risky portfolio. The particular point chosen on the CML will depend on the individual's utility function, which, in turn, will be determined by his risk and return preferences.

EXAMPLE 2

Risk and Return of a Leveraged Portfolio with Equal Lending and Borrowing Rates

1. Mr. Miles decides to set aside a small part of his wealth for investment in a portfolio that has greater risk than his previous investments because he anticipates that the overall market will generate attractive returns in the future. He assumes that he can borrow money at 5 percent and achieve the same return on the S&P 500 as before: an expected return of 15 percent with a standard deviation of 20 percent.

   Calculate his expected risk and return if he borrows 25 percent, 50 percent, and 100 percent of his initial investment amount.

Solution:

The leveraged portfolio's standard deviation and return can be calculated in the same manner as before with the following equations:

$$E(R_p) = w_1 R_f + (1 - w_1)E(R_m)$$

and

$\sigma_p = (1 - w_1)\sigma_m$

The proportion invested in T-bills becomes negative instead of positive because Mr. Miles is borrowing money. If 25 percent of the initial investment is borrowed, $w_1 = -0.25$, and $(1 - w_1) = 1.25$, etc.

Return with $w_1 = -0.25 = (-0.25 \times 5\%) + (1.25 \times 15\%) = 17.5\%$.

Standard deviation with $w_1 = -0.25 = 1.25 \times 20\% = 25\%$.

Return with $w_1 = -0.50 = (-0.50 \times 5\%) + (1.50 \times 15\%) = 20.0\%$.

Standard deviation with $w_1 = -0.50 = 1.50 \times 20\% = 30\%$.

Return with $w_1 = -1.00 = (-1.00 \times 5\%) + (2.00 \times 15\%) = 25.0\%$.

Standard deviation with $w_1 = -1.00 = 2.00 \times 20\% = 40\%$.

Note that negative investment (borrowing) in the risk-free asset provides a higher expected return for the portfolio but that higher return is also associated with higher risk.

Leveraged Portfolios with Different Lending and Borrowing Rates

Although we assumed that Mr. Miles can borrow at the same rate as the US government, it is more likely that he will have to pay a higher interest rate than the government because his ability to repay is not as certain as that of the government. Now consider that although Mr. Miles can invest (lend) at R_f, he can borrow at only R_b, a rate that is higher than the risk-free rate.

With different lending and borrowing rates, the CML will no longer be a single straight line. The line will have a slope of $[E(R_m) - R_f]/\sigma_m$ between Points R_f and M, where the lending rate is R_f, but will have a smaller slope of $[E(R_m) - R_b]/\sigma_m$ at points to the right of M, where the borrowing rate is R_b. Exhibit 5 illustrates the CML with different lending and borrowing rates.

Exhibit 5: CML with Different Lending and Borrowing Rates

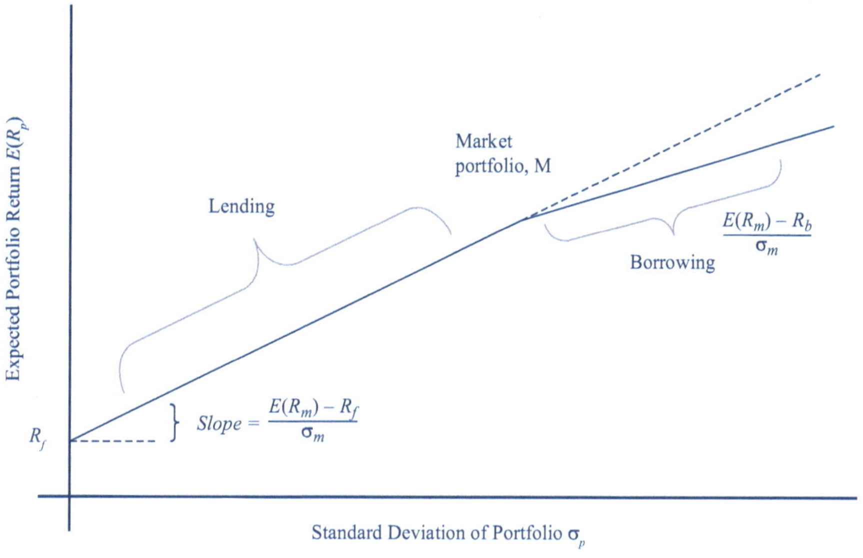

The equations for the two lines are given below.

$$w_1 \geq 0: E\left(R_p\right) = R_f + \left(\frac{E\left(R_m\right) - R_f}{\sigma_m}\right) \times \sigma_p$$

and

$$w_1 < 0: E\left(R_p\right) = R_b + \left(\frac{E\left(R_m\right) - R_b}{\sigma_m}\right) \times \sigma_p$$

The first equation is for the line where the investment in the risk-free asset is zero or positive—that is, at M or to the left of M in Exhibit 5. The second equation is for the line where borrowing, or negative investment in the risk-free asset, occurs. Note that the only difference between the two equations is in the interest rates used for borrowing and lending.

All passive portfolios will lie on the kinked CML, although the investment in the risk-free asset may be positive (lending), zero (no lending or borrowing), or negative (borrowing). Leverage allows less risk-averse investors to increase the amount of risk they take by borrowing money and investing more than 100 percent in the passive portfolio.

EXAMPLE 3

Leveraged Portfolio with Different Lending and Borrowing Rates

1. Mr. Miles approaches his broker to borrow money against securities held in his portfolio. Even though Mr. Miles' loan will be secured by the securities in his portfolio, the broker's rate for lending to customers is 7 percent. Assuming a risk-free rate of 5 percent and a market return of 15 percent with a standard deviation of 20 percent, estimate Mr. Miles' expected return and risk if he invests 25 percent and 75 percent in the market and if he decides

to borrow 25 percent and 75 percent of his initial investment and invest the money in the market.

Solution:

The unleveraged portfolio's standard deviation and return are calculated using the same equations as before:

$$E(R_p) = w_1 R_f + (1 - w_1)E(R_m),$$

and

$$\sigma_p = (1 - w_1)\sigma_m$$

The results are unchanged. The slope of the line for the unleveraged portfolio is 0.50, just as before:

Return with 25 percent invested in the market = (0.75 × 5%) + (0.25 × 15%) = 7.5%.

Standard deviation with 25 percent invested in the market = 0.25 × 20% = 5%.

Return with 75 percent invested in the market = (0.25 × 5%) + (0.75 × 15%) = 12.5%.

Standard deviation with 75 percent invested in the market = 0.75 × 20% = 15%.

For the leveraged portfolio, everything remains the same except that R_f is replaced with R_b.

$$E(R_p) = w_1 R_b + (1 - w_1)E(R_m),$$

and

$$\sigma_p = (1 - w_1)\sigma_m.$$

Return with w_1 = –0.25 = (–0.25 × 7%) + (1.25 × 15%) = 17.0%.

Standard deviation with w_1 = –0.25 = 1.25 × 20% = 25%.

Return with w_1 = –0.75 = (–0.75 × 7%) + (1.75 × 15%) = 21.0%.

Standard deviation with w_1 = –0.75 = 1.75 × 20% = 35%.

The risk and return of the leveraged portfolio is higher than that of the unleveraged portfolio. As Mr. Miles borrows more money to invest in the market, the expected return increases but so does the standard deviation of the portfolio. The slope of the line for the leveraged portfolio is 0.40, compared with 0.50 for the unleveraged portfolio, which means that for every 1 percent increase in risk, the investor gets a 0.40 percent increase in expected return in the leveraged part of the portfolio, compared with a 0.50 percent increase in expected return in the unleveraged part of the portfolio. Only investors who are less risk averse will choose leveraged portfolios.

SYSTEMATIC AND NONSYSTEMATIC RISK

5

- [ ] explain systematic and nonsystematic risk, including why an investor should not expect to receive additional return for bearing nonsystematic risk

In constructing a portfolio, it is important to understand the concept of correlation and how less than perfect correlation can diversify the risk of a portfolio. As a consequence, the risk of an asset held alone may be greater than the risk of that same asset when it is part of a portfolio. Because the risk of an asset varies from one environment to another, which kind of risk should an investor consider and how should that risk be priced? This section addresses the question of pricing of risk by decomposing the total risk of a security or a portfolio into systematic and nonsystematic risk. The meaning of these risks, how they are computed, and their relevance to the pricing of assets are also discussed.

Systematic Risk and Nonsystematic Risk

Systematic risk, also known as non-diversifiable or market risk, is the risk that affects the entire market or economy. In contrast, nonsystematic risk is the risk that pertains to a single company or industry and is also known as company-specific, industry-specific, diversifiable, or idiosyncratic risk.

Systematic risk is risk that cannot be avoided and is inherent in the overall market. It is non-diversifiable because it includes risk factors that are innate within the market and affect the market as a whole. Examples of factors that constitute systematic risk include interest rates, inflation, economic cycles, political uncertainty, and widespread natural disasters. These events affect the entire market, and there is no way to avoid their effect. Systematic risk can be magnified through selection or by using leverage, or diminished by including securities that have a low correlation with the portfolio, assuming they are not already part of the portfolio.

Nonsystematic risk is risk that is local or limited to a particular asset or industry that need not affect assets outside of that asset class. Examples of nonsystematic risk could include the failure of a drug trial or an airliner crash. All these events will directly affect their respective companies and possibly industries, but have no effect on assets that are far removed from these industries. Investors can avoid nonsystematic risk through diversification by forming a portfolio of assets that are not highly correlated with one another.

We will derive expressions for each kind of risk later in this reading. You will see that the sum of systematic variance and nonsystematic variance equals the total variance of the security or portfolio:

Total variance = Systematic variance + Nonsystematic variance

Although the equality relationship is between variances, you will find frequent references to total risk as the sum of systematic risk and nonsystematic risk. In those cases, the statements refer to variance, not standard deviation.

Pricing of Risk

Pricing or valuing an asset is equivalent to estimating its expected rate of return. If an asset has a known terminal value, such as the face value of a bond, then a lower current price implies a higher future return and a higher current price implies a lower future return. The relationship between price and return can also be observed in the valuation expression shown in Section 2.1.2. Therefore, we will occasionally use price and return interchangeably when discussing the price of risk.

Consider an asset with both systematic and nonsystematic risk. Assume that both kinds of risk are priced—that is, you receive a return for both systematic risk and non-systematic risk. What will you do? Realizing that nonsystematic risk can be diversified away, you would buy assets that have a large amount of nonsystematic risk. Once you have bought those assets with nonsystematic risk, you would diversify, or reduce that risk, by including other assets that are not highly correlated. In the process, you will minimize nonsystematic risk and eventually eliminate it altogether from your portfolio. You would now have a diversified portfolio with only systematic risk, yet you would be compensated for nonsystematic risk that you no longer have. Just like everyone else, you would have an incentive to take on more and more diversifiable risk because you are compensated for it even though you can get rid of it. The demand for diversifiable risk would keep increasing until its price becomes infinite and its expected return falls to zero. This means that our initial assumption of a non-zero return for diversifiable risk was incorrect and that the correct assumption is zero return for diversifiable risk. Therefore, according to theory, in an efficient market no incremental reward is earned for taking on diversifiable risk.

We have argued that investors should not be compensated for taking on nonsystematic risk. Therefore, investors who have nonsystematic risk must diversify it away by investing in many industries, many countries, and many asset classes. Because future returns are unknown and it is not possible to pick only winners, diversification helps in offsetting poor returns in one asset class by garnering good returns in another asset class, thereby reducing the overall risk of the portfolio. In contrast, investors must be compensated for accepting systematic risk because that risk cannot be diversified away. If investors do not receive a return commensurate with the amount of systematic risk they are taking, they will refuse to accept systematic risk.

In summary, according to theory, systematic or non-diversifiable risk is priced and investors are compensated for holding assets or portfolios based only on that investment's systematic risk. Investors do not receive any return for accepting non-systematic or diversifiable risk. Therefore, it is in the interest of risk-averse investors to hold only well-diversified portfolios.

EXAMPLE 4

Systematic and Nonsystematic Risk

1. Describe the systematic and nonsystematic risk components of the following assets:
   - **A.** A risk-free asset, such as a three-month Treasury bill
   - **B.** The market portfolio, such as the S&P 500.
2. Consider two assets, A and B. Asset A has twice the amount of total risk as Asset B. For Asset A, systematic risk comprises two-thirds of total risk. For Asset B, all of total risk is systematic risk. Which asset should have a higher expected rate of return?

Solution to 1A:

By definition, a risk-free asset has no risk. Therefore, a risk-free asset has zero systematic risk and zero nonsystematic risk.

Solution to 1B:

As we mentioned earlier, a market portfolio is a diversified portfolio, one in which no more risk can be diversified away. We have also described it as an efficient portfolio. Therefore, a market portfolio does not contain any nonsystematic risk.

Solution to 2:

Based on the facts given, Asset A's systematic risk is one-third greater than Asset B's systematic risk. Because only systematic risk is priced or receives a return, the expected rate of return must be higher for Asset A.

RETURN GENERATING MODELS

6

- [ ] explain return generating models (including the market model) and their uses

As previously mentioned, in order to form the market portfolio, you should combine all available risky assets. Knowledge of the correlations among those assets allows us to estimate portfolio risk. You also learned that a fully diversified portfolio will include all asset classes and essentially all assets in those asset classes. The work required for construction of the market portfolio is formidable. For example, for a portfolio of 1,000 assets, we will need 1,000 return estimates, 1,000 standard deviation estimates, and 499,500 (1,000 × 999 ÷ 2) correlations. Other related questions that arise with this analysis are whether we really need all 1,000 assets and what happens if there are errors in these estimates.

An alternate method of constructing an optimal portfolio is simpler and easier to implement. An investor begins with a known portfolio, such as the S&P 500, and then adds other assets one at a time on the basis of the asset's standard deviation, expected return, and impact on the portfolio's risk and return. This process continues until the addition of another asset does not have a significant impact on the performance of the portfolio. The process requires only estimates of systematic risk for each asset because investors will not be compensated for nonsystematic risk. Expected returns can be calculated by using return-generating models, as we will discuss in this section. In addition to using return generating models, we will also decompose total variance into systematic variance and nonsystematic variance and establish a formal relationship between systematic risk and return. In the next section, we will expand on this discussion and introduce the CAPM as the preferred return-generating model.

Return-Generating Models

A **return-generating model** is a model that can provide an estimate of the expected return of a security given certain parameters. If systematic risk is the only relevant parameter for return, then the return-generating model will estimate the expected return for any asset given the level of systematic risk.

As with any model, the quality of estimates of expected return will depend on the quality of input estimates and the accuracy of the model. Because it is difficult to decide which factors are appropriate for generating returns, the most general form of a return-generating model is a multi-factor model. A **multi-factor model** allows more than one variable to be considered in estimating returns and can be built using different kinds of factors, such as macroeconomic, fundamental, and statistical factors.

Macroeconomic factor models use economic factors that are correlated with security returns. These factors may include economic growth, the interest rate, the inflation rate, productivity, employment, and consumer confidence. Past relationships with returns are estimated to obtain parameter estimates, which are, in turn, used for computing expected returns. Fundamental factor models analyze and use relationships between security returns and the company's underlying fundamentals, such as, for example, earnings, earnings growth, cash flow generation, investment in research, advertising, and number of patents. Finally, in a statistical factor model, historical and cross-sectional return data are analyzed to identify factors that explain variance or covariance in observed returns. These statistical factors, however, may or may not have an economic or fundamental connection to returns. For example, the conference to which the American football Super Bowl winner belongs, whether the American Football Conference or the National Football Conference, may be a factor in US stock returns, but no obvious economic connection seems to exist between the winner's conference and US stock returns. Moreover, data mining may generate many spurious factors that are devoid of any economic meaning. Because of this limitation, analysts prefer the macroeconomic and fundamental factor models for specifying and estimating return-generating models.

A general return-generating model is expressed in the following manner:

$$E(R_i) - R_f = \sum_{j=1}^{k} \beta_{ij} E(F_j) = \beta_{i1}[E(R_m) - R_f] + \sum_{j=2}^{k} \beta_{ij} E(F_j)$$

The model has k factors, $E(F_1)$, $E(F_2)$, ... $E(F_k)$. The coefficients, β_{ij}, are the factor weights (sometimes called factor loadings) associated with each factor. The left-hand side of the model has the expected excess return (i.e., the expected return over the risk-free rate). The right-hand side provides the risk factors that would generate the return or premium required to assume that risk. We have separated out one factor, $E(R_m)$, which represents the market return. All models contain return on the market portfolio as a key factor.

Three-Factor and Four-Factor Models

Eugene Fama and Kenneth French[1] suggested that a return-generating model for stock returns should include relative market capitalization of the company ("size") relative book-to-market value of the company in addition to beta. Fama and French found that past returns could be explained better with their model than with other models available at that time, most notably, the capital asset pricing model. Mark Carhart (1997) extended the Fama and French model by adding another factor: momentum, defined as relative past stock returns.

The Single-Index Model

The simplest form of a return-generating model is a single-factor linear model, in which only one factor is considered. The most common implementation is a single-index model, which uses the market factor in the following form: $E(R_i) - R_f = \beta_i[E(R_m) - R_f]$.

Although the single-index model is simple, it fits nicely with the capital market line. Recall that the CML is linear, with an intercept of R_f and a slope of $[E(R_m) - R_f]/\sigma_m$. We can rewrite the CML by moving the intercept to the left-hand side of the equation, rearranging the terms, and generalizing the subscript from p to i, for any security:

$$E(R_i) - R_f = \left(\frac{\sigma_i}{\sigma_m}\right)[E(R_m) - R_f]$$

1 Fama and French (1992).

The factor loading or factor weight, σ_i/σ_m, refers to the ratio of total security risk to total market risk. To obtain a better understanding of factor loading and to illustrate that the CML reduces to a single-index model, we decompose total risk into its components.

Decomposition of Total Risk for a Single-Index Model

With the introduction of return-generating models, particularly the single-index model, we are able to decompose total variance into systematic and nonsystematic variances. Instead of using expected returns in the single index, let us use realized returns. The difference between expected returns and realized returns is attributable to non-market changes, as an error term, e_i, in the second equation below:

$$E(R_i) - R_f = \beta_i[E(R_m) - R_f]$$

and

$$R_i - R_f = \beta_i(R_m - R_f) + e_i$$

The variance of realized returns can be expressed in the equation below (note that R_f is a constant). We can further drop the covariance term in this equation because, by definition, any non-market return is uncorrelated with the market. Thus, we are able to decompose total variance into systematic and nonsystematic variances in the second equation below:

$$\sigma_i^2 = \beta_i^2\sigma_m^2 + \sigma_e^2 + 2Cov\left(R_m, e_i\right)$$

Total variance = Systematic variance + Nonsystematic variance, which can be written as

$$\sigma_i^2 = \beta_i^2\sigma_m^2 + \sigma_e^2$$

Total risk can be expressed as

$$\sigma_i = \sqrt{\beta_i^2\sigma_m^2 + \sigma_e^2}$$

Because nonsystematic risk is zero for well-diversified portfolios, such as the market portfolio, the total risk of a market portfolio and other similar portfolios is only systematic risk, which is $\beta_i\sigma_m$. We can now return to the CML discussed in the previous subsection and replace σ_i with $\beta_i\sigma_m$ because the CML assumes that the market is a diversified portfolio. By making this substitution for the above equation, we get the following single-index model:

$$E\left(R_i\right) - R_f = \left(\frac{\sigma_i}{\sigma_m}\right) \times \left[E\left(R_m\right) - R_f\right] = \left(\frac{\beta_i\sigma_m}{\sigma_m}\right) \times \left[E\left(R_m\right) - R_f\right],$$

$$E(R_i) - R_f = \beta_i[E(R_m) - R_f]$$

Thus, the CML, which holds only for well-diversified portfolios, is fully consistent with a single-index model.

In summary, total variance may be decomposed into systematic and nonsystematic variances and the CML is the same as a single-index model for diversified portfolios.

Return-Generating Models: The Market Model

The most common implementation of a single-index model is the **market model**, in which the market return is the single factor or single index. In principle, the market model and the single-index model are similar. The difference is that the market model is easier to work with and is normally used for estimating beta risk and computing abnormal returns. The market model is

$$R_i = \alpha_i + \beta_i R_m + e_i$$

To be consistent with the previous section, $\alpha_i = R_f(1 - \beta)$. The intercept, α_i, and slope coefficient, β_i, can be estimated by using historical security and market returns. These parameter estimates are then used to predict company-specific returns that a security may earn in a future period. Assume that a regression of Wal-Mart's historical daily returns on S&P 500 daily returns gives an α_i of 0.0001 and a β_i of 0.9. Thus, Wal-Mart's expected daily return = 0.0001 + 0.90 × R_m. If, on a given day the market rises by 1 percent and Wal-Mart's stock rises by 2 percent, then Wal-Mart's company-specific return (e_i) for that day = $R_i - E(R_i) = R_i - (\alpha_i + \beta_i R_m) = 0.02 - (0.0001 + 0.90 \times 0.01) = 0.0109$, or 1.09%. In other words, Wal-Mart earned an abnormal return of 1.09 percent on that day.

7 CALCULATION AND INTERPRETATION OF BETA

☐ calculate and interpret beta

We begin with the single-index model introduced earlier using realized returns and rewrite it as

$$R_i = (1 - \beta_i)R_f + \beta_i \times R_m + e_i$$

Because systematic risk depends on the correlation between the asset and the market, we can arrive at a measure of systematic risk from the covariance between R_i and R_m, where R_i is defined using the above equation. Note that the risk-free rate is a constant, so the first term in R_i drops out.

$$\begin{aligned}\text{Cov}\left(R_i, R_m\right) &= \text{Cov}\left(\beta_i \times R_m + e_i, R_m\right)\\ &= \beta_i \text{Cov}\left(R_m, R_m\right) + \text{Cov}\left(e_i, R_m\right)\\ &= \beta_i \sigma_m^2 + 0\end{aligned}$$

The first term is beta multiplied by the variance of R_m. Because the error term is uncorrelated with the market, the second term drops out. Then, we can rewrite the equation in terms of beta as follows:

$$\beta_i = \frac{Cov\left(R_i, R_m\right)}{\sigma_m^2} = \frac{\rho_{i,m}\sigma_i\sigma_m}{\sigma_m^2} = \frac{\rho_{i,m}\sigma_i}{\sigma_m}$$

The above formula shows the expression for beta, β_i, which is similar to the factor loading in the single-index model presented earlier. For example, if the correlation between an asset and the market is 0.70 and the asset and market have standard deviations of return of 0.25 and 0.15, respectively, the asset's beta would be (0.70)(0.25)/0.15 = 1.17. If the asset's covariance with the market and market variance were given as 0.026250 and 0.02250, respectively, the calculation would be 0.026250/0.02250 = 1.17. The beta in the market model includes an adjustment for the correlation between asset *i* and the market because the market model covers all assets whereas the CML works only for fully diversified portfolios.

As shown in the above equation, **beta** is a measure of how sensitive an asset's return is to the market as a whole and is calculated as the covariance of the return on *i* and the return on the market divided by the variance of the market return; that expression is equivalent to the product of the asset's correlation with the market with a ratio of standard deviations of return (i.e., the ratio of the asset's standard deviation to the market's). As we have shown, beta captures an asset's systematic risk, or the portion of an asset's risk that cannot be eliminated by diversification. The variances and correlations required for the calculation of beta are usually based on historical returns.

A positive beta indicates that the return of an asset follows the general market trend, whereas a negative beta shows that the return of an asset generally follows a trend that is opposite to that of the market. In other words, a positive beta indicates that the return of an asset moves in the same direction of the market, whereas a negative beta indicates that the return of an asset moves in the opposite direction of the market. A risk-free asset's beta is zero because its covariance with other assets is zero. In other words, a beta of zero indicates that the asset's return has no correlation with movements in the market. The market's beta can be calculated by substituting σ_m for σ_i in the numerator. Also, any asset's correlation with itself is 1, so the beta of the market is 1:

$$\beta_i = \frac{\rho_{i,m}\sigma_i}{\sigma_m} = \frac{\rho_{m,m}\sigma_m}{\sigma_m} = 1$$

Because the market's beta is 1, the average beta of stocks in the market, by definition, is 1. In terms of correlation, most stocks, especially in developed markets, tend to be highly correlated with the market, with correlations in excess of 0.70. Some US broad market indexes, such as the S&P 500, the Dow Jones 30, and the NASDAQ 100, have even higher correlations that are in excess of 0.90. The correlations among different sectors are also high, which shows that companies have similar reactions to the same economic and market changes. As a consequence and as a practical matter, finding assets that have a consistently negative beta is unusual because of the market's broad effects on all assets.

EXAMPLE 5

Calculation of Beta

Assuming that the risk (standard deviation) of the market is 25 percent, calculate the beta for the following assets:

We use the formula for beta in answering the above questions: $\beta_i = \frac{\rho_{i,m}\sigma_i}{\sigma_m}$

1. A short-term US Treasury bill.

Solution:

By definition, a short-term US Treasury bill has zero risk. Therefore, its beta is zero.

2. Gold, which has a standard deviation equal to the standard deviation of the market but a zero correlation with the market.

Solution:

Because the correlation of gold with the market is zero, its beta is zero.

3. A new emerging market that is not currently included in the definition of "market"—the emerging market's standard deviation is 60 percent, and the correlation with the market is –0.1.

Solution:

Beta of the emerging market is –0.1 × 0.60 ÷ 0.25 = –0.24.

4. An initial public offering or new issue of stock with a standard deviation of 40 percent and a correlation with the market of 0.7 (IPOs are usually very risky but have a relatively low correlation with the market).

Solution:

Beta of the initial public offering is 0.7 × 0.40 ÷ 0.25 = 1.12.

Estimation of Beta

An alternative and more practical approach is to estimate beta directly by using the market model described above. The market model, $R_i = \alpha_i + \beta_i R_m + e_i$, is estimated by using regression analysis, which is a statistical process that evaluates the relationship between a given variable (the dependent variable) and one or more other (independent) variables. Historical security returns (R_i) and historical market returns (R_m) are inputs used for estimating the two parameters α_i and β_i.

Regression analysis is similar to plotting all combinations of the asset's return and the market return (R_i, R_m) and then drawing a line through all points such that it minimizes the sum of squared linear deviations from the line. Exhibit 6 illustrates the market model and the estimated parameters. The intercept, α_i (sometimes referred to as the constant), and the slope term, β_i, are all that is needed to define the security characteristic line and obtain beta estimates.

Exhibit 6: Beta Estimation Using a Plot of Security and Market Returns

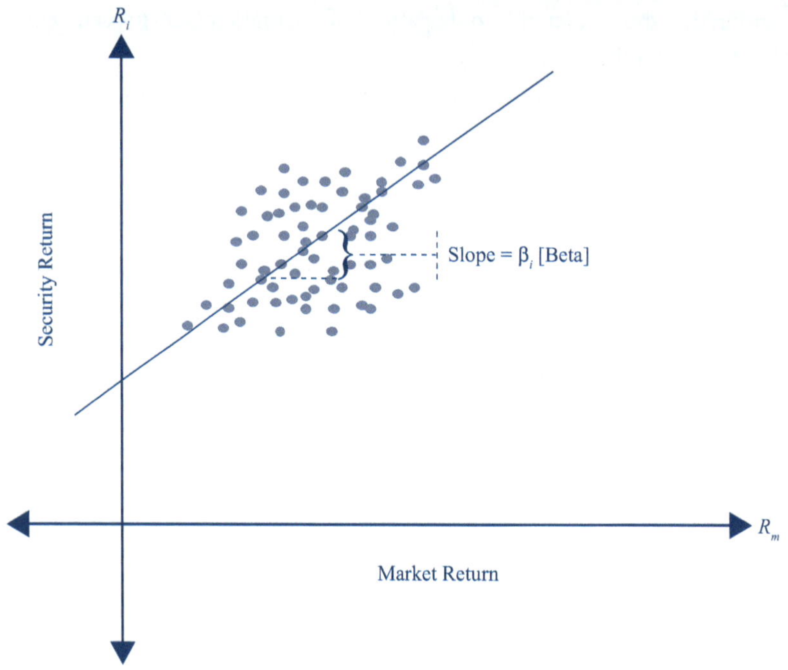

Although beta estimates are important for forecasting future levels of risk, there is much concern about their accuracy. In general, shorter periods of estimation (e.g., 12 months) represent betas that are closer to the asset's current level of systematic risk. Shorter period beta estimates, however, are also less accurate than beta estimates measured over three to five years because they may be affected by special events in that short period. Although longer period beta estimates are more accurate, they may be a poor representation of future expectations, especially if major changes in the asset have occurred. Therefore, it is necessary to recognize that estimates of beta, whether obtained through calculation or regression analysis, may or may not represent current or future levels of an asset's systematic risk.

Beta and Expected Return

Although the single-index model, also called the **capital asset pricing model** (CAPM), will be discussed in greater detail in the next section, we will use the CAPM in this section to estimate returns, given asset betas. The CAPM is usually written with the risk-free rate on the right-hand side:

$$E(R_i) = R_f + \beta_i[E(R_m) - R_f]$$

The model shows that the primary determinant of expected return for a security is its beta, or how well the security correlates with the market. The higher the beta of an asset, the higher its expected return will be. Assets with a beta greater than 1 have an expected return that is higher than the market return, whereas assets with a beta of less than 1 have an expected return that is less than the market return.

In certain cases, assets may require a return less than the risk-free return. For example, if an asset's beta is negative, the required return will be less than the risk-free rate. When combined with the market, the asset reduces the risk of the overall portfolio, which makes the asset very valuable. Insurance is one such asset. Insurance gives a positive return when the insured's wealth is reduced because of a catastrophic loss. In the absence of such a loss or when the insured's wealth is growing, the insured is required to pay an insurance premium. Thus, insurance has a negative beta and a negative expected return, but helps in reducing overall risk.

EXAMPLE 6

Calculation of Expected Return

Alpha Natural Resources (ANR), a coal producer, buys a large but privately held coal producer in China. As a result of the cross-border acquisition of a private company, ANR's standard deviation of returns is reduced from 50 percent to 30 percent and its correlation with the market falls from 0.95 to 0.75. Assume that the standard deviation and return of the market remain unchanged at 25 percent and 10 percent, respectively, and that the risk-free rate is 3 percent.

1. Calculate the beta of ANR stock and its expected return before the acquisition.

Solution:

Using the formula for β_i, we can calculate β_i and then the return.

$$\beta_i = \frac{\rho_{i,m}\sigma_i}{\sigma_m} = \frac{0.95 \times 0.50}{0.25} = 1.90$$

$$E(R_i) = R_f + \beta_i[E(R_m) - R_f] = 0.03 + 1.90 \times (0.10 - 0.03) = 0.163 = 16.3\%$$

2. Calculate the expected return after the acquisition.

Solution:

We follow the same procedure but with the after-acquisition correlation and risk.

$$\beta_i = \frac{\rho_{i,m}\sigma_i}{\sigma_m} = \frac{0.75 \times 0.30}{0.25} = 0.90$$

$$E(R_i) = R_f + \beta_i[E(R_m) - R_f] = 0.03 + 0.90 \times (0.10 - 0.03) = 0.093 = 9.3\%$$

The market risk premium is 7 percent (10% – 3%). As the beta changes, the change in the security's expected return is the market risk premium multiplied by the change in beta. In this scenario, ANR's beta decreased by 1.0, so the new expected return for ANR is 7 percentage points lower.

Mr. Miles observes the strong demand for iPods and iPhones and wants to invest in Apple stock. Unfortunately, Mr. Miles doesn't know the return he should expect from his investment. He has been given a risk-free rate of 3 percent, a market return of 10 percent, and Apple's beta of 1.5.

3. Calculate Apple's expected return.

Solution:

$$E(R_i) = R_f + \beta_i[E(R_m) - R_f] = 0.03 + 1.5 \times (0.10 - 0.03) = 0.135 = 13.5\%$$

4. An analyst looking at the same information decides that the past performance of Apple is not representative of its future performance. He decides that, given the increase in Apple's market capitalization, Apple acts much more like the market than before and thinks Apple's beta should be closer to 1.1. What is the analyst's expected return for Apple stock?

Solution:

$$E(R_i) = R_f + \beta_i[E(R_m) - R_f] = 0.03 + 1.1 \times (0.10 - 0.03) = 0.107 = 10.7\%$$

This example illustrates the lack of connection between estimation of past returns and projection into the future. Investors should be aware of the limitations of using past returns for estimating future returns.

8 CAPITAL ASSET PRICING MODEL: ASSUMPTIONS AND THE SECURITY MARKET LINE

- ☐ explain the capital asset pricing model (CAPM), including its assumptions, and the security market line (SML)
- ☐ calculate and interpret the expected return of an asset using the CAPM

The capital asset pricing model is one of the most significant innovations in portfolio theory. The model is simple, yet powerful; is intuitive, yet profound. The CAPM was introduced independently by William Sharpe, John Lintner, Jack Treynor, and Jan Mossin and builds on Harry Markowitz's earlier work on diversification and modern portfolio theory.[2] The model provides a linear expected return–beta relationship that

2 See, for example, Markowitz (1952), Sharpe (1964), Lintner (1965a, 1965b), Treynor (1961, 1962), and Mossin (1966).

precisely determines the expected return given the beta of an asset. In doing so, it makes the transition from total risk to systematic risk, the primary determinant of expected return. Recall the following equation:

$$E(R_i) = R_f + \beta_i[E(R_m) - R_f]$$

The CAPM asserts that the expected returns of assets vary only by their systematic risk as measured by beta. Two assets with the same beta will have the same expected return irrespective of the nature of those assets. Given the relationship between risk and return, all assets are defined only by their beta risk, which we will explain as the assumptions are described.

In the remainder of this section, we will examine the assumptions made in arriving at the CAPM and the limitations those assumptions entail. Second, we will implement the CAPM through the security market line to price any portfolio or asset, both efficient and inefficient. Finally, we will discuss ways in which the CAPM can be applied to investments, valuation, and capital budgeting.

Assumptions of the CAPM

Similar to all other models, the CAPM ignores many of the complexities of financial markets by making simplifying assumptions. These assumptions allow us to gain important insights into how assets are priced without complicating the analysis. Once the basic relationships are established, we can relax the assumptions and examine how our insights need to be altered. Some of these assumptions are constraining, whereas others are benign. And other assumptions affect only a particular set of assets or only marginally affect the hypothesized relationships.

1. ***Investors are risk-averse, utility-maximizing, rational individuals.***

   Risk aversion means that investors expect to be compensated for accepting risk. Note that the assumption does not require investors to have the same degree of risk aversion; it only requires that they are averse to risk. Utility maximization implies that investors want higher returns, not lower returns, and that investors always want more wealth (i.e., investors are never satisfied). Investors are understood to be rational in that they correctly evaluate and analyze available information to arrive at rational decisions. Although rational investors may use the same information to arrive at different estimates of expected risk and expected returns, homogeneity among investors (see Assumption 4) requires that investors be rational individuals.

   Risk aversion and utility maximization are generally accepted as reflecting a realistic view of the world. Yet, rationality among investors has been questioned because investors may allow their personal biases and experiences to disrupt their decision making, resulting in suboptimal investments. Nonetheless, the model's results are unaffected by such irrational behavior as long as it does not affect prices in a significant manner (i.e., the trades of irrational investors cancel each other or are dominated by the trades of rational investors).

2. ***Markets are frictionless, including no transaction costs and no taxes.***

   Frictionless markets allow us to abstract the analysis from the operational characteristics of markets. In doing so, we do not allow the risk–return relationship to be affected by, for example, the trading volume on the New York Stock Exchange or the difference between buying and selling prices. Specifically, frictionless markets do not have transaction costs, taxes, or any costs or restrictions on short selling. We also assume that borrowing and lending at the risk-free rate is possible.

The transaction costs of many large institutions are negligible, and many institutions do not pay taxes. Even the presence of non-zero transaction costs, taxes, or the inability to borrow at the risk-free rate does not materially affect the general conclusions of the CAPM. Costs of short selling or restrictions on short selling, however, can introduce an upward bias in asset prices, potentially jeopardizing important conclusions of the CAPM.

3. ***Investors plan for the same single holding period.***

   The CAPM is a single-period model, and all investor decisions are made on the basis of that one period. The assumption of a single period is applied for convenience because working with multi-period models is more difficult. A single-period model, however, does not allow learning to occur, and bad decisions can persist. In addition, maximizing utility at the end of a multi-period horizon may require decisions in certain periods that may seem suboptimal when examined from a single-period perspective. Nonetheless, the single holding period does not severely limit the applicability of the CAPM to multi-period settings.

4. ***Investors have homogeneous expectations or beliefs.***

   This assumption means that all investors analyze securities in the same way using the same probability distributions and the same inputs for future cash flows. In addition, given that they are rational individuals, the investors will arrive at the same valuations. Because their valuations of all assets are identical, they will generate the same optimal risky portfolio, which we call the market portfolio.

   The assumption of homogeneous beliefs can be relaxed as long as the differences in expectations do not generate significantly different optimal risky portfolios.

5. ***All investments are infinitely divisible.***

   This assumption implies that an individual can invest as little or as much as he or she wishes in an asset. This supposition allows the model to rely on continuous functions rather than on discrete jump functions. The assumption is made for convenience only and has an inconsequential impact on the conclusions of the model.

6. ***Investors are price takers.***

   The CAPM assumes that there are many investors and that no investor is large enough to influence prices. Thus, investors are price takers, and we assume that security prices are unaffected by investor trades. This assumption is generally true because even though investors may be able to affect prices of small stocks, those stocks are not large enough to affect the primary results of the CAPM.

The main objective of these assumptions is to create a marginal investor who rationally chooses a mean–variance-efficient portfolio in a predictable fashion. We assume away any inefficiency in the market from both operational and informational perspectives. Although some of these assumptions may seem unrealistic, relaxing most of them will have only a minor influence on the model and its results. Moreover, the CAPM, with all its limitations and weaknesses, provides a benchmark for comparison and for generating initial return estimates.

The Security Market Line

In this subsection, we apply the CAPM to the pricing of securities. The **security market line** (SML) is a graphical representation of the capital asset pricing model with beta, reflecting systematic risk, on the *x*-axis and expected return on the *y*-axis. Using the same concept as the capital market line, the SML intersects the *y*-axis at the risk-free rate of return, and the slope of this line is the market risk premium, $R_m - R_f$. Recall that the capital market line (CML) does not apply to all securities or assets but only to portfolios on the efficient frontier. The efficient frontier gives optimal combinations of expected return and total risk. In contrast, the security market line applies to any security, efficient or not. Total risk and systematic risk are equal only for efficient portfolios because those portfolios have no diversifiable risk remaining.

Exhibit 7 is a graphical representation of the CAPM, the security market line. As shown earlier in this reading, the beta of the market is 1 (*x*-axis) and the market earns an expected return of R_m (*y*-axis). Using this line, it is possible to calculate the expected return of an asset. The next example illustrates the beta and return calculations.

Exhibit 7: The Security Market Line

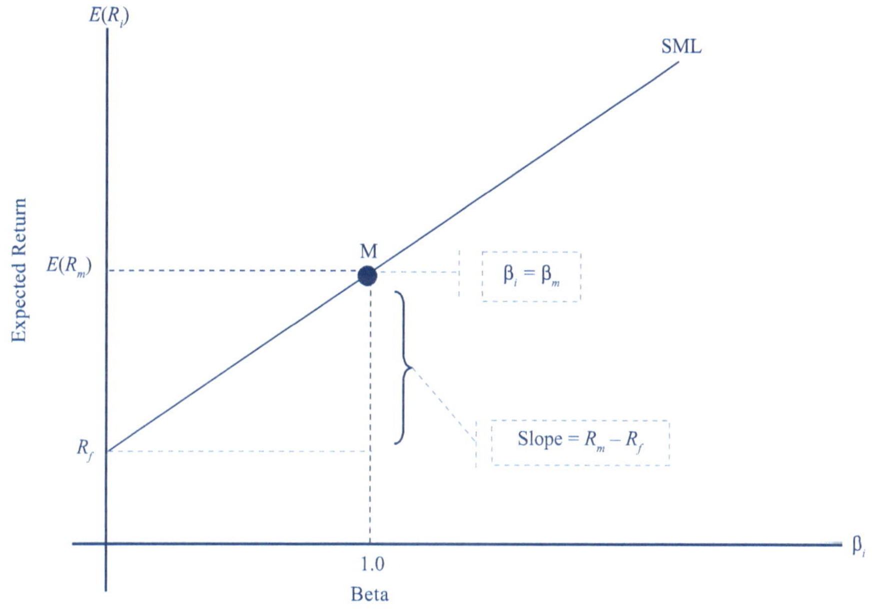

EXAMPLE 7

Security Market Line and Expected Return

1. Suppose the risk-free rate is 3 percent, the expected return on the market portfolio is 13 percent, and its standard deviation is 23 percent. An Indian company, Bajaj Auto, has a standard deviation of 50 percent but is uncorrelated with the market. Calculate Bajaj Auto's beta and expected return.

Solution:

Using the formula for β_i, we can calculate β_i and then the return.

$$\beta_i = \frac{\rho_{i,m}\sigma_i}{\sigma_m} = \frac{0.0 \times 0.50}{0.23} = 0$$

$$E(R_i) = R_f + \beta_i[E(R_m) - R_f] = 0.03 + 0 \times (0.13 - 0.03) = 0.03 = 3.0\%$$

Because of its zero correlation with the market portfolio, Bajaj Auto's beta is zero. Because the beta is zero, the expected return for Bajaj Auto is the risk-free rate, which is 3 percent.

2. Suppose the risk-free rate is 3 percent, the expected return on the market portfolio is 13 percent, and its standard deviation is 23 percent. A German company, Mueller Metals, has a standard deviation of 50 percent and a correlation of 0.65 with the market. Calculate Mueller Metal's beta and expected return.

Solution:

Using the formula for β_i, we can calculate β_i and then the return.

$$\beta_i = \frac{\rho_{i,m}\sigma_i}{\sigma_m} = \frac{0.65 \times 0.50}{0.23} = 1.41$$

$$E(R_i) = R_f + \beta_i[E(R_m) - R_f] = 0.03 + 1.41\times (0.13 - 0.03) = 0.171 = 17.1\%$$

Because of the high degree of correlation with the market, the beta for Mueller Metals is 1.41 and the expected return is 17.1 percent. Because Mueller Metals has systematic risk that is greater than that of the market, it has an expected return that exceeds the expected return of the market.

Portfolio Beta

As we stated above, the security market line applies to all securities. But what about a combination of securities, such as a portfolio? Consider two securities, 1 and 2, with a weight of w_i in Security 1 and the balance in Security 2. The return for the two securities and return of the portfolio can be written as:

$$E(R_1) = R_f + \beta_1\left[E(R_m) - R_f\right]$$
$$E(R_2) = R_f + \beta_2\left[E(R_m) - R_f\right]$$
$$E\left(R_p\right) = w_1 E(R_1) + w_2 E(R_2)$$
$$= w_1 R_f + w_1\beta_1\left[E(R_m) - R_f\right] + w_2 R_f + w_2\beta_2\left[E(R_m) - R_f\right]$$
$$= R_f + (w_1\beta_1 + w_2\beta_2)\left[E(R_m) - R_f\right]$$

The last equation gives the expression for the portfolio's expected return. From this equation, we can conclude that the portfolio's beta = $w_1\beta_1 + w_2\beta_2$. In general, the portfolio beta is a weighted sum of the betas of the component securities and is given by:

$$\beta_p = \sum_{i=1}^{n} w_i\beta_i;\ \sum_{i=1}^{n} w_i = 1$$

The portfolio's return given by the CAPM is

$$E(R_p) = R_f + \beta_p[E(R_m) - R_f]$$

This equation shows that a linear relationship exists between the expected return of a portfolio and the systematic risk of the portfolio as measured by β_p.

EXAMPLE 8

Portfolio Beta and Return

1. You invest 20 percent of your money in the risk-free asset, 30 percent in the market portfolio, and 50 percent in RedHat, a US stock that has a beta of 2.0. Given that the risk-free rate is 4 percent and the market return is 16 percent, what are the portfolio's beta and expected return?

Solution:

The beta of the risk-free asset = 0, the beta of the market = 1, and the beta of RedHat is 2.0. The portfolio beta is

$$\beta_p = w_1\beta_1 + w_2\beta_2 + w_3\beta_3 = (0.20 \times 0.0) + (0.30 \times 1.0) + (0.50 \times 2.0) = 1.30$$

$$E(R_i) = R_f + \beta_i[E(R_m) - R_f] = 0.04 + 1.30 \times (0.16 - 0.04) = 0.196 = 19.6\%$$

The portfolio beta is 1.30, and its expected return is 19.6 percent.

Alternate Method:

Another method for calculating the portfolio's return is to calculate individual security returns and then use the portfolio return formula (i.e., weighted average of security returns) to calculate the overall portfolio return.

Return of the risk-free asset = 4 percent; return of the market = 16 percent

RedHat's return based on its beta = 0.04 + 2.0 × (0.16 – 0.04) = 0.28

Portfolio return = (0.20 × 0.04) + (0.30 × 0.16) + (0.50 × 0.28) = 0.196 = 19.6%

Not surprisingly, the portfolio return is 19.6 percent, as calculated in the first method.

CAPITAL ASSET PRICING MODEL: APPLICATIONS 9

- ☐ calculate and interpret the expected return of an asset using the CAPM
- ☐ describe and demonstrate applications of the CAPM and the SML

The CAPM offers powerful and intuitively appealing predictions about risk and the relationship between risk and return. The CAPM is not only important from a theoretical perspective but is also used extensively in practice. In this section, we will discuss some common applications of the model. When applying these tools to different scenarios, it is important to understand that the CAPM and the SML are functions that give an indication of what the return in the market *should* be, given a certain level of risk. The actual return may be quite different from the expected return.

Applications of the CAPM include estimates of the expected return for capital budgeting, comparison of the actual return of a portfolio or portfolio manager with the CAPM return for performance appraisal, and the analysis of alternate return estimates and the CAPM returns as the basis for security selection. The applications are discussed in more detail in this section.

Estimate of Expected Return

Given an asset's systematic risk, the expected return can be calculated using the CAPM. Recall that the price of an asset is the sum of all future cash flows discounted at the required rate of return, where the discount rate or the required rate of return is commensurate with the asset's risk. The expected rate of return obtained from the CAPM is normally the first estimate that investors use for valuing assets, such as stocks, bonds, real estate, and other similar assets. The required rate of return from the CAPM is also used for capital budgeting and determining the economic feasibility of projects. Again, recall that when computing the net present value of a project, investments and net revenues are considered cash flows and are discounted at the required rate of return. The required rate of return, based on the project's risk, is calculated using the CAPM.

Because risk and return underlie almost all aspects of investment decision making, it is not surprising that the CAPM is used for estimating expected return in many scenarios. Other examples include calculating the cost of capital for regulated companies by regulatory commissions and setting fair insurance premiums. The next example shows an application of the CAPM to capital budgeting.

EXAMPLE 9

Application of the CAPM to Capital Budgeting

GlaxoSmithKline Plc is examining the economic feasibility of developing a new medicine. The initial investment in Year 1 is \$500 million. The investment in Year 2 is \$200 million. There is a 50 percent chance that the medicine will be developed and will be successful. If that happens, GlaxoSmithKline must spend another \$100 million in Year 3, but its income from the project in Year 3 will be \$500 million, not including the third-year investment. In Years 4, 5, and 6, it will earn \$400 million a year if the medicine is successful. At the end of Year 6, it intends to sell all rights to the medicine for \$600 million. If the medicine is unsuccessful, none of GlaxoSmithKline's investments can be salvaged. Assume that the market return is 12 percent, the risk-free rate is 2 percent, and the beta risk of the project is 2.3. All cash flows occur at the end of each year.

1. Calculate the expected annual cash flows using the probability of success.

Solution:

There is a 50 percent chance that the cash flows in Years 3–6 will occur. Taking that into account, the expected annual cash flows are:

Year 1: –\$500 million (outflow)

Year 2: –\$200 million (outflow)

Year 3: 50% of –\$100 million (outflow) + 50% of \$500 million = \$200 million

Year 4: 50% of \$400 million = \$200 million

Year 5: 50% of \$400 million = \$200 million

Year 6: 50% of \$400 million + 50% of \$600 million = \$500 million

2. Calculate the expected return.

Solution:

The expected or required return for the project can be calculated using the CAPM, which is = 0.02 + 2.3 × (0.12 – 0.02) = 0.25.

3. Calculate the net present value.

Solution:

The net present value is the discounted value of all cash flows:

$$NPV = \sum_{t=0}^{T} \frac{CF_t}{(1+r_t)^t}$$

$$= \frac{-500}{(1+0.25)} + \frac{-200}{(1+0.25)^2} + \frac{200}{(1+0.25)^3} + \frac{200}{(1+0.25)^4}$$

$$+ \frac{200}{(1+0.25)^5} + \frac{500}{(1+0.25)^6}$$

$$= -400 - 128 + 102.40 + 81.92 + 65.54 + 131.07 = -147.07.$$

Because the net present value is negative (–\$147.07 million), the project should not be accepted by GlaxoSmithKline.

BEYOND CAPM: LIMITATIONS AND EXTENSIONS OF CAPM 10

☐ describe and demonstrate applications of the CAPM and the SML

In general, return-generating models allow us to estimate an asset's return given its characteristics, where the asset characteristics required for estimating the return are specified in the model. Estimating an asset's return is important for investment decision making. These models are also important as a benchmark for evaluating portfolio, security, or manager performance. The return-generating models were briefly introduced in Section 3.2.1, and one of those models, the capital asset pricing model, was discussed in detail in Section 4.

The purpose of this section is to make readers aware that, although the CAPM is an important concept and model, the CAPM is not the only return-generating model. In this section, we revisit and highlight the limitations of the CAPM and preview return-generating models that address some of those limitations.

Limitations of the CAPM

The CAPM is subject to theoretical and practical limitations. Theoretical limitations are inherent in the structure of the model, whereas practical limitations are those that arise in implementing the model.

Theoretical Limitations of the CAPM

- Single-factor model: Only systematic risk or beta risk is priced in the CAPM. Thus, the CAPM states that no other investment characteristics should be considered in estimating returns. As a consequence, it is prescriptive and easy to understand and apply, although it is very restrictive and inflexible.
- Single-period model: The CAPM is a single-period model that does not consider multi-period implications or investment objectives of future periods, which can lead to myopic and suboptimal investment decisions. For example, it may be optimal to default on interest payments in the current period to maximize current returns, but the consequences may be negative in the next period. A single-period model like the CAPM is unable to capture factors that vary over time and span several periods.

Practical Limitations of the CAPM

In addition to the theoretical limitations, implementation of the CAPM raises several practical concerns, some of which are listed below.

- Market portfolio: The true market portfolio according to the CAPM includes all assets, financial and nonfinancial, which means that it also includes many assets that are not investable, such as human capital and assets in closed economies. Richard Roll[3] noted that one reason the CAPM is not testable is that the true market portfolio is unobservable.
- Proxy for a market portfolio: In the absence of a true market portfolio, market participants generally use proxies. These proxies, however, vary among analysts, the country of the investor, etc. and generate different return estimates for the same asset, which is impermissible in the CAPM.
- Estimation of beta risk: A long history of returns (three to five years) is required to estimate beta risk. The historical state of the company, however, may not be an accurate representation of the current or future state of the company. More generally, the CAPM is an *ex ante* model, yet it is usually applied using *ex post* data. In addition, using different periods for estimation results in different estimates of beta. For example, a three-year beta is unlikely to be the same as a five-year beta, and a beta estimated with daily returns is unlikely to be the same as the beta estimated with monthly returns. Thus, we are likely to estimate different returns for the same asset depending on the estimate of beta risk used in the model.
- The CAPM is a poor predictor of returns: If the CAPM is a good model, its estimate of asset returns should be closely associated with realized returns. However, empirical support for the CAPM is weak.[4] In other words, tests of the CAPM show that asset returns are not determined only by systematic risk. Poor predictability of returns when using the CAPM is a serious limitation because return-generating models are used to estimate future returns.
- Homogeneity in investor expectations: The CAPM assumes that homogeneity exists in investor expectations for the model to generate a single optimal risky portfolio (the market) and a single security market line. Without this assumption, there will be numerous optimal risky portfolios and numerous security market lines. Clearly, investors can process the same information in a rational manner and arrive at different optimal risky portfolios.

---

3 Roll (1977).

4 See, for example, Fama and French (1992).

Extensions to the CAPM

Given the limitations of the CAPM, it is not surprising that other models have been proposed to address some of these limitations. These new models are not without limitations of their own, which we will mention while discussing the models. We divide the models into two categories—theoretical models and practical models—and provide one example of each type.

Theoretical Models

Theoretical models are based on the same principle as the CAPM but expand the number of risk factors. The best example of a theoretical model is the arbitrage pricing theory (APT), which was developed by Stephen Ross.[5] Like the CAPM, APT proposes a linear relationship between expected return and risk:

$$E(R_p) = R_F + \lambda_1\beta_{p,1} + \ldots + \lambda_K\beta_{p,K}$$

where

$E(R_p)$ = the expected return of portfolio p

R_F = the risk-free rate

λ_j = the risk premium (expected return in excess of the risk-free rate) for factor j

$\beta_{p,j}$ = the sensitivity of the portfolio to factor j

K = the number of risk factors

Unlike the CAPM, however, APT allows numerous risk factors—as many as are relevant to a particular asset. Moreover, other than the risk-free rate, the risk factors need not be common and may vary from one asset to another. A no-arbitrage condition in asset markets is used to determine the risk factors and estimate betas for the risk factors.

Although it is theoretically elegant, flexible, and superior to the CAPM, APT is not commonly used in practice because it does not specify any of the risk factors and it becomes difficult to identify risk factors and estimate betas for each asset in a portfolio. So from a practical standpoint, the CAPM is preferred to APT.

Practical Models

If beta risk in the CAPM does not explain returns, which factors do? Practical models seek to answer this question through extensive research. As mentioned in Section 3.2.1, the best example of such a model is the four-factor model proposed by Fama and French (1992) and Carhart (1997).

Based on an analysis of the relationship between past returns and a variety of different factors, Fama and French (1992) proposed that three factors seem to explain asset returns better than just systematic risk. Those three factors are relative size, relative book-to-market value, and beta of the asset. With Carhart's (1997) addition of relative past stock returns, the model can be written as follows:

$$E(R_{it}) = \alpha_i + \beta_{i,MKT}MKT_t + \beta_{i,SMB}SMB_t + \beta_{i,HML}HML_t + \beta_{i,UMD}UMD_t$$

5 Ross (1976).

where

$E(R_i)$ = the return on an asset in excess of the one-month T-bill return

MKT = the excess return on the market portfolio

SMB = the difference in returns between small-capitalization stocks and large-capitalization stocks (size)

HML = the difference in returns between high-book-to-market stocks and low-book-to-market stocks (value versus growth)

UMD = the difference in returns of the prior year's winners and losers (momentum)

Historical analysis shows that the coefficient on *MKT* is not significantly different from zero, which implies that stock return is unrelated to the market. The factors that explain stock returns are size (smaller companies outperform larger companies), book-to-market ratio (value companies outperform glamour companies), and momentum (past winners outperform past losers).

The four-factor model has been found to predict asset returns much better than the CAPM and is extensively used in estimating returns for US stocks.

Two observations are in order. First, the model is not underpinned by a theory of market equilibrium, as is the case for the CAPM. Second, there is no assurance that the model will continue to work well in the future.

11 PORTFOLIO PERFORMANCE APPRAISAL MEASURES

- [ ] calculate and interpret the Sharpe ratio, Treynor ratio, M^2, and Jensen's alpha

In the investment industry, **performance evaluation** refers to the measurement, attribution, and appraisal of investment results. In particular, performance evaluation provides information about the return and risk of investment portfolios over specified investment period(s). By providing accurate data and analysis on investment decisions and their consequences, performance evaluation allows portfolio managers to take corrective measures to improve investment decision-making and management processes. Performance evaluation information helps in understanding and controlling investment risk and should, therefore, lead to improved risk management. Performance evaluation seeks to answer the following questions:

- What was the investment portfolio's past performance, and what may be expected in the future?

Answering this question is the subject of performance measurement. *Performance measurement is concerned with the measurement of return and risk.*

- How did the investment portfolio produce its observed performance, and what are the expected sources of expected future performance?

Answering this question is the subject of performance attribution. *Performance attribution is concerned with identifying and quantifying the sources of performance of a portfolio.*

- Was the observed investment portfolio's performance the result of investment skill or luck?

Answering this question is the subject of performance appraisal. *Performance appraisal is concerned with identifying and measuring investment skill.*

The information provided by performance evaluation is of great interest to all stakeholders in the investment management process because of its value in evaluating the overall quality of the investment management process as well as individual investment decisions.

In this reading, performance appraisal is based only on the CAPM. However, it is easy to extend this analysis to multi-factor models that may include industry or other special factors. Four ratios are commonly used in performance appraisal.

The Sharpe Ratio

Performance has two components, risk and return. Although return maximization is a laudable objective, comparing just the return of a portfolio with that of the market is not sufficient. Because investors are risk averse, they will require compensation for higher risk in the form of higher returns. A commonly used measure of performance is the **Sharpe ratio**, which is defined as the portfolio's risk premium divided by its risk. An appealing feature of the Sharpe ratio is that its use can be justified on a theoretical *ex ante* (before the fact) basis and *ex post* (after the fact) values can easily be determined by using readily available market data. The Sharpe ratio is also easy to interpret, essentially being an efficiency ratio relating reward to risks taken. It is the most widely recognized and used appraisal measure.

The equation below defines the *ex ante* Sharpe ratio in terms of three inputs: (1) the portfolio's expected return, $E(R_p)$; (2) the risk-free rate of interest, R_f; and (3) the portfolio's *ex ante* standard deviation of returns (return volatility), σ_p, a quantitative measure of total risk.

$$\text{SR} = \frac{E\left(R_p\right) - R_F}{\sigma_p}$$

The Sharpe ratio can also be used on an *ex post* basis to evaluate historical risk-adjusted returns. Assume we have a sample of historical data that can be used to determine the sample mean portfolio return, $\overline{R}_p$; the standard deviation of the sample returns, here denoted by $\hat{\sigma}_p$ (s_p is a familiar notation in other contexts); and the sample mean risk-free rate, $\overline{R}_f$. The *ex post* (or realized or historical) Sharpe ratio can then be determined by using the following:

$$\widehat{SR} = \frac{\overline{R}_p - \overline{R}_F}{\hat{\sigma}_p}$$

Recalling the CAL from earlier in the reading, one can see that the Sharpe ratio, also called the reward-to-variability ratio, is simply the slope of the capital allocation line. Note, however, that the ratio uses the *total risk* of the portfolio, not its systematic risk. The use of total risk is appropriate if the portfolio is an investor's total portfolio—that is, the investor does not own any other assets. Sharpe ratios of the market and other portfolios can also be calculated in a similar manner. The portfolio with the highest Sharpe ratio has the best risk-adjusted performance, and the one with the lowest Sharpe ratio has the worst risk-adjusted performance, provided that the numerator is positive for all comparison portfolios. If the numerator is negative, the ratio will be less negative for riskier portfolios, resulting in incorrect rankings.

The Sharpe ratio, however, suffers from two limitations. First, it uses total risk as a measure of risk when only systematic risk is priced. Second, the ratio itself (e.g., 0.2 or 0.3) is not informative. To rank portfolios, the Sharpe ratio of one portfolio must be compared with the Sharpe ratio of another portfolio. Nonetheless, the ease of computation makes the Sharpe ratio a popular tool.

The Treynor Ratio

The **Treynor ratio** is a simple extension of the Sharpe ratio and resolves the Sharpe ratio's first limitation by substituting beta (systematic risk) for total risk. The *ex ante* and *ex post* Treynor ratios are provided below.

$$TR = \frac{E(R_p) - R_f}{\beta_p}$$

$$\widehat{TR} = \frac{\overline{R}_p - \overline{R}_f}{\hat{\beta}_p}$$

Just like the Sharpe ratio, the numerators must be positive for the Treynor ratio to give meaningful results. In addition, the Treynor ratio does not work for negative-beta assets—that is, the denominator must also be positive for obtaining correct estimates and rankings. Although both the Sharpe and Treynor ratios allow for ranking of portfolios, neither ratio gives any information about the economic significance of differences in performance. For example, assume the Sharpe ratio of one portfolio is 0.75 and the Sharpe ratio for another portfolio is 0.80. The second portfolio is superior, but is that difference meaningful? In addition, we do not know whether either of the portfolios is better than the passive market portfolio. The remaining two measures, M^2 and Jensen's alpha, attempt to address that problem by comparing portfolios while also providing information about the extent of the overperformance or underperformance.

M^2: Risk-Adjusted Performance (RAP)

M^2 provides a measure of portfolio return that is adjusted for the total risk of the portfolio relative to that of some benchmark. In 1997, Nobel Prize winner Franco Modigliani and his granddaughter, Leah Modigliani, developed what they called a risk-adjusted performance measure, or RAP. The RAP measure has since become more commonly known as M^2 reflecting the Modigliani names. It is related to the Sharpe ratio and ranks portfolios identically, but it has the useful advantage of being denominated in familiar terms of percentage return advantage assuming the same level of total risk as the market.

M^2 borrows from capital market theory by assuming a portfolio is leveraged or de-leveraged until its volatility (as measured by standard deviation) matches that of the market. This adjustment produces a portfolio-specific leverage ratio that equates the portfolio's risk to that of the market. The portfolio's excess return times the leverage ratio plus the risk-free rate is then compared with the markets actual return to determine whether the portfolio has outperformed or underperformed the market on a risk-adjusted basis.

The equations below provide the *ex ante* and *ex post* formulas for M^2, where σ_m is the standard deviation of the market portfolio and σ_m/σ_p is the portfolio-specific leverage ratio. Because the Sharpe ratio is defined as

$$\frac{E(R_p) - R_f}{\sigma_p}$$

the equation shows that M^2 can be thought of as a rescaling of the Sharpe ratio that allows for easier comparisons among different portfolios. The reason that M^2 and Sharpe ratios rank portfolios identically is because, in a given time period—and for any given comparison of the market portfolio—both the risk-free rate and the market volatility are constant across all comparisons. Only the Sharpe ratio differs, so it determines all rankings.

$$M^2 = \left[E\left(R_p\right) - R_f\right]\frac{\sigma_m}{\sigma_p} + R_f = \text{SR} \times \sigma_m + R_f \text{(ex ante)}$$

$$\widehat{M^2} = \left(\bar{R}_p - \bar{R}_f\right)\frac{\hat{\sigma}_m}{\hat{\sigma}_p} + R_f = \widehat{\text{SR}} \times \hat{\sigma}_m + R_f \text{(ex post)}$$

For example, assume that $\bar{R}_f = 4.0\%$, $\bar{R}_p = 14.0\%$, $\hat{\sigma}_p = 25.0\%$ and $\hat{\sigma}_m = 20.0\%$. The Sharpe ratio is 0.4,

$$\widehat{\text{SR}} = \frac{0.14 - 0.04}{0.25} = 0.4,$$

and $\widehat{M^2}$ is 12.0%, $\widehat{M^2} = 0.4(0.2) + 0.04 = 0.12 = 12.0\%$. If the market return was 10%, then the portfolio outperformed the market on a risk-adjusted basis by 12.0% – 10.0% = 2.0%. This difference between the risk-adjusted performance of the portfolio and the performance of the market is frequently referred to as **M^2 alpha**.

The Sharpe ratio of the market portfolio is

$$\widehat{\text{SR}} = \frac{0.10 - 0.04}{0.20}$$

= 0.3. Comparing the Sharpe ratio of the portfolio with the Sharpe ratio of the market portfolio shows that the fund outperformed the market. But the 2.0% difference between M^2 and the market's return tells us the risk-adjusted outperformance as a percentage return.

Jensen's Alpha

Like the Treynor ratio, Jensen's alpha is based on systematic risk. We can measure a portfolio's systematic risk by estimating the market model, which is done by regressing the portfolio's daily return on the market's daily return. The coefficient on the market return is an estimate of the beta risk of the portfolio. We can calculate the risk-adjusted return of the portfolio using the beta of the portfolio and the CAPM. The difference between the actual portfolio return and the calculated risk-adjusted return is a measure of the portfolio's performance relative to the market portfolio and is called Jensen's alpha. By definition, α_m of the market is zero. Jensen's alpha is also the vertical distance from the SML measuring the excess return for the same risk as that of the market and is given by

$$\alpha_p = R_p - \{R_f + \beta_p[E(R_m) - R_f]\}$$

If the period is long, it may contain different risk-free rates, in which case R_f represents the average risk-free rate. Furthermore, the returns in the equation are all realized, actual returns. The sign of α_p indicates whether the portfolio has outperformed the market. If α_p is positive, then the portfolio has outperformed the market; if α_p is negative, the portfolio has underperformed the market. Jensen's alpha is commonly used for evaluating most institutional managers, pension funds, and mutual funds. Values of alpha can be used to rank different managers and the performance of their portfolios, as well as the magnitude of underperformance or overperformance. For example, if a portfolio's alpha is 2 percent and another portfolio's alpha is 5 percent, the second portfolio has outperformed the first portfolio by 3 percentage points and the market by 5 percentage points. Jensen's alpha is the maximum amount that you should be willing to pay the manager to manage your money. As with other performance appraisal measures, Jensen's alpha has *ex ante* and *ex post* forms. The use context usually clarifies which one is being referred to. Where we want to underscore a reference to *ex post* Jensen's alpha based on an estimated beta, $\hat{\beta}_p$, and an average market return, the notation $\hat{\alpha}_p$ is used.

EXAMPLE 10

Portfolio Performance Evaluation

1. A British pension fund has employed three investment managers, each of whom is responsible for investing in one-third of all asset classes so that the pension fund has a well-diversified portfolio. Information about the managers is given below.

Manager	Average Return	$\hat{\sigma}$	$\hat{\beta}$
X	10%	20%	1.1
Y	11	10	0.7
Z	12	25	0.6
Market (M)	9	19	
Risk-free rate (R_f)	3		

Calculate the expected return for each manager, based on using the average market return and the CAPM. Then also calculate for the managers (ex post) Sharpe ratio, Treynor ratio, M^2 alpha, and Jensen's alpha. Analyze your results and plot the returns and betas of these portfolios.

Solution:

In each case, the calculations are shown only for Manager X. All answers are tabulated below. Note that the β of the market is 1 and the σ and β of the risk-free rate are both zero.

Expected return: $E(R_X) = R_f + \beta_X\left[E(R_m) - R_f\right] = 0.03 + 1.10 \times (0.09 - 0.03) = 0.096 = 9.6\%$

$$\widehat{SR} = \frac{\bar{R}_x - \bar{R}_f}{\hat{\sigma}_x} = \frac{0.10 - 0.03}{0.20} = 0.35$$

$$\widehat{TR} = \frac{\bar{R}_x - \bar{R}_f}{\hat{\beta}_x} = \frac{0.10 - 0.03}{1.1} = 0.064$$

$$\widehat{M^2} = \left(\bar{R}_x - \bar{R}_f\right)\frac{\hat{\sigma}_m}{\hat{\sigma}_x} + \bar{R}_f = \widehat{SR} \times \hat{\sigma}_m + \bar{R}_f$$

$$= 0.35 \times 0.19 + 0.03 = 0.0965 = 9.65\%$$

Since the market return is 9%, M^2 alpha is 0.65% (9.65% – 9%).

$$\hat{\alpha}_X = R_X - \left[\bar{R}_f + \hat{\beta}_X\left(\bar{R}_m - \bar{R}_f\right)\right] = 0.10 - (0.03 + 1.1 \times 0.06)$$

$$= 0.004 = 0.40\%$$

Exhibit 8: Measures of Portfolio Performance Evaluation

Manager	$\bar{R}_i$	$\hat{\sigma}_i$	$\hat{\beta}_i$	$E(R_i)$	Sharpe Ratio	Treynor Ratio	M² alpha	$\hat{\alpha}_i$
X	10.0%	20.0%	1.10	9.6%	0.35	0.064	0.65%	0.40%
Y	11.0	10.0	0.70	7.2	0.80	0.114	9.20	3.80
Z	12.0	25.0	0.60	6.6	0.36	0.150	0.84	5.40
M	9.0	19.0	1.00	9.0	0.32	0.060	0.00	0.00
R_f	3.0	0.0	0.00	3.0	–	–	–	0.00

Let us begin with an analysis of the risk-free asset. Because the risk-free asset has zero risk and a beta of zero, calculating the Sharpe ratio, Treynor ratio, or M^2 is not possible because they all require the portfolio risk in the denominator. The risk-free asset's alpha, however, is zero. Turning to the market portfolio, we see that the absolute measures of performance, the Sharpe ratio and the Treynor ratio, are positive for the market portfolio. These ratios are positive as long as the portfolio earns a return that is in excess of that of the risk-free asset. $\widehat{M}^2$ alpha and $\hat{\alpha}_i$ are performance measures relative to the market, so they are both equal to zero for the market portfolio.

All three managers have Sharpe and Treynor ratios greater than those of the market, and all three managers' M^2 alpha and α_i are positive; therefore, the pension fund should be satisfied with their performance. Among the three managers, Manager X has the worst performance, irrespective of whether total risk or systematic risk is considered for measuring performance. The relative rankings are depicted in Exhibit 9.

Exhibit 9: Ranking of Portfolios by Performance Measure

Rank	Sharpe Ratio	Treynor Ratio	M² alpha	α_i
1	Y	Z	Y	Z
2	Z	Y	Z	Y
3	X	X	X	X
4	M	M	M	M
5	–	–	–	R_f

Comparing Y and Z, we can observe that Y performs much better than Z when total risk is considered. Y has a Sharpe ratio of 0.80, compared with a Sharpe ratio of 0.36 for Z. Similarly, M^2 alpha is higher for Y (9.20 percent) than for Z (0.84 percent). In contrast, when systematic risk is used, Z outperforms Y. The Treynor ratio is higher for Z (0.150) than for Y (0.114), and Jensen's alpha is also higher for Z (5.40 percent) than for Y (3.80 percent), which indicates that Z has done a better job of generating excess return relative to systematic risk than Y.

Exhibit 10 confirms these observations in that all three managers outperform the benchmark because all three points lie above the SML. Among the three portfolios, Z performs the best when we consider risk-adjusted returns because it is the point in Exhibit 10 that is located northwest relative to the portfolios X and Y.

Exhibit 10: Portfolios Along the SML

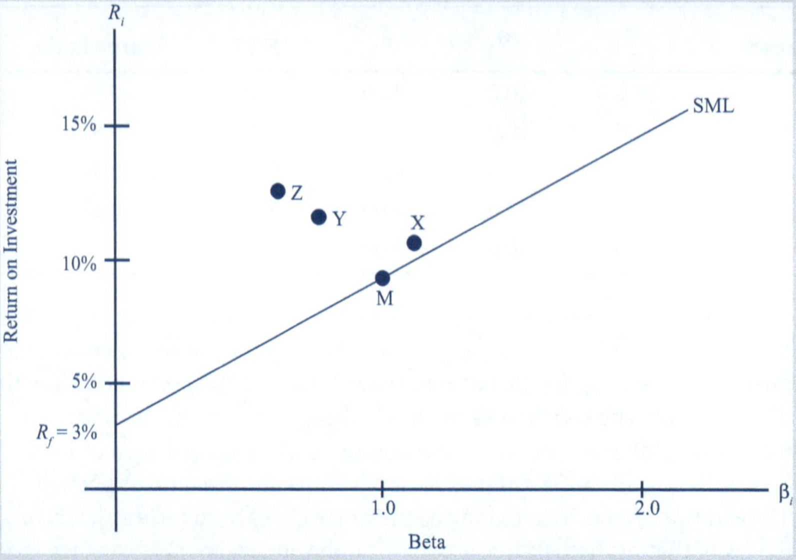

When do we use total risk performance measures like the Sharpe ratio and M^2, and when do we use beta risk performance measures like the Treynor ratio and Jensen's alpha? Total risk is relevant for an investor when he or she holds a portfolio that is not fully diversified, which is not a desirable portfolio. In such cases, the Sharpe ratio and M^2 are appropriate performance measures. Thus, if the pension fund were to choose only one fund manager to manage all its assets, it should choose Manager Y. Performance measures relative to beta risk—Treynor ratio and Jensen's alpha—are relevant when the investor holds a well-diversified portfolio with negligible diversifiable risk. In other words, if the pension fund is well diversified and only the systematic risk of the portfolio matters, the fund should choose Manager Z.

The measures of performance evaluation assume that the market portfolio is the correct benchmark. As a result, an error in the benchmark may cause the results to be misleading. For example, evaluating a real estate fund against the S&P 500 is incorrect because real estate has different characteristics than equity. In addition to errors in benchmarking, errors could occur in the measurement of risk and return of the market portfolio and the portfolios being evaluated. Finally, many estimates are based on historical data. Any projections based on such estimates assume that this level of performance will continue in the future.

12 APPLICATIONS OF THE CAPM IN PORTFOLIO CONSTRUCTION

- ☐ calculate and interpret the expected return of an asset using the CAPM
- ☐ describe and demonstrate applications of the CAPM and the SML

This section introduces applications of the CAPM in portfolio construction. First, the security characteristic line, which graphically indicates *ex post* Jensen's alpha, is described. If we relax the assumption that investors have the same expectations about risk and return, a positive Jensen's alpha can be interpreted as an indication of superior information or investment ability. The section on security selection covers that possibility. The last section summarizes how the CAPM and related concepts can be applied to portfolio construction.

Security Characteristic Line

Similar to the SML, we can draw a **security characteristic line** (SCL) for a security. The SCL is a plot of the excess return of the security on the excess return of the market. In Exhibit 8, Jensen's alpha is the intercept and the beta is the slope. The equation of the line can be obtained by rearranging the terms in the expression for Jensen's alpha and replacing the subscript p with i:

$$R_i - R_f = \alpha_i + \beta_i(R_m - R_f)$$

As an example, the SCL is drawn in Exhibit 11 using Manager X's portfolio from Exhibit 8. The security characteristic line can also be estimated by regressing the excess security return, $R_i - R_f$, on the excess market return, $R_m - R_f$.

Exhibit 11: The Security Characteristic Line

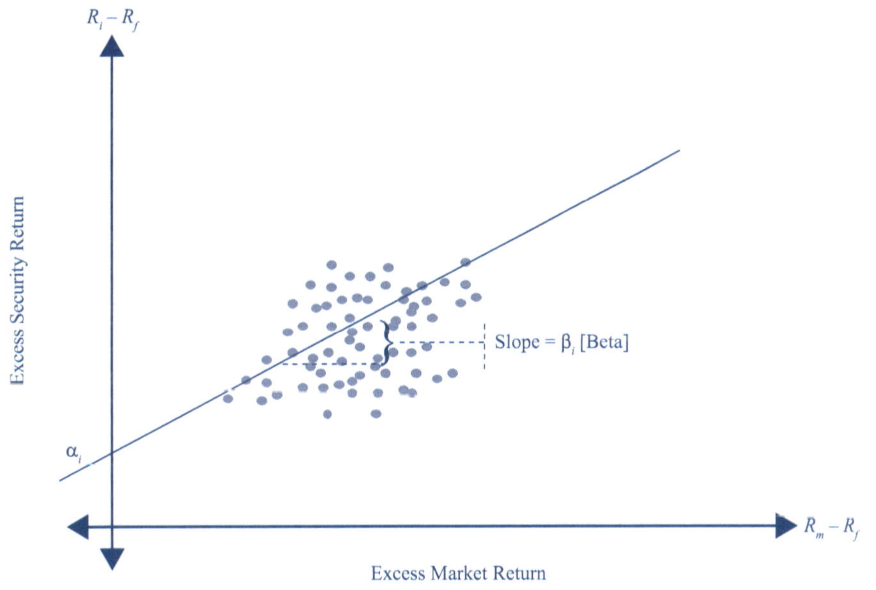

Security Selection

When discussing the CAPM, we assumed that investors have homogeneous expectations and are rational, risk-averse, utility-maximizing investors. With these assumptions, we were able to state that all investors assign the same value to all assets and, therefore, have the same optimal risky portfolio, which is the market portfolio. In other words, we assumed that there is commonality among beliefs about an asset's future cash flows and the required rate of return. Given the required rate of return, we can discount the future cash flows of the asset to arrive at its current value, or price, which is agreed upon by all or most investors.

In this section, we introduce heterogeneity in beliefs of investors. Because investors are price takers, it is assumed that such heterogeneity does not significantly affect the market price of an asset. The difference in beliefs can relate to future cash flows, the systematic risk of the asset, or both. Because the current price of an asset is the discounted value of the future cash flows, the difference in beliefs could result in an investor-estimated price that is different from the CAPM-calculated price. The CAPM-calculated price is the current market price because it reflects the beliefs of all other investors in the market. If the investor-estimated current price is higher (lower) than the market price, the asset is considered undervalued (overvalued). Therefore, the CAPM is an effective tool for determining whether an asset is undervalued or overvalued and whether an investor should buy or sell the asset.

Although portfolio performance evaluation is backward looking and security selection is forward looking, we can apply the concepts of portfolio evaluation to security selection. The best measure to apply is Jensen's alpha because it uses systematic risk and is meaningful even on an absolute basis. A positive Jensen's alpha indicates a superior security, whereas a negative Jensen's alpha indicates a security that is likely to underperform the market when adjusted for risk.

Another way of presenting the same information is with the security market line. Potential investors can plot a security's expected return and beta against the SML and use this relationship to decide whether the security is overvalued or undervalued in the market.[6] Exhibit 12 shows a number of securities along with the SML. All securities that reflect the consensus market view are points directly on the SML (i.e., properly valued). If a point representing the estimated return of an asset is above the SML (Points A and C), the asset has a low level of risk relative to the amount of expected return and would be a good choice for investment. In contrast, if the point representing a particular asset is below the SML (Point B), the stock is considered overvalued. Its return does not compensate for the level of risk and should not be considered for investment. Of course, a short position in Asset B can be taken if short selling is permitted.

6 In this reading, we do not consider transaction costs, which are important whenever deviations from a passive portfolio are considered. Thus, the magnitude of undervaluation or overvaluation should be considered in relation to transaction costs prior to making an investment decision.

Exhibit 12: Security Selection Using SML

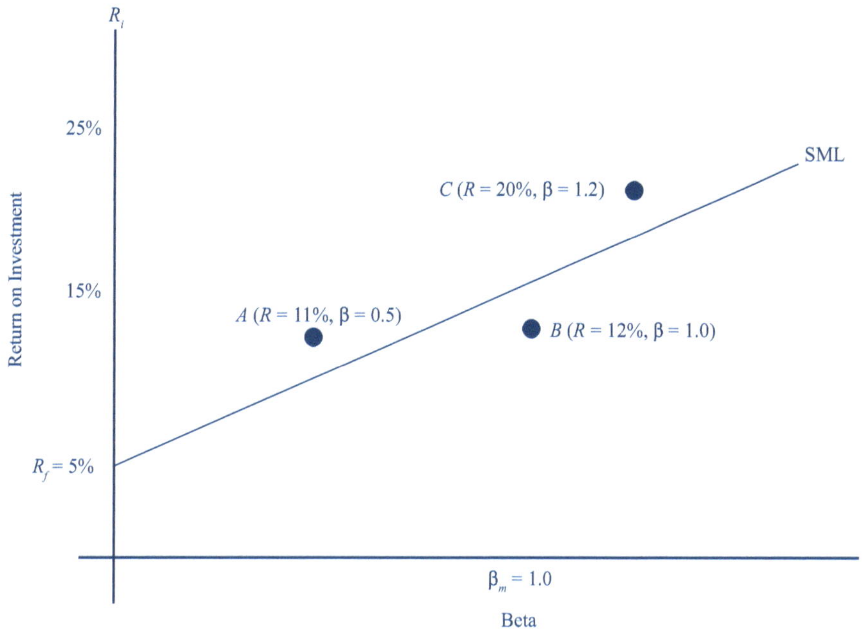

Implications of the CAPM for Portfolio Construction

Based on the CAPM, investors should hold a combination of the risk-free asset and the market portfolio. The true market portfolio consists of a large number of securities, and an investor would have to own all of them in order to be completely diversified. Because owning all existing securities is not practical, in this section, we will consider an alternate method of constructing a portfolio that may not require a large number of securities and will still be sufficiently diversified. Exhibit 13 shows the reduction in risk as we add more and more securities to a portfolio. As can be seen from the exhibit, much of the nonsystematic risk can be diversified away in as few as 30 securities. These securities, however, should be randomly selected and represent different asset classes for the portfolio to effectively diversify risk. Otherwise, one may be better off using an index (e.g., the S&P 500 for a diversified large-cap equity portfolio and other indexes for other asset classes).

Exhibit 13: Diversification with Number of Stocks

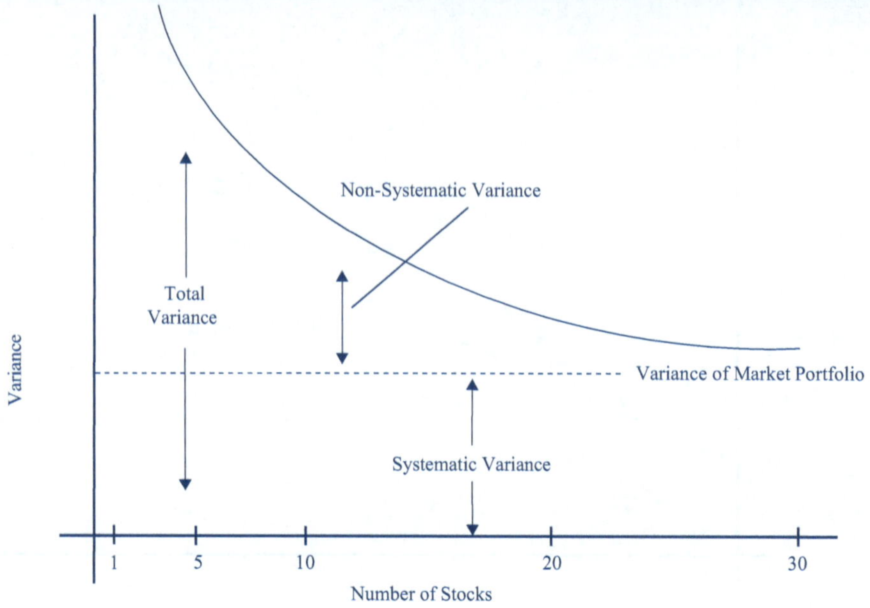

Let's begin constructing the optimal portfolio with a portfolio of securities like the S&P 500. Although the S&P 500 is a portfolio of 500 securities, it is a good starting point because it is readily available as a single security for trading. In contrast, it represents only the large corporations that are traded on the US stock markets and, therefore, does not encompass the global market entirely. Because the S&P 500 is the base portfolio, however, we treat it is as the market for the CAPM.

Any security not included in the S&P 500 can be evaluated to determine whether it should be integrated into the portfolio. That decision is based on the α_i of the security, which is calculated using the CAPM with the S&P 500 as the market portfolio. Note that security i may not necessarily be priced incorrectly for it to have a non-zero α_i; α_i can be positive merely because it is not well correlated with the S&P 500 and its return is sufficient for the amount of systematic risk it contains. For example, assume a new stock market, ABC, opens to foreign investors only and is being considered for inclusion in the portfolio. We estimate ABC's model parameters relative to the S&P 500 and find an α_i of approximately 3 percent, with a β_i of 0.60. Because α_i is positive, ABC should be added to the portfolio. Securities with a significantly negative α_i may be short sold to maximize risk-adjusted return. For convenience, however, we will assume that negative positions are not permitted in the portfolio.

In addition to the securities that are correctly priced but enter the portfolio because of their risk–return superiority, securities already in the portfolio (S&P 500) may be undervalued or overvalued based on investor expectations that are incongruent with the market. Securities in the S&P 500 that are overvalued (negative α_i) should be dropped from the S&P 500 portfolio, if it is possible to exclude individual securities, and positions in securities in the S&P 500 that are undervalued (positive α_i) should be increased.

This brings us to the next question: What should the relative weight of securities in the portfolio be? Because we are concerned with maximizing risk-adjusted return, securities with a higher α_i should have a higher weight, and securities with greater nonsystematic risk should be given less weight in the portfolio. A complete analysis of portfolio optimization is beyond the scope of this reading, but the following principles are helpful. The weight in each nonmarket security should be proportional to $\frac{\alpha_i}{\sigma_{ei}^2}$, where the denominator is the nonsystematic variance of security i. The total weight of nonmarket securities in the portfolio is proportional to

$$\frac{\sum_{i=1}^{N} w_i \alpha_i}{\sum_{i=1}^{N} w_i^2 \sigma_{ei}^2}.$$

The weight in the market portfolio is a function of

$$\frac{E(R_m)}{\sigma_m^2}.$$

The information ratio, $\frac{\alpha_i}{\sigma_{ei}}$ (i.e., alpha divided by nonsystematic risk), measures the abnormal return per unit of risk added by the security to a well-diversified portfolio. The larger the information ratio is, the more valuable the security.

EXAMPLE 11

Optimal Investor Portfolio with Heterogeneous Beliefs

A Japanese investor is holding the Nikkei 225 index, which is her version of the market. She thinks that three stocks, P, Q, and R, which are not in the Nikkei 225, are undervalued and should form a part of her portfolio. She has the following information about the stocks, the Nikkei 225, and the risk-free rate (the information is given as expected return, standard deviation, and beta):

P: 15%, 30%, 1.5

Q: 18%, 25%, 1.2

R: 16%, 23%, 1.1

Nikkei 225: 12%, 18%, 1.0

Risk-free rate: 2%, 0%, 0.0

1. Calculate Jensen's alpha for P, Q, and R.

Solution:

Stock P's α: $R_i - [R_f + \beta_i(R_m - R_f)] = 0.15 - (0.02 + 1.5 \times 0.10) = -0.02$

Stock Q's α: $R_i - [R_f + \beta_i(R_m - R_f)] = 0.18 - (0.02 + 1.2 \times 0.10) = 0.04$

Stock R's α: $R_i - [R_f + \beta_i(R_m - R_f)] = 0.16 - (0.02 + 1.1 \times 0.10) = 0.03$

2. Calculate nonsystematic variance for P, Q, and R.

Solution:

Total variance = Systematic variance + Nonsystematic variance. From Section 3.2.2, we write the equation as $\sigma_{ei}^2 = \sigma_i^2 - \beta_i^2 \sigma_m^2$.

Stock P's nonsystematic variance = (0.30 × 0.30) – (1.5 × 1.5 × 0.18 × 0.18) = 0.09 – 0.0729

= 0.0171

Stock Q's nonsystematic variance = (0.25 × 0.25) – (1.2 × 1.2 × 0.18 × 0.18) = 0.0625 – 0.0467

= 0.0158

Stock R's nonsystematic variance = (0.23 × 0.23) – (1.1 × 1.1 × 0.18 × 0.18) = 0.0529 – 0.0392

= 0.0137

3. Should any of the three stocks be included in the portfolio? If so, which stock should have the highest weight in the portfolio?

Solution:

Stock P has a negative α and should not be included in the portfolio, unless a negative position can be assumed through short selling. Stocks Q and R have a positive α; therefore, they should be included in the portfolio with positive weights.

The relative weight of Q is 0.04/0.0158 = 2.53.

The relative weight of R is 0.03/0.0137 = 2.19.

Stock Q will have the largest weight among the nonmarket securities to be added to the portfolio. In relative terms, the weight of Q will be 15.5 percent greater than the weight of R (2.53/2.19 = 1.155). As the number of securities increases, the analysis becomes more complex. However, the contribution of each additional security toward improvement in the risk–return trade-off will decrease and eventually disappear, resulting in a well-diversified portfolio.

SUMMARY

In this reading, we discussed the capital asset pricing model in detail and covered related topics such as the capital market line. The reading began with an interpretation of the CML, uses of the market portfolio as a passive management strategy, and leveraging of the market portfolio to obtain a higher expected return. Next, we discussed systematic and nonsystematic risk and why one should not expect to be compensated for taking on nonsystematic risk. The discussion of systematic and nonsystematic risk was followed by an introduction to beta and return-generating models. This broad topic was then broken down into a discussion of the CAPM and, more specifically, the relationship between beta and expected return. The final section included applications of the CAPM to capital budgeting, portfolio performance evaluation, and security selection. The highlights of the reading are as follows:

- The capital market line is a special case of the capital allocation line, where the efficient portfolio is the market portfolio.
- Obtaining a unique optimal risky portfolio is not possible if investors are permitted to have heterogeneous beliefs because such beliefs will result in heterogeneous asset prices.

- Investors can leverage their portfolios by borrowing money and investing in the market.
- Systematic risk is the risk that affects the entire market or economy and is not diversifiable.
- Nonsystematic risk is local and can be diversified away by combining assets with low correlations.
- Beta risk, or systematic risk, is priced and earns a return, whereas nonsystematic risk is not priced.
- The expected return of an asset depends on its beta risk and can be computed using the CAPM, which is given by $E(R_i) = R_f + \beta_i[E(R_m) - R_f]$.
- The security market line is an implementation of the CAPM and applies to all securities, whether they are efficient or not.
- Expected return from the CAPM can be used for making capital budgeting decisions.
- Portfolios can be evaluated by several CAPM-based measures, such as the Sharpe ratio, the Treynor ratio, M^2, and Jensen's alpha.
- The SML can assist in security selection and optimal portfolio construction.

By successfully understanding the content of this reading, you should feel comfortable decomposing total variance into systematic and nonsystematic variance, analyzing beta risk, using the CAPM, and evaluating portfolios and individual securities.

REFERENCES

Carhart, Mark. 1997. "On Persistence in Mutual Fund Performance." *Journal of Finance* 52, vol. , no. 1:57–82. 10.2307/2329556

Fama, Eugene and Kenneth French. 1992. "The Cross-Section of Expected Stock Returns." *Journal of Finance* 47, vol. , no. 2:427–466. 10.2307/2329112

PRACTICE PROBLEMS

1. The line depicting the total risk and expected return of portfolio combinations of a risk-free asset and any risky asset is the:

   A. security market line.

   B. capital allocation line.

   C. security characteristic line.

2. The portfolio of a risk-free asset and a risky asset has a better risk-return tradeoff than investing in only one asset type because the correlation between the risk-free asset and the risky asset is equal to:

   A. −1.0.

   B. 0.0.

   C. 1.0.

3. With respect to capital market theory, an investor's optimal portfolio is the combination of a risk-free asset and a risky asset with the highest:

   A. expected return.

   B. indifference curve.

   C. capital allocation line slope.

4. Highly risk-averse investors will *most likely* invest the majority of their wealth in:

   A. risky assets.

   B. risk-free assets.

   C. the optimal risky portfolio.

5. The capital market line (CML) is the graph of the risk and return of portfolio combinations consisting of the risk-free asset and:

   A. any risky portfolio.

   B. the market portfolio.

   C. the leveraged portfolio.

6. Which of the following statements *most accurately* defines the market portfolio in capital market theory? The market portfolio consists of all:

   A. risky assets.

   B. tradable assets.

   C. investable assets.

7. With respect to capital market theory, the optimal risky portfolio:

   A. is the market portfolio.

B. has the highest expected return.

C. has the lowest expected variance.

8. Relative to portfolios on the CML, any portfolio that plots above the CML is considered:

   A. inferior.

   B. inefficient.

   C. unachievable.

9. A portfolio on the capital market line with returns greater than the returns on the market portfolio represents a(n):

   A. lending portfolio.

   B. borrowing portfolio.

   C. unachievable portfolio.

10. With respect to the capital market line, a portfolio on the CML with returns less than the returns on the market portfolio represents a(n):

    A. lending portfolio.

    B. borrowing portfolio.

    C. unachievable portfolio.

11. Which of the following types of risk is *most likely* avoided by forming a diversified portfolio?

    A. Total risk.

    B. Systematic risk.

    C. Nonsystematic risk.

12. Which of the following events is *most likely* an example of nonsystematic risk?

    A. A decline in interest rates.

    B. The resignation of chief executive officer.

    C. An increase in the value of the US dollar.

13. With respect to the pricing of risk in capital market theory, which of the following statements is *most accurate*?

    A. All risk is priced.

    B. Systematic risk is priced.

    C. Nonsystematic risk is priced.

14. The sum of an asset's systematic variance and its nonsystematic variance of returns is equal to the asset's:

    A. beta.

B. total risk.

C. total variance.

The following information relates to questions 15-17

An analyst gathers the following information:

Security	Expected Annual Return (%)	Expected Standard Deviation (%)	Correlation between Security and the Market
Security 1	11	25	0.6
Security 2	11	20	0.7
Security 3	14	20	0.8
Market	10	15	1.0

15. Which security has the *highest* total risk?

A. Security 1.

B. Security 2.

C. Security 3.

16. Which security has the *highest* beta measure?

A. Security 1.

B. Security 2.

C. Security 3.

17. Which security has the *least* amount of market risk?

A. Security 1.

B. Security 2.

C. Security 3.

---

18. With respect to return-generating models, the intercept term of the market model is the asset's estimated:

A. beta.

B. alpha.

C. variance.

19. With respect to return-generating models, the slope term of the market model is an estimate of the asset's:

A. total risk.

B. systematic risk.

C. nonsystematic risk.

20. With respect to return-generating models, which of the following statements is *most accurate*? Return-generating models are used to directly estimate the:

A. expected return of a security.

B. weights of securities in a portfolio.

C. parameters of the capital market line.

21. With respect to capital market theory, the average beta of all assets in the market is:

A. less than 1.0.

B. equal to 1.0.

C. greater than 1.0.

22. With respect to the capital asset pricing model, the primary determinant of expected return of an individual asset is the:

A. asset's beta.

B. market risk premium.

C. asset's standard deviation.

23. With respect to the capital asset pricing model, which of the following values of beta for an asset is *most likely* to have an expected return for the asset that is less than the risk-free rate?

A. −0.5

B. 0.0

C. 0.5

24. With respect to the capital asset pricing model, the market risk premium is:

A. less than the excess market return.

B. equal to the excess market return.

C. greater than the excess market return.

25. The graph of the capital asset pricing model is the:

A. capital market line.

B. security market line.

C. security characteristic line.

26. With respect to capital market theory, correctly priced individual assets can be plotted on the:

A. capital market line.

B. security market line.

C. capital allocation line.

The following information relates to questions 27-30

An analyst gathers the following information:

Security	Expected Standard Deviation (%)	Beta
Security 1	25	1.50
Security 2	15	1.40
Security 3	20	1.60

27. With respect to the capital asset pricing model, if the expected market risk premium is 6% and the risk-free rate is 3%, the expected return for Security 1 is *closest* to:

    A. 9.0%.

    B. 12.0%.

    C. 13.5%.

28. With respect to the capital asset pricing model, if expected return for Security 2 is equal to 11.4% and the risk-free rate is 3%, the expected return for the market is *closest* to:

    A. 8.4%.

    B. 9.0%.

    C. 10.3%.

29. With respect to the capital asset pricing model, if the expected market risk premium is 6% the security with the *highest* expected return is:

    A. Security 1.

    B. Security 2.

    C. Security 3.

30. With respect to the capital asset pricing model, a decline in the expected market return will have the *greatest* impact on the expected return of:

    A. Security 1.

    B. Security 2.

    C. Security 3.

31. With respect to capital market theory, which of the following statements *best* describes the effect of the homogeneity assumption? Because all investors have the same economic expectations of future cash flows for all assets, investors will invest in:

A. the same optimal risky portfolio.

B. the Standard and Poor's 500 Index.

C. assets with the same amount of risk.

32. With respect to capital market theory, which of the following assumptions allows for the existence of the market portfolio? All investors:

A. are price takers.

B. have homogeneous expectations.

C. plan for the same, single holding period.

33. Three equity fund managers have performance records summarized in the following table:

	Mean Annual Return (%)	Standard Deviation of Return (%)
Manager 1	14.38	10.53
Manager 2	9.25	6.35
Manager 3	13.10	8.23

Given a risk-free rate of return of 2.60%, which manager performed best based on the Sharpe ratio?

A. Manager 1

B. Manager 2

C. Manager 3

34. Which of the following performance measures is consistent with the CAPM?

A. M^2.

B. Sharpe ratio.

C. Jensen's alpha.

35. Which of the following performance measures does *not* require the measure to be compared to another value?

A. Sharpe ratio.

B. Treynor ratio.

C. Jensen's alpha.

36. Which of the following performance measures is *most* appropriate for an investor who is *not* fully diversified?

A. M^2.

B. Treynor ratio.

C. Jensen's alpha.

37. The slope of the security characteristic line is an asset's:

A. beta.

B. excess return.

C. risk premium.

38. Analysts who have estimated returns of an asset to be greater than the expected returns generated by the capital asset pricing model should consider the asset to be:

A. overvalued.

B. undervalued.

C. properly valued.

39. The intercept of the best fit line formed by plotting the excess returns of a manager's portfolio on the excess returns of the market is *best* described as Jensen's:

A. beta.

B. ratio.

C. alpha.

40. Portfolio managers who are maximizing risk-adjusted returns will seek to invest *more* in securities with:

A. lower values of Jensen's alpha.

B. values of Jensen's alpha equal to 0.

C. higher values of Jensen's alpha.

41. Portfolio managers, who are maximizing risk-adjusted returns, will seek to invest *less* in securities with:

A. lower values for nonsystematic variance.

B. values of nonsystematic variance equal to 0.

C. higher values for nonsystematic variance.

SOLUTIONS

1. B is correct. A capital allocation line (CAL) plots the expected return and total risk of combinations of the risk-free asset and a risky asset (or a portfolio of risky assets).

2. B is correct. A portfolio of the risk-free asset and a risky asset or a portfolio of risky assets can result in a better risk-return tradeoff than an investment in only one type of an asset, because the risk-free asset has zero correlation with the risky asset.

3. B is correct. Investors will have different optimal portfolios depending on their indifference curves. The optimal portfolio for each investor is the one with highest utility; that is, where the CAL is tangent to the individual investor's highest possible indifference curve.

4. B is correct. Although the optimal risky portfolio is the market portfolio, highly risk-averse investors choose to invest most of their wealth in the risk-free asset.

5. B is correct. Although the capital allocation line includes all possible combinations of the risk-free asset and any risky portfolio, the capital market line is a special case of the capital allocation line, which uses the market portfolio as the optimal risky portfolio.

6. A is correct. The market includes all risky assets, or anything that has value; however, not all assets are tradable, and not all tradable assets are investable.

7. A is correct. The optimal risky portfolio is the market portfolio. Capital market theory assumes that investors have homogeneous expectations, which means that all investors analyze securities in the same way and are rational. That is, investors use the same probability distributions, use the same inputs for future cash flows, and arrive at the same valuations. Because their valuations of all assets are identical, all investors will invest in the same optimal risky portfolio (i.e., the market portfolio).

8. C is correct. Theoretically, any point above the CML is not achievable and any point below the CML is dominated by and inferior to any point on the CML.

9. B is correct. As one moves further to the right of point M on the capital market line, an increasing amount of borrowed money is being invested in the market portfolio. This means that there is negative investment in the risk-free asset, which is referred to as a leveraged position in the risky portfolio.

10. A is correct. The combinations of the risk-free asset and the market portfolio on the CML where returns are less than the returns on the market portfolio are termed 'lending' portfolios.

11. C is correct. Investors are capable of avoiding nonsystematic risk by forming a portfolio of assets that are not highly correlated with one another, thereby reducing total risk and being exposed only to systematic risk.

12. B is correct. Nonsystematic risk is specific to a firm, whereas systematic risk affects the entire economy.

13. B is correct. Only systematic risk is priced. Investors do not receive any return for accepting nonsystematic or diversifiable risk.

14. C is correct. The sum of systematic variance and nonsystematic variance equals the total variance of the asset. References to total risk as the sum of systematic risk and nonsystematic risk refer to variance, not to risk.

15. A is correct. Security 1 has the highest total risk = 0.25 compared to Security 2 and Security 3 with a total risk of 0.20.

16. C is correct. Security 3 has the highest beta value;

$$1.07 = \frac{\rho_{3,m}\sigma_3}{\sigma_m} = \frac{(0.80)\ (20\%)}{15\%}$$

compared to Security 1 and Security 2 with beta values of 1.00 and 0.93, respectively.

17. B is correct. Security 2 has the lowest beta value;

$$0.93 = \frac{\rho_{2,m}\sigma_2}{\sigma_m} = \frac{(0.70)\ (20\%)}{15\%}$$

compared to Security 1 and 3 with beta values of 1.00 and 1.07, respectively.

18. B is correct. In the market model, $R_i = \alpha_i + \beta_i R_m + e_i$, the intercept, α_i, and slope coefficient, β_i, are estimated using historical security and market returns.

19. B is correct. In the market model, $R_i = \alpha_i + \beta_i R_m + e_i$, the slope coefficient, β_i, is an estimate of the asset's systematic or market risk.

20. A is correct. In the market model, $R_i = \alpha_i + \beta_i R_m + e_i$, the intercept, α_i, and slope coefficient, β_i, are estimated using historical security and market returns. These parameter estimates then are used to predict firm-specific returns that a security may earn in a future period.

21. B is correct. The average beta of all assets in the market, by definition, is equal to 1.0.

22. A is correct. The CAPM shows that the primary determinant of expected return for an individual asset is its beta, or how well the asset correlates with the market.

23. A is correct. If an asset's beta is negative, the required return will be less than the risk-free rate in the CAPM. When combined with a positive market return, the asset reduces the risk of the overall portfolio, which makes the asset very valuable. Insurance is an example of a negative beta asset.

24. B is correct. In the CAPM, the market risk premium is the difference between the return on the market and the risk-free rate, which is the same as the return in excess of the market return.

25. B is correct. The security market line (SML) is a graphical representation of the capital asset pricing model, with beta risk on the x-axis and expected return on the y-axis.

26. B is correct. The security market line applies to any security, efficient or not. The CAL and the CML use the total risk of the asset (or portfolio of assets) rather than its systematic risk, which is the only risk that is priced.

27. B is correct. The expected return of Security 1, using the CAPM, is 12.0% = 3% + 1.5(6%); $E(R_i) = R_f + \beta_i[E(R_m) - R_f]$.

28. B is correct. The expected risk premium for Security 2 is 8.4%, (11.4% – 3%), indicates that the expected market risk premium is 6%; therefore, since the risk-free

rate is 3% the expected rate of return for the market is 9%. That is, using the CAPM, $E(R_i) = R_f + \beta_i[E(R_m) - R_f]$, 11.4% = 3% + 1.4(X%), where X% = (11.4% – 3%)/1.4 = 6.0% = market risk premium.

29. C is correct. Security 3 has the highest beta; thus, regardless of the value for the risk-free rate, Security 3 will have the highest expected return:

$$E(R_i) = R_f + \beta_i[E(R_m) - R_f]$$

30. C is correct. Security 3 has the highest beta; thus, regardless of the risk-free rate the expected return of Security 3 will be most sensitive to a change in the expected market return.

31. A is correct. The homogeneity assumption refers to all investors having the same economic expectation of future cash flows. If all investors have the same expectations, then all investors should invest in the same optimal risky portfolio, therefore implying the existence of only one optimal portfolio (i.e., the market portfolio).

32. B is correct. The homogeneous expectations assumption means that all investors analyze securities in the same way and are rational. That is, they use the same probability distributions, use the same inputs for future cash flows, and arrive at the same valuations. Because their valuation of all assets is identical, they will generate the same optimal risky portfolio, which is the market portfolio.

33. C is correct. The Sharpe ratio $\left(\widehat{\text{SR}}\right)$ is the mean excess portfolio return per unit of risk, where a higher Sharpe ratio indicates better performance:

$$\widehat{SR}_1 = \frac{\bar{R}_p - \bar{R}_f}{\hat{\sigma}_p} = \frac{14.38 - 2.60}{10.53} = 1.12$$

$$\widehat{SR}_2 = \frac{\bar{R}_p - \bar{R}_f}{\hat{\sigma}_p} = \frac{9.25 - 2.60}{6.35} = 1.05$$

$$\widehat{SR}_3 = \frac{\bar{R}_p - \bar{R}_f}{\hat{\sigma}_p} = \frac{13.10 - 2.60}{8.23} = 1.28$$

34. C is correct. Jensen's alpha adjusts for systematic risk, and M^2 and the Sharpe Ratio adjust for total risk.

35. C is correct. The sign of Jensen's alpha indicates whether or not the portfolio has outperformed the market. If alpha is positive, the portfolio has outperformed the market; if alpha is negative, the portfolio has underperformed the market.

36. A is the correct. M^2 adjusts for risk using standard deviation (i.e., total risk).

37. A is correct. The security characteristic line is a plot of the excess return of the security on the excess return of the market. In such a graph, Jensen's alpha is the intercept and the beta is the slope.

38. B is correct. If the estimated return of an asset is above the SML (the expected return), the asset has a lower level of risk relative to the amount of expected return and would be a good choice for investment (i.e., undervalued).

39. C is correct. This is because of the plot of the excess return of the security on the excess return of the market. In such a graph, Jensen's alpha is the intercept and the beta is the slope.

40. C is correct. Since managers are concerned with maximizing risk-adjusted returns, securities with a higher value of Jensen's alpha, α_i, should have a higher weight.

41. C is correct. Since managers are concerned with maximizing risk-adjusted returns, securities with greater nonsystematic risk should be given less weight in the portfolio.

LEARNING MODULE

3

Portfolio Management: An Overview

by Owen M. Concannon, CFA, Robert M. Conroy, DBA, CFA, Alistair Byrne, PhD, CFA, and Vahan Janjigian, PhD, CFA.

Owen M. Concannon, CFA, is at Neuberger Berman (USA). Robert M. Conroy, DBA, CFA, is at the Darden School of Business, University of Virginia (USA). Alistair Byrne, PhD, CFA, is at State Street Global Advisors (United Kingdom). Vahan Janjigian, PhD, CFA, is at Greenwich Wealth Management, LLC (USA).

LEARNING OUTCOMES

Mastery	*The candidate should be able to:*
☐	describe the portfolio approach to investing
☐	describe the steps in the portfolio management process
☐	describe types of investors and distinctive characteristics and needs of each
☐	describe defined contribution and defined benefit pension plans
☐	describe aspects of the asset management industry
☐	describe mutual funds and compare them with other pooled investment products

INTRODUCTION

1

This reading provides an overview of portfolio management and the asset management industry, including types of investors and investment plans and products. A portfolio approach is important to investors in achieving their financial objectives. We outline the steps in the portfolio management process in managing a client's investment portfolio. We next compare the financial needs of different types of investors: individual and institutional investors. We then describe both defined contribution and defined benefit pension plans. The asset management[1] industry, which serves as a critical

1 Note that both "investment management" and "asset management" are commonly used throughout the CFA Program curriculum. The terms are often used interchangeably in practice.

link between providers and seekers of investment capital around the world, is broadly discussed. Finally, we describe mutual funds and other types of pooled investment products offered by asset managers.

2 PORTFOLIO PERSPECTIVE: DIVERSIFICATION AND RISK REDUCTION

- [ ] describe the portfolio approach to investing

One of the biggest challenges faced by individuals and institutions is to decide how to invest for future needs. For individuals, the goal might be to fund retirement needs. For such institutions as insurance companies, the goal is to fund future liabilities in the form of insurance claims, whereas endowments seek to provide income to meet the ongoing needs of such institutions as universities. Regardless of the ultimate goal, all face the same set of challenges that extend beyond just the choice of what asset classes to invest in. They ultimately center on formulating basic principles that determine how to think about investing. One important question is: Should we invest in individual securities, evaluating each in isolation, or should we take a portfolio approach? By "portfolio approach," we mean evaluating individual securities in relation to their contribution to the investment characteristics of the whole portfolio. In the following section, we illustrate a number of reasons why a diversified portfolio perspective is important.

Historical Example of Portfolio Diversification: Avoiding Disaster

Portfolio diversification helps investors avoid disastrous investment outcomes. This benefit is most convincingly illustrated by examining what may happen when individuals have *not* diversified.

We are usually not able to observe how individuals manage their personal investments. However, in the case of US 401(k) individual retirement portfolios,[2] it is possible to see the results of individuals' investment decisions. When we examine their retirement portfolios, we find that some individual participants make sub-optimal investment decisions.

During the 1990s, Enron Corporation was one of the most admired corporations in the United States. A position in Enron shares returned over 27 percent per year from 1990 to September 2000, compared to 13 percent for the S&P 500 Index for the same time period.

2 In the United States, 401(k) plans are employer-sponsored individual retirement savings plans. They allow individuals to save a portion of their current income and defer taxation until the time when the savings and earnings are withdrawn. In some cases, the sponsoring firm will also make matching contributions in the form of cash or shares. Individuals within certain limits have control of the invested funds and consequently can express their preferences as to which assets to invest in.

Exhibit 1: Value of US$1 Invested from January 1990 to September 2000 Enron vs. S&P 500 Composite Index (01/01/1990 = US$1.00)

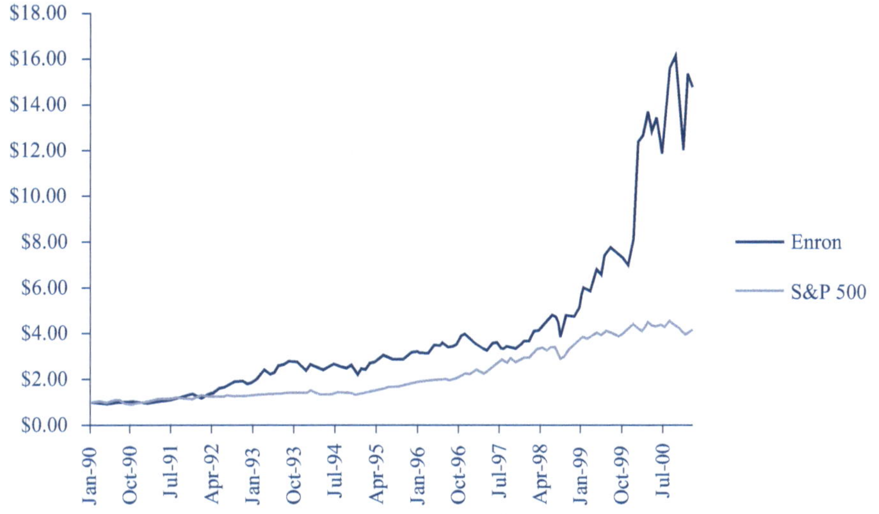

Source: Thomson Reuters Datastream.

During this time period, thousands of Enron employees participated in the company's 401(k) retirement plan. The plan allowed employees to set aside some of their earnings in a tax-deferred account. Enron participated by matching the employees' contributions. Enron made the match by depositing required amounts in the form of Enron shares. Enron restricted the sale of its contributed shares until an employee turned 50 years old. In January 2001, the employees' 401(k) retirement accounts were valued at over US$2 billion, of which US$1.3 billion (or 62 percent) was in Enron shares. Although Enron restricted the sale of shares it contributed, less than US$150 million of the total of US$1.3 billion in shares had this restriction. The implication was that Enron employees continued to hold large amounts of Enron shares even though they were free to sell them and invest the proceeds in other assets.

A typical individual was Roger Bruce,[3] a 67-year-old Enron retiree who held all of his US$2 million in retirement funds in Enron shares. Between January 2001 and January 2002, Enron's share price fell from about US$90 per share to zero.

3 Singletary (2001).

Exhibit 2: Value of US$1 Invested from January 1990 to January 2002 Enron vs. S&P 500 Composite Index (1/1/1990 = US$1.00)

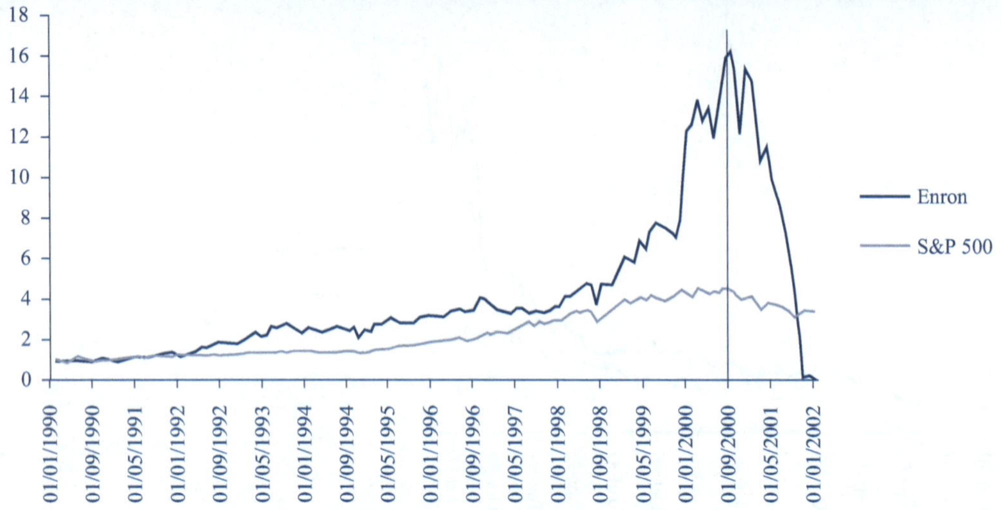

Source: Thomson Reuters Datastream.

Employees and retirees who had invested all or most of their retirement savings in Enron shares, just like Mr. Bruce, experienced financial ruin. The hard lesson that the Enron employees learned from this experience was to "not put all your eggs in one basket."[4] Unfortunately, the typical Enron employee did have most of his or her eggs in one basket. Most employees' wages and financial assets were dependent on Enron's continued viability; hence, any financial distress on Enron would have a material impact on an employee's financial health. The bankruptcy of Enron resulted in the closing of its operations, the dismissal of thousands of employees, and its shares becoming worthless. Hence, the failure of Enron was disastrous to the typical Enron employee.

Enron employees were not the only ones to be victims of over-investment in a single company's shares. In the defined contribution retirement plans at Owens Corning, Northern Telecom, Corning, and ADC Telecommunications, employees all held more than 25 percent of their assets in the company's shares during a time (March 2000 to December 2001) in which the share prices in these companies fell by almost 90 percent. The good news in this story is that the employees participating in employer-matched 401(k) plans since 2001 have significantly reduced their holdings of their employers' shares.

Thus, by taking a diversified portfolio approach, investors can spread away some of the risk. Rational investors are concerned about the risk–return trade-off of their investments. The portfolio approach provides investors with a way to reduce the risk associated with their wealth without necessarily decreasing their expected rate of return.

Portfolios: Reduce Risk

In addition to avoiding a potential disaster associated with over investing in a single security, portfolios also generally offer equivalent expected returns with lower overall **volatility** of returns—as represented by a measure such as standard deviation. Consider

4 This expression, which most likely originated in England in the 1700s, has a timeless sense of wisdom.

this simple example: Suppose you wish to make an investment in companies listed on the Hong Kong Stock Exchange (HKSE) and you start with a sample of five companies.[5] The cumulative returns for 16 fiscal quarters are shown in Exhibit 3.

Exhibit 3: Cumulative Wealth Index of Sample of Shares Listed on HKSE (initial amount= US$1.00)

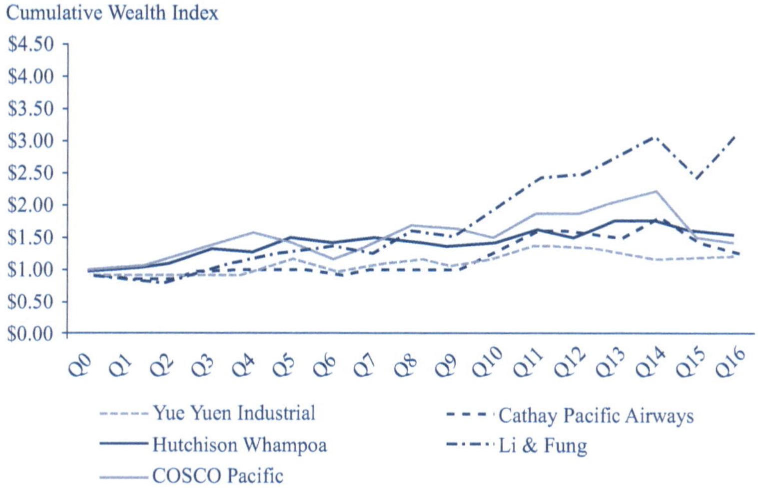

Source: Thomson Reuters Datastream.

The individual quarterly returns for each of the five shares are shown in Exhibit 4. The annualized means and annualized standard deviations for each are also shown.[6]

Exhibit 4: Quarterly Returns (in Percent) for Sample of HKSE Listed Shares over 16 Fiscal Quarters

	Yue Yuen Industrial	Cathay Pacific Airways	Hutchison Whampoa	Li & Fung	COSCO Pacific	Equally Weighted Portfolio
Q1	−11.1%	−2.3%	0.6%	−13.2%	−1.1%	−5.4%
Q2	−0.5	−5.4	10.8	1.7	21.0	5.5
Q3	5.7	6.8	19.1	13.8	15.5	12.2
Q4	5.3	4.6	−2.1	16.9	12.4	7.4
Q5	17.2	2.4	12.6	14.5	−7.9	7.8
Q6	−17.6	−10.4	−0.9	4.4	−16.7	−8.2
Q7	12.6	7.4	4.2	−10.9	15.4	5.7
Q8	7.5	−0.4	−3.6	29.2	21.9	10.9
Q9	−7.9	1.3	−5.1	−2.0	−1.6	−3.1
Q10	8.2	27.5	0.1	26.0	−10.1	10.3
Q11	18.3	24.3	16.5	22.8	25.7	21.5
Q12	0.1	−2.6	−6.7	−0.4	0.3	−1.8

5 A sample of five companies from a similar industry group was arbitrarily selected for illustration purposes.
6 Mean quarterly returns are annualized by multiplying the quarterly mean by 4. Quarterly standard deviations are annualized by taking the quarterly standard deviation and multiplying it by 2.

	Yue Yuen Industrial	Cathay Pacific Airways	Hutchison Whampoa	Li & Fung	COSCO Pacific	Equally Weighted Portfolio
Q13	−6.2	−4.2	16.7	11.9	11.1	5.8
Q14	−8.0	17.9	−1.8	12.4	8.4	5.8
Q15	3.5	−20.1	−8.5	−20.3	−31.5	−15.4
Q16	2.1	−11.8	−2.6	24.2	−6.1	1.2
Mean annual return	7.3%	8.7%	12.3%	32.8%	14.2%	15.1%
Annual standard deviation	20.2%	25.4%	18.1%	29.5%	31.3%	17.9%
Diversification ratio						71.9%

Source: Thomson Reuters Datastream.

Suppose you want to invest in one of these five securities next year. There is a wide variety of risk–return trade-offs for the five shares selected. If you believe that the future will replicate the past, then choosing Li & Fung would be a good choice. For the prior four years, Li & Fung provided the best trade-off between return and risk. In other words, it provided the most return per unit of risk. However, if there is no reason to believe that the future will replicate the past, it is more likely that the risk and return on the one security selected will be more like selecting one randomly. When we randomly selected one security each quarter, we found an average annualized return of 15.1 percent and an average annualized standard deviation of 24.9 percent, which would now become your expected return and standard deviation, respectively.

Alternatively, you could invest in an equally weighted portfolio of the five shares, which means that you would invest the same dollar amount in each security for each quarter. The quarterly returns on the equally weighted portfolio are just the average of the returns of the individual shares. As reported in Exhibit 4, the equally weighted portfolio has an average return of 15.1 percent and a standard deviation of 17.9 percent. As expected, the equally weighted portfolio's return is the same as the return on the randomly selected security. However, the same does not hold true for the portfolio standard deviation. That is, the standard deviation of an equally weighted portfolio is not simply the average of the standard deviations of the individual shares. In a more advanced reading we will demonstrate in greater mathematical detail how such a portfolio offers a lower standard deviation of return than the average of its individual components due to the correlations or interactions between the individual securities.

Because the mean return is the same, a simple measure of the value of diversification is calculated as the ratio of the standard deviation of the equally weighted portfolio to the standard deviation of the randomly selected security. This ratio may be referred to as the **diversification ratio**. In this case, the equally weighted portfolio's standard deviation is approximately 72 percent of the average standard deviation of the 5 stocks (24.9%). The diversification ratio of the portfolio's standard deviation to the individual asset's standard deviation measures the risk reduction benefits of a simple portfolio construction method, equal weighting. Even though the companies were chosen from a similar industry grouping, we see significant risk reduction. An even greater portfolio effect (i.e., lower diversification ratio) could have been realized if we had chosen companies from completely different industries.

This example illustrates one of the critical ideas about portfolios: Portfolios affect risk more than returns. In the prior section portfolios helped avoid the effects of downside risk associated with investing in a single company's shares. In this section we extended the notion of risk reduction through portfolios to illustrate why individuals and institutions should hold portfolios.

PORTFOLIO PERSPECTIVE: RISK-RETURN TRADE-OFF, DOWNSIDE PROTECTION, MODERN PORTFOLIO THEORY

3

☐ describe the portfolio approach to investing

In the previous section we compared an equally weighted portfolio to the selection of a single security. In this section we examine additional combinations of the same set of shares and observe the trade-offs between portfolio volatility of returns and expected return (for short, their risk–return trade-offs). If we select the portfolios with the best combination of risk and return (taking historical statistics as our expectations for the future), we produce the set of portfolios shown in Exhibit 5.

Exhibit 5: Optimal Portfolios for Sample of HKSE Listed Shares

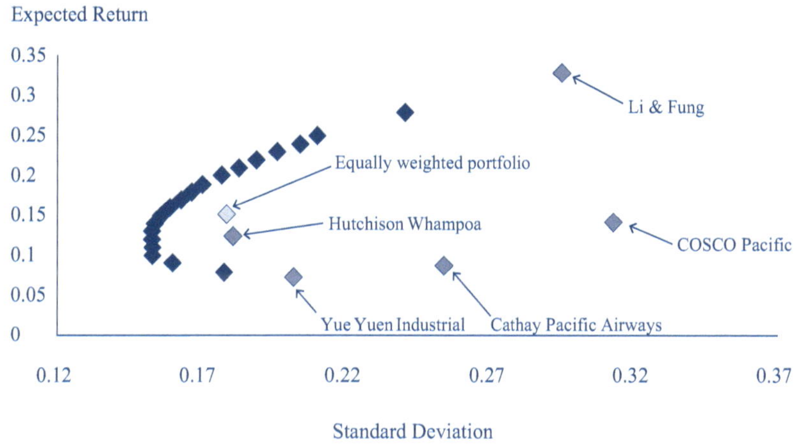

Source: Thomson Reuters Datastream.

In addition to illustrating that the diversified portfolio approach reduces risk, Exhibit 5 also shows that the composition of the portfolio matters. For example, an equally weighted portfolio (20 percent of the portfolio in each security) of the five shares has an expected return of 15.1 percent and a standard deviation of 17.9 percent. Alternatively, a portfolio with 25 percent in Yue Yuen Industrial (Holdings), 3 percent in Cathay Pacific, 52 percent in Hutchison Whampoa, 20 percent in Li & Fung, and 0 percent in COSCO Pacific produces a portfolio with an expected return of 15.1 percent and a standard deviation of 15.6 percent. Compared to a simple equally weighted portfolio, this provides an improved trade-off between risk and return because a lower level of risk was achieved for the same level of return.

Historical Portfolio Example: Not Necessarily Downside Protection

A major reason that portfolios can effectively reduce risk is that combining securities whose returns do not move together provides diversification. Sometimes a subset of assets will go up in value at the same time that another will go down in value. The fact that these may offset each other creates the potential diversification benefit we attribute to portfolios. However, an important issue is that the co-movement or correlation pattern of the securities' returns in the portfolio can change in a manner unfavorable to the investor. We use historical return data from a set of global indexes to show the impact of changing co-movement patterns.

When we examine the returns of a set of global equity indexes over the last 15 years, we observe a reduction in the diversification benefit due to a change in the pattern of co-movements of returns. Exhibit 6 and Exhibit 7 show the cumulative returns for a set of five global indexes[7] for two different time periods. Comparing the first time period, from Q4 1993 through Q3 2000 (as shown in Exhibit 6), with the last time period, from Q1 2006 through Q1 2009 (as shown in Exhibit 7), we show that the degree to which these global equity indexes moved together increased over time.

Exhibit 6: Returns to Global Equity Indexes Q4 1993–Q3 2000

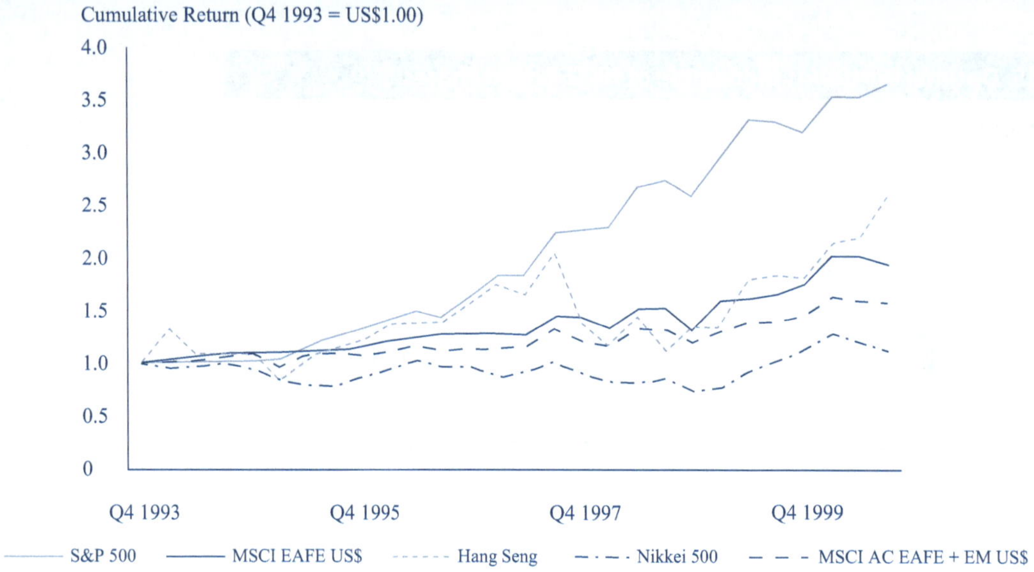

Source: Thomson Reuters Datastream.

7 The S&P 500, Hang Seng, and Nikkei 500 are broad-based composite equity indexes designed to measure the performance of equities in the United States, Hong Kong SAR, and Japan. MSCI stands for Morgan Stanley Capital International. EAFE refers to developed markets in Europe, Australasia, and the Far East. AC indicates all countries, and EM is emerging markets. All index returns are in US dollars.

Exhibit 7: Returns to Global Equity Indexes Q1 2006–Q1 2009

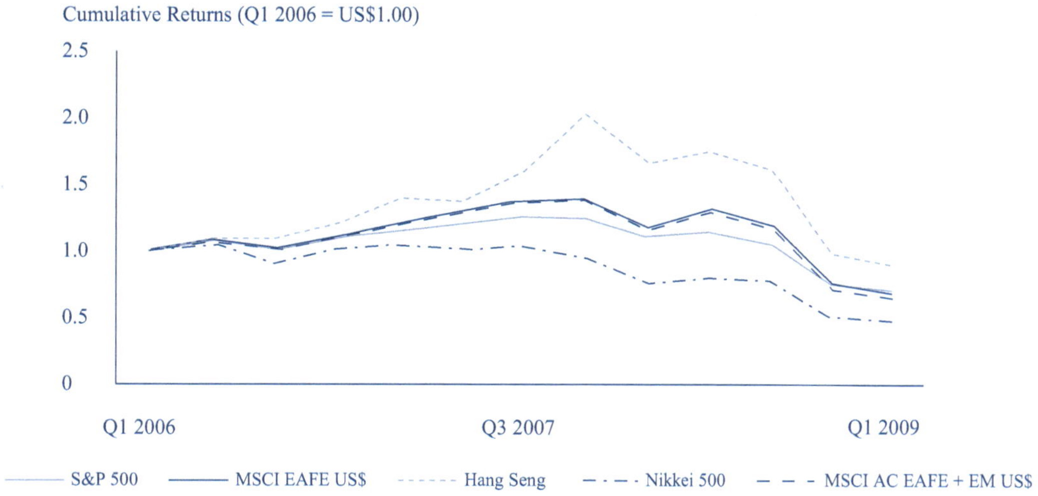

Source: Thomson Reuters Datastream.

The latter part of the second time period, from Q4 2007 to Q1 2009, was a period of dramatic declines in global share prices. Exhibit 8 shows the mean annual returns and standard deviation of returns for this time period.

Exhibit 8: Returns to Global Equity Indexes

	Q4 1993–Q3 2000		Q1 2006–Q1 2009		Q4 2007–Q1 2009	
Global Index	**Mean**	**Stand. Dev.**	**Mean**	**Stand. Dev.**	**Mean**	**Stand. Dev.**
S&P 500	20.5%	13.9%	–6.3%	21.1%	–40.6%	23.6%
MSCI EAFE US$	10.9	14.2	–3.5	29.4	–48.0	35.9
Hang Seng	20.4	35.0	5.1	34.2	–53.8	34.0
Nikkei 500	3.3	18.0	–13.8	27.6	–48.0	30.0
MSCI AC EAFE + EM US$	7.6	13.2	–4.9	30.9	–52.0	37.5
Randomly selected index	12.6%	18.9%	–4.7%	28.6%	–48.5%	32.2%
Equally weighted portfolio	12.6%	14.2%	–4.7%	27.4%	–48.5%	32.0%
Diversification ratio		75.1%		95.8%		99.4%

Source: Thomson Reuters Datastream.

During the period Q4 2007 through Q1 2009, the average return for the equally weighted portfolio, including dividends, was –48.5 percent. Other than reducing the risk of earning the return of the worst performing market, the diversification benefits were small. Exhibit 9 shows the cumulative quarterly returns of each of the five indexes over this time period. All of the indexes declined in unison. The lesson is that although portfolio diversification generally does reduce risk, it does not necessarily provide the same level of risk reduction during times of severe market turmoil as it does when the economy and markets are operating 'normally'. In fact, if the economy or markets fail totally (which has happened numerous times around the world), then diversification is a false promise. In the face of a worldwide contagion, diversification was ineffective, as illustrated at the end of 2008.

Exhibit 9: Return to Global Equity Indexes Q4 2007–Q1 2009

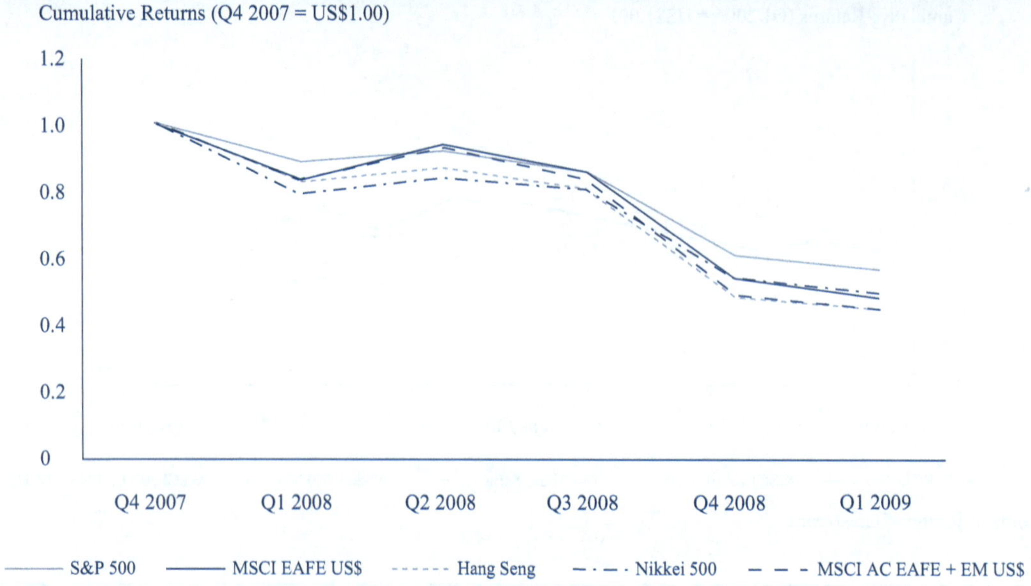

Source: Thomson Reuters Datastream.

KNOWLEDGE CHECK

Portfolios are *most likely* to provide:

A. risk reduction.

B. risk elimination.

C. downside protection.

Solution:

A is correct. Combining assets into a portfolio should reduce the portfolio's volatility. However, the portfolio approach does not necessarily provide downside protection or eliminate all risk.

Portfolios: Modern Portfolio Theory

The concept of diversification has been around for a long time and has a great deal of intuitive appeal. However, the actual theory underlying this basic concept and its application to investments only emerged in 1952 with the publication of Harry Markowitz's classic article on portfolio selection.[8] The article provided the foundation for what is now known as **modern portfolio theory** (MPT). The main conclusion of MPT is that investors should not only hold portfolios but should also focus on how individual securities in the portfolios are related to one another. In addition to the diversification benefits of portfolios to investors, the work of William Sharpe (1964), John Lintner (1965), and Jack Treynor (1961) demonstrated the role that portfolios play in determining the appropriate individual asset risk premium (i.e., the return in excess of the risk-free return expected by investors as compensation for the asset's

8 Markowitz (1952).

risk). According to capital market theory, the priced risk of an individual security is affected by holding it in a well-diversified portfolio. The early research provided the insight that an asset's risk should be measured in relation to the remaining systematic or non-diversifiable risk, which should be the only risk that affects the asset's price. This view of risk is the basis of the capital asset pricing model, or CAPM, which is discussed in greater detail in other readings. Although MPT has limitations, the concepts and intuitions illustrated in the theory continue to be the foundation of knowledge for portfolio managers.

STEPS IN THE PORTFOLIO MANAGEMENT PROCESS 4

☐ describe the steps in the portfolio management process

In the previous section we discussed a portfolio approach to investing. When establishing and managing a client's investment portfolio, certain critical steps are followed in the process. We describe these steps in this section.

- The Planning Step
  - Understanding the client's needs
  - Preparation of an investment policy statement (IPS)
- The Execution Step
  - Asset allocation
  - Security analysis
  - Portfolio construction
- The Feedback Step
  - Portfolio monitoring and rebalancing
  - Performance measurement and reporting

Step One: The Planning Step

The first step in the investment process is to understand the client's needs (objectives and constraints) and develop an **investment policy statement** (IPS). A portfolio manager is unlikely to achieve appropriate results for a client without a prior understanding of the client's needs. The IPS is a written planning document that describes the client's investment objectives and the constraints that apply to the client's portfolio. The IPS may state a benchmark—such as a particular rate of return or the performance of a particular market index—that can be used in the feedback stage to assess the performance of the investments and whether objectives have been met. The IPS should be reviewed and updated regularly (for example, either every three years or when a major change in a client's objectives, constraints, or circumstances occurs).

Step Two: The Execution Step

The next step is for the portfolio manager to construct a suitable portfolio based on the IPS of the client. The portfolio execution step consists of first deciding on a target asset allocation, which determines the weighting of asset classes to be included in the portfolio. This step is followed by the analysis, selection, and purchase of individual investment securities.

Asset Allocation

The next step in the process is to assess the risk and return characteristics of the available investments. The analyst forms economic and capital market expectations that can be used to form a proposed allocation of asset classes suitable for the client. Decisions that need to be made in the **asset allocation** of the portfolio include the distribution between equities, fixed-income securities, and cash; sub-asset classes, such as corporate and government bonds; and geographical weightings within asset classes. Alternative assets—such as real estate, commodities, hedge funds, and private equity—may also be included.

Economists and market strategists may set the top down view on economic conditions and broad market trends. The returns on various asset classes are likely to be affected by economic conditions; for example, equities may do well when economic growth has been unexpectedly strong whereas bonds may do poorly if inflation increases. The economists and strategists will attempt to forecast these conditions.

Top down—A **top-down analysis** begins with consideration of macroeconomic conditions. Based on the current and forecasted economic environment, analysts evaluate markets and industries with the purpose of investing in those that are expected to perform well. Finally, specific companies within these industries are considered for investment.

Bottom up—Rather than emphasizing economic cycles or industry analysis, a **bottom-up analysis** focuses on company-specific circumstances, such as management quality and business prospects. It is less concerned with broad economic trends than is the case for top-down analysis, but instead focuses on company specifics.

Security Analysis

The top-down view can be combined with the bottom-up insights of security analysts who are responsible for identifying attractive investments in particular market sectors. They will use their detailed knowledge of the companies and industries they cover to assess the expected level and risk of the cash flows that each security will produce. This knowledge allows the analysts to assign a valuation to the security and identify preferred investments.

Portfolio Construction

The portfolio manager will then construct the portfolio, taking account of the target asset allocation, security analysis, and the client's requirements as set out in the IPS. A key objective will be to achieve the benefits of diversification (i.e., to avoid putting all the eggs in one basket). Decisions need to be taken on asset class weightings, sector weightings within an asset class, and the selection and weighting of individual securities or assets. The relative importance of these decisions on portfolio performance depends at least in part on the investment strategy selected; for example, consider an investor that actively adjusts asset sector weights in relation to forecasts of sector performance and one who does not. Although all decisions have an effect on portfolio performance, the asset allocation decision is commonly viewed as having the greatest impact.

Exhibit 10 shows the broad portfolio weights of the endowment funds of Yale University and the University of Virginia as of June 2017. As you can see, the portfolios have a heavy emphasis on such alternative assets as hedge funds, private equity, and real estate—Yale University particularly so.

Exhibit 10: Endowment Portfolio Weights, June 2017

Asset Class	Yale University Endowment	University of Virginia Endowment
Public equity	19.1%	26.7%
Fixed income	4.6	9.1
Private equity	14.2	15.7
Real assets (e.g., real estate)	18.7	12.1
Absolute return (e.g., hedge funds)	25.1	19.6
Cash	1.2	2.3
Other	17.2	14.5
Portfolio value	US$27.2bn	US$8.6bn

Sources: "2017 Yale Endowment Annual Report" (p. 2): www.yale.edu/investments/Yale_Endowment_17.pdf; "University of Virginia Investment Management Company Annual Report 2017" (p. 26): http://uvm-web.eservices.virginia.edu/public/reports/FinancialStatements_2017.pdf.

Risk management is an important part of the portfolio construction process. The client's risk tolerance will be set out in the IPS, and the portfolio manager must make sure the portfolio is consistent with it. As noted above, the manager will take a diversified portfolio perspective: What is important is not the risk of any single investment, but rather how all the investments perform as a portfolio.

The endowments shown above are relatively risk tolerant investors. Contrast the asset allocation of the endowment funds with the portfolio mix of the insurance companies shown in Exhibit 11. You will notice that the majority of the insurance assets are invested in fixed-income investments, typically of high quality. Note that the Yale University portfolio has less than 5 percent invested in fixed income, with the remainder invested in such growth assets as equity, real estate, and hedge funds. This allocation is in sharp contrast to the Massachusetts Mutual Life Insurance Company (MassMutual) portfolio, which is 80 percent invested in bonds, mortgages, loans, and cash—reflecting the differing risk tolerance and constraints (life insurers face regulatory constraints on their investments).

Exhibit 11: MassMutual Portfolio, December 2017[9]

Asset Classes	Portfolio %
Bonds	56%
Preferred and common shares	9
Mortgages	14
Real estate	1
Policy loans	8
Partnerships	5
Other assets	5
Cash	2

Source: "MassMutual Financial Group 2017 Annual Report" (p. 8): www.massmutual.com/mmfg/docs/annual_report/index.html.

The portfolio construction phase also involves trading. Once the portfolio manager has decided which securities to buy and in what amounts, the securities must be purchased. In many investment firms, the portfolio manager will pass the trades to a buy-side trader—a colleague who specializes in securities trading—who will contact a stockbroker or dealer to have the trades executed.

Step Three: The Feedback Step

Finally, the feedback step assists the portfolio manager in rebalancing the portfolio due to a change in, for example, market conditions or the circumstances of the client.

Portfolio Monitoring and Rebalancing

Once the portfolio has been constructed, it needs to be monitored and reviewed and the composition revised as the security analysis changes because of changes in security prices and changes in fundamental factors. When security and asset weightings have drifted from the intended levels as a result of market movements, some rebalancing may be required. The portfolio may also need to be revised if it becomes apparent that the client's needs or circumstances have changed.

Performance Evaluation and Reporting

Finally, the performance of the portfolio must be evaluated, which will include assessing whether the client's objectives have been met. For example, the investor will wish to know whether the return requirement has been achieved and how the portfolio has performed relative to any benchmark that has been set. Analysis of performance may suggest that the client's objectives need to be reviewed and perhaps changes made to the IPS. As we will discuss in the next section, there are numerous investment products that clients can use to meet their investment needs. Many of these products are diversified portfolios that an investor can purchase.

9 Asset class definitions: Bonds—Debt instruments of corporations and governments as well as various types of mortgage- and asset-backed securities; Preferred and Common Shares—Investments in preferred and common equities; Mortgages—Mortgage loans secured by various types of commercial property as well as residential mortgage whole loan pools; Real Estate—Investments in real estate; Policy Loans—Loans by policyholders that are secured by insurance and annuity contracts; Partnerships—Investments in partnerships and limited liability companies; Cash—Cash, short-term investments, receivables for securities, and derivatives. Cash equivalents have short maturities (less than one year) or are highly liquid and able to be readily sold.

TYPES OF INVESTORS

5

- ☐ describe types of investors and distinctive characteristics and needs of each
- ☐ describe defined contribution and defined benefit pension plans

The portfolio management process described in the previous section may apply to different types of investment clients. Such clients are broadly divided among individual (or retail) and institutional investors. Each of these segments has distinctive characteristics and needs, as discussed in the following sub-sections.

Individual Investors

Individual investors have a variety of motives for investing and constructing portfolios. Short-term goals can include providing for children's education, saving for a major purchase (such as a vehicle or a house), or starting a business. The retirement goal—investing to provide for an income in retirement—is a major part of the investment planning of most individuals. Many employees of public and private companies invest for retirement through **defined contribution pension plans** (DC plans). DC plans are retirement plans in the employee's name usually funded by both the employee and the employer. Examples include 401(k) plans in the United States, group personal pension schemes in the United Kingdom, and superannuation plans in Australia. With DC plans, individuals will invest part of their wages while working, expecting to draw on the accumulated funds to provide income during retirement or to transfer some of their wealth to their heirs. The key to a DC plan is that the employee accepts the investment and inflation risk and is responsible for ensuring that there are enough assets in the plan to meet their needs upon retirement.

Some individuals will be investing for growth and will therefore seek assets that have the potential for capital gains. Others, such as retirees, may need to draw an income from their assets and may therefore choose to invest more in fixed-income and dividend-paying shares. The investment needs of individuals will depend in part on their broader financial circumstances, such as their employment prospects and whether or not they own their own residence. They may also need to consider such issues as building up a cash reserve and the purchase of appropriate insurance policies before undertaking longer-term investments.

Asset managers serving individual investors typically distribute their products directly to investors or through intermediaries such as financial advisers and/or retirement plan providers. The distribution network for individual investors varies globally. In the United States, financial advisers are independent or employed by national or regional broker–dealers, banks, and trust companies. Additionally, many asset managers distribute investment strategies to investors through major online brokerage and custodial firms.

In Europe, retail investment product distribution is fragmented and, in turn, varies by country/region. In continental Europe, for example, distribution is primarily driven through financial advisers affiliated with retail and private banks. In the United Kingdom, products are sold through independent advisers as well as through advisers representing a bank or insurance group. Retail distribution in Switzerland and in the Nordic countries is driven mainly through large regional and private banks. In contrast to the United States and Europe, in many Asian markets retail distribution is dominated by large regional retail banks and global banks with private banking divisions.

Globally, many wealth management firms and asset managers target high-net-worth investors. These clients often require more customized investment solutions alongside tax and estate planning services.

Institutional Investors

Institutional investors primarily include defined benefit pension plans, endowments and foundations, banks, insurance companies, investment companies, and sovereign wealth funds. Each of these has unique goals, asset allocation preferences, and investment strategy needs.

Defined Benefit Pension Plans

Pension plans are typically categorized as either defined contribution (DC) or defined benefit (DB). We previously described DC plans, which relate to individual investors. **Defined benefit pension plans** (DB plans) are company-sponsored plans that offer employees a predefined benefit on retirement. The future benefit is defined because the DB plan requires the plan sponsor to specify the obligation stated in terms of the retirement income benefits owed to participants. Generally, employers are responsible for the contributions made to a DB plan and bear the risk associated with adequately funding the benefits offered to employees. Plans are committed to paying pensions to members, and the assets of these plans are there to fund those payments. Plan managers need to ensure that sufficient assets will be available to pay pension benefits as they come due. The plan may have an indefinitely long time horizon if new plan members are being admitted or a finite time horizon if the plan has been closed to new members. In some cases, the plan managers attempt to match the fund's assets to its liabilities by, for example, investing in bonds that will produce cash flows corresponding to expected future pension payments. There may be many different investment philosophies for pension plans, depending on funded status and other variables.

An ongoing trend is that plan sponsors increasingly favor DC plans over DB plans because DC plans typically have lower costs/risk to the company. As a result, DB plans have been losing market share of pension assets to DC plans. Nevertheless, DB plans, both public and private, remain sizable sources of investment funds for asset managers. As Exhibit 12 shows, global pension assets totaled more than US$41 trillion by the end of 2017. The United States, United Kingdom, and Japan represent the three largest pension markets in the world, comprising more than 76% of global pension assets.

Exhibit 12: Global Pension Assets (as of year-end 2017)

Country/Region	Total Assets (US$ billions)
United States	25,411
United Kingdom	3,111
Japan	3,054
Australia	1,924
Canada	1,769
Netherlands	1,598
Switzerland	906
South Korea	725
Germany	472
Brazil	269
South Africa	258

Country/Region	Total Assets (US$ billions)
Finland	233
Malaysia	227
Chile	205
Mexico	177
Italy	184
France	167
Chinese mainland	177
Hong Kong SAR	164
Ireland	157
India	120
Spain	44
Total	**41,355**

Note: Column does not sum precisely because of rounding.
Source: Willis Towers Watson.

By geography, the United States and Australia have a higher proportion of pension assets in DC plans, whereas Canada, Japan, the Netherlands, and the United Kingdom remain weighted toward DB plans (see Exhibit 13).

Exhibit 13: Pension Plan Type by Geography

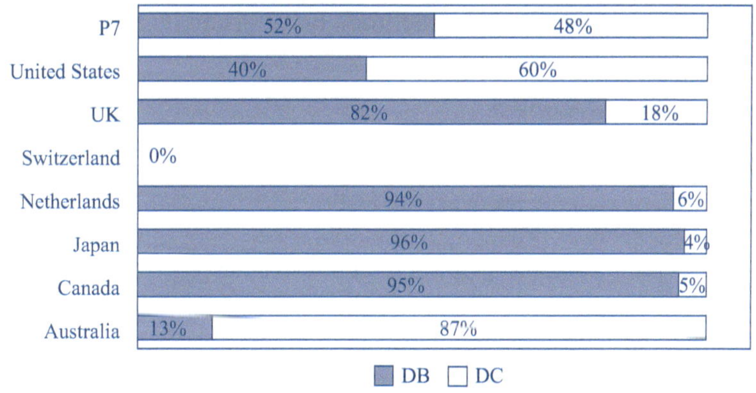

Notes: "P7" represents the combination of the seven countries listed. No data were available for Switzerland for this study.

Sources: Willis Towers Watson and secondary sources.

Endowments and Foundations

Endowments are funds of non-profit institutions that help the institutions provide designated services. In contrast, foundations are grant-making entities. Endowments and foundations collectively represent an estimated US$1.6 trillion in assets in the United States, which is the primary market for endowments and foundations.

Endowments and foundations typically allocate a sizable portion of their assets in alternative investments (Exhibit 14). This large allocation to alternative investments primarily reflects the typically long time horizon of endowments and foundations, as well as the popularity of endowment-specific asset allocation models developed by Yale University's endowment managers David Swensen and Dean Takahashi.

Exhibit 14: Asset Allocations for US College and University Endowments and Affiliated Foundations (as of 30 June 2017, dollar weighted)

Asset Class	Percentage Allocation
Domestic equity	15
Fixed income	7
Foreign equity	20
Alternatives	54
Cash	4

Source: National Association of College and University Budget Officers and Commonfund Institute.

A typical investment objective of an endowment or a foundation is to maintain the real (inflation-adjusted) capital value of the fund while generating income to fund the objectives of the institution. Most foundations and endowments are established with the intent of having perpetual lives. Exhibit 15 describes the Yale University endowment's approach to balancing short-term spending needs with ensuring that future generations also benefit from the endowment, and it also shows the Wellcome Trust's approach. The investment approach undertaken considers the objectives and constraints of the institution (for example, no tobacco investments for a medical endowment).

Exhibit 15: Spending Rules

The following examples of spending rules are excerpts from the Yale University endowment (in the United States) and from the Wellcome Trust (in the United Kingdom).

Yale University Endowment

> The spending rule is at the heart of fiscal discipline for an endowed institution. Spending policies define an institution's compromise between the conflicting goals of providing substantial support for current operations and preserving purchasing power of Endowment assets. The spending rule must be clearly defined and consistently applied for the concept of budget balance to have meaning.
>
> The Endowment spending policy, which allocates Endowment earnings to operations, balances the competing objectives of providing a stable flow of income to the operating budget and protecting the real value of the Endowment over time. The spending policy manages the trade-of between these two objectives by combining a long-term spending rate target with a smoothing rule, which adjusts spending in any given year gradually in response to changes in Endowment market value.
>
> The target spending rate approved by the Yale Corporation currently stands at 5.25%. According to the smoothing rule, Endowment spending in a given year sums to 80% of the previous year's spending and 20% of the targeted long-term spending rate applied to the fiscal year-end market value two years prior.

Source: 2017 Yale Endowment Annual Report (p.18) [http://investments.yale.edu/endowment-update/]

Wellcome Trust

> Our overall investment objective is to generate 4.5% percent real return over the long term.
>
> This is to provide for real increases in annual expenditure while reserving the Trust's capital base to balance the needs of current and future beneficiaries.
>
> We use this absolute return strategy because it aligns asset allocation with funding requirements and provides a competitive framework in which to judge individual investments.

Source: Wellcome Trust website (https://wellcome.ac.uk/about-us/investments)

Banks

Banks are financial intermediaries that accept deposits and lend money. Banks often have excess reserves that are invested in relatively conservative and very short-duration fixed-income investments, with a goal of earning an excess return above interest obligations due to depositors. Liquidity is a paramount concern for banks that stand ready to meet depositor requests for withdrawals. Many large banks have asset management divisions that offer retail and institutional products to their clients.

Insurance Companies

Insurance companies receive premiums for the policies they write, and they need to invest these premiums in a manner that will allow them to pay claims.

Insurance companies can be segmented into two broad types: life insurers and property and casualty (P&C) insurers. Insurance premiums from policyholders comprise an insurance company's general account. To pay claims to policyholders, regulatory guidelines maintain that an insurance company's general account is typically invested conservatively in a diverse allocation of fixed-income securities. General account portfolio allocations differ among life, P&C, and other specialty insurers (e.g., reinsurance) because of both the varying duration of liabilities and the unique liquidity considerations across insurance type.[10] In contrast to the general account, an insurer's surplus account is the difference between its assets and liabilities. An insurer's surplus account typically targets a higher return than the general account and thus often invests in less-conservative asset classes, such as public and private equities, real estate, infrastructure, and hedge funds.

Many insurance companies have in-house portfolio management teams responsible for managing general account assets. Some insurance companies offer portfolio management services and products in addition to their insurance offerings. An increasing trend among insurers (particularly in the United States) is outsourcing some of the portfolio management responsibilities—primarily sophisticated alternative asset classes—to unaffiliated asset managers. Several insurers manage investments for third-party clients, often through separately branded subsidiaries.

Sovereign Wealth Funds

Sovereign wealth funds (SWFs) are state-owned investment funds or entities that invest in financial or real assets. SWFs do not typically manage specific liability obligations, such as pensions, and have varying investment horizons and objectives based on funding the government's goals (for example, budget stabilization or future

---

10 For example, life insurers tend to invest in longer-term assets (e.g., 30-year government and corporate bonds) relative to P&C insurers because of the longer-term nature of their liabilities.

development projects). SWF assets more than doubled from 2007 to March 2018, totaling more than US$7.6 trillion.[11] Exhibit 16 lists the 10 largest SWFs in the world. The largest SWFs tend to be concentrated in Asia and in natural resource-rich places.

Exhibit 16: Largest Sovereign Wealth Funds (as of August 2018, in US$ billions)

Place	Sovereign Wealth Fund (Inception Year)	Assets
Norway	Government Pension Fund—Global (1990)	1,058
Chinese Mainland	China Investment Corporation (2007)	941
UAE – Abu Dhabi	Abu Dhabi Investment Authority (1976)	683
Kuwait	Kuwait Investment Authority (1953)	592
Hong Kong SAR	Hong Kong Monetary Authority Investment Portfolio (1993)	523
Saudi Arabia	SAMA Foreign Holdings (1952)	516
Chinese Mainland	SAFE Investment Company (1997)	441
Singapore	Government of Singapore Investment Authority (1981)	390
Singapore	Temasek Holdings (1974)	375
Saudi Arabia	Public Investment Fund (2008)	360
Total SWF Assets under Management		**8,109**

Source: SWF Institute (www.swfinstitute.org).

Investment needs vary across client groups. With some groups of clients, generalizations are possible. In other groups, needs vary by client. Exhibit 17 summarizes needs within each group.

Exhibit 17: Summary of Investment Needs by Client Type

Client	Time Horizon	Risk Tolerance	Income Needs	Liquidity Needs
Individual investors	Varies by individual	Varies by individual	Varies by individual	Varies by individual
Defined benefit pension plans	Typically long term	Typically quite high	High for mature funds; low for growing funds	Varies by maturity of the plan
Endowments and foundations	Very long term	Typically high	To meet spending commitments	Typically quite low
Banks	Short term	Quite low	To pay interest on deposits and operational expenses	High to meet repayment of deposits
Insurance companies	Short term for property and casualty; long term for life insurance companies	Typically quite low	Typically low	High to meet claims

11 SWFI, "Sovereign Wealth Fund Rankings" (https://www.swfinstitute.org/sovereign-wealth-fund-rankings/ ; retrieved October 2018).

Client	Time Horizon	Risk Tolerance	Income Needs	Liquidity Needs
Investment companies	Varies by fund	Varies by fund	Varies by fund	High to meet redemptions
Sovereign wealth funds	Varies by fund	Varies by fund	Varies by fund	Varies by fund

THE ASSET MANAGEMENT INDUSTRY

6

☐ describe aspects of the asset management industry

The portfolio management process and investor types are broad components of the asset management industry, which is an integral component of the global financial services sector. At the end of 2017, the industry managed more than US$79 trillion of assets owned by a broad range of institutional and individual investors (Exhibit 18).[12] Although nearly 80% of the world's professionally managed assets are in North America and Europe, the fastest-growing markets are in Asia and Latin America.

Exhibit 18: Global Assets under Management (AUM) by Region (year-end 2017)

	Market Size (US$ trillions)	Market Share (%)
North America	37.4	47%
Europe	22.2	28
Japan and Australia	6.2	8
Chinese mainland	4.2	5
Asia (excluding Japan, Australia, and Chinese mainland)	3.5	4
Latin America	1.8	2
Middle East and Africa	1.4	2
Total Global AUM	79.2	100%

Notes: Total Global AUM in this exhibit represents assets professionally managed in exchange for a fee. The total of US$79.2 trillion includes certain offshore assets that are not represented in the specific regional categories above.
Source: Boston Consulting Group.

The asset management industry is highly competitive. The universe of firms in the industry is broad, ranging from "pure-play" independent asset managers to diversified commercial banks, insurance companies, and brokerages that offer asset management services in addition to their core business activities. Given the increasingly global nature of the industry, many asset managers have investment research and distribution offices around the world. An asset manager is commonly referred to as a

12 http://image-src.bcg.com/Images/BCG-Seizing-the-Analytics-Advantage-June-2018-R-3_tcm9-194512.pdf (accessed on 6 September 2018).

buy-side firm given that it uses (buys) the services of sell-side firms. A **sell-side firm** is a broker/dealer that sells securities and provides independent investment research and recommendations to their clients (i.e., buy-side firms).

Asset managers offer a broad range of strategies. Specialist asset managers may focus on a specific asset class (e.g., emerging market equities) or style (e.g., quantitative investing), while "full service" managers typically offer a wide variety of asset classes and styles. Another type of asset manager firm is a "multi-boutique," in which a holding company owns several asset management firms that typically have specialized investment strategies. The multi-boutique structure allows individual asset management firms to retain their own unique investment cultures—and often equity ownership stakes—while also benefiting from the centralized, shared services of the holding company (e.g., technology, sales and marketing, operations, and legal services).

Active versus Passive Management

Asset managers may offer either active or passive management. As of year-end 2017, active management considerably exceeded passive management in terms of global assets under management and industry revenue (Exhibit 19), although passive management has demonstrated significant growth.

Exhibit 19: Global Asset Management Industry Assets and Revenue (as of year-end 2017)

Category	Assets (US$ trillions)	Revenue (US$ billions)	Market Share by Assets (%)	Market Share by Revenue (%)
Actively Managed	**64**	**258**	**80%**	**94%**
Alternatives	12	117	15	43
Active Specialties	15	55	19	20
Multi Asset Class	11	27	14	10
Core	26	59	33	21
Passively Managed	**16**	**17**	**20%**	**6%**
Total	**80**	**275**	**100%**	**100%**

Note: Some columns may not sum precisely because of rounding.
Source: Boston Consulting Group.

Through fundamental research, quantitative research, or a combination of both, active asset managers generally attempt to outperform either predetermined performance benchmarks, such as the S&P 500, or, for multi-asset class portfolios, a combination of benchmarks. In contrast to active managers, passive managers attempt to replicate the returns of a market index. Despite the rise of passive management in asset share, its share of industry revenue remains small given the low management fees relative to active management. As Exhibit 19 illustrates, passive management represents a fifth of global assets under management but only 6% of industry revenue.

Asset managers are increasingly offering other strategies beyond traditional market-cap-weighted exposures. Some of these other strategies, commonly known as **smart beta**, are based on such factors as size, value, momentum, or dividend characteristics. Smart beta involves the use of simple, transparent, rules-based strategies as a basis for investment decisions. Typically, smart beta strategies feature somewhat higher management fees and higher portfolio turnover relative to passive market-cap weighted strategies.

Traditional versus Alternative Asset Managers

Asset managers are typically categorized as either "traditional" or "alternative." Traditional managers generally focus on long-only equity, fixed-income, and multi-asset investment strategies, generating most of their revenues from asset-based management fees. Alternative asset managers, however, focus on hedge fund, private equity, and venture capital strategies, among others, while generating revenue from both management and performance fees (or "carried interest"). As Exhibit 19 demonstrates, alternative asset managers have a relatively low proportion of total global assets under management but generate a disproportionately high total of industry revenue.

Increasingly, the line between traditional and alternative managers has blurred. Many traditional managers have introduced higher-margin alternative products to clients. Concurrently, alternative managers seeking to reduce the revenue volatility associated with performance fees have increasingly offered retail versions of their institutional alternative strategies (typically referred to as "liquid alternatives") as well as long-only investment strategies. These liquid alternatives are often offered through highly regulated pooled investment products (e.g., mutual funds) and typically feature less leverage, no performance fees, and more liquid holdings than typical alternative products.

Ownership Structure

The ownership structure of an asset manager can play an important role in retaining and incentivizing key personnel. Portfolio managers who have personal capital invested in their firms or investment strategies are often viewed favorably by potential investors because of perceived alignment of management and client interests.

The majority of asset management firms are privately owned, typically by individuals who either established their firms or play key roles in their firms' management. Privately owned firms are typically structured as limited liability companies or limited partnerships.

While less common than privately owned managers, publicly traded asset managers have substantial assets under management. A prevalent ownership form in the industry is represented by asset management divisions of large, diversified financial services companies that offer asset management alongside insurance and banking services.

Asset Management Industry Trends

The asset management industry is evolving and continues to be shaped by socio-economic trends, shifting investor demands, advances in technology, and the expansion of global capital markets. Three key trends that we discuss in this section include the growth of passive investing, "big data" in the investment process, and the emergence of robo-advisers in the wealth management industry.

Growth of Passive Investing

As we saw in Exhibit 19, passively managed assets comprised nearly a fifth of global assets under management at the end of 2017. Management of passive assets is concentrated among a reasonably small group of asset managers and tends to be concentrated in equity strategies. As shown in Exhibit 20, the top three managers account for 70% of industry's assets. One key catalyst supporting the growth of passive investing is low cost for investors—management fees for index (or other passive) funds are often a fraction of those for active strategies. Another catalyst is the challenge that many active asset managers face in generating ex ante alpha, especially in somewhat more-efficiently priced markets, such as large-cap US equities.

Exhibit 20: Top Five ETP Managers Globally (as of 30 July 2017)

ETP Provider	Assets (US$ billions)	Market Share (%)
iShares	1,583	37
Vanguard	803	19
State Street Global Advisors	596	14
PowerShares	132	3
Nomura	100	2

Source: ETFGI.

Use of "Big Data" in the Investment Process

The prevalence of new data is extraordinary: In 2013, IBM estimated that 90% of the world's entire universe of data was created in the previous two years. The digitization of data and an exponential increase in computing power and data storage capacity have expanded additional information sources for asset managers. Massive amounts of data containing information of potential value to investors are created and captured daily. These data include both structured data—such as order book data and security returns—and data lacking recognizable structure, which is generated by a vast number of activities on the internet and elsewhere (e.g., compiled search information). The term "big data" is used to refer to these massively large datasets and their analysis.

Asset managers are using advanced statistical and machine-learning techniques to help process and analyze these new sources of data. Such techniques are used in both fundamentally driven and quantitatively driven investment processes. For example, computers are used to "read" earnings and economic data releases much faster than humans can and react with short-term trading strategies.

Third-party research vendors are supplying a vast range of relevant new data for asset managers, such as data used for time-series and predictive models. Among the most popular new sources of data are social media data and imagery and sensor data.

- **Social media data**. Real-time media and content outlets, such as Twitter and Facebook, provide meaningful market and company-specific announcements for investors and asset managers. In addition, the aggregation and analysis of social media users can aid key market sentiment indicators (e.g., short-term directional market movements) and indicate potential specific user trends related to products and services.
- **Imagery and sensor data**. Satellite imagery and geolocation devices provide vast real-time data to investment professionals. As the cost of launching and maintaining satellites has decreased, more satellites have been launched to track sensors and imagery that are relevant to economic considerations (e.g., weather conditions, cargo ship traffic patterns) and company-specific considerations (e.g., retailer parking capacity/usage, tracking of retail customers).

The challenge for asset managers is to discover data with predictive potential and to do so faster than fellow market participants. Many market participants are participating in an "information arms race" that has required substantial investments in specialized human capital (e.g., programmers, data scientists), technology, and information technology infrastructure to effectively convert various forms of structured and unstructured data into alpha-generating portfolio and security-level decisions.

Robo-Advisers: An Expanding Wealth Management Channel

Robo-advisers represent technology solutions that use automation and investment algorithms to provide several wealth management services—notably, investment planning, asset allocation, tax loss harvesting, and investment strategy selection. Investment and advice services provided by robo-advisers typically reflect an investor's general investment goals and risk tolerance preferences (often obtained from an investor questionnaire). Robo-adviser platforms range from exclusively digital investment advice platforms to hybrid offerings that offer both digital investment advice and the services of a human financial adviser.

At the end of 2017, robo-advisers managed an estimated US$180 billion in assets,[13] and market participants expect that number to grow considerably over time. This expected rapid growth in robo-advisory assets is based on several industry trends:

- **Growing demand from "mass affluent" and younger investors**: Traditional investment advice has often underserved younger and "mass affluent" investors with lower relative levels of investable assets. Given the efficiencies of robo-advisers and the scalability of technology, customized but standardized investment advice now can be offered to a wide range and size of investors.
- **Lower fees**: The cost of digital investment advice provided by robo-advisers is often a fraction of traditional investment advice channels because of scalability. For example, in the United States, a typical financial adviser may charge a 1% annual advisory fee[14] based on a client's assets, while robo-adviser fees typically average 0.20% annually.[15] Additionally, robo-advisers often rely on lower fee underlying portfolio investment options, such as index funds or ETFs, when constructing portfolios for clients.
- **New entrants**: Reflecting low barriers to entry, large wealth management firms have introduced robo-adviser solutions to service certain customer segments and appeal to a new generation of investors. In addition to these large wealth managers, other less-traditional entrants, such as insurance companies and asset managers, are developing solutions to cross-sell into their existing clients. Many market observers expect that non-financial firms (large technology leaders) will also become key players in the robo-adviser industry as they look to monetize their access to user data.

POOLED INTEREST - MUTUAL FUNDS 7

☐ describe mutual funds and compare them with other pooled investment products

In the asset management industry, a challenge faced by all investors is to find the right set of investment products to meet their needs. There is a diverse set of investment products available to investors, ranging from a simple brokerage account in which

13 S&P Global Market Intelligence.

14 http://www.riainabox.com/blog/2016-ria-industry-study-average-investment-advisory-fee-is-0-99-percent.

15 Deloitte, "Robo-Advisors Capitalizing on a Growing Opportunity" (https://www2.deloitte.com/content/dam/Deloitte/us/Documents/strategy/us-cons-robo-advisors.pdf).

the individual creates her own portfolio by assembling individual securities, to large institutions that employ individual portfolio managers to meet clients' investment management needs. Among the major investment products offered by asset managers are mutual funds and other pooled investment products, such as separately managed accounts, exchange-traded funds, hedge funds, and private equity/venture capital funds.

Mutual Funds

Rather than assemble a portfolio on their own, individual investors and institutions can turn over the selection and management of their investment portfolio to a third party. One way of doing this is through a **mutual fund**. This type of fund is a commingled investment pool in which investors in the fund each have a pro-rata claim on the income and value of the fund. The value of a mutual fund is referred to as the "net asset value." It is computed daily based on the closing price of the securities in the portfolio.

Mutual funds represent a primary investment product of individual investors globally. According to the International Investment Funds Association, worldwide regulated open-end fund assets totaled US$50 trillion as of the first quarter of 2018. Exhibit 21 shows the growth of global open-end funds over the past five years by region. Mutual funds provide several advantages, including low investment minimums, diversified portfolios, daily liquidity, and standardized performance and tax reporting.

Exhibit 21: Worldwide Regulated Open-End Funds: Total Net Assets (as of year-end, in US$ trillions)

	2011	2012	2013	2014	2015	2016	Q1 2018
World	**27.9**	**31.9**	**36.3**	**38.0**	**38.2**	**40.4**	**50.0**
Americas	14.6	16.5	18.9	20.0	19.6	21.1	24.9
Europe	10.3	11.9	13.6	13.8	13.7	14.1	18.1
Asia and Pacific	2.9	3.3	3.7	4.1	4.7	5.0	6.8
Africa	0.1	0.1	0.1	0.1	0.1	0.1	0.2

Notes: Components may not add to the total because of rounding. Regulated open-end funds include mutual funds, exchange-traded funds (ETFs), and institutional funds.
Source: International Investment Funds Association (IIFA).

Mutual funds are one of the most important investment vehicles for individuals and institutions. The best way to understand how a mutual fund works is to consider a simple example. Suppose that an investment firm wishes to start a mutual fund with a target amount of US$10 million. It is able to reach this goal through investments from five individuals and two institutions. The investment of each is as follows:

Investor	Amount Invested (US$)	Percent of Total	Number of Shares
Individuals			
A	$1.0 million	10%	10,000
B	1.0	10	10,000
C	0.5	5	5,000
D	2.0	20	20,000
E	0.5	5	5,000
Institutions			
X	2.0	20	20,000

Investor	Amount Invested (US$)	Percent of Total	Number of Shares
Y	3.0	30	30,000
Totals	**$10.0 million**	**100%**	**100,000**

Based on the US$10 million value (net asset value), the investment firm sets a total of 100,000 shares at an initial value of US$100 per share (US$10 million/100,000 = US$100). The investment firm will appoint a portfolio manager to be responsible for the investment of the US$10 million. Going forward, the total value of the fund or net asset value will depend on the value of the assets in the portfolio.

The fund can be set up as an open-end fund or a closed-end fund. If it is an **open-end fund**, it will accept new investment money and issue additional shares at a value equal to the net asset value of the fund at the time of investment. For example, assume that at a later date the net asset value of the fund increases to US$12 million and the new net asset value per share is US$120. A new investor, F, wishes to invest US$0.96 million in the fund. If the total value of the assets in the fund is now US$12 million or US$120 per share, in order to accommodate the new investment the fund would create 8,000 (US$0.96 million/US$120) new shares. After this investment, the net asset value of the fund would be US$12.96 million and there would be a total of 108,000 shares.

Funds can also be withdrawn at the net asset value per share. Suppose on the same day Investor E wishes to withdraw all her shares in the mutual fund. To accommodate this withdrawal, the fund will have to liquidate US$0.6 million in assets to retire 5,000 shares at a net asset value of US$120 per share (US$0.6 million/US$120). The combination of the inflow and outflow on the same day would be as follows:

Type	Investment (US$)	Shares
Inflow (Investor F buys)	$960,000	8,000
Outflow (Investor E sells)	–$600,000	–5,000
Net	$360,000	3,000

The net of the inflows and outflows on that day would be US$360,000 of new funds to be invested and 3,000 new shares created. However, the number of shares held and the value of the shares of all remaining investors, except Investor E, would remain the same.

An alternative to setting the fund up as an open-end fund would be to create a **closed-end fund** in which no new investment money is accepted into the fund. New investors invest by buying existing shares, and investors in the fund liquidate by selling their shares to other investors. Hence, the number of outstanding shares does not change. One consequence of this fixed share base is that, unlike open-end funds in which new shares are created and sold at the current net asset value per share, closed-end funds can sell for a premium or discount to net asset value depending on the demand for the shares.

There are advantages and disadvantages to each type of fund. The open-end fund structure makes it easy to grow in size but creates pressure on the portfolio manager to manage the cash inflows and outflows. One consequence of this structure is the need to liquidate assets that the portfolio manager might not want to sell at the time to meet redemptions. Conversely, the inflows require finding new assets in which to invest. As such, open-end funds tend not to be fully invested but rather keep some cash for redemptions not covered by new investments. Closed-end funds do not have these problems, but they do have a limited ability to grow. Of the total net asset value of all US mutual funds at the end of 2017 (US$19 trillion), only approximately 1 percent were in the form of closed-end funds.

In addition to open-end or closed-end funds, mutual funds can be classified as load or no-load funds. The primary difference between the two is whether the investor pays a sales charge (a "load") to purchase, hold, or redeem shares in the fund. In the case of the **no-load fund**, there is no fee for investing in the fund or for redemption but there is an annual fee based on a percentage of the fund's net asset value. **Load funds** are funds in which, in addition to the annual fee, a percentage fee is charged to invest in the fund and/or for redemptions from the fund. In addition, load funds are usually sold through retail brokers who receive part of the upfront fee. Overall, the number and importance of load funds has declined over time.

8 POOLED INTEREST - TYPE OF MUTUAL FUNDS

☐ describe mutual funds and compare them with other pooled investment products

The following section introduces the major types of mutual funds differentiated by the asset type that they invest in: money market funds, bond mutual funds, stock mutual funds, and hybrid or balanced funds.

Money Market Funds

Money market funds are mutual funds that invest in short-term money market instruments such as treasury bills, certificates of deposit, and commercial paper. They aim to provide security of principal, high levels of liquidity, and returns in line with money market rates. Many funds operate on a constant net asset value (CNAV) basis where the share price is maintained at $1 (or local currency equivalent). Others operate on a variable net asset value (VNAV) basis where the unit price can vary. In the United States, there are two basic types of money market funds: taxable and tax-free. Taxable money market funds invest in high-quality, short-term corporate debt and federal government debt. Tax-free money market funds invest in short-term state and local government debt. Although money market funds have been a substitute for bank savings accounts since the early 1980s, they are not insured in the same way as bank deposits.

Bond Mutual Funds

A bond mutual fund is an investment fund consisting of a portfolio of individual bonds and, occasionally, preferred shares. The net asset value of the fund is the sum of the value of each bond in the portfolio divided by the number of shares. Investors in the mutual fund hold shares, which account for their pro-rata share or interest in the portfolio. The major difference between a bond mutual fund and a money market fund is the maturity of the underlying assets. In a money market fund the maturity is as short as overnight and rarely longer than 90 days. A bond mutual fund, however, holds bonds with maturities as short as one year and as long as 30 years (or more). Exhibit 22 illustrates the general categories of bond mutual funds.[16]

16 In the United States, judicial rulings on federal powers of taxation have created a distinction between (federally) taxable and (federally) tax-exempt bonds and a parallel distinction for US bond mutual funds.

Exhibit 22: Bond Mutual Funds

Type of Bond Mutual Fund	Securities Held
Global	Domestic and non-domestic government, corporate, and securitized debt
Government	Government bonds and other government-affiliated bonds
Corporate	Corporate debt
High yield	Below investment-grade corporate debt
Inflation protected	Inflation-protected government debt
National tax-free bonds	National tax-free bonds (e.g., US municipal bonds)

Stock Mutual Funds

Historically, the largest types of mutual funds based on market value of assets under management are stock (equity) funds.

There are two types of stock mutual funds. The first is an actively managed fund in which the portfolio manager seeks outstanding performance through the selection of the appropriate stocks to be included in the portfolio. Passive management is followed by index funds that are very different from actively managed funds. Their goal is to match or track the performance of different indexes. The first index fund was introduced in 1976 by the Vanguard Group.

There are several major differences between actively managed funds and index funds. First, management fees for actively managed funds are higher than for index funds. The higher fees for actively managed funds reflect its goal to outperform an index, whereas the index fund simply aims to match the return on the index. Higher fees are required to pay for the research conducted to actively select securities. A second difference is that the level of trading in an actively managed fund is much higher than in an index fund, which depending on the jurisdiction, has tax implications. Mutual funds are often required to distribute all income and capital gains realized in the portfolio, so the actively managed fund tends to have more opportunity to realize capital gains. This results in higher taxes relative to an index fund, which uses a buy-and-hold strategy. Consequently, there is less buying and selling in an index fund and less likelihood of realizing capital gains distributions.

Hybrid/Balanced Funds

Hybrid or balanced funds are mutual funds that invest in both bonds and stocks. These types of funds represent a small fraction of the total investment in US mutual funds but are more common in Europe. These types of funds, however, have gained popularity with the growth of lifecycle funds. Lifecycle or Target Date funds manage the asset mix based on a desired retirement date. For example, if an investor is 40 years old in 2019 and planned to retire at the age of 67, he could invest in a mutual fund with a target date of 2046 and the fund would manage the appropriate asset mix over the next 27 years. In 2019 it might be 90 percent invested in shares and 10 percent in bonds. As time passes, however, the fund would gradually change the mix of shares and bonds to reflect the appropriate mix given the time to retirement.

9 POOLED INTEREST - OTHER INVESTMENT PRODUCTS

☐ describe mutual funds and compare them with other pooled investment products

A fund management service for institutions or individual investors with substantial assets is the **separately managed account** (SMA), which is also commonly referred to as a "managed account," "wrap account," or "individually managed account."

SMAs are managed exclusively for the benefit of a single individual or institution. Unlike a mutual fund, the assets of an SMA are owned directly by the individual or institution. The main disadvantage of an SMA is that the required minimum investment is usually much higher than with a mutual fund.

Large institutional investors are generally the dominant users of SMAs. SMAs enable asset managers to implement an investment strategy that matches an investor's specific objectives, portfolio constraints, and tax considerations, where applicable. For example, a public pension plan investing in an asset manager's large value equity strategy might have a socially responsible investment preference. In this case, the plan sponsor may wish to exclude certain industries, such as tobacco and defense, while also including additional companies that are deemed favorable according to other environmental, social, and governance (ESG) considerations.

Exchange-Traded Funds

Exchange-traded funds (ETFs) are investment funds that trade on exchanges (similar to individual stocks) and are generally structured as open-end funds. ETFs represent one of the fastest-growing investment products in the asset management industry. According to BlackRock, global ETF assets increased from US$428 billion in 2005 to US$4.9 trillion as of June 2018. Long-term investors—both institutional and retail—use ETFs in building a diversified asset allocation. While ETFs are structured similarly to open-end mutual funds, some key differences exist between the two products. One difference relates to transaction price. Because they are traded on exchanges, ETFs can be transacted (and are priced) intraday. That is, ETF investors buy the shares from other investors just as if they were buying or selling shares of stock. ETF investors can also short shares or purchase the shares on margin. In contrast, mutual funds typically can be purchased or sold only once a day, and short sales or purchasing shares on margin is not allowed. Mutual fund investors buy the fund shares directly from the fund, and all investments are settled at the net asset value. In practice, the market price of the ETF is likely to be close to the net asset value of the underlying investments.

Other key differences between ETFs and mutual funds relate to transaction costs and treatment of dividends and the minimum investment amount. Dividends on ETFs are paid out to the shareholders whereas mutual funds usually reinvest the dividends. Finally, the minimum required investment in ETFs is usually smaller than that of mutual funds.

Hedge Funds

Hedge funds are private investment vehicles that typically use leverage, derivatives, and long and short investment strategies. The origin of hedge funds can be traced back as far as 1949 to a fund managed by A.W. Jones & Co. It offered a strategy of a non-correlated offset to the "long-only" position typical of most portfolios. Since then, the hedge fund industry has grown considerably, with global hedge fund assets totaling US$3.3 trillion as of May 2017.

Hedge fund investment strategies are diverse and can range from specific niche strategies (e.g., long–short financial services) to global multi-strategy approaches. Consequently, hedge funds are often used by investors for portfolio diversification purposes. In general, hedge funds share a few distinguishing characteristics:

- *Short selling*: Many hedge funds implement short positions directly or synthetically using such derivatives as options, futures, and credit default swaps.
- *Absolute return seeking:* Hedge funds often seek positive returns in all market environments.
- *Leverage:* Many hedge funds use financial leverage (bank borrowing) or implicit leverage (using derivatives). The use and amount of leverage are dependent on the investment strategy being implemented.
- *Low correlation:* Some hedge funds have historically exhibited low return correlations with traditional equity and/or fixed-income asset classes.
- *Fee structures:* Hedge funds typically charge two distinct fees: a traditional asset-based management fee (AUM fee) and an incentive (or performance) fee in which the hedge fund earns a portion of the fund's realized capital gains.[17] Hedge funds have traditionally charged management fees of 2% and incentive fees of up to 20%, although there has been downward pressure on those fees amid increased competition and the availability of competing products.

Hedge funds are not readily available to all investors. They typically require a high minimum investment and often have restricted liquidity by allowing only periodic (e.g., quarterly) withdrawals or having a long fixed-term commitment.

Private Equity and Venture Capital Funds

Private equity funds and **venture capital funds** are alternative funds that seek to buy, optimize, and ultimately sell portfolio companies to generate profits. As of December 2017, assets under management in the private equity industry totaled US$3.1 trillion, a historical high point.[18] Most private equity and venture capital funds have a lifespan of approximately 7–10 years (but usually subject to contractual extensions). Unlike most traditional asset managers that trade in public securities, private equity and venture firms often take a "hands-on" approach to their portfolio companies through a combination of financial engineering (e.g., realizing expense synergies, changing capital structures), installment of executive management and board members, and significant contributions to the development of a target company's business strategy. The final investment stage, often referred to as the "exit" or "harvesting" stage, occurs when a private equity or venture capital fund divests its portfolio companies through a merger with another company, the acquisition by another company, or an initial public offering (IPO).

17 Performance fees are often subject to high-water mark provisions, which preclude a manager from earning a performance fee unless the value of a fund at the end of a predefined measurement period is higher than the value of the fund at the beginning of the measurement period. The unpredictability of future performance leads to uncertainty in performance fee revenue, which is regarded as less reliable than revenue derived from management fees.

18 https://www.pionline.com/article/20180724/ONLINE/180729930/preqin-private-equity-aum-grows-20-in-2017-to-record-306-trillion# (accessed 13 November 2018)

As with most alternative funds, the majority of private equity and venture capital funds are structured as limited partnerships. These limited partnership agreements exist between the fund manager, called the general partner (GP), and the fund's investors, called limited partners (LPs). The funds generate revenue through several types of fees:

- *Management fees:* Fees are based on committed capital (or sometimes net asset value or invested capital) and typically range from 1–3% annually. Sometimes these fees step down several years into the investment period of a fund.
- *Transaction fees:* Fees are paid by portfolio companies to the fund for various corporate and structuring services. Typically, a percentage of the transaction fee is shared with the LPs by offsetting the management fee.
- *Carried interest:* Carried interest is the GP's share of profits (typically 20%) on sales of portfolio companies. Most GPs do not earn the incentive fee until LPs have recovered their initial investment.
- *Investment income.* Investment income includes profits generated on capital contributed to the fund by the GP.

SUMMARY

- A portfolio approach to investing could be preferable to simply investing in individual securities.
- The problem with focusing on individual securities is that this approach may lead to the investor "putting all her eggs in one basket."
- Portfolios provide important diversification benefits, allowing risk to be reduced without necessarily affecting or compromising return.
- Understanding the needs of your client and preparing an investment policy statement represent the first steps of the portfolio management process. Those steps are followed by asset allocation, security analysis, portfolio construction, portfolio monitoring and rebalancing, and performance measurement and reporting.
- Types of investors include individual and institutional investors. Institutional investors include defined benefit pension plans, endowments and foundations, banks, insurance companies, and sovereign wealth funds.
- The asset management industry is an integral component of the global financial services sector. Asset managers offer either active management, passive management, or both. Asset managers are typically categorized as traditional or alternative, although the line between traditional and alternative has blurred.
- Three key trends in the asset management industry include the growth of passive investing, "big data" in the investment process, and robo-advisers in the wealth management industry.
- Investors use different types of investment products in their portfolios. These include mutual funds, separately managed accounts, exchange-traded funds, hedge funds, and private equity and venture capital funds.

REFERENCES

Lintner, John. 1965. "The Valuation of Risk Assets and the Selection of Risky Investments in Stock Portfolios and Capital Budgets." *Review of Economics and Statistics* 47, vol. , no. 1 (February):13–37. 10.2307/1924119

Markowitz, Harry M. 1952. "Portfolio Selection." *Journal of Finance* 7, vol. , no. 1 (March):77–91. 10.2307/2975974

Sharpe, William F. 1964. "Capital Asset Prices: A Theory of Market Equilibrium under Conditions of Risk." *Journal of Finance* 19, vol. , no. 3 (September):425–442. 10.2307/2977928

Singletary, Michelle. 2001. "Cautionary Tale of an Enron Employee Who Went for Broke." Seattlepi.com (10 December): http://www.seattlepi.com/money/49894_singletary10.shtml.

Treynor, J. L. 1961. "Toward a Theory of Market Value of Risky Assets." Unpublished manuscript.

PRACTICE PROBLEMS

1. Investors should use a portfolio approach to:

   A. reduce risk.

   B. monitor risk.

   C. eliminate risk.

2. Which of the following is the *best* reason for an investor to be concerned with the composition of a portfolio?

   A. Risk reduction.

   B. Downside risk protection.

   C. Avoidance of investment disasters.

3. With respect to the formation of portfolios, which of the following statements is *most accurate*?

   A. Portfolios affect risk less than returns.

   B. Portfolios affect risk more than returns.

   C. Portfolios affect risk and returns equally.

4. With respect to the portfolio management process, the asset allocation is determined in the:

   A. planning step.

   B. feedback step.

   C. execution step.

5. The planning step of the portfolio management process is *least likely* to include an assessment of the client's

   A. securities.

   B. constraints.

   C. risk tolerance.

6. With respect to the portfolio management process, the rebalancing of a portfolio's composition is *most likely* to occur in the:

   A. planning step.

   B. feedback step.

   C. execution step.

7. An analyst gathers the following information for the asset allocations of three

portfolios:

Portfolio	Fixed Income (%)	Equity (%)	Alternative Assets (%)
1	25	60	15
2	60	25	15
3	15	60	25

Which of the portfolios is *most likely* appropriate for a client who has a high degree of risk tolerance?

A. Portfolio 1.

B. Portfolio 2.

C. Portfolio 3.

8. Which of the following institutions will *on average* have the greatest need for liquidity?

   A. Banks.

   B. Investment companies.

   C. Non-life insurance companies.

9. Which of the following institutional investors will *most likely* have the longest time horizon?

   A. Defined benefit plan.

   B. University endowment.

   C. Life insurance company.

10. A defined benefit plan with a large number of retirees is *likely* to have a high need for:

    A. income.

    B. liquidity.

    C. insurance.

11. Which of the following institutional investors is *most likely* to manage investments in mutual funds?

    A. Insurance companies.

    B. Investment companies.

    C. University endowments.

12. Which of the following investment products is *most likely* to trade at their net asset value per share?

    A. Exchange traded funds.

    B. Open-end mutual funds.

    C. Closed-end mutual funds.

13. Which of the following financial products is *least likely* to have a capital gain distribution?

   A. Exchange traded funds.

   B. Open-end mutual funds.

   C. Closed-end mutual funds.

14. Which of the following forms of pooled investments is subject to the *least* amount of regulation?

   A. Hedge funds.

   B. Exchange traded funds.

   C. Closed-end mutual funds.

15. Which of the following pooled investments is *most likely* characterized by a few large investments?

   A. Hedge funds.

   B. Buyout funds.

   C. Venture capital funds.

SOLUTIONS

1. A is correct. Combining assets into a portfolio should reduce the portfolio's volatility. Specifically, "individuals and institutions should hold portfolios to reduce risk." As illustrated in the reading, however, risk reduction may not be as great during a period of dramatic economic change.

2. A is correct. Combining assets into a portfolio should reduce the portfolio's volatility. The portfolio approach does not necessarily provide downside protection or guarantee that the portfolio always will avoid losses.

3. B is correct. As illustrated in the reading, portfolios reduce risk more than they increase returns.

4. C is correct. The client's objectives and constraints are established in the investment policy statement and are used to determine the client's target asset allocation, which occurs in the execution step of the portfolio management process.

5. A is correct. Securities are analyzed in the execution step. In the planning step, a client's objectives and constraints are used to develop the investment policy statement.

6. B is correct. Portfolio monitoring and rebalancing occurs in the feedback step of the portfolio management process.

7. C is correct. Portfolio 3 has the same equity exposure as Portfolio 1 and has a higher exposure to alternative assets, which have greater volatility (as discussed in the section of the reading comparing the endowments from Yale University and the University of Virginia).

8. A is correct. The excess reserves invested by banks need to be relatively liquid. Although investment companies and non-life insurance companies have high liquidity needs, the liquidity need for banks is on average the greatest.

9. B is correct. Most foundations and endowments are established with the intent of having perpetual lives. Although defined benefit plans and life insurance companies have portfolios with a long time horizon, they are not perpetual.

10. A is correct. Income is necessary to meet the cash flow obligation to retirees. Although defined benefit plans have a need for income, the need for liquidity typically is quite low. A retiree may need life insurance; however, a defined benefit plan does not need insurance.

11. B is correct. Investment companies manage investments in mutual funds. Although endowments and insurance companies may own mutual funds, they do not issue or redeem shares of mutual funds.

12. B is correct. Open-end funds trade at their net asset value per share, whereas closed-end funds and exchange traded funds can trade at a premium or a discount.

13. A is correct. Exchange traded funds do not have capital gain distributions. If an investor sells shares of an ETF (or open-end mutual fund or closed-end mutual fund), the investor may have a capital gain or loss on the shares sold; however, the gain (or loss) from the sale is not a distribution.

14. A is correct. Hedge funds are currently exempt from the reporting requirements of a typical public investment company.

15. B is correct. Buyout funds or private equity firms make only a few large investments in private companies with the intent of selling the restructured companies in three to five years. Venture capital funds also have a short time horizon; however, these funds consist of many small investments in companies with the expectation that only a few will have a large payoff (and that most will fail).

LEARNING MODULE

4

Basics of Portfolio Planning and Construction

by Alistair Byrne, PhD, CFA, and Frank E. Smudde, MSc, CFA.

Alistair Byrne, PhD, CFA, is at State Street Global Advisors (United Kingdom). Frank E. Smudde, MSc, CFA, is at APG Asset Management (Netherlands).

LEARNING OUTCOMES

Mastery	*The candidate should be able to:*
☐	describe the reasons for a written investment policy statement (IPS)
☐	describe the major components of an IPS
☐	describe risk and return objectives and how they may be developed for a client
☐	explain the difference between the willingness and the ability (capacity) to take risk in analyzing an investor's financial risk tolerance
☐	describe the investment constraints of liquidity, time horizon, tax concerns, legal and regulatory factors, and unique circumstances and their implications for the choice of portfolio assets
☐	explain the specification of asset classes in relation to asset allocation
☐	describe the principles of portfolio construction and the role of asset allocation in relation to the IPS
☐	describe how environmental, social, and governance (ESG) considerations may be integrated into portfolio planning and construction

CFA Institute would like to thank Hardik Sanjay Shah, CFA, for his contributions to the 2022 update of this reading.

1 INTRODUCTION

To build a suitable portfolio for a client, investment advisers should first seek to understand the client's investment goals, resources, circumstances, and constraints. Investors can be categorized into broad groups based on shared characteristics with respect to these factors (e.g., various types of individual investors and institutional investors). Even investors within a given type, however, will invariably have a number of distinctive requirements. In this reading, we consider in detail the planning for investment success based on an individualized understanding of the client.

This reading is organized as follows: Section 2 discusses the investment policy statement, a written document that captures the client's investment objectives and the constraints. Section 3 discusses the portfolio construction process, including the first step of specifying a strategic asset allocation for the client. Section 4 concludes and summarizes the reading.

2 THE INVESTMENT POLICY STATEMENT

- ☐ describe the reasons for a written investment policy statement (IPS)
- ☐ describe the major components of an IPS

Portfolio planning can be defined as a program developed in advance of constructing a portfolio that is expected to define the client's investment objectives. The written document governing this process is the investment policy statement (IPS). The IPS is sometimes complemented by a document outlining policy on responsible investing—the broadest (umbrella) term used to describe principles that typically address one or more environmental, social, and governance themes that an investor requires to be considered when evaluating whether to invest in a particular company, as well as during the period of ownership. Sustainable investing, a term used in a similar context to responsible investing, focuses on factoring in sustainability issues during the investment process. Policies on responsible investing may also be integrated within the IPS itself. In the remainder of this reading, the integration of responsible investing within the IPS will be our working assumption.

The Investment Policy Statement

The IPS is the starting point of the portfolio management process. Without a full understanding of the client's situation and requirements, it is unlikely that successful results will be achieved. "Success" can be defined as a client achieving his important investment goals using means that he is comfortable with (in terms of risks taken and other concerns). The IPS essentially communicates a plan for achieving investment success.

The IPS is typically developed following a fact-finding discussion with the client. This discussion can include the use of a questionnaire designed to articulate the client's risk tolerance as well as address expectations in connection with specific circumstances. In the case of institutional clients, the fact finding may involve asset–liability management reviews, identification of liquidity needs, and a wide range of tax, legal, and other considerations.

The IPS can take a variety of forms.[1] A typical format will include the client's investment objectives and the constraints that apply to the client's portfolio.

The client's objectives are specified in terms of risk tolerance and return requirements. These elements must be consistent with each other: a client is unlikely to be able to find a portfolio that offers a relatively high expected return without taking on a relatively high level of expected risk. As part of their financial planning, clients may specify specific spending goals, which need to be considered when setting risk tolerance and return requirements.

The constraints section covers factors that need to be taken into account when constructing a portfolio for the client that meets the objectives. The typical categories are liquidity requirements, time horizon, regulatory requirements, tax status, and unique needs. The constraints may be either internal (i.e., set by the client) or external (i.e., set by law or regulation), as we discuss in detail later.

Having a well-constructed IPS for all clients should be standard procedure for an investment manager. The investment manager should build the portfolio with reference to the IPS and be able to refer to it to assess a particular investment's suitability for the client. In some cases, the need for the IPS goes beyond simply being a matter of standard procedure. In certain countries, the IPS (or an equivalent document) is a legal or regulatory requirement. For example, UK pension schemes must have a statement of investment principles under the Pensions Act 1995 (Section 35), and this statement is in essence an IPS. The UK Financial Services Authority also has requirements for investment firms to "know their customers." The European Union's Markets in Financial Instruments Directive ("MiFID") requires firms to assign clients to categories (eligible counterparties, institutional clients, or retail clients), with the category type determining the types of protections and limitations relevant for the client by law.

In the case of an institution, such as a pension plan or university endowment, the IPS may set out the governance arrangements that apply to the investment portfolio. For example, this information could cover the investment committee's approach to appointing and reviewing investment managers for the portfolio, and the discretion that those managers have.

The IPS should be reviewed on a regular basis to ensure that it remains consistent with the client's circumstances and requirements. For example, the UK Pensions Regulator suggests that a pension scheme's statements of investment principles—a form of IPS—should be reviewed at least every three years. The IPS should also be reviewed if the manager becomes aware of a material change in the client's circumstances, as well as on the initiative of the client when her objectives, time horizon, or liquidity needs change.

Major Components of an IPS

There is no single standard format for an IPS. Many IPS and investment governance documents with a similar purpose (as noted previously), however, include the following sections:

- *Introduction.* This section describes the client.
- *Statement of Purpose.* This section states the purpose of the IPS.

1 In this reading, an IPS is assumed to be a document governing investment management activities covering all or most of a client's financial wealth. In many practical contexts, investment professionals work with investment mandates that cover only parts of a client's wealth or financial risk. Governance documents such as "Limited Partnership Agreements" and "Investment Management Agreements" will govern such mandates. Their contents are to a large degree comparable to the contents of the IPS as described in this reading.

- *Statement of Duties and Responsibilities*. This section details the duties and responsibilities of the client, the custodian of the client's assets, and the investment managers.
- *Procedures*. This section explains the steps to take to keep the IPS current and the procedures to follow to respond to various contingencies.
- *Investment Objectives*. This section explains the client's objectives in investing.
- *Investment Constraints*. This section presents the factors that constrain the client in seeking to achieve the investment objectives.
- *Investment Guidelines*. This section provides information about how policy should be executed (e.g., on the permissible use of leverage and derivatives) and on specific types of assets excluded from investment, if any.
- *Evaluation and Review*. This section provides guidance on obtaining feedback on investment results.
- *Appendices*: (A) Strategic Asset Allocation and (B) Rebalancing Policy. Many investors specify a strategic asset allocation (SAA), also known as the policy portfolio, which is the baseline allocation of portfolio assets to asset classes in view of the investor's investment objectives and the investor's policy with respect to rebalancing asset class weights. This SAA may include a statement of policy concerning hedging risks such as currency risk and interest rate risk.

The sections that are most closely linked to the client's distinctive needs, and probably the most important from a planning perspective, are those dealing with investment objectives and constraints. An IPS focusing on these two elements has been called an IPS in an "objectives and constraints" format.

In the following sections, we discuss the investment objectives and constraints format of an IPS beginning with risk and return objectives. The process of developing the IPS is the basic mechanism for evaluating and trying to improve an investor's overall expected return–risk stance. In a portfolio context, return objectives and expectations must be tailored to be consistent with risk objectives. The risk and return objectives must also be consistent with the constraints that apply to the portfolio. A growing proportion of investors explicitly include non-financial considerations when formulating their investment policies. This approach is often referred to as responsible investing (discussed earlier alongside related terms), which reflects environmental, social, and governance (ESG) considerations. Responsible investing recognizes that ESG considerations may eventually affect the portfolio's financial risk–return profile and may express the investor's societal convictions. In this reading, we discuss responsible investing aspects of investment policy, where relevant.

3 IPS RISK AND RETURN OBJECTIVES

- ☐ describe the major components of an IPS
- ☐ describe risk and return objectives and how they may be developed for a client
- ☐ explain the difference between the willingness and the ability (capacity) to take risk in analyzing an investor's financial risk tolerance

When constructing a portfolio for a client, it is important to ensure that the risk of the portfolio is suitable for the client. The IPS should state clearly the risk tolerance of the client. Risk objectives are specifications for portfolio risk that reflect the client's risk tolerance. Quantitative risk objectives can be absolute, relative, or a combination of the two.

Examples of an absolute risk objective would be a desire not to suffer any loss of capital or not to lose more than a given percentage of capital in any 12-month period. Note that these objectives are unrelated to investment market performance, good or bad, and are absolute in the sense of being self-standing. The fulfillment of such objectives could be achieved by not taking any risk—for example, by investing in an insured bank certificate of deposit at a creditworthy bank. If investments in risky assets are undertaken, however, such statements could be restated as a probability statement to be more operational (i.e., practically useful). For example, the desire not to lose more than 4% of capital in any 12-month period might be restated as an objective that with 95% probability the portfolio not lose more than 4% in any 12-month period. Measures of absolute risk include the variance or standard deviation of returns and **value at risk**.[2]

Some clients may choose to express relative risk objectives, which relate risk relative to one or more benchmarks perceived to represent appropriate risk standards. For example, investments in large-cap UK equities could be benchmarked to an equity market index, such as the FTSE 100 Index. The S&P 500 Index could be used as a benchmark for large-cap US equities; for investments with cash-like characteristics, the benchmark could be an interest rate such as Treasury bill rate. For risk relative to a benchmark, the measure could be **tracking risk**, or **tracking error**.[3] In practice, such risk objectives are used in situations where the total wealth management activities on behalf of a client are divided into partial mandates.

Other clients take both the investor's assets and liabilities into consideration when establishing an IPS risk objective. In some cases where the size, timing and/or relative certainty of future investor financial obligations are known, an IPS may be tailored to meet these objectives in what is called a **liability-driven investment (LDI)** approach. Examples of LDI include life insurance companies, defined benefit pension plans or an individual's budget after retirement. For example, a pension plan must meet the pension payments as they come due, and the risk objective will be to minimize the probability that it will fail to do so. A related return objective might be to outperform the discount rate used in finding the present value of liabilities over a multi-year time horizon.

When a policy portfolio (that is, a specified set of long-term asset class weightings and hedge ratios) is used, the risk objective may be expressed as a desire for the portfolio return to be within a band of plus or minus X% of the benchmark return calculated by assigning an index or benchmark to represent each asset class present in the policy portfolio. Again, this objective may be more usefully interpreted as a statement of probability—for example, a 95% probability that the portfolio return will be within X% of the benchmark return over a stated period. Example 1 reviews this material.

2 **Value at risk** is a money measure of the minimum value of losses expected during a specified period at a given level of probability.

3 **Tracking risk** (sometimes called **tracking error**) is the standard deviation of the differences between a portfolio's returns and its benchmark's returns.

EXAMPLE 1

Types of Risk Objectives

A Japanese institutional investor has a portfolio valued at ¥10 billion. The investor expresses her first risk objective as a desire not to lose more than ¥1 billion in the coming 12-month period. She specifies a second risk objective of achieving returns within 4% of the return to the TOPIX stock market index, which is her benchmark. Based on this information, address the following:

1.

a. Characterize the first risk objective as absolute or relative.

b. Give an example of how the risk objective could be restated in a practical manner.

Solution

a. This is an absolute risk objective.

b. This risk objective could be restated in a practical manner by specifying that the 12-month 95% value at risk of the portfolio must be no more than ¥1 billion.

2.

a. Characterize the second risk objective as absolute or relative.

b. Identify a measure for quantifying the risk objective.

Solution

a. This is a relative risk objective.

b. This risk objective could be quantified using the tracking risk as a measure. For example, assuming returns follow a normal distribution, an expected tracking risk of 2% would imply a return within 4% of the index return approximately 95% of the time. Remember that tracking risk is stated as a one standard deviation measure.

A client's overall risk tolerance is a function of the client's ability to bear (accept) risk and her "risk attitude," which might be considered as the client's willingness to take risk. For ease of expression, from this point on we will refer to ability to bear risk and willingness to take risk as the two components of risk tolerance. Above-average ability to bear risk and above-average willingness to take risk imply above-average risk tolerance. Below-average ability to bear risk and below-average willingness to take risk imply below-average risk tolerance. These interactions are shown in Exhibit 1.

Exhibit 1: Risk Tolerance

	Ability to Bear Risk	
Willingness to Take Risk	**Below Average**	**Above Average**
Below Average	Below-average risk tolerance	Resolution needed
Above Average	Resolution needed	Above-average risk tolerance

The *ability* to bear risk is measured mainly in terms of objective factors, such as time horizon, expected income, and level of wealth relative to liabilities. For example, an investor with a 20-year time horizon can be considered to have a greater ability to bear risk, other things being equal, than an investor with a 2-year horizon. This difference is because over 20 years, there is more scope for losses to be recovered or other adjustments made to circumstances than there is over 2 years.

Similarly, an investor whose assets are comfortably in excess of their liabilities has more ability to bear risk than an investor whose wealth and expected future expenditure are more closely balanced. For example, a wealthy individual who can sustain a comfortable lifestyle after a very substantial investment loss has a relatively high ability to bear risk. A pension plan that has a large surplus of assets over liabilities has a relatively high ability to bear risk.

The *willingness* to take risk, or risk attitude, is a more subjective factor based on the client's psychology and perhaps also his current circumstances. Although the list of factors related to an individual's risk attitude remains open to debate, it is believed that some psychological factors, such as personality type, self-esteem, and inclination to independent thinking, are correlated with risk attitude. Some individuals are comfortable taking financial and investment risk, whereas others find it distressing. Although there is no single agreed-upon method for measuring risk tolerance, a willingness to take risk may be gauged by discussing risk with the client or by asking the client to complete a psychometric questionnaire. For example, financial planning academic John Grable and collaborators have developed 13-item and 5-item risk attitude questionnaires that have undergone some level of technical validation. The five-item questionnaire is shown in Exhibit 2.

Exhibit 2: A Five-Item Risk Assessment Instrument

1. Investing is too difficult to understand.
   a. Strongly agree
   b. Tend to agree
   c. Tend to disagree
   d. Strongly disagree
2. I am more comfortable putting my money in a bank account than in the stock market.
   a. Strongly agree
   b. Tend to agree
   c. Tend to disagree
   d. Strongly disagree
3. When I think of the word "risk," the term "loss" comes to mind immediately.
   a. Strongly agree
   b. Tend to agree
   c. Tend to disagree
   d. Strongly disagree
4. Making money in stocks and bonds is based on luck.
   a. Strongly agree
   b. Tend to agree
   c. Tend to disagree
   d. Strongly disagree
5. In terms of investing, safety is more important than returns.
   a. Strongly agree

b. Tend to agree

c. Tend to disagree

d. Strongly disagree

Source: Grable and Joo (2004).

The responses, a), b), c), and d), are coded 1, 2, 3, and 4, respectively, and summed. The lowest score is 5 and the highest score is 20, with higher scores indicating greater risk tolerance. For two random samples drawn from the faculty and staff of large US universities (n = 406), the mean score was 12.86 with a standard deviation of 3.01 and a median score (i.e., the middle score) of 13.

Note that a question, such as the first one in Exhibit 2, indicates that risk attitude may be associated with non-psychological factors (such as level of financial knowledge and understanding and decision-making style) as well as psychological factors.

The adviser needs to examine whether a client's ability to accept risk is consistent with the client's willingness to take risk. For example, a wealthy investor with a 20-year time horizon, who is thus able to take risk, may also be comfortable taking risk; in this case the factors are consistent. If the wealthy investor has a low willingness to take risk, there would be a conflict.

The conflict between ability and willingness to take risk can also arise in the institutional context. In addition, different stakeholders within the institution may take different views. For example, the trustees of a well-funded pension plan may desire a low-risk approach to safeguard the funding of the scheme and beneficiaries of the scheme may take a similar view. The sponsor, however, may wish a higher-risk/higher-return approach in an attempt to reduce future funding costs. When a trustee bears a fiduciary responsibility to pension beneficiaries and the interests of the pension sponsor and the pension beneficiaries conflict, the trustee should act in the best interests of the beneficiaries.

When both the ability and willingness to take risk are consistent, the investment adviser's task is the simplest. When ability to take risk is below average and willingness to take risk is above average, the investor's risk tolerance should be assessed as below average overall. When ability to take risk is above average but willingness is below average, the portfolio manager or adviser may seek to counsel the client and explain the conflict and its implications. For example, the adviser could outline the reasons why the client is considered to have a high ability to take risk and explain the likely consequences, in terms of reduced expected return, of not taking risk. The investment adviser, however, should not aim to change a client's willingness to take risk that is not a result of a miscalculation or misperception. Modification of elements of personality is not within the purview of the investment adviser's role. The prudent approach is to reach a conclusion about risk tolerance consistent with the lower of the two factors (ability and willingness) and to document the decisions made.

Example 2 is the first of a set that follows the analysis of an investment client through the preparation of the major elements of an IPS.

EXAMPLE 2

The Case of Henri Gascon: Risk Tolerance

1. Henri Gascon is an energy trader who works for a major French oil company based in Paris. He is 30 years old and married with one son, aged 5. Gascon has decided that it is time to review his financial situation and consults a financial adviser, who notes the following aspects of Gascon's situation:

   - Gascon's annual salary of €250,000 is more than sufficient to cover the family's outgoings.

- Gascon owns his apartment outright and has €1,000,000 of savings.
- Gascon perceives that his job is reasonably secure.
- Gascon has a good knowledge of financial matters and is confident that equity markets will deliver positive returns over the long term.
- In the risk tolerance questionnaire, Gascon strongly disagrees with the statements that "making money in stocks and bonds is based on luck" and "in terms of investing, safety is more important than returns."
- Gascon expects that most of his savings will be used to fund his retirement, which he hopes to start at age 50.

Based only on the information given, which of the following statements is *most* accurate?

A. Gascon has a low ability to take risk but a high willingness to take risk.

B. Gascon has a high ability to take risk but a low willingness to take risk.

C. Gascon has a high ability to take risk and a high willingness to take risk.

Solution:

C is correct. Gascon has a high income relative to outgoings, a high level of assets, a secure job, and a time horizon of 20 years. This information suggests a high *ability* to take risk. At the same time, Gascon is knowledgeable and confident about financial markets and responds to the questionnaire with answers that suggest risk tolerance. This result suggests he also has a high *willingness* to take risk.

EXAMPLE 3

The Case of Jacques Gascon: Risk Tolerance

1. Marie Gascon is so pleased with the services provided by her financial adviser that she suggests to her brother Jacques that he should also consult the adviser. Jacques thinks it is a good idea. Jacques, a self-employed computer consultant also based in Paris, is 40 years old and divorced with four children, aged between 12 and 16. The financial adviser notes the following aspects of Jacques' situation:

   - Jacques' consultancy earnings average €40,000 per annum but are quite volatile.
   - Jacques is required to pay €10,000 per year to his ex-wife and children.
   - Jacques has a mortgage on his apartment of €100,000 and €10,000 of savings.
   - Jacques has a good knowledge of financial matters and expects that equity markets will deliver very high returns over the long term.
   - In the risk tolerance questionnaire, Jacques strongly disagrees with the statements "I am more comfortable putting my money in a bank account than in the stock market" and "When I think of the word 'risk,' the term 'loss' comes to mind immediately."

- Jacques expects that most of his savings will be required to support his children at university.

Based only on the information given, which statement is correct?

A. Jacques has a low ability to take risk but a high willingness to take risk.

B. Jacques has a high ability to take risk but a low willingness to take risk.

C. Jacques has a high ability to take risk and a high willingness to take risk.

Solution:

A is correct. Jacques does not have a particularly high income, his income is unstable, and he has reasonably high outgoings for his mortgage and maintenance payments. His investment time horizon is approximately two to six years given the ages of his children and his desire to support them at university. This finely balanced financial situation and short time horizon suggests a low ability to take risk. In contrast, his expectations for financial market returns and risk tolerance questionnaire answers suggest a high willingness to take risk. The financial adviser may wish to explain to Jacques how finely balanced his financial situation is and suggest that, despite his desire to take more risk, a relatively cautious portfolio might be the most appropriate approach to take.

Return Objectives

A client's return objectives can be stated in a number of ways. Similar to risk objectives, return objectives may be stated on an absolute or a relative basis.

As an example of an absolute objective, the client may want to achieve a particular percentage rate of return. This objective could be a nominal rate of return or could be expressed in real (inflation-adjusted) terms.

Alternatively, the return objective can be stated on a relative basis—for example, relative to a benchmark return. The benchmark could be an equity market index, such as the S&P 500 or the FTSE 100, or a cash rate of interest such as the market reference rate (MRR). A relative return objective might be stated as, for example, a desire to outperform the benchmark index by one percentage point per year.

Some institutions also set their return objectives relative to a peer group or universe of managers—for example, an endowment aiming for a return that is in the top 50% of returns of similar institutions, or a private equity mandate aiming for returns in the top quartile among the private equity universe. This objective can be problematic when limited information is known about the investment strategies or the return calculation methodology being used by peers, and we must bear in mind the impossibility of *all* institutions being "above average." Furthermore, a good benchmark should be investable—that is, able to be replicated by the investor—and a peer benchmark typically does not meet that criterion.

In each case, the return requirement can be stated before or after fees. Care should be taken that the fee basis used is clear and understood by both the manager and client. The return can also be stated on either a pre- or post-tax basis when the investor is required to pay tax. For a taxable investor, the baseline is to state and analyze returns on an after-tax basis.

The return objective could be a required return—that is, the amount the investor needs to earn to meet a particular future goal—such as a certain level of retirement income.

The manager or adviser must ensure that the return objective is realistic. Care should be taken that client and manager are in agreement on whether the return objective is nominal (which is more convenient for measurement purposes) or real (i.e., inflation-adjusted, which usually relates better to the objective). It must be consistent with the client's risk objective (high expected returns are unlikely to be possible without high levels of risk) and also with the current economic and market environment. For example, 15% nominal returns might be possible when inflation is 10% but will be unlikely when inflation is 3%.

When a client has unrealistic return expectations, the manager or adviser will need to counsel her about what is achievable in the current market environment and within the client's tolerance for risk.

EXAMPLE 4

The Case of Marie Gascon: Return Objectives

Having assessed her risk tolerance, Marie Gascon now begins to discuss her retirement income needs with the financial adviser. She wishes to retire at age 50, which is 20 years from now. Her salary meets current and expected future expenditure requirements, but she does not expect to be able to make any additional pension contributions to her fund. Gascon sets aside €100,000 of her savings as an emergency fund to be held in cash. The remaining €900,000 is invested for her retirement.

Gascon estimates that a before-tax amount of €2,000,000 in today's money will be sufficient to fund her retirement income needs. The financial adviser expects inflation to average 2% per year over the next 20 years. Pension fund contributions and pension fund returns in France are exempt from tax, but pension fund distributions are taxable upon retirement.

1. Which of the following is closest to the amount of money Gascon will have to accumulate in nominal terms by her retirement date to meet her retirement income objective (i.e., expressed in money of the day in 20 years)?

   A. €900,000

   B. €2,000,000

   C. €3,000,000

Solution:

C is correct. At 2% annual inflation, €2,000,000 in today's money equates to €2,971,895 in 20 years measured in money of the day [$€2,000,000 \times (1 + 2\%)^{20}$].

2. Which of the following is closest to the annual rate of return that Gascon must earn on her pension portfolio to meet her retirement income objective?

   A. 2.0%

   B. 6.2%

   C. 8.1%

Solution:

B is correct. €900,000 growing at 6.2% per year for 20 years will accumulate to €2,997,318, which is just above the required amount. (The solution of

6.2% comes from €2,997,318/€900,000 = $(1 + X)^{20}$, where X is the required rate of return.)

4 IPS CONSTRAINTS

- ☐ describe the major components of an IPS
- ☐ describe the investment constraints of liquidity, time horizon, tax concerns, legal and regulatory factors, and unique circumstances and their implications for the choice of portfolio assets

In the following sections, we analyze five major types of constraints on portfolio selection: liquidity, time horizon, tax concerns, legal and regulatory factors, and unique circumstances.

Liquidity Requirements

The IPS should state what the likely requirements are to withdraw funds from the portfolio. Examples for an individual investor would be outlays for covering healthcare payments or tuition fees. For institutions, it could be spending rules and requirements for endowment funds, the existence of claims coming due in the case of property and casualty insurance, or benefit payments for pension funds and life insurance companies.

When the client does have such a requirement, the manager should allocate part of the portfolio to cover the liability. This part of the portfolio will be invested in assets that are liquid—that is, easily converted to cash—and have low risk when the liquidity need is actually present (e.g., a bond maturing at the time when private education expenses will be incurred), so that their value is known with reasonable certainty. For example, the asset allocation in the insurance portfolios of US insurer Progressive Corporation (see Exhibit 3) shows a large allocation to fixed-income investments (called "Fixed maturities" by the company), some of which are either highly liquid or have a short maturity. These investments enable the company, in the case of automobile insurance, to pay claims for which the timing is unpredictable.

Exhibit 3: Asset Allocation of Progressive Corporation

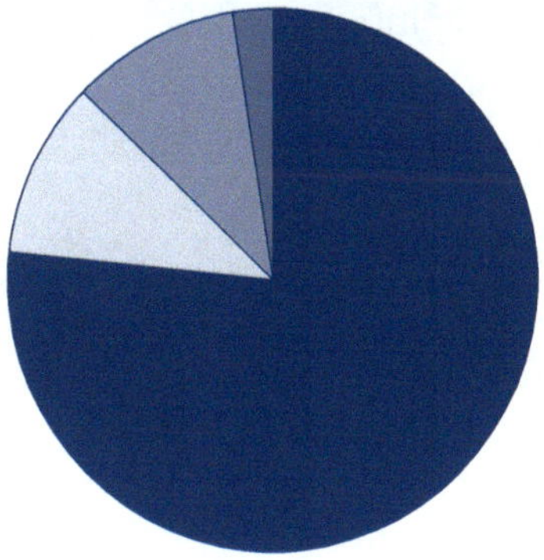

Source: Progressive Corporation, 2018 Second Quarter Report.

Time Horizon

The IPS should state the time horizon over which the investor is investing. It may be the period over which the portfolio is accumulating before any assets need to be withdrawn; it could also be the period until the client's circumstances are likely to change. For example, a 55-year-old pension plan investor hoping to retire at age 65 has a 10-year horizon. The portfolio may not be liquidated at age 65, but its structure may need to change, for example, as the investor begins to draw an income from the fund.

The time horizon of the investor will affect the nature of investments used in the portfolio. Illiquid or risky investments may be unsuitable for an investor with a short time horizon because the investor may not have enough time to recover from investment losses, for example. Such investments, however, may be suitable for an investor with a longer horizon, especially if the risky investments are expected to have higher returns.

EXAMPLE 5

Investment Time Horizon

1. Frank Johnson is investing for retirement and has a 20-year horizon. He has an average risk tolerance. Which investment is likely to be the *least* suitable for a major allocation in Johnson's portfolio?

   A. Listed equities

   B. Private equity

   C. US Treasury bills

Solution:

C is correct. With a 20-year horizon and average risk tolerance, Johnson can accept the additional risk of listed equities and private equity compared with US Treasury bills.

2. Al Smith has to pay a large tax bill in six months and wants to invest the money in the meantime. Which investment is likely to be the *least* suitable for a major allocation in Smith's portfolio?

   A. Listed equities

   B. Private equity

   C. US Treasury bills

Solution:

B is correct. Private equity is risky, has no public market, and is the least liquid among the assets mentioned.

Tax Concerns

Tax status varies among investors. Some investors will be subject to taxation on investment returns and some will not. For example, in many countries, returns to pension funds are exempt from tax. Some investors will face a different tax rate on income (dividends and interest payments) than they do on capital gains (associated with increases in asset prices). Typically, when there is a differential, income is taxed more highly than gains. Gains may be subject to a lower tax rate, or part or all of the gain may be exempt from taxation. Furthermore, income may be taxed as it is earned, whereas gains may be taxed when they are realized. Hence, in such cases there is a time value of money benefit in the deferment of taxation of gains relative to income.

In many cases, the portfolio should reflect the tax status of the client. For example, a taxable investor may wish to hold a portfolio that emphasizes capital gains and receives little income. A taxable investor based in the United States is also likely to consider including US municipal bonds ("munis") in his portfolio because interest income from munis, unlike from Treasuries and corporate bonds, is exempt from taxes. A tax-exempt investor, such as a pension fund, will be relatively indifferent to the form of returns.

Legal and Regulatory Factors

The IPS should state any legal and regulatory restrictions that constrain how the portfolio is invested.

In some countries, such institutional investors as pension funds are subject to restrictions on portfolio composition. For example, there may be a limit on the proportion of equities or other risky assets in the portfolio or on the proportion of the portfolio that may be invested overseas. The United States has no limits on pension fund asset allocation, but some countries do, examples of which are shown in Exhibit 4. Pension funds also often face restrictions on the percentage of assets that can be invested in securities issued by the plan sponsor, so called **self-investment limits**.

Exhibit 4: Examples of Pension Fund Investment Restrictions

Country	Listed Equity	Real Estate	Government Bonds	Corporate Bonds	Foreign Currency Exposure
Switzerland	50%	30%	100%	100%	Unhedged 30%
Japan	100%	Not permitted	100%	100%	No limits
South Africa	75%	25%	100%	75%	25%

Source: OECD "Survey of Investment Regulations of Pension Funds," July 2018.

When an individual has access to material nonpublic information about a particular security, this situation may also form a constraint. For example, the directors of a public company may need to refrain from trading the company's stock at certain points of the year before financial results are published. The IPS should note this constraint so that the portfolio manager does not inadvertently trade the stock on the client's behalf.

Unique Circumstances and ESG Considerations

This section of the IPS should cover any other aspect of the client's circumstances, including beliefs and values, that is likely to have a material impact on portfolio composition. A client may have considerations derived from her faith or moral values that could constrain investment choices. For instance, an investor seeking compliance with Shari'a (the Islamic law) will avoid investing in businesses and financial instruments inconsistent with Shari'a, such as casinos and bonds, because Shari'a prohibits gambling and lending money on interest. Similarly, an investor may wish to avoid investments that he believes are inconsistent with his faith. Charitable and pension fund investors may have constituencies that want to express their values in an investment portfolio.

Whether rooted in religious beliefs or not, a client may have personal objections to certain products (e.g., weapons, tobacco, gambling) or practices (e.g., environmental impact of business activities, human impact of government policies, labor standards), which could lead to the exclusion of certain companies, countries, or types of securities (e.g., interest-bearing debt) from the investable universe as well as the client's benchmark. Investing in accordance with such considerations is referred to as socially responsible investing (SRI).

Specific ESG investment approaches can be classified in a variety of ways, and the investment community lacks clear consensus on terminology. We define six generic ESG investment approaches:

- *Negative screening*: Excluding companies or sectors based on business activities or environmental or social concerns;
- *Positive screening*: Including sectors or companies based on specific ESG criteria, typically ESG performance relative to industry peers;
- *ESG integration*: Systematic consideration of material ESG factors in asset allocation, security selection, and portfolio construction decisions;
- *Thematic investing*: Investing in themes or assets related to ESG factors;
- *Engagement/active ownership*: Using shareholder power to influence corporate behavior to achieve targeted ESG objectives along with financial returns; and
- *Impact investing*: Investments made with the intention to generate positive, measurable social and environmental impact alongside a financial return.

These ESG investment approaches may impact a portfolio manager's investment universe and may also require the investment management firm to put in place a process to systematically incorporate ESG factors into the investment process.

EXAMPLE 6

Ethical Preferences

The BMO Responsible UK Equity Fund is designed for investors who wish to have ethical and ESG principles applied to the selection of their investments. The fund's managers apply both positive (features to be emphasized in the portfolio) and negative (features to be avoided in the portfolio) screening criteria:

Product-Based Screening Criteria

- Alcohol
- Arctic and oil sands
- Coal mining
- Gambling
- Nuclear power generation
- Pornography
- Tobacco
- Weapons

Conduct-Based Screening Criteria

Environmental

- Environmental management

Social

- Animal welfare
- Health and safety
- Human rights and oppressive regimes
- Labor standards

Governance

- Business ethics

[Excerpted from BMO Responsible UK Equity Fund documents; https://www.bmogam.com/gb-en/intermediary/bmo-responsible-uk-equity-2-inc/.]

When the portfolio represents only part of the client's total wealth, there may be aspects or portions of wealth not under the control of the manager that have implications for the portfolio. For example, an employee of a public company whose labor income and retirement income provision are reliant on that company, and who may have substantial investment exposure to the company through employee share options and stock holdings, may decide that his portfolio should not invest additional amounts in that stock. An entrepreneur may be reluctant to see her portfolio invested in the shares of competing businesses or in any business that has risk exposures aligned with her entrepreneurial venture.

A client's income may rely on a particular industry or asset class. Appropriate diversification requires that industry or asset class to be de-emphasized in the client's investments. For example, a stockbroker should consider having a relatively low weighting in equities, as his skills and thus his income-generating ability are worth less when equities do not perform well. Employees should similarly be wary of having concentrated share positions in the equity of the company where they work. If the employer encounters difficulties, not only may its employees lose their jobs but their investment portfolios could also suffer a significant loss of value.

GATHERING CLIENT INFORMATION

5

- ☐ describe risk and return objectives and how they may be developed for a client
- ☐ describe the investment constraints of liquidity, time horizon, tax concerns, legal and regulatory factors, and unique circumstances and their implications for the choice of portfolio assets

As noted earlier, it is important for portfolio managers and investment advisers to know their clients. For example, in the EU, MiFID II requires financial intermediaries to undertake substantial fact finding. This is required not only in the case of full-service wealth management or in the context of an IPS but also in "lighter" forms of financial intermediation, such as advisory relationships (in which clients make investment decisions after consultation with their investment adviser or broker) or execution-only relationships (in which the client makes investment decisions independently).

An exercise in fact finding about the customer should take place at the beginning of the client relationship. This process will involve gathering information about the client's circumstances as well as discussing the client's objectives and requirements.

Important data to gather from a client should cover family and employment situation as well as financial information. If the client is an individual, it may also be necessary to know about the situation and requirements of the client's spouse or other family members. The health of the client and her dependents is also relevant information. In an institutional relationship, it will be important to know about key stakeholders in the organization and what their perspective and requirements are. Information gathering may be done in an informal way or may involve structured interviews, questionnaires, or analysis of data. Many advisers will capture data electronically and use special systems that record data and produce customized reports.

Good recordkeeping is very important and may be crucial in a case in which any aspect of the client relationship comes into dispute at a later stage.

EXAMPLE 7

Marie Gascon: Description of Constraints

Marie Gascon continues to discuss her investment requirements with her financial adviser. The adviser begins to draft the constraints section of the IPS.

Gascon expects that she will continue to work for the oil company and that her relatively high income will continue for the foreseeable future. Gascon and her husband plan to have no additional children but expect that their son will go to a university at age 18. They expect that their son's education costs can be met out of their salary income.

Gascon's emergency reserve of €100,000 is considered to be sufficient as a reserve for unforeseen expenditures and emergencies. Her retirement savings of €900,000 has been contributed to her defined-contribution pension plan account to fund her retirement. Under French regulation, pension fund contributions are paid from gross income (i.e., income prior to deduction of tax), and pension fund returns are exempt from tax, but pension payments from a fund to retirees are taxed as income to the retiree.

With respect to Gascon's retirement savings portfolio, refer back to Example 2 as needed and address the following:

1. As concerns liquidity,

   A. a maximum of 50% of the portfolio should be invested in liquid assets.

   B. the portfolio should be invested entirely in liquid assets because of high spending needs.

   C. the portfolio has no need for liquidity because there are no short-term spending requirements.

Solution:

C is correct. The assets are for retirement use, which is 20 years away. Any short-term spending needs will be met from other assets or income.

2. The investment time horizon is closest to

   A. 5 years.

   B. 20 years.

   C. 40 years.

Solution:

B is correct. The relevant time horizon is to the retirement date, which is 20 years away. The assets may not be liquidated at that point, but a restructuring of the portfolio is to be expected as Gascon starts to draw an income from it.

3. As concerns taxation, the portfolio

   A. should emphasize capital gains because income is taxable.

   B. should emphasize income because capital gains are taxable.

   C. is tax exempt and thus indifferent between income and capital gains.

Solution:

C is correct. Because no tax is paid in the pension fund, it does not matter whether returns come in the form of income or capital gains.

4. The principle legal and regulatory factors applying to the portfolio are

   A. US securities laws.

   B. European banking laws.

   C. French pension fund regulations.

Solution:

C is correct. Management of the portfolio will have to comply with any rules relating to French pension funds.

5. As concerns unique needs, the portfolio should

   A. have a high weighting in oil and other commodity stocks.

   B. be invested only in responsible and sustainable investments.

C. not have significant exposure to oil and other commodity stocks.

Solution:

C is correct. Gascon's human capital (i.e., future labor income) is affected by the prospects of the oil industry. If her portfolio has significant exposure to oil stocks, she would be increasing a risk exposure she already has.

Example 8, the final one based on Marie Gascon, shows how the information obtained from the fact-finding exercises might be incorporated into the objectives and constraints section of an IPS.

EXAMPLE 8

Marie Gascon: Outline of an IPS

Following is a simplified excerpt from the IPS the adviser prepares for Marie Gascon, covering objectives and constraints.

Risk Objectives:

- The portfolio may take on relatively high amounts of risk in seeking to meet the return requirements. With a 20-year time horizon and significant assets and income, the client has an above-average ability to take risk. The client is a knowledgeable investor, with an above-average willingness to take risk. Hence, the client's risk tolerance is above average, explaining the aforementioned portfolio risk objective.
- The portfolio should be well diversified with respect to asset classes and concentration of positions within an asset class. Although the client has above-average risk tolerance, his investment assets should be diversified to control the risk of catastrophic loss.

Return Objectives:

- The portfolio's long-term return requirement is 6.2% per year, in nominal terms and net of fees, to meet the client's retirement income goal.

Constraints:

- *Liquidity*: The portfolio consists of pension fund assets, and there is no need for liquidity in the short to medium term.
- *Time Horizon*: The portfolio will be invested with a 20-year time horizon. The client intends to retire in 20 years, at which time an income will be drawn from the portfolio.
- *Tax Status*: Under French law, contributions to the fund are made gross of tax and returns in the fund are tax-free. Hence, the client is indifferent between income and capital gains in the fund.
- *Legal and Regulatory Factors*: Management of the portfolio must comply with French pension fund regulations.
- *Unique Needs*: The client is an executive in the oil industry. The portfolio should strive to minimize additional exposures to oil and related stocks.

6 PORTFOLIO CONSTRUCTION AND CAPITAL MARKET EXPECTATIONS

- ☐ explain the specification of asset classes in relation to asset allocation
- ☐ describe the principles of portfolio construction and the role of asset allocation in relation to the IPS

Once the IPS has been compiled, the investment manager can construct a suitable portfolio. Strategic asset allocation is a traditional focus of the first steps in portfolio construction. The strategic asset allocation is stated in terms of percentage allocations to asset classes. An **asset class** is a category of assets that have similar characteristics, attributes, and risk–return relationships. The **strategic asset allocation** (SAA) is the set of exposures to IPS-permissible asset classes that is expected to achieve the client's long-term objectives given the client's risk profile and investment constraints. An SAA could include a policy of hedging portfolio risks not explicitly covered by asset class weights. The obvious examples are hedge ratios for foreign currency exposure, or the management of interest rate risk resulting from asset-liability mismatch, and the hedging of inflation risk. So-called "overlay" portfolios of derivatives are often used for this purpose.

The focus on the SAA is the result of a number of important investment principles. One principle is that a portfolio's systematic risk accounts for most of its change in value over the long term. **Systematic risk** is risk related to the economic system (e.g., risk related to business cycle) that cannot be eliminated by holding a diversified portfolio. This risk is different from **nonsystematic risk**, defined as the unique risks of particular assets, which may be avoided by holding other assets with offsetting risks. A second principle is that the returns to groups of similar assets (e.g., long-term debt claims) predictably reflect exposures to certain sets of systematic factors (e.g., for the debt claims, unexpected changes in the interest rate). Thus, the SAA is a means of providing the investor with exposure to the systematic risks of asset classes in proportions that meet the risk and return objectives.

The process of formulating a strategic asset allocation is based on the IPS, already discussed, and capital market expectations.

Capital Market Expectations

Capital market expectations are the investor's expectations concerning the risk and return prospects of asset classes, however broadly or narrowly the investor defines those asset classes. When associated with the client's investment objectives, the result is the strategic asset allocation that is expected to allow the client to achieve his investment objectives (at least under normal capital market conditions).

Traditionally, capital market expectations are quantified in terms of asset class expected returns, standard deviation of returns, and correlations among pairs of asset classes. Formally, the expected return of an asset class consists of the risk-free rate and one or more risk premium(s) associated with the asset class. Expected returns are in practice developed in a variety of ways, including the use of historical estimates, economic analysis, and various kinds of valuation models. Standard deviations and correlation estimates are frequently based on historical data and risk models.

STRATEGIC ASSET ALLOCATION 7

- ☐ explain the specification of asset classes in relation to asset allocation
- ☐ describe the principles of portfolio construction and the role of asset allocation in relation to the IPS

Traditionally, investors have distinguished cash, equities, bonds (government and corporate), and real estate as the major asset classes. In recent years, this list has been expanded with private equity, hedge funds, high-yield and emerging market bonds, and commodities. In addition, such assets as art and intellectual property rights may be considered asset classes for those investors prepared to take a more innovative approach and to accept some illiquidity. Combining such new asset classes as well as hedge funds and private equity under the header "alternative investments" has become accepted practice.

As the strategic asset allocation is built up by asset classes, the decision about how to define those asset classes is an important one. Defining the asset classes also determines the extent to which the investor controls the risk and return characteristics of the eventual investment portfolio. For example, separating bonds into government bonds and corporate bonds, and then further separating corporate bonds into investment grade and non-investment grade (high yield) and government bonds into domestic and foreign government bonds, creates four bond categories. For these categories, risk–return expectations can be expressed and correlations with other asset classes (and, in an asset–liability management context, with the liabilities) can be estimated. An investment manager who wants to explicitly consider the risk–return characteristics of those bond categories in the strategic asset allocation may choose to treat them as distinct asset classes. Similarly, in equities, some investors distinguish between emerging market and developed market equities, between domestic and international equities, or between large-cap and small-cap equities. In some regulatory environments for institutional investors, asset class definitions are mandatory, thereby forcing investment managers to articulate risk–return expectations (and apply risk management) on the asset classes specified. Conversely, a broader categorization of asset classes leaves the allocation between different categories of bonds and equities, for example, to managers responsible for these asset classes.

When defining asset classes, a number of criteria apply. Intuitively, an asset class should contain relatively homogeneous assets while providing diversification relative to other asset classes. In statistical terms, risk and return expectations should be similar, and paired correlations of assets should be relatively high within an asset class but should be lower versus assets in other asset classes. Also, the asset classes, while being mutually exclusive, should add up to a sufficient approximation of the relevant investable universe. Applying these criteria ensures that the strategic asset allocation process has considered all available investment alternatives.

EXAMPLE 9

Specifying Asset Classes

The strategic asset allocations of many institutional investors make a distinction between domestic equities and international equities or between developed market equities and emerging market equities. Often, equities are separated into different market capitalization brackets, resulting, for example, in an asset class such as domestic small-cap equity.

The correlation matrix in Exhibit 5 shows the paired correlations of monthly returns between different equity asset classes and other asset classes. Specifically, these correlations are measured over the period from December 2000 through August 2018. In addition, the exhibit shows the annualized volatility of monthly returns.

Exhibit 5: Asset Class Correlation Matrix

Correlations	US Equities	Emerging Markets	European Equities	Japanese Equities	US Small-Cap Equities	Commod-ities	European Gov't. Bonds	US Treasuries	US Credits	US High-Yield Credit
US Equities	1.00	0.78	0.88	0.59	0.89	0.32	0.08	−0.37	0.19	0.66
Emerging Markets Equities	0.78	1.00	0.84	0.64	0.75	0.46	0.21	−0.24	0.34	0.70
European Equities	0.88	0.84	1.00	0.64	0.79	0.43	0.16	−0.28	0.29	0.68
Japanese Equities	0.59	0.64	0.64	1.00	0.57	0.32	0.24	−0.18	0.29	0.52
US Small-Cap Equities	0.89	0.75	0.79	0.57	1.00	0.32	0.09	−0.36	0.19	0.69
Commodities	0.32	0.46	0.43	0.32	0.32	1.00	0.13	−0.18	0.12	0.36
European Gov't. Bonds	0.08	0.21	0.16	0.24	0.09	0.13	1.00	0.45	0.60	0.30
US Treasuries	−0.37	−0.24	−0.28	−0.18	−0.36	−0.18	0.45	1.00	0.58	−0.19
US Credits	0.19	0.34	0.29	0.29	0.19	0.12	0.60	0.58	1.00	0.54
US High-Yield Credit	0.66	0.70	0.68	0.52	0.69	0.36	0.30	−0.19	0.54	1.00
Volatility	14.3%	21.6%	18.4%	15.6%	18.4%	22.3%	4.9%	4.4%	5.5%	9.3%

Correlations and volatilities have been calculated using monthly returns from December 2000 through August 2018, unhedged, in USD.

Source: MSCI Bloomberg, S&P

Based only on the information given, address the following:

1. Contrast the correlations between equity asset classes with the correlations between equity asset classes and US Treasuries.

Solution:

The matrix reveals very strong correlation between the equity asset classes. For example, the correlation between European equities and US equities is 0.88. The correlation of equities with bonds, however, is much lower. For example, US equities, emerging markets equities, European equities, and Japanese equities all have negative correlation with US government bonds (−0.37, −0.24 and −0.28, and −0.18, respectively). It is worth noting, however, that correlations can vary through time and the values shown may be specific to the sample period used.

2. The monthly returns of which equity asset class differ the most from US equities?

Solution:

Among equity asset classes as listed in the table, the correlation between US and Japanese equities is the lowest, at 0.59. By contrast, correlations between US equities and emerging markets, European, and US small cap equities are 0.78 or higher.

Using correlation as a metric, Example 9 tends to indicate that only emerging markets were well differentiated from European equities. So, why do investors still often subdivide equities? Apart from any regulatory reasons, one explanation might be that this decomposition into smaller asset classes corresponds to the way the asset allocation is structured in portfolios. Many investment managers have expertise exclusively in specific areas of the market, such as emerging market equities, US small-cap equity, or international investment-grade credit. Bringing the asset class definitions of the asset allocation in line with investment products actually available in the market may simplify matters from an organizational perspective.

The risk–return profile of the strategic asset allocation depends on the expected returns and risks of the individual asset classes, as well as the correlation between those asset classes. In general, adding assets classes with low correlation improves the risk–return trade-off (more return for similar risk). Typically, the strategic asset allocation for risk-averse investors will have a large weight in government bonds and cash, whereas those with more willingness and ability to take risk will have more of their assets in risky asset classes, such as equities and many types of alternative investments.

It is customary to represent asset classes using benchmarks and universes calculated by providers such as FTSE, MSCI, or Bloomberg. A negative screening or a **best-in-class** policy (discussed previously) limits the number of securities to choose from, potentially impacting the risk and expected return estimates for these asset classes. Some examples of exclusions may be controversial weaponry or tobacco companies, or investments in certain countries. When such exclusions apply, risk and return estimates based on non-traditional ("off-the-shelf") asset class benchmarks may not be applicable. Separate benchmark indices reflecting the exclusions may be available from the providers to mitigate this issue.

ABP is the pension fund for the Dutch government sector employees. The fund offers teachers, police officers, members of the military, and other civil servants a defined benefit pension plan, aiming for a pension of 70% of the average career real income for employees. As of the first quarter of 2018, ABP had €405 billion under management. The strategic asset allocation as of this period is shown in Exhibit 6.

Exhibit 6: Strategic Asset Allocation for ABP

Equity	
Equities, developed countries	27%
Equities, emerging markets	9%
Total equity	***36%***

Equity	
Alternatives	
Real estate	10%
Private equity	5%
Hedge funds	4%
Commodities	5%
Infrastructure	3%
Total alternatives	***27%***
Fixed-income securities	
Government bonds	13%
Corporate bonds	13%
Inflation-linked bonds	8%
Emerging market bonds	3%
Total fixed income	***37%***
Total	100%

Source: ABP Quarterly Report Q1 2018

A strategic asset allocation results from combining the constraints and objectives articulated in the IPS and long-term capital market expectations regarding the asset classes. The strategic asset allocation or policy portfolio will subsequently be implemented into real portfolios. Exhibit 7 illustrates conceptually how investment objectives and constraints and long-term capital market expectations combine into a policy portfolio.

Exhibit 7: Strategic Asset Allocation Process

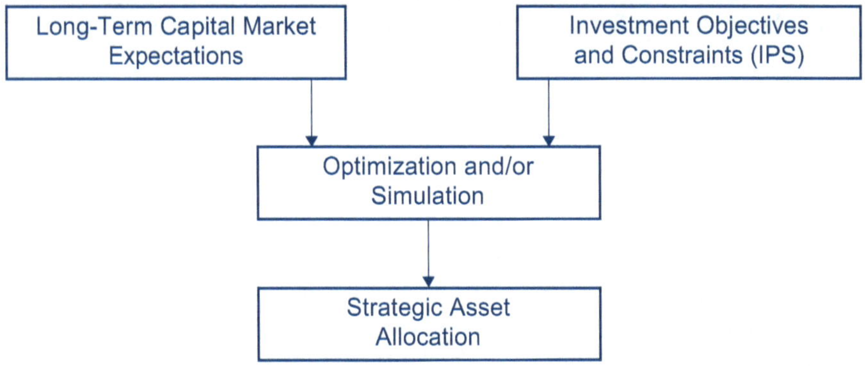

In some frameworks used in practice, the asset allocation is an integral part of the investment policy statement. This presentation, however, keeps the asset allocation separate from the investment policy statement because clients' investment objectives and constraints qualitatively differ in nature from capital market expectations, thus requiring different types of analysis, different sources of information, and different review cycles.

The combination of investment objectives/constraints and capital market expectations theoretically occurs using optimization techniques. In this section, we apply mean–variance optimization to a sample set of investment objectives and constraints, using an investment universe with associated market expectations. We assume that investors choosing from a range of asset allocations with similar returns would prefer those with lower risk. Choosing from allocations with similar levels of risk, investors would prefer those with the highest return. Formally, investors' risk and return objectives can be described as a utility function, in which utility increases with higher expected returns and lower risk. This assumption could yield an expected utility equation such as that shown in Equation 1.[4]

$$U_p = E\left(R_p\right) - \lambda \sigma_p^2 \quad (1)$$

where

U_p = the investor's expected utility from the portfolio

$E(R_p)$ = the expected return of the portfolio

σ_p = the standard deviation of returns of the portfolio

λ = a measure of the investor's risk aversion

This utility function expresses a positive relationship between utility and expected portfolio return (i.e., higher expected return increases utility, all else equal) and a negative relationship between utility and volatility of portfolio return as measured by the variance of portfolio returns. The stronger the negative relationship, the greater the investor's risk aversion. The portfolio is understood to represent a particular asset allocation. The asset allocation providing the highest expected utility is the one that is optimal for the investor given his or her risk aversion.

For different values of U_p, a line can be plotted that links those combinations of risk and expected return that produces that level of utility: an indifference curve. An investor would attain equal utility from all risk–return combinations on that curve.

Capital market expectations, specified in asset classes' expected returns, standard deviations of return, and correlations, translate into an efficient frontier of portfolios. A multi-asset class portfolio's expected return is given by

$$E\left(R_p\right) = \sum_{i=1}^{n} w_i E\left(R_i\right) \quad (2)$$

where w_i equals the weight of asset class i in the portfolio, and its risk is given by

$$\sigma_p = \sqrt{\sum_{i=1}^{n}\sum_{j=1}^{n} w_{p,i} w_{p,j} \text{Cov}\left(R_i, R_j\right)} \quad (3)$$

The covariance between the returns on asset classes i and j is given by the product of the correlation between the two asset classes and their standard deviations of return:

$$\text{Cov}(R_i,R_j) = \rho_{i,j}\sigma_i\sigma_j \quad (4)$$

where

$\text{Cov}(R_i,R_j)$ = the covariance between the return of asset classes i and j

$\rho_{i,j}$ = the correlation between the returns of asset classes i and j

The resulting portfolios can be represented as a scatter of dots in a chart depicting their risk and expected return. Because a portfolio's risk is a positive function of the risk of its assets and the correlations among them, a portfolio consisting of risky assets with low correlation has lower risk than one with similarly risky assets with high correlation. It is therefore possible to construct different portfolios with equal expected returns but with different levels of risk. The line that connects those

4 Sharpe, Chen, Pinto, and McLeavey (2007).

portfolios with the minimal risk for each level of expected return (above that of the **minimum-variance portfolio**—the portfolio with the minimum variance for each given level of expected return) is the efficient frontier. Clearly, the efficient frontier will move "upward" as more low-correlation assets with sufficient expected return are added to the mix because it lowers the risk in the portfolios for equal expected returns. Similarly, when return expectations increase for asset classes while volatility and correlation assumptions remain unchanged, the efficient frontier will move upward because each portfolio is able to generate higher returns for the same level of risk.

Both the efficient frontier and a range of indifference curves can be plotted in the risk–return space. In Exhibit 8, the dark-colored curves that are concave from below represent efficient frontiers associated with different assumed expected returns. The lighter-colored curves are indifference curves. The point where the efficient frontier intersects with the indifference curve with the highest utility attainable (i.e., the point of tangency) represents the optimal asset allocation for the client/investor. In Exhibit 8, efficient frontier 1 has a point of tangency with indifference curve 1. Higher levels of utility, such as those associated with indifference curve 0, can apparently not be reached with the assets underlying the efficient frontier. It is clear that when capital market expectations change, this change moves the efficient frontier away from its original location. In the chart, this movement is illustrated by efficient frontier 2, which incorporates different capital market expectations. This new efficient frontier has a point of tangency with indifference curve 2, which is associated with a lower level of expected utility. Because the point of tangency represents the strategic asset allocation, it implies the asset allocation should be adjusted. Similarly, should investment objectives or constraints change, the indifference curves will change their shape and location. This change will again move the point of tangency, and hence change the asset allocation.

Exhibit 8: Strategic Asset Allocation Efficient Frontier

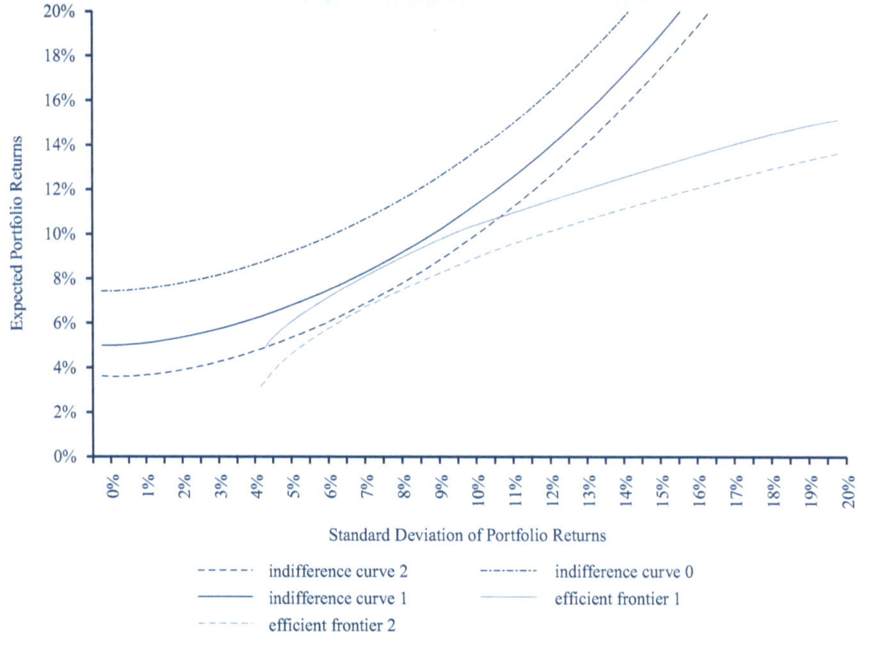

This framework describes how investor objectives and capital market expectations should theoretically be reconciled. It will, however, not be the exact procedure that in practice will be followed. First, an IPS does not necessarily translate the client's investment objectives and constraint into a utility function. Rather, an IPS gives threshold levels for risk and expected return, combined with a number of additional constraints that cannot be captured in this model. Second, the model illustrated is a single-period model, whereas in practice, the constraints from the IPS will make it more appropriate to use multi-period models. Multi-period problems can be more effectively addressed using simulation.

EXAMPLE 10

Approaching a SAA for a Private Investor

1. Rainer Gottschalk recently sold his local home construction company in the south of Germany to a large homebuilder with a nationwide reach. Upon selling his company, he accepted a job as regional manager for that nationwide homebuilder. Gottschalk is now considering his and his family's financial future. He looks forward to his new job—he likes his new role, and the position provides him with income to fulfill his family's short-term and medium-term liquidity needs. Gottschalk feels strongly that he should not invest the proceeds of the sale of his company in real estate because his income already depends on the state of the real estate market. Also, reflecting family values, he feels strongly that his savings should not support the tobacco industry. He therefore wants his equity allocation to exclude any stocks of tobacco product manufacturers or retailers. Gottschalk consults a financial adviser from his bank about how to invest his money to retire in good wealth in 20 years.

   The IPS developed by his adviser suggests a return objective of 5%, with a standard deviation of 10%. The bank's asset management division provides Gottschalk and his adviser with the following data (Exhibit 9, Panel 1) on market expectations. The adviser estimates that excluding the tobacco industry from the investment universe affects expected equity returns of European equities by −0.2% and annual standard deviation by +0.1%. The impact on emerging market equities, and on the correlation structure, was considered negligible. Gottschalk accepts the results of these calculations as shown in Exhibit 9, Panel 2.

Exhibit 9: Risk, Return, and Correlation Estimates

			Correlation Matrix		
	Expected Return	Standard Deviation	European Equities	Emerging Mkt Equities	European Govt Bonds
Panel 1					
European equities	6.0%	15.0%	1.00	0.78	−0.08
Emerging market equities	8.0%	20.1%	0.78	1.00	−0.07
European government bonds	2.0%	7.8%	−0.08	−0.07	1.00
Panel 2					

	Expected Return	Standard Deviation	Correlation Matrix European Equities	Emerging Mkt Equities	European Govt Bonds
European equities	5.8%	15.1%	1.00	0.78	−0.08
Emerging market equities	8.0%	20.1%	0.78	1.00	−0.07
European government bonds	2.00%	7.8%	−0.08	−0.07	1.00

Standard deviation and correlation calculated over the period March 1999–August 2018. All data in unhedged euros.

Sources: MSCI, Bloomberg

To illustrate the possibilities, the adviser presents Gottschalk with the following plot (Exhibit 10), in which the points forming the shaded curve outline the risk–return characteristics of the portfolios that can be constructed out of the three asset classes. An imaginary line linking the points with the lowest standard deviation for each attainable level of return would be the efficient frontier. The two straight lines show the risk and return objectives. Gottschalk should aim for portfolios that offer an expected return of at least 6% (the straight horizontal line or above) and a standard deviation of return of 12% or lower (the straight vertical line to the left).

Exhibit 10: Efficient Frontier

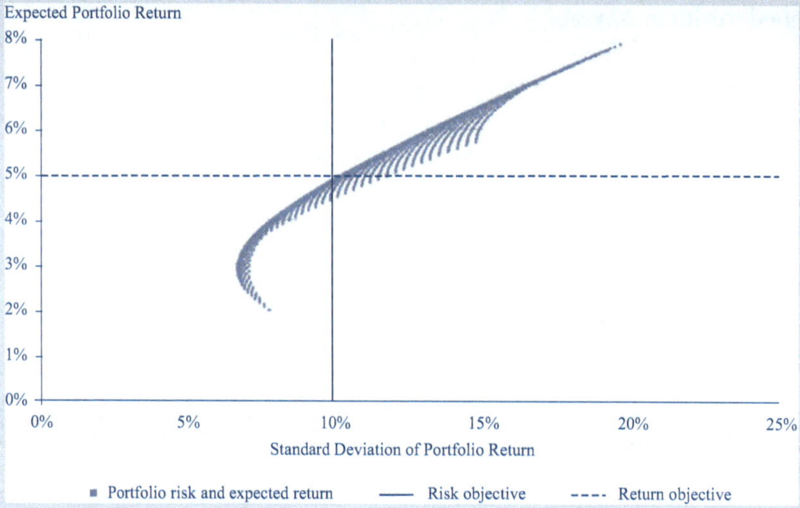

Exhibit 10 shows that no portfolio satisfies the two objectives (return of 5% and standard deviation of 10%) exactly, because the highest expected return that can be attained at a maximum volatility of 10% is 4.9%. This difference, Gottschalk and the adviser agree, is acceptable. The portfolio that would correspond with this expected return consists of 16% European stocks, 38% emerging market equities, and 46% government bonds.

PORTFOLIO CONSTRUCTION PRINCIPLES

8

☐ describe the principles of portfolio construction and the role of asset allocation in relation to the IPS

The strategic asset allocation in itself does not yet represent an actual investment portfolio. It is the first step in implementing an investment strategy. For quantitatively oriented portfolio managers, the next step is often risk budgeting.

As used in this reading, **risk budgeting** is the process of deciding on the amount of risk to assume in a portfolio (the overall risk budget) and subdividing that risk over the sources of investment return (e.g., strategic asset allocation, tactical asset allocation, and security selection). Because the decision about the total amount of risk to be taken is made in constructing the IPS, at this stage we are concerned about the subdivision of that risk.

Apart from the exposures to systematic risk factors specified in the strategic asset allocation, the returns of an investment strategy depend on two other sources: tactical asset allocation and security selection. **Tactical asset allocation** is the decision to deliberately deviate from the policy exposures to systematic risk factors (i.e., the policy weights of asset classes) with the intent to add value based on forecasts of the near-term returns of those asset classes. For instance, an investor may decide to temporarily invest more of the portfolio in equities than the SAA prescribes if the investor anticipates that equities will deliver a higher return over the short term than other asset classes. **Security selection** is an attempt to generate higher returns than the asset class benchmark by selecting securities with a higher expected return. For example, an investment manager may decide to add more IBM stock in her portfolio than the weight in her equity benchmark if she expects this stock to do better than the benchmark. To fund this purchase, she may sell another stock expected to do worse than either the benchmark or IBM. Obviously, deciding to deviate from policy weights or to select securities aiming to beat the benchmark creates additional uncertainty about returns. This risk is over and above the risk inherent in the policy portfolio. Hence, an investment policy should set risk limits and desired payoffs for each of these three activities.

Risk budgeting implies that the portfolio manager has to choose, for every asset class, whether to deploy security selection as a return generator. This choice is generally referred to as the choice between active or passive management. Contrary to strategic asset allocation, where exposures to sources of systematic risk are selected and sized, security selection is not rewarded with a long-run payoff to risk. Security selection is a zero-sum game: All investors in an asset class are competing with each other to identify a typically limited number of assets that are misvalued. In total, the gross returns of all market participants average out to the market return (the reward for taking systematic risk). This implies that the average active investor will match the market return and that one investor's gain versus the market return is the other investor's loss versus the market return. Because active managers tend to trade more and have to pay people (including themselves) to generate investment ideas or information leading to such ideas, however, the average active manager will underperform the market, net of costs. This fact does not imply that there are no skillful investment managers who, with some consistency, beat their benchmarks. Neither does it imply that all passive managers will be able to match the benchmark. The higher the turnover of an index, the more trading costs a passive manager will incur, making the task of matching the return of an index more difficult.

The likelihood of adding a significant amount of value from security selection depends on the skills of the manager and the informational efficiency of the market for the asset class his skill relates to. The more efficient an asset class or a subset of that asset class (such as a regional stock, bond, or real estate market or a size category within the stock market), the more skillful an asset manager has to be to add value. Broadly speaking, an efficient market is a market in which prices, on average, very quickly reflect newly available information. That requires a sizeable participation of investors trading risk against expected return, acting on rational expectations, using the same or similar pricing models, and having equal opportunities to access relevant information. Clearly, the market for US large-capitalization equities would be quite efficient. By contrast, some regional bond and equity markets do not have the technical and regulatory systems for information dissemination that are sufficient to serve all investors on a timely basis. Skilled managers should be able to exploit the resulting inefficiencies.

Sometimes the choice between active and passive management is actually made implicitly when the asset class is included in the asset allocation. The markets for some assets—such as those for non-listed real estate and infrastructure assets—are so illiquid that it is very difficult to buy a diversified exposure. As a result, participating in that market is not possible without engaging in security selection.

As the portfolio is constructed and its value changes with the returns of the asset classes and securities in which it is invested, the weights of the asset classes will gradually deviate from the policy weights in the strategic asset allocation. This process is referred to as drift. Periodically, or when a certain threshold deviation from the policy weight (the bandwidth) has been breached, the portfolio should be rebalanced back to the policy weights. The set of rules that guide the process of restoring the portfolio's original exposures to systematic risk factors is known as the **rebalancing policy**. Even absent a formal risk budget, formulating a rebalancing policy is an important element of risk management, as the following example illustrates.

EXAMPLE 11

Strategic and Tactical Asset Allocation for a European Charity

A European charity has an asset allocation at the beginning of the year consisting of the asset classes and weights shown in Exhibit 11.

Exhibit 11: Asset Allocation of a European Charity (beginning of year)

Asset Class	Policy Weight	Corridor (+/–)	Upper Limit	Lower Limit
European equities	30.0%	2.0%	32.0%	28.0%
International equities	15.0%	2.0%	17.0%	13.0%
European government bonds	20.0%	2.0%	22.0%	18.0%
Corporate bonds	20.0%	2.0%	22.0%	18.0%
Cash and money market instruments	15.0%	2.0%	17.0%	13.0%
Total	100.0%			

As Exhibit 11 reveals, the charity has a policy that the asset class weights cannot deviate from the policy weights by more than 2% (the corridor). The resulting upper and lower limits for the asset class weights are shown in the rightmost columns of the table. There are two reasons for asset class actual weights to deviate from policy weights: by deliberate choice (tactical asset allocation or market timing) and as a result of divergence of the returns of the different asset classes (drift). In this example, the asset class weights start the year exactly in line with policy weights.

After half a year, the investment portfolio is as shown in Exhibit 12.

Exhibit 12: Asset Allocation for a European Charity (six months later)

Asset Class	Policy Weight	Corridor (+/–)	Upper Limit	Lower Limit	Period Return	Ending Weight
European equities	30.0%	2.0%	32.0%	28.0%	15.0%	32.4%
International equities	15.0%	2.0%	17.0%	13.0%	10.0%	15.5%
European government bonds	20.0%	2.0%	22.0%	18.0%	0.5%	18.9%
Corporate bonds	20.0%	2.0%	22.0%	18.0%	1.5%	19.1%
Cash and money market instruments	15.0%	2.0%	17.0%	13.0%	1.0%	14.2%
Total	100.0%				6.6%	100.0%

1. Discuss the returns of the portfolio and comment on the main asset weight changes.

Solution to 1:

The investment portfolio generated a return calculated on beginning (policy) weights of 6.55%, rounded to 6.6% (= 0.30 × 15% + 0.15 × 10% + 0.20 × 0.5% + 0.20 × 1.5% + 0.15 × 1.0%), mainly driven by a strong equity market. Bond returns were more subdued, leading to considerable drift in asset class weights. In particular, the European equity weight breached the upper limit of its allowed actual weight.

2. The investment committee decides against reducing European equities back to policy weight and adding to the fixed income and cash investments toward policy weights. Although this rebalancing would be prudent, the committee decides to engage in tactical asset allocation based on the view that this market will continue to be strong over the course of the year. It decides to just bring European equities back to within its bandwidth (a 32% portfolio weight) and add the proceeds to cash. Exhibit 13 shows the outcome after another half year.

Exhibit 13: Asset Allocation for a European Charity (an additional six months later)

Asset Class	Policy Weight	Starting Weight	Corridor (+/–)	Upper Limit	Lower Limit	Period Return	Ending Weight
European equities	30.0%	32.0%	2.0%	32.0%	28.0%	–9.0%	29.7%
International equities	15.0%	15.5%	2.0%	17.0%	13.0%	–6.0%	14.9%
European government bonds	20.0%	18.9%	2.0%	22.0%	18.0%	4.0%	20.0%
Corporate bonds	20.0%	19.1%	2.0%	22.0%	18.0%	4.0%	20.2%

Asset Class	Policy Weight	Starting Weight	Corridor (+/–)	Upper Limit	Lower Limit	Period Return	Ending Weight
Cash and money market instruments	15.0%	14.6%	2.0%	17.0%	13.0%	2.0%	15.2%
Total	100.0%					–2.0%	100.0%

The prior decision not to rebalance to policy weights did not have a positive result. Contrary to the investment committee's expectations, both European and international equities performed poorly while bonds recovered. The return of the portfolio was –2.0%.

How much of this return can be attributed to tactical asset allocation?

Solution to 2:

Because tactical asset allocation is the deliberate decision to deviate from policy weights, the return contribution from tactical asset allocation equals the difference between the actual return and the return that would have been made if the asset class weights were equal to the policy weights. Exhibit 14 shows this difference to be –0.30%.

Exhibit 14: Returns to Tactical Asset Allocation

Asset Class	Policy Weight I	Starting Weight II	Weights Difference III (= II – I)	Period Return IV	TAA Contribution V(= III × IV)
European equities	30.0%	32.0%	2.0%	–9.0%	–0.18%
International equities	15.0%	15.5%	0.5%	–6.0%	–0.03%
European government bonds	20.0%	18.9%	–1.1%	4.0%	–0.05%
Corporate bonds	20.0%	19.1%	–0.9%	4.0%	–0.04%
Cash and money market instruments	15.0%	14.6%	–0.4%	2.0%	–0.01%
Total	100.0%			–2.0%	–0.30%

The process of executing an investment strategy continues with selecting the appropriate manager(s) for each asset class and allocating funds to them. The investment portfolio management process is then well into the execution stage.

The investment managers' performance will be monitored, as well as the results of the tactical and strategic asset allocation. When asset class weights move outside their corridors, money is transferred from the asset classes that have become too large compared with the SAA to those that fall short. Managers as well as the strategic asset allocation will be reviewed on the basis of the outcome of the monitoring process. In addition, capital market expectations may change, as may the circumstances and objectives of the client. These changes could result in an adjustment of the strategic asset allocation.

New Developments in Portfolio Management

The portfolio planning and construction framework presented so far relies on a somewhat rigid process. Nonetheless, there are two newer, less structured developments that deserve specific mention.

The first development is the growth in the offering of exchange traded funds, or ETFs, in combination with algorithm-based financial advice (or robo-advice). ETFs are funds that track the performance of an asset class index or sub-index, are easily tradable, and are relatively cheap compared with actively managed funds or managed accounts. The broad array of ETF offerings, covering the main equity and fixed-income indices as well as commodities, enable retail investors to obtain fast, inexpensive, and liquid exposure to asset classes. Robo-advice has further reduced the costs for retail investors to create a well-diversified portfolio.

The second development relates to criticism of asset class return forecasts over relevant time horizons, as well as the perceived instability of asset class correlations and volatilities. Some market participants argue that poor investment portfolio results reflect the sensitivity of modern portfolio theory-based portfolio construction methodologies to small errors in return forecasts or estimated correlations. In response, practitioners developed an investment approach where asset classes were weighted according to risk contribution. This approach is known as *risk parity investing*. Proponents of risk parity investing argue that traditionally constructed portfolios have considerable risk from equities. That is, the typically high (60% or more) weight of equities in institutional portfolios understates the risk impact: equities tend to be much more volatile than fixed income. Opponents of risk parity argue that following the global financial crisis of 2007–2009, favorable results of risk parity portfolios were caused by the long period of decline in interest rates that benefited bond market performance.

ESG CONSIDERATIONS IN PORTFOLIO PLANNING AND CONSTRUCTION 9

☐ describe how environmental, social, and governance (ESG) considerations may be integrated into portfolio planning and construction

The implementation of a policy on responsible investing affects both strategic asset allocation and implementation of the portfolio construction process. The ESG investment approaches described previously require a set of instructions for investment managers with regard to the selection of securities, the exercise of shareholder rights, and the selection of investment strategies. Examples of issues driving the integration of environmental and social factors in the investment process include scarcity of natural resources, physical impacts of climate change, global economic and demographic trends, diversity and inclusion, and the rise of social media. ESG investment approaches can be implemented with structured, numeric data for many of these issues (e.g., executive salaries and bonuses, carbon footprint, employee turnover, lost time injuries and fatalities, and employee absenteeism). Although companies often are not required to disclose such data, that is changing as many stock exchanges and other regulatory bodies across developed and emerging markets have set up guidelines related to corporate sustainability disclosures for listed companies. In addition, many organizations and regulatory bodies have derived frameworks setting out standards on a number of these issues—examples include the Principles of Responsible Investment, the UN Global Compact, and the OECD Guidelines for Multinational Enterprises. These standards help form the basis of responsible investing policies for asset owners. In turn, asset owners may exclude or engage with companies in accordance with these issues, or demand from their selected investment managers consider these issues in their investment process.

We previously discussed that the limitation in the investment universe from using negative screening policies affects the expected returns and risk. When selecting or instructing active or passive managers, these managers will clearly prefer to see their performance measured against a benchmark that reflects the limited universe. There are benchmarks and investment vehicles (both active and passive) available, particularly in equities, that reflect many commonly excluded companies or sectors. It is also worth noting that with the proliferation of the ESG integration approach, more and more asset owners expect their asset managers to beat the regular benchmarks, because integration of ESG factors into traditional financial analysis and portfolio construction is viewed more as a process enhancement rather than an entirely new way to invest.

EXAMPLE 12

ESG Factors Directly Impacting Portfolio Construction

1. Based in South Africa, Mountain Materials (Mountain) is a fictitious cement manufacturing company that ranks as one of the largest cement and concrete manufacturers in the world. Mountain operates mostly in South Africa, where environmental regulations have been gradually strengthening since 2015. Because of the large scale of its operations, Mountain is a significant emitter of greenhouse gases (GHGs). During 2019, by setting a carbon price on the country's largest GHG emitters, South Africa launched a new, crucial endeavor in its efforts to tackle air pollution and climate change. Despite having some ad hoc initiatives to manage its carbon emissions, the company lacks firmwide programs to limit energy use or carbon emissions, thereby remaining exposed to increased costs to offset excess emissions. The average price on carbon across seven pilot markets in South Africa was between \$5 and \$15 per ton of carbon dioxide. In addition, the company's performance in managing toxic air emissions as well as employee health and safety falls short of industry best practices, leaving Mountain exposed to related risks.

   Ved Disha, CFA, is analyzing the effects of the environmental and social factors on Mountain's financial statements. Exhibit 15 illustrates Disha's expected internal rate of return (IRR) in the base, bear, and bull case scenarios for Mountain based on his fundamental analysis, and Exhibit 16 illustrates the same scenarios following the integration of these material environmental and social risks.

Exhibit 15: Pre-ESG Integration: Bear/Base/Bull Case Scenario

	Bear Case	Base Case	Bull Case
Revenue growth	0.0%	10.0%	15.0%
Margin improvement	–5.0%	3.0%	5.0%
Cash dividend	1.0%	2.0%	2.0%

	Bear Case	Base Case	Bull Case
Multiple expansion	–10.0%	0.0%	5.0%
IRR	–14.0%	15.0%	27.0%

Exhibit 16: Post-ESG Integration: Bear/Base/Bull Case Scenario

	Bear Case	Base Case	Bull Case
Revenue growth	–5.0%	10.0%	20.0%
Margin improvement	–10.0%	–3.0%	0.0%
Cash dividend	0.0%	0.0%	2.0%
Multiple expansion	–5.0%	–2.0%	0.0%
IRR	–20.0%	5.0%	22.0%

Disha assumed that compliance with national and provincial carbon regulations would require the company to increase spending on equipment, resulting in a 1% erosion in operating margin. Moreover, to limit toxic emissions, the company would have to switch to relatively cleaner sources of energy such as gas-based powered plants. This change is expected to further dampen operating margin by 2% because of increased fuel costs. As a result of higher spending, it was assumed that the previously stable cash dividend policy would turn conservative in the short term, and hence Disha reduced the expected dividend from 2% to 0% for the base case. Lastly, there is a downside to multiples as a result of the concerns related to management of health and safety risks, because the company's performance is below that of its peers and capital markets tend to discount the share price in the event of safety incidents. Based on all of these changes, the base case IRR for the cement company case became less attractive. This outlook led Disha to undertake a relatively smaller position of 0.5% (versus 1.5% in the absence of ESG risks) in his portfolio because of the various unmanaged ESG risks at Mountain. Disha also decided to engage with company management to influence better disclosures and management of these environmental and social risks. In this manner, key ESG risks and growth opportunities were integrated with traditional financial analysis to help arrive at a more robust investment decision.

In this example, a high level of unmanaged ESG risks led to a significant change in expected IRR following the ESG integration and hence impacted the position size significantly. It is prudent to note, however, that ESG is one of the many factors that influence investment decision making. Therefore, in many cases, ESG risk and opportunities may have limited effect on a company's financial attractiveness and thereby may not cause a large change in the portfolio. These risks and opportunities have to be analyzed and interpreted on a case-by-case basis.

Shareholder engagement requires good cooperation between investor (client) and investment manager. Engagement efforts are time-consuming, and the interest in such efforts is often that of the clients rather than that of the investment managers. Clients and investment managers must be clear with each other about the exercise of voting rights, filing of shareholder proposals, or entering into conversations with company management. It may be that the engagement and voting is delegated by the client to the investment manager and implemented according to the manager's stewardship policy. Alternatively, the client may instruct some proxy agent to vote on its behalf and according to its own stewardship policies, or the client may instruct voting and maintain dialogue with its investee companies through either individual engagements or collaborative engagements. Collaborative engagement initiatives have gained popularity because it is easier to gain the attention of and encourage positive action from corporations on material ESG issues through collective action. Climate Action 100+ is one such initiative that aims to ensure the world's largest corporate GHG emitters take necessary action on climate change. The initiative aims to engage with more than 100 systemically important carbon emitters, accounting for two-thirds of annual global industrial emissions, alongside more than 60 other companies with significant opportunity to drive the clean energy transition.

Selecting thematic investments, particularly in liquid asset classes, requires finding specialist managers who can identify the right opportunities and manage thematic investment portfolios. In particular, an allocation to thematic investments will bias the total asset class portfolio toward a particular theme, so it is important for the investment manager to demonstrate the impact of the thematic investment on the total risk–return profile of the portfolio. Impact investing specifically selects investment opportunities based on their intention to create a positive environmental and social impact.

The effort and costs associated with limiting the investment universe as part of responsible investing may suggest a negative impact on investment returns. Responsible investing proponents argue, however, that potential improvements in governance, as well as the avoidance of material risks by companies that screen, favorably improve returns. Significant empirical research has been conducted on the performance of ESG factors in equities, including the return differences of ESG equity portfolios relative to mainstream equity portfolios. Academic research remains mixed on the impact of ESG factors on portfolio returns. Nevertheless, ESG investing continues to see strong adoption, with nearly US$31 trillion of AUM dedicated toward responsible investment mandates at the start of 2018. The ESG integration approach that integrates material qualitative and quantitative environmental, social, and governance factors into traditional security and industry analysis as well as portfolio construction is now widely adopted across mainstream funds and not just limited to client-specific separate accounts.

SUMMARY

In this reading, we have discussed construction of a client's investment policy statement, including discussion of risk and return objectives and the various constraints that will apply to the portfolio. We have also discussed the portfolio construction process, with emphasis on the strategic asset allocation decisions that must be made.

- The IPS is the starting point of the portfolio management process. Without a full understanding of the client's situation and requirements, it is unlikely that successful results will be achieved.
- The IPS can take a variety of forms. A typical format will include the client's investment objectives and also list the constraints that apply to the client's portfolio.
- The client's objectives are specified in terms of risk tolerance and return requirements.

- The constraints section covers factors that need to be considered when constructing a portfolio for the client that meets the objectives. The typical constraint categories are liquidity requirements, time horizon, regulatory requirements, tax status, and unique needs.
- Clients may have personal objections to certain products or practices, which could lead to the exclusion of certain companies, countries, or types of securities from the investable universe as well as the client's benchmark. Such considerations are often referred to as ESG (environmental, social, governance).
- ESG considerations can be integrated into an investment policy by negative screening, positive screening, ESG integration, thematic investing, engagement/active ownership, and impact investing.
- Risk objectives are specifications for portfolio risk that reflect the risk tolerance of the client. Quantitative risk objectives can be absolute, relative, or a combination of the two.
- The client's overall risk tolerance is a function of both the client's ability to accept risk and the client's "risk attitude," which can be considered the client's willingness to take risk.
- The client's return objectives can be stated on an absolute or a relative basis. As an example of an absolute objective, the client may want to achieve a particular percentage rate of return. Alternatively, the return objective can be stated on a relative basis—for example, relative to a benchmark return.
- The liquidity section of the IPS should state what the client's requirements are to draw cash from the portfolio.
- The time horizon section of the IPS should state the time horizon over which the investor is investing. This horizon may be the period during which the portfolio is accumulating before any assets need to be withdrawn.
- Tax status varies among investors, and a client's tax status should be stated in the IPS.
- The IPS should state any legal or regulatory restrictions that constrain the investment of the portfolio.
- The unique circumstances section of the IPS should cover any other aspect of a client's circumstances that is likely to have a material impact on portfolio composition. Certain ESG implementation approaches may be discussed in this section.
- Asset classes are the building blocks of an asset allocation. An asset class is a category of assets that have similar characteristics, attributes, and risk–return relationships. Traditionally, investors have distinguished cash, equities, bonds, and real estate as the major asset classes.
- A strategic asset allocation results from combining the constraints and objectives articulated in the IPS and capital market expectations regarding the asset classes.
- As time goes on, a client's asset allocation will drift from the target allocation, and the amount of allowable drift as well as a rebalancing policy should be formalized.
- In addition to taking systematic risk, an investment committee may choose to take tactical asset allocation risk or security selection risk. The amount of return attributable to these decisions can be measured.

- ESG considerations may be integrated into the portfolio planning and construction process. ESG implementation approaches require a set of instructions for investment managers with regard to the selection of securities, the exercise of shareholder rights, and the selection of investment strategies.

PRACTICE PROBLEMS

1. Which of the following is *least* important as a reason for a written investment policy statement (IPS)?

   A. The IPS may be required by regulation.

   B. Having a written IPS is part of best practice for a portfolio manager.

   C. Having a written IPS ensures the client's risk and return objectives can be achieved.

2. Which of the following *best* describes the underlying rationale for a written investment policy statement (IPS)?

   A. A written IPS communicates a plan for trying to achieve investment success.

   B. A written IPS provides investment managers with a ready defense against client lawsuits.

   C. A written IPS allows investment managers to instruct clients about the proper use and purpose of investments.

3. A written investment policy statement (IPS) is *most* likely to succeed if:

   A. it is created by a software program to assure consistent quality.

   B. it is a collaborative effort of the client and the portfolio manager.

   C. it reflects the investment philosophy of the portfolio manager.

4. The section of the investment policy statement (IPS) that provides information about how policy may be executed, including restrictions and exclusions, is *best* described as the:

   A. *Investment Objectives.*

   B. *Investment Guidelines.*

   C. *Statement of Duties and Responsibilities.*

5. Which of the following is *least* likely to be placed in the appendices to an investment policy statement (IPS)?

   A. *Rebalancing Policy.*

   B. *Strategic Asset Allocation.*

   C. *Statement of Duties and Responsibilities.*

6. Which of the following typical topics in an investment policy statement (IPS) is *most* closely linked to the client's "distinctive needs"?

   A. *Procedures.*

   B. *Investment Guidelines.*

   C. *Statement of Duties and Responsibilities.*

7. An investment policy statement that includes a return objective of outperforming the FTSE 100 by 120 basis points is *best* characterized as having a(n):
   A. relative return objective.
   B. absolute return objective.
   C. arbitrage-based return objective.

8. Risk assessment questionnaires for investment management clients are *most* useful in measuring:
   A. value at risk.
   B. ability to take risk.
   C. willingness to take risk.

9. Which of the following is *best* characterized as a relative risk objective?
   A. Value at risk for the fund will not exceed US$3 million.
   B. The fund will not underperform the DAX by more than 250 basis points.
   C. The fund will not lose more than €2.5 million in the coming 12-month period.

10. In preparing an investment policy statement, which of the following is *most* difficult to quantify?
   A. Time horizon.
   B. Ability to accept risk.
   C. Willingness to accept risk.

11. A client who is a 34-year old widow with two healthy young children (aged 5 and 7) has asked you to help her form an investment policy statement. She has been employed as an administrative assistant in a bureau of her national government for the previous 12 years. She has two primary financial goals—her retirement and providing for the college education of her children. This client's time horizon is *best* described as being:
   A. long term.
   B. short term.
   C. medium term.

12. The timing of payouts for property and casualty insurers is unpredictable ("lumpy") in comparison with the timing of payouts for life insurance companies. Therefore, in general, property and casualty insurers have:
   A. lower liquidity needs than life insurance companies.
   B. greater liquidity needs than life insurance companies.
   C. a higher return objective than life insurance companies.

13. A client who is a director of a publicly listed corporation is required by law to refrain from trading that company's stock at certain points of the year when dis-

closure of financial results are pending. In preparing a written investment policy statement (IPS) for this client, this restriction on trading:

A. is irrelevant to the IPS.

B. should be included in the IPS.

C. makes it illegal for the portfolio manager to work with this client.

14. After interviewing a client in order to prepare a written investment policy statement (IPS), you have established the following:

- The client has earnings that vary dramatically between £30,000 and £70,000 (pre-tax) depending on weather patterns in Britain.
- In three of the previous five years, the after-tax income of the client has been less than £20,000.
- The client's mother is dependent on her son (the client) for approximately £9,000 per year support.
- The client's own subsistence needs are approximately £12,000 per year.
- The client has more than 10 years' experience trading investments including commodity futures, stock options, and selling stock short.
- The client's responses to a standard risk assessment questionnaire suggest he has above average risk tolerance.

The client is *best* described as having a:

A. low ability to take risk, but a high willingness to take risk.

B. high ability to take risk, but a low willingness to take risk.

C. high ability to take risk and a high willingness to take risk.

15. After interviewing a client in order to prepare a written investment policy statement (IPS), you have established the following:

- The client has earnings that have exceeded €120,000 (pre-tax) each year for the past five years.
- She has no dependents.
- The client's subsistence needs are approximately €45,000 per year.
- The client states that she feels uncomfortable with her lack of understanding of securities markets.
- All of the client's current savings are invested in short-term securities guaranteed by an agency of her national government.
- The client's responses to a standard risk assessment questionnaire suggest she has low risk tolerance.

The client is *best* described as having a:

A. low ability to take risk, but a high willingness to take risk.

B. high ability to take risk, but a low willingness to take risk.

C. high ability to take risk and a high willingness to take risk.

16. Returns on asset classes are *best* described as being a function of:

A. the failure of arbitrage.

B. exposure to the idiosyncratic risks of those asset classes.

C. exposure to sets of systematic factors relevant to those asset classes.

17. Consider the pairwise correlations of monthly returns of the following asset classes:

	Brazilian Equities	East Asian Equities	European Equities	US Equities
Brazilian equities	1.00	0.70	0.85	0.76
East Asian equities	0.70	1.00	0.91	0.88
European equities	0.85	0.91	1.00	0.90
US equities	0.76	0.88	0.90	1.00

Based solely on the information in the above table, which equity asset class is *most* sharply distinguished from US equities?

A. Brazilian equities.

B. European equities.

C. East Asian equities.

18. In defining asset classes as part of the strategic asset allocation decision, pairwise correlations within asset classes should generally be:

A. equal to correlations among asset classes.

B. lower than correlations among asset classes.

C. higher than correlations among asset classes.

19. Tactical asset allocation is *best* described as:

A. attempts to exploit arbitrage possibilities among asset classes.

B. the decision to deliberately deviate from the policy portfolio.

C. selecting asset classes with the desired exposures to sources of systematic risk in an investment portfolio.

SOLUTIONS

1. C is correct. Depending on circumstances, a written IPS or its equivalent may be required by law or regulation and a written IPS is certainly consistent with best practices. The mere fact that a written IPS is prepared for a client, however, does not *ensure* that risk and return objectives will in fact be achieved.

2. A is correct. A written IPS is best seen as a communication instrument allowing clients and portfolio managers to mutually establish investment objectives and constraints.

3. B is correct. A written IPS, to be successful, must incorporate a full understanding of the client's situation and requirements. As stated in the reading, "The IPS will be developed following a fact finding discussion with the client."

4. B is correct. The major components of an IPS are listed in Section 2 of the reading. *Investment Guidelines* are described as the section that provides information about how policy may be executed, including restrictions on the permissible use of leverage and derivatives and on specific types of assets excluded from investment, if any. *Statement of Duties and Responsibilities* "detail[s] the duties and responsibilities of the client, the custodian of the client's assets, the investment managers, and so forth." *Investment Objectives* is "a section explaining the client's objectives in investing."

5. C is correct. The major components of an IPS are listed in Section 2 of the reading. Strategic Asset Allocation (also known as the policy portfolio) and Rebalancing Policy are often included as appendices to the IPS. The *Statement of Duties and Responsibilities*, however, is an integral part of the IPS and is unlikely to be placed in an appendix.

6. B is correct. According to the reading, "The sections of an IPS that are most closely linked to the client's distinctive needs are those dealing with investment objectives and constraints." *Investment Guidelines* "[provide] information about how policy may be executed, including investment constraints." *Procedures* "[detail] the steps to be taken to keep the IPS current and the procedures to follow to respond to various contingencies." *Statement of Duties and Responsibilities* "detail[s] the duties and responsibilities of the client, the custodian of the client's assets, the investment managers, and so forth."

7. A is correct. Because the return objective specifies a target return *relative to* the FTSE 100 Index, the objective is best described as a relative return objective.

8. C is correct. Risk attitude is a subjective factor and measuring risk attitude is difficult. Oftentimes, investment managers use psychometric questionnaires, such as those developed by Grable and Joo (2004), to assess a client's willingness to take risk.

9. B is correct. The reference to the DAX marks this response as a relative risk objective. Value at risk establishes a minimum value of loss expected during a specified time period at a given level of probability. A statement of maximum allowed absolute loss (€2.5 million) is an absolute risk objective.

10. C is correct. Measuring willingness to take risk (risk tolerance, risk aversion) is an exercise in applied psychology. Instruments attempting to measure risk attitudes exist, but they are clearly less objective than measurements of ability to take risk.

Ability to take risk is based on relatively objective traits such as expected income, time horizon, and existing wealth relative to liabilities.

11. A is correct. The client's financial objectives are long term. Her stable employment indicates that her immediate liquidity needs are modest. The children will not go to college until 10 or more years later. Her time horizon is best described as being long term.

12. B is correct. The unpredictable nature of property and casualty (P&C) claims forces P&C insurers to allocate a substantial proportion of their investments into liquid, short maturity assets. This need for liquidity also forces P&C companies to accept investments with relatively low expected returns. Liquidity is of less concern to life insurance companies given the greater predictability of life insurance payouts.

13. B is correct. When a client has a restriction in trading, such as this obligation to refrain from trading, the IPS "should note this constraint so that the portfolio manager does not inadvertently trade the stock on the client's behalf."

14. A is correct. The volatility of the client's income and the significant support needs for his mother and himself suggest that the client has a low ability to take risk. The client's trading experience and his responses to the risk assessment questionnaire indicate that the client has an above average willingness to take risk.

15. B is correct. On the one hand, the client has a stable, high income and no dependents. On the other hand, she exhibits above average risk aversion. Her ability to take risk is high, but her willingness to take risk is low.

16. C is correct. Strategic asset allocation depends on several principles. As stated in the reading, "One principle is that a portfolio's systematic risk accounts for most of its change in value over the long run." A second principle is that, "the returns to groups of like assets... predictably reflect exposures to certain sets of systematic factors." This latter principle establishes that returns on asset classes primarily reflect the systematic risks of the classes.

17. A is correct. The correlation between US equities and Brazilian equities is 0.76. The correlations between US equities and East Asian equities and the correlation between US equities and European equities both exceed 0.76. Lower correlations indicate a greater degree of separation between asset classes. Therefore, using solely the data given in the table, returns on Brazilian equities are most sharply distinguished from returns on US equities.

18. C is correct. As the reading states, "an asset class should contain homogeneous assets... paired correlations of securities would be high within an asset class, but should be lower versus securities in other asset classes."

19. B is correct. Tactical asset allocation allows actual asset allocation to deviate from that of the strategic asset allocation (policy portfolio) of the IPS. Tactical asset allocation attempts to take advantage of temporary dislocations from the market conditions and assumptions that drove the policy portfolio decision.

LEARNING MODULE

5

The Behavioral Biases of Individuals

by Michael M. Pompian, CFA.

Michael M. Pompian, CFA, is at Sunpointe Investments (USA).

LEARNING OUTCOMES

Mastery	The candidate should be able to:
☐	compare and contrast cognitive errors and emotional biases
☐	discuss commonly recognized behavioral biases and their implications for financial decision making
☐	describe how behavioral biases of investors can lead to market characteristics that may not be explained by traditional finance

INTRODUCTION

1

Research has demonstrated that when people face complex decisions, they often rely on basic judgments and preferences to simplify the situation rather than acting completely rationally. Although such approaches are quick and intuitively appealing, they may lead to suboptimal outcomes. In contrast to this body of research, traditional economic and financial theory generally assumes that individuals act rationally by considering all available information in the decision-making process, leading them to optimal outcomes and supporting the efficiency of markets. Behavioral finance challenges these assumptions by incorporating research on how individuals and markets actually behave. In this reading, we explore a foundational concept of behavioral finance: behavioral biases. Investment professionals may be able to improve economic outcomes by understanding these biases, recognizing them in themselves and others, and learning strategies to mitigate them.

The reading proceeds as follows. Section 2 describes and broadly characterizes behavioral biases. Sections 3 and 4 discuss specific behavioral biases within two broad categories: cognitive errors and emotional biases. The discussion includes a description of each bias, potential consequences, and guidance on detecting and mitigating the effects of the bias. Section 5 discusses market anomalies, which are essentially aggregate expressions of individual biases among financial market participants. A summary and practice problems conclude the reading.

2 BEHAVIORAL BIAS CATEGORIES

☐ compare and contrast cognitive errors and emotional biases

In general, behavioral biases come in two forms: faulty cognitive reasoning, known as **cognitive errors**, and those based on feelings or emotions, known as **emotional biases**. Both forms of bias, regardless of their source, may cause decisions to deviate from what is assumed by traditional finance theory.

Cognitive errors can often be corrected or eliminated through better information, education, and advice. Emotional biases, on the other hand, are harder to correct because they stem from impulses and intuitions. They arise spontaneously rather than through conscious effort and may even be undesired to the individual feeling them. Thus, it is often possible only to recognize an emotional bias and adapt to it. The cognitive–emotional distinction will help us determine when and how to adjust for behavioral biases in financial decision making.

Researchers have identified numerous behavioral biases. This reading does not attempt to catalog all of them. Rather, it discusses some of the more publicized and recognized biases within the cognitive–emotional framework. Additionally, we limit our focus to gauging the presence or absence—not the magnitude—of each bias discussed. That is, we will not try to measure how strongly the bias is exhibited, but rather we will describe the behavioral bias, its potential consequences, and the detection of and correction for the behavioral bias. In detecting a bias, we will identify statements or thought processes that may indicate the bias. Diagnostic tests of varying degrees of complexity are available to detect biases but are beyond the scope of this reading.

Finally, the individuals of interest in this reading are "financial market participants" (FMPs) engaged in financial decision making. These include both individual investors and financial services professionals.

3 COGNITIVE ERRORS

☐ discuss commonly recognized behavioral biases and their implications for financial decision making

We classify cognitive errors into two categories: "belief perseverance biases" and "processing errors."

Belief perseverance is the tendency to cling to one's previously held beliefs by committing statistical, information-processing, or memory errors. The belief perseverance biases discussed are conservatism, confirmation, representativeness, illusion of control, and hindsight.

Processing errors describe how information may be processed and used illogically or irrationally in financial decision making. The processing errors discussed are anchoring and adjustment, mental accounting, framing, and availability.

Belief Perseverance Biases

Belief perseverance biases result from the mental discomfort that occurs when new information conflicts with previously held beliefs or cognitions, known as **cognitive dissonance**. To resolve this discomfort, people may ignore or modify conflicting information and consider only information that confirms their existing beliefs or thoughts.

Conservatism Bias

Conservatism bias is a belief perseverance bias in which people maintain their prior views or forecasts by inadequately incorporating new, conflicting information. In Bayesian terms, they tend to overweight their prior probability of the event and underweight the new information, resulting in revised beliefs about probabilities and outcomes that underreact to the new information.

Consequences of Conservatism Bias

As a result of conservatism bias, FMPs may do the following:

- Maintain or be slow to update a view or a forecast, even when presented with new information; and
- Maintain a prior belief rather than deal with the mental stress of updating beliefs given complex data. This behavior relates to an underlying difficulty in processing new information.

Detection of and Guidance for Overcoming Conservatism Bias

The effect of conservatism bias may be corrected for or reduced by properly analyzing and weighting new information. The first step is to be aware that a bias exists, especially about information that is technical, abstract, and/or statistical, because the **cognitive cost** involved in processing those forms of information is higher than for other types.

When new information is presented, the FMP should ask such questions as, "How does this information change my forecast?" or "What effect does this information have on my forecast?" FMPs should conduct careful analysis incorporating the new information and then respond appropriately. This updating of prior beliefs in light of new information is consistent with the tenets of Bayes' Rule, in which updated probabilities are derived by systematically combining previous estimates and new information.

If information is difficult to interpret or understand, FMPs should seek guidance from someone who can either explain how to interpret the information or can explain its implications.

Confirmation Bias

Confirmation bias refers to the tendency to look for and notice what confirms prior beliefs and to ignore or undervalue whatever contradicts them. A response to cognitive dissonance, confirmation bias reflects a predisposition to justify to ourselves what we want to believe.

Most experienced private wealth advisers have dealt with a client who conducts some research and insists on adding a particular investment to the portfolio. The client may insist on continuing to hold the investment, even when the adviser recommends otherwise, because the client's follow-up research seeks only information that confirms his belief that the investment is still a good value. The confirmation bias is not limited to individual investors; all FMPs should be wary of the potential confirmation biases within themselves.

EXAMPLE 1

Confirmation Bias

A portfolio manager at Sarter Investment Advisors recommended shares of Real Media Inc., a hypothetical television production and distribution company, largely on the basis of compelling analytical and valuation work from a top equity research analyst. Sarter's clients have owned the shares for several years.

Recently, the shares have underperformed significantly as a result of the company missing analysts' earnings estimates and also in response to executive management turnover. The portfolio manager's colleagues believe this underperformance is a result of Real Media losing market share to a competitor with superior technology and distribution. The competitor is publicly traded, but Sarter's portfolio managers and analysts have not done research on it.

After another poor earnings release from Real Media, the portfolio manager speaks with the equity research analyst whose work was the primary source of the investment. The equity research analyst, who maintains a buy rating on the stock, believes that Real Media is now a more compelling investment than ever because its share price has fallen while its earnings estimates remain unchanged. As a result of the conversation, the portfolio manager feels reassured and holds the position.

The portfolio manager is subject to confirmation bias. Rather than speaking with a research analyst who has a sell rating on the stock or conducting research on the competitor to consider a different perspective, the portfolio manager speaks with someone who has an opinion she already shares.

Consequences of Confirmation Bias

As a result of confirmation bias, FMPs may do the following:

- Consider only the positive information about an existing investment while ignoring any negative information about the investment.
- Develop screening criteria while ignoring information that either refutes the validity of the criteria or supports other criteria. As a result, some good investments that do not meet the screening criteria may be ignored, and conversely, some bad investments that do meet the screening criteria may be made.
- Under-diversify portfolios. FMPs may become convinced of the value of a single company's stock. They ignore negative news, and they gather and process only information confirming that the company is a good investment. They build a larger position than appropriate and hold an under-diversified portfolio.
- Hold a disproportionate amount of their investment assets in their employing company's stock, because they believe in their company and are convinced of its favorable prospects. Favorable information is cited, and unfavorable information is ignored. If the employee were to acknowledge unfavorable information, the associated mental discomfort might make work very difficult for the employee.

Detection of and Guidance for Overcoming Confirmation Bias

The effect of confirmation bias may be corrected for or reduced by actively seeking out information that challenges existing beliefs.

Another useful step is to corroborate an investment decision. For example, if investment selections are based on criteria confirming an existing belief, such as stocks breaking through 52-week highs, it is usually advisable to corroborate that decision with research from another perspective or source (e.g., fundamental research on the company, industry, or sector).

Representativeness Bias

Representativeness bias refers to the tendency to classify new information based on past experiences and classifications. New information may resemble or seem *representative* of familiar elements already classified, but in reality, it can be very different. In these instances, the classification reflex can deceive, producing an incorrect understanding that biases all future thinking about the information. *Base-rate neglect* and *sample-size neglect* are two types of representativeness bias that apply to FMPs.

In **base-rate neglect**, a phenomenon's rate of incidence in a larger population—its base rate—is neglected in favor of specific information. The specific, individual information may be misleading relative to the more appropriate base rate or general information. FMPs often follow this erroneous path because diligent research is often conducted on an individual security or strategy, leading FMPs to overlook or ignore general information about the "class" to which an investment belongs, such as an industry, sector, or geography.

A second type of representativeness bias is **sample-size neglect**, in which FMPs incorrectly assume that small sample sizes are *representative* of populations. Individuals prone to sample-size neglect are quick to treat properties reflected in small samples as properties that accurately describe large pools of data, overweighting the information in the small sample.

EXAMPLE 2

Representativeness Bias

Jacques Verte is evaluating the future prospects of APM Company, a large auto parts manufacturer having some difficulties. During the last 50 years, very few auto part manufacturers have failed, even during periods of difficulty. A number of recent headlines have highlighted APM's business and financial difficulties, however, with some commentators suggesting that APM may go out of business.

1. Which of the following scenarios is more likely? Explain why.

   A. APM will solve its difficulties.

   B. APM will go out of business.

Solution:

Scenario A is more likely. The base rate, based on 50 years of data, is that more auto parts companies survive difficult times than fail. Thus, it is more likely that APM will solve its difficulties than go out of business.

2. If Verte is subject to representativeness bias, is he more likely to classify APM into A or B? Explain why.

Solution:

If Verte is subject to representativeness bias, he is likely to choose Scenario B, predicting that the company will go out of business because of the headlines he has read. In classifying APM as likely to go out of business, Verte would be guilty of base-rate neglect by ignoring the low base rate of auto parts manufacturers failing even during times of difficulty.

Consequences of Representativeness Bias

As a result of representativeness bias, FMPs may do the following:

- Adopt a view or a forecast based almost exclusively on individual, specific information or a small sample; and
- Update beliefs using simple classifications rather than deal with the mental stress of updating beliefs given the high cognitive costs of complex data.

Detection of and Guidance on Overcoming Representativeness Bias

When FMPs sense that base-rate or sample-size neglect may be a problem, they should ask the following question: "What is the probability that X (the investment under consideration) belongs to Group A (the group it resembles or is considered representative of) versus Group B (the group it is statistically more likely to belong to)?" This question, or a similar question, will help FMPs think through whether they are failing to consider base-rate probabilities or neglecting the law of small numbers and thus inaccurately assessing a particular situation. It may be necessary to do more research to obtain base-rate information and/or widen the sample size of observations.

Illusion of Control Bias

In **illusion of control bias**, people tend to believe that they can control or influence outcomes when, in fact, they cannot. Many researchers have uncovered situations where people perceived themselves as possessing more control than they did, inferred causal connections where none existed, or displayed surprisingly great certainty in their predictions for the outcomes of chance events. A classic example is that people prefer choosing their own lottery numbers over random numbers selected for them.

EXAMPLE 3

Illusion of Control Bias

Adelia Scott is a wealth adviser at Sarter Investment Advisors (Sarter), an investment advisory firm for high-net-worth individuals. Scott meets with a client who has 30% of his account in shares of his employer's stock. The client is not subject to any employee holding requirement.

Prior meeting notes indicate that the client initially agreed to diversify the concentrated position over a five-year period. Scott recommends a faster schedule, however, based on recent research indicating that the company's future growth prospects have considerably worsened as a result of industry trends and macroeconomic conditions.

When presented with this information, the client is reluctant to change his diversification plan, citing the company's history of double-digit growth and his belief that this rate of growth will continue for the foreseeable future. The client remarks, "Trust me, my team and I are not going to let those forecasts you're citing come true."

The client is subject to illusion of control bias. He is unwilling to believe Scott's opinion because he believes that he and his team can control the company's performance and stock price.

Consequences of Illusion of Control

As a result of illusion of control bias, FMPs may do the following:

- Inadequately diversify portfolios. Research has found that some investors prefer to invest in companies that they feel they have control over, such as the companies they work for, leading them to hold concentrated positions. In fact, most investors have little or no control over the companies they work for. If the company performs poorly, these investors may experience both the loss of employment and investment losses.
- Trade more than is prudent. Researchers have found that portfolio turnover is negatively correlated with investment returns.
- Construct financial models and forecasts that are overly detailed. FMPs may require detailed models before making an investment decision, believing that forecasts from these models control uncertainty. Although a greater understanding of an investment, issuer, or industry is often useful, increased model complexity does not control the inherent risk and uncertainty of investment outcomes.

Detection of and Guidelines for Overcoming Illusion of Control Bias

The first and most basic idea that investors need to recognize is that investing is a probabilistic activity. Even the largest investment management firms have little control over the outcomes of the investments they make. Companies are subject to macroeconomic and industry forces, as well as the actions of competitors, customers, and suppliers.

Second, it is advisable to seek contrary viewpoints. As you contemplate a new investment, take a moment to think about considerations that might weigh against making the investment. Ask yourself: What are the downside risks? What might go wrong? When will I sell? It is often useful to speak with someone who has an opposing view, such as an equity research analyst with a sell rating on the subject stock.

Hindsight Bias

Hindsight bias refers to believing past events as having been predictable and reasonable to expect. This behavior results from the obvious fact that outcomes that did occur are more readily evident than outcomes that did not. Similarly, people tend to remember their own predictions of the future as more accurate than they actually were because they are biased by the knowledge of what actually occurred. Poorly reasoned decisions with positive results may be remembered as brilliant tactical moves, and poor results of well-reasoned decisions may be described as avoidable mistakes.

EXAMPLE 4

Hindsight Bias

Beverly Bolo, an analyst at an investment advisory firm, is giving a presentation to clients that, among other topics, explains the firm's investment results during past macroeconomic downturns. In the presentation, Bolo points out that the "occurrence of the last recession was obvious upon inspection of the yield curve and other leading indicators eight months before the downturn started."

Bolo's comment exhibits hindsight bias. Recessions, like any other event, appear obvious in hindsight but are hardly ever accurately predicted. Bolo could augment her remarks by exploring how often these leading indicators suggested that a recession is imminent against how often a recession subsequently occurred.

Consequences of Hindsight Bias

As a result of hindsight bias, FMPs may do the following:

- Overestimate the degree to which they correctly predicted an investment outcome, or the predictability of an outcome generally. This bias is closely related to overconfidence bias, which is discussed later in the reading.
- Unfairly assess money manager or security performance. Based on the ability to look back at what has taken place in securities markets, performance is compared against what has happened as opposed to expectations at the time the investment was made.

Detection of and Guidelines for Overcoming Hindsight Bias

Once understood, hindsight bias should be recognizable. FMPs should ask such questions as, "Am I re-writing history or being honest with myself about the mistakes I made?"

To guard against hindsight bias, FMPs should carefully record their investment decisions and key reasons for making those decisions in writing at or around the time the decision is made. Consulting these written records rather than memory will often produce a far more accurate examination of past decisions.

Processing Errors

Processing errors refer to information being processed and used illogically or irrationally. As opposed to belief perseverance biases, processing errors are less related to errors of memory or in assigning and updating probabilities; rather, they relate more closely to flaws in how information itself is processed.

Anchoring and Adjustment Bias

Anchoring and adjustment bias refers to relying on an initial piece of information to make subsequent estimates, judgments, and decisions. When required to estimate a value with unknown magnitude, people generally begin with some initial default number—an "anchor"—which they then adjust up or down. Regardless of how the initial anchor was chosen, people tend to adjust their anchors insufficiently and produce end approximations that are, consequently, biased. Anchoring and adjustment bias is closely related to conservatism bias. Bayes Rule again provides guidance for how new information should be incorporated into changing prior beliefs.

EXAMPLE 5

Anchoring and Adjustment Bias

Aiden Smythe is an equity research analyst at a brokerage firm. Smythe covers Industrial Lift Plc, a company that manufactures construction machinery. The company's business is sensitive to macroeconomic conditions, particularly non-residential construction activity. Last year, Industrial Lift reported £1.00 in EPS amid mostly strong non-residential construction activity levels. Smythe is updating his EPS estimate for this year. Non-residential construction activity has severely declined in the last two months, and some economists fear that a recession is likely. As a result, Smythe forecasts that EPS will fall 10% from the prior-year level, publishing a £0.90 estimate for the year.

Smythe's estimate exhibits anchoring and adjustment. Smythe's anchor is the prior year's EPS of £1.00, despite the possibility of a material change in underlying conditions.

Consequences of Anchoring and Adjustment Bias

As a result of anchoring and adjustment bias, FMPs may stick too closely to their original estimates when learning new information. This mindset is not limited to downside adjustments; the same phenomenon occurs with upside adjustments as well.

Detection of and Guidelines for Overcoming Anchoring and Adjustment Bias

The primary action FMPs can take is consciously asking questions that may reveal an anchoring and adjustment bias. Examples of such questions include, "Am I holding onto this stock based on rational analysis, or am I trying to attain a price that I am anchored to, such as the purchase price or a high water mark?" and "Am I making this forecast based on previously observed quantities or based on future expected conditions?"

It is important to remember that a company's revenues and earnings for a given period reflect conditions in that period. If the conditions in the future differ from the past, revenues and earnings will likely differ as well, sometimes radically. Similarly, security prices reflect investors' perception of the future at a given point in time; a given investor's cost basis, past market levels, and other conditions based in the past are often irrelevant. FMPs should look at the basis for any investment recommendation to see whether it is anchored to previous estimates or some "default" number.

Mental Accounting Bias

Mental accounting bias refers to mentally dividing money into "accounts" that influence decisions, even though money is **fungible** (Thaler 1980). Despite traditional finance theory assuming that FMPs consider their entire portfolio holistically in a risk–return context, Statman (1999, 2008) contends that the difficulty individuals have in addressing the interaction of different investments leads to mental accounting: Investors construct portfolios in a layered pyramid format, with each layer addressing a specific financial goal.

EXAMPLE 6

Mental Accounting Bias

Kendra Liu, an individual investor, owns shares in New Horizons Ltd., a pharmaceutical company. A drug in that company's research and development pipeline unexpectedly succeeds in a clinical trial, resulting in the shares doubling overnight. Liu sells half of her position in New Horizons and uses the proceeds to purchase shares of Cutting Edge Ltd., a small-cap biotechnology company. Liu believes that an investment in Cutting Edge is a "high-risk, high-reward bet" that could result in a total loss, but she is comfortable making the investment because she is using the proceeds from the sale of New Horizons Ltd., money that she did not expect to have anyway.

Liu's investment in Cutting Edge exhibits mental accounting bias. She has sorted the gains from New Horizons into a mental account based on its source, even though the money is fungible. Liu should invest the proceeds in a manner consistent with a holistic portfolio strategy.

Consequences of Mental Accounting Bias

As a result of mental accounting bias, FMPs may do the following:

- Neglect opportunities to reduce risk by combining assets with low correlations. Offsetting positions across various portfolio layers or mental accounts can lead to suboptimal aggregate performance.

- Irrationally distinguish between returns derived from income and those derived from capital appreciation. Although many investors feel the need to preserve principal, they focus on the idea of spending income that the principal generates. As a result, many FMPs chase income streams, unwittingly risking principal in the process.
- Irrationally bifurcate wealth or a portfolio into investment principal and investment returns. Some FMPs may believe that greater risk can be taken with returns (from either income or capital appreciation) than the principal initially contributed. A common euphemism for this scenario, from the casino world, is "playing with house money."

Detection of and Guidelines for Overcoming Mental Accounting Bias

An effective way to detect and overcome mental accounting behavior is to recognize its drawbacks. The primary drawback is that correlations between investments are not considered, leading to unintentional risk taking. FMPs should go through the exercise of combining all of their assets onto one spreadsheet (without headings or account labels) to see the holistic asset allocation. This exercise often produces information that is surprising when seen as a whole, such as higher cash balances than expected. The logical next step would be to create a portfolio strategy taking all assets into consideration.

Framing Bias

Framing bias is an information-processing bias in which a person answers a question differently based on the way in which it is asked or framed. It is often possible to frame a given decision problem in more than one way.

For example, a situation may be presented within a *gain* context (one in four start-up companies succeed) or within a *loss* context (three out of four start-ups fail). Given the first frame, an FMP may adopt a positive outlook and make venture capital investments. Given the second frame, the FMP might not.

Narrow framing occurs when people evaluate information based on a *narrow frame* of reference—that is, losing sight of the big picture in favor of one or two specific points. For example, an investor might focus solely on a company's executive management team, overlooking or even dismissing other important properties such as industry characteristics, fundamental performance, and valuation.

EXAMPLE 7

Effects of Framing Bias

Decision-making frames are quite prevalent in the context of investor behavior. Risk tolerance questionnaires can demonstrate how framing bias may occur in practice and how FMPs should be aware of its effects.

Suppose an investor is to take a risk tolerance questionnaire for the purpose of determining which "risk category" she is in. The risk category will determine asset allocations and the appropriate types of investments. The following information is provided to each questionnaire taker:

Over a 10-year period, Portfolio ABC has averaged an annual return of 10% with an annual standard deviation of 16%. Assuming a normal return distribution, in a given year there is a 67% probability that the return will fall within one standard deviation of the mean, a 95% probability that the return will fall within two standard deviations of the mean, and a 99.7% probability that the return will fall within three standard deviations of the mean. Thus, there is a

67% chance that the return earned by Portfolio ABC will be between −6% and 26%, a 95% chance that the return will be between −22% and 42%, and a 99.7% chance that the return will be between −38% and 58%.

The following two questions focus on hypothetical Portfolio ABC, DEF, and XYZ. The risk and return for each portfolio are the same in each of the two questions, but the presentation of information differs.

1. Based on the following chart, which investment portfolio fits your risk tolerance and desire for long-term return?

Portfolio	95% Probability Return Range	10-Year Average Return
XYZ	0.5% to 6.5%	3.5%
DEF	−18.0% to 30.0%	6.0%
ABC	−22.0% to 42.0%	10.0%

2. Based on the following chart, which investment portfolio fits your risk tolerance and desire for long-term return?

Portfolio	10-Year Average Return	Standard Deviation of Returns
XYZ	3.5%	1.5%
DEF	6.0%	12.0%
ABC	10.0%	16.0%

An investor may choose different portfolios when asked Question 1 compared with Question 2. Portfolio XYZ may appear more attractive in the first question, which uses two standard deviations to define the range of returns and show the risk, than in the second, which shows only the standard deviations. Also, in the second question, the returns are presented first and the measure of risk second. Thus, how questions are framed and the order in which they are presented can significantly affect how they are answered. FMPs should be acutely aware of how framing can affect investment choices.

Consequences of Framing Bias

As a result of framing bias, FMPs may do the following:

- Misidentify risk tolerances because of how questions about risk tolerance were framed, becoming more risk-averse when presented with a gain frame of reference and more risk-seeking when presented with a loss frame of reference. This misidentification may result in suboptimal portfolios.
- Focus on short-term price fluctuations, which may result in long-run considerations being ignored in the decision-making process.

Detection of and Guidelines for Overcoming Framing Bias

Framing bias is detected by asking such questions as, "Is the decision the result of focusing on a net gain or net loss position?" As discussed earlier, an investor who has framed the decision as a potential net loss is more likely to select a riskier investment; if the decision is framed as a potential net gain, however, the investor is more likely to go with a less risky investment. When making decisions, FMPs should try to eliminate any reference to gains and losses already incurred. Instead, they should focus on the future prospects of an investment and try to be as neutral and open-minded as possible when interpreting investment-related situations.

Availability Bias

Availability bias is an information-processing bias in which people estimate the probability of an outcome or the importance of a phenomenon based on how easily information is recalled. Various sources of availability bias exist; the four most applicable to FMPs are retrievability, categorization, narrow range of experience, and resonance.

Retrievability: If an answer or idea comes to mind more quickly than another answer or idea, the first answer or idea will likely be chosen as correct even if it is not the reality.

Categorization: When solving problems, people gather information from what they perceive as relevant search sets. Different problems require different search sets, which are often based on familiar categorizations. If it is difficult to come up with a search set, because the object of the search is difficult to characterize, the estimated probability of an event may be biased.

Narrow Range of Experience: When making an estimate, a person may use only a narrow range of experience instead of considering multiple perspectives. For example, assuming a product or service that has launched successfully in one country will be globally successful.

Resonance: People are often biased by how closely a situation parallels their own personal situation.

EXAMPLE 8

Availability Bias

A portfolio manager asks an analyst to research and present a list of companies that have "strong growth potential." The manager suggests looking for companies that sell a product or service different from its competitors—but with a compelling value proposition for customers—and that have a small share of a large market.

The analyst is familiar with technology companies, software in particular, based on prior work experience. The analyst has also seen a lot of news articles covering various software companies that, he believes, fit the criteria. The analyst begins screening among technology companies that have high revenue growth rates for the last two quarters. Although the analyst is aware that other companies in other sectors probably fit the criteria as well, the criteria are qualitative and vague such that they cannot be easily translated as screening input.

The analyst's behavior exhibits availability bias from by considering only technology companies in the search because he is familiar with them. The analyst should consult colleagues and/or external resources to widen his search to include all sectors and for help with creatively specifying screening criteria.

Consequences of Availability Bias

As a result of availability bias, FMPs may do the following:

- Limit their investment opportunity set. This limitation may result because they use familiar classification schemes. They may restrict investments to stocks or bonds, securities of one country or one sector, and so on.
- Choose an investment, investment adviser, or mutual fund based on advertising or the quantity of news coverage. For instance, when asked to name potential mutual fund companies to invest with, many people will name only the funds that do extensive advertising. The choice of mutual fund should be based on a variety of factors that make it a good fit given the investor's objectives and risk–return profile.

- Fail to diversify. This failure may occur because they make their choices based on a narrow range of experience. For example, an investor who works for a company in a particular industry may overweight investments in that industry.

Detection of and Guidelines for Overcoming Availability Bias

To overcome availability bias, investors need to develop an appropriate investment policy strategy, carefully research and analyze investment decisions before making them, and focus on long-term historical data. Questions such as, "How did you decide which investments to consider? Did you choose investments based on your familiarity with the industry or country? Did you see them in an article or research report?" and "Did you choose your investments because you like the companies' products?" can help identify issues of categorization, narrow range of experience, and resonance as sources of availability bias. Availability bias may cause FMPs to think that events that receive heavy media attention are more important than they actually are.

EXAMPLE 9

The following information relates to Questions 1–5

Luca Gerber recently became the chief investment officer for the Ludwigs Family Charity, a mid-size private foundation in Switzerland. Prior to assuming this role, Gerber was a well-known health care industry analyst. The Ludwigs's family fortune is primarily the result of entrepreneurship. Gerhard Ludwigs founded ABC Innovations (ABC), a biotech company dedicated to small cell lung cancer research. The foundation's portfolio is 15% invested in ABC.

Gerber initially feels that the 15% investment in ABC is high. Upon review, however, he decides it is appropriate based on the Ludwigs's involvement and their past success with similar ventures. Gerber makes a mental note to closely monitor the investment in ABC because he is unfamiliar with small-cap start-up companies. The remaining 85% of the foundation's portfolio is invested in equity of high-quality large-cap pharmaceutical companies. Gerber deems this allocation appropriate and is excited that he can continue to use his superior knowledge of the health care industry.

For the past two years, ABC has been dedicated to Project M, an effort directed at developing a drug to treat relapses in small cell lung cancer. Project M has delayed its Phase Two trials twice. Published results from Phase One trials have raised some concerns regarding the drug. In its last two quarterly investors' conference calls, ABC's CEO was very cautious in discussing expectations for Project M. ABC's stock price decreased by more than 20% during the past six months. Gerber believes that the research setbacks are temporary because of ABC's past success with projects. He expects that ABC will begin Phase Two within a year, and he also believes that once Project M goes into Phase Two, ABC's stock price should reach a new 52-week high of CHF80.

Soon after deciding to hold the stock, Gerber reads an article by ABC's chief scientist that details certain scientific results from Project M. As a conclusion, the article states: "Although we still have some major obstacles to overcome, the Project M team has seen positive signs that a treatment for small cell lung cancer is achievable." Although Gerber has difficulty interpreting the scientific results, he feels reassured after reading the concluding statement.

Today, ABC announces the news that it will no longer pursue Project M, citing early signs of the project's failure. In response to the announcement, the stock price drops by 50%. Gerber is stunned. He reviews the company's history and notes that ABC had made numerous comments on its struggles to solve Project M issues, which make the failure seem predictable at the time.

1. Gerber's assessment of the foundation's 100% allocation to biotechnology and pharmaceutical companies is most likely an example of which bias?

   A. Framing

   B. Availability

   C. Hindsight

   Solution:

   B is correct. A consequence of availability bias is a limited investment opportunity set, based on the narrow range of experience of the FMP. Gerber's prior experience has likely resulted in perceiving a portfolio concentrated in a single sector as appropriate because that sector reflects what he knows.

2. Gerber's belief that the research setbacks were merely temporary given ABC's success with past projects is most likely an example of which bias?

   A. Availability

   B. Mental accounting

   C. Conservatism

   Solution:

   C is correct. Conservatism bias can result in FMPs maintaining or only slowly updating their views when presented with new information, especially when the information is complex. Faced with complex information in the form of clinical trial delays that should have reduced his assessment of Project M's probability of success, Gerber elected to maintain his original views.

3. Researching the biotechnology industry average probability of success of Phase 2 trials, particularly those that have experienced delays, is a strategy that Gerber could have used to most likely mitigate which behavioral bias?

   A. Hindsight

   B. Representativeness

   C. Framing

   Solution:

   B is correct. A form of representativeness bias is base-rate neglect, in which general information, such as the rate of incidence of a phenomenon for its "reference class" of phenomena, is ignored in favor of individual, specific information. Gerber did not consider the "base rate" of the success of Phase 2 trials.

4. Gerber's approach to reading the article by ABC's chief scientist could best be described by exhibiting which behavioral bias?

   A. Representativeness

   B. Confirmation

C. Mental accounting

Solution:

B is correct. Confirmation bias refers to the tendency to seek confirming information and ignore contradictory information. Gerber did not adequately interpret the scientific results or the broader message of the article, choosing instead to focus on the reassuring concluding message that confirmed his existing beliefs.

5. Gerber's conclusion, upon re-examining ABC's history, is most likely an example of which behavioral bias?

   A. Confirmation

   B. Hindsight

   C. Conservatism

Solution:

B is correct. Hindsight bias is the result of selectively interpreting the past using knowledge of the present. Although Gerber should have implemented various mitigation strategies over the life of the investment, it is also true that investing, especially investing in a small-cap biotechnology company, is a probabilistic activity. Had Project M succeeded, Gerber may have been tempted to see the investment as evidence of his investment acumen, which would also be biased. The most useful examination of the past for Gerber would be investigating whether any mitigating actions or strategies would have been useful and putting them in place for subsequent investments.

EMOTIONAL BIASES 4

☐ discuss commonly recognized behavioral biases and their implications for financial decision making

We will now review six emotional biases, their implications for investment decision making, and suggestions for managing the effects of these biases. Emotional biases are harder to correct than cognitive errors because they originate from impulse or intuition rather than conscious calculations. It is often possible only to recognize the bias and adapt to it. The six emotional biases discussed are loss aversion, overconfidence, self-control, status quo, endowment, and regret aversion.

Loss-Aversion Bias

Loss-aversion bias refers to the tendency to strongly prefer avoiding losses to achieving gains. Rational FMPs should accept more risk to increase gains, not to mitigate losses. Paradoxically, in real life, FMPs instead tend to accept more risk to avoid losses than to achieve gains. Loss aversion leads FMPs to hold their losers to avoid recognizing losses and sell their winners to lock in profits.

Kahneman and Tversky (1979) describe loss-averse investor behavior as the evaluation of gains and losses based on a reference point. A utility function that passes through this reference point appears in Exhibit 1. It is S-shaped and asymmetric, implying a greater impact of losses than of gains on utility for the same variation in absolute value. This utility function implies risk-seeking behavior in the domain of losses (below the horizontal axis) and risk avoidance in the domain of gains (above the horizontal axis). An important concept embedded in this utility representation is what has been termed the **disposition effect**: the holding of investments that have experienced losses too long, and the selling of investments that have experienced gains too quickly (i.e., holding on to losers and selling winners). The resulting portfolio may be riskier than the optimal portfolio based on the investor's risk–return objectives.

Exhibit 1: Value Function of Loss Aversion

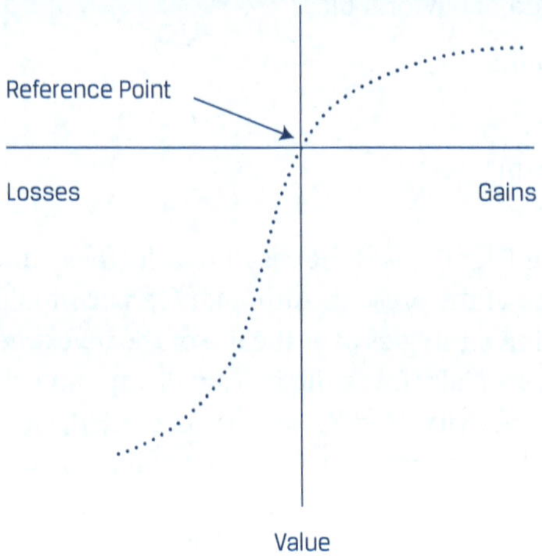

EXAMPLE 10

Effects of Loss-Aversion Bias

Loss-aversion bias, executed in practice as the disposition effect, is observed often by wealth management practitioners. The classic case of this bias is when an investor opens her monthly account statement and scans the individual investments for winners and losers. Seeing that some investments have lost money and others have gained, the investor is likely to respond by continuing to hold the losing investments. The idea of actually losing money is so painful that the first reaction is to hold the investment until it breaks even.

The investor is acting based on emotions, not cognitive reasoning. In this case, if she did some research, the investor might learn that the company in question is experiencing difficulty and that holding the investment actually adds to the risk in the portfolio (hence the term risk-seeking in the domain of losses).

Conversely, the winners are making money. Loss-averse FMPs tend to sell these investments and realize their gains to avoid seeing gains evaporate. In this case, if the investor did some research, she might learn that the company in question actually improves the portfolio's risk–return profile. By selling the investment, not only is the potential for future losses eliminated but the potential for future gains is also eliminated. Combining the added risk of holding the losers with the elimination of potential gains from selling the winners may make investors' portfolios less efficient than portfolios based on fundamental analysis.

Consequences of Loss Aversion

As a result of loss-aversion bias, FMPs may do the following:

- Hold investments in a loss position longer than justified by fundamental analysis, in the hope that they will return to breakeven.
- Sell investments in a gain position earlier than justified by fundamental analysis, out of fear that the gains will erode.

Detection of and Guidelines for Overcoming Loss Aversion

A disciplined approach to investment is a good way to alleviate the impact of the loss-aversion bias. It is impossible to make experiencing losses any less painful emotionally, but analyzing investments and realistically considering the probabilities of future losses and gains may help guide the FMP to a rational decision.

Overconfidence Bias

Overconfidence bias is a bias in which people demonstrate unwarranted faith in their own abilities. Overconfidence may be intensified when combined with **self-attribution bias**, in which people take too much credit for successes (*self-enhancing*) and assign responsibility to others for failures (*self-protecting*). Overconfidence has aspects of both cognitive and emotional errors but is classified as emotional because the bias primarily results from emotion.

Overconfidence bias has two forms: *prediction overconfidence* and *certainty overconfidence*. Both types demonstrate faulty reasoning combined with "gut feel" and hope. Prediction overconfidence occurs when the confidence intervals that FMPs assign to their investment predictions are too narrow. For example, when estimating the future value of a stock, overconfident FMPs will incorporate far too little variation—using a narrower range of expected payoffs and a lower standard deviation of returns—than justified by historical results and fundamental analysis.

Certainty overconfidence occurs when the probabilities that FMPs assign to outcomes are too high. This certainty is often an emotional response rather than a cognitive evaluation.

EXAMPLE 11

Overconfidence Bias

An analyst estimates that the price of oil will increase by 40% over the next 12 months because prevailing prices are lower than many oil producers' cost of production. Unprofitable producers reducing production will eventually put upward pressure on prices so long as oil demand remains stable or increases. Based on this forecast, the analyst recommends several high-yield bonds of oil producers to a portfolio manager.

The portfolio manager asks the analyst for an estimate of downside risk: "How much could we lose if, say, the oil price falls another 10%?" The analyst replies, "That is unrealistic. The current oil price is as low as it can go, and yields on these bonds are as attractive as they will ever be. We must make the investment now. There is no credible downside case."

The analyst is exhibiting overconfidence bias by placing excessive certainty in his prediction and not considering the likelihood or impact of variance from that prediction.

Consequences of Overconfidence Bias

As a result of overconfidence bias, FMPs may do the following:

- Underestimate risks and overestimate expected returns.
- Hold poorly diversified portfolios, which may result in significant downside risk.

Detection of and Guidelines for Overcoming Overconfidence Bias

FMPs should review their trading records, identify *both* the winners and losers, and calculate portfolio performance over at least two years. Investors with an unfounded belief in their own ability to identify good investments may recall winners and their results but underestimate the number and results of their losers. This review will also identify the amount of trading. Overconfidence is also a cognitive error, and so more-complete information can often help FMPs understand the error of their ways.

It is critical that investors be objective when making and evaluating investment decisions. As an old Wall Street adage states, "Don't confuse brains with a bull market." It is advisable to view the reasoning behind and the results of investments, both winners and losers, as objectively as possible. When did you make money? When did you lose money? Mentally separate your good money-making decisions from your bad ones. Then, review the beneficial decisions and try to discern what, exactly, you did correctly. Did you purchase an investment at a particularly advantageous time based on fundamentals, or did you luck out by timing a market upswing? Similarly, review the decisions that you categorized as poor. Did you invest aptly based on fundamentals and then make an error when it came time to sell, or was the market going through a correction?

When reviewing unprofitable decisions, look for patterns or common mistakes that perhaps you were unaware you were making. Note any such tendencies that you discover, and try to remain mindful of them by brainstorming a rule or reminder such as: "I will do X in the future" or "I will not do Y in the future."

Self-Control Bias

Self-control bias is a bias in which people fail to act in pursuit of their long-term, overarching goals in favor of short-term satisfaction. For example, individuals pursuing the CFA charter may fail to study sufficiently because of short-term competing demands on their time. Rational behavior suggests that people would do whatever is necessary to achieve their long-term goals, but it often does not happen.

When it comes to money, many people are willing and able to save for the future, but they often have difficulty sacrificing present consumption because of a lack of self-control. This apparent lack of self-control may also be a function of hyperbolic discounting, the human tendency to prefer small payoffs now compared with larger payoffs in the future. Sacrifices in the present require much greater payoffs in the future; otherwise, people will be unwilling to make current sacrifices.

Consequences of Self-Control Bias

As a result of self-control bias, FMPs may do the following:

- Save insufficiently for the future, which may, in turn, result in accepting too much risk in portfolios in an attempt to generate higher returns.
- Borrow excessively to finance present consumption.

Detection of and Guidelines for Overcoming Self-Control Bias

FMPs should ensure that a proper investment plan is in place and should have a personal budget. Plans need to be in writing, so that they can be reviewed regularly. Similarly, FMPs should look to maintain a strategic asset allocation based on a thorough evaluation.

Status Quo Bias

Status quo bias is an emotional bias in which people choose to do nothing (i.e., maintain the "status quo") instead of making a change, even when change is warranted. Status quo bias is often discussed in tandem with endowment and regret-aversion biases because an outcome of the biases, maintaining existing positions, is similar. The reasons for maintaining the existing positions differ, however. In the status quo bias, positions are maintained largely because of inertia rather than conscious choice. In endowment and regret-aversion biases, positions are maintained because of conscious, but possibly incorrect, choices.

EXAMPLE 12

The Path of Least Resistance

Using data from three firms, Choi et al. (2001) studied the impact of automatically enrolling employees in a defined contribution pension plan and how default contribution rates and investment options affect participants' behavior.

Automatic enrollment increased employee participation in the defined contribution plan from 26%–43% after six months' tenure and 57%–69% after three years' tenure to >85% for both tenures at all three firms.

Although automatic enrollment increased participation, more than 65% of employees tended to contribute the employer-specified default amount—2% or 3%—and remained in the default investment option. Although this percentage declined slowly over time, even after two years of tenure, more than 40% of participants continued to use the default.

Consequences of Status Quo Bias

As a result of status quo bias, FMPs may do the following:

- Unknowingly maintain portfolios with risk characteristics that are inappropriate for their circumstances.
- Fail to explore other opportunities.

Detection of and Guidelines for Overcoming Status Quo Bias

Status quo bias may be exceptionally strong and difficult to overcome. Education is essential. FMPs should quantify the risk-reducing and return-enhancing advantages of diversification and proper asset allocation. For example, with a concentrated stock position, showing what can happen to overall wealth levels if the stock collapses may persuade an FMP to diversify.

Endowment Bias

Endowment bias is an emotional bias in which people value an asset more when they own it than when they do not. Endowment bias is inconsistent with standard economic theory, which asserts that the price a person is *willing to pay* for a good should equal the price at which that person would be *willing to sell* the same good. Psychologists have found, however, that people tend to state minimum selling prices for a good that exceed maximum purchase prices that they are willing to pay for the same good. Effectively, ownership "endows" the asset with added value.

Endowment bias may be the result of several other behavioral biases, such as loss aversion, anchoring and adjustment, and overconfidence. Despite the name, purchased as well as inherited securities can be subject to endowment bias.

EXAMPLE 13

Endowment Bias

Several of an investment analyst's recommended stocks have done well for the past five years, prompting the portfolio manager to ask for a brief update on each, including valuations. For each stock, the analyst estimates that fair value is at least another 40% above the current price. The portfolio manager challenges the analyst by pointing out that the fair value estimates imply valuation multiples that are at least two standard deviations above the five-year average and are well above even the most bullish sell-side analyst's target price. The analyst responds by saying that the market is overlooking these companies' fundamentals. The portfolio manager then asks, "Would you buy these shares today?" The analyst answers, "Probably not."

The analyst is likely exhibiting endowment bias by overestimating the value of shares already owned in the portfolio. This bias is likely the result of having successfully invested in the shares.

Consequences of Endowment Bias

Endowment bias may lead FMPs to do the following:

- Fail to sell certain assets and replace them with other assets.
- Continue to hold classes of assets with which they are familiar. FMPs may believe they understand the characteristics of the investments they already own and may be reluctant to purchase assets with which they have less experience. Familiarity adds to owners' perceived value of a security.
- As a result, the FMP may maintain an inappropriate asset allocation. The portfolio may be inappropriate for investors' levels of risk tolerance and financial goals.

Detection of and Guidelines for Overcoming Endowment Bias

Many wealth management practitioners have encountered clients who are reluctant to sell securities bequeathed by previous generations. Often in these situations, investors cite feelings of disloyalty associated with the prospect of selling inherited securities, general uncertainty in determining the right choice, and concerns about tax issues. An FMP should ask, "If an equivalent sum to the value of the investments inherited had been received in cash, how would you invest the cash?" Often, the answer is into a very different investment portfolio than the one inherited. It may also be useful to explore the deceased's intent in owning the investment and bequeathing it. "Was the primary intent to leave the specific investment portfolio because it was perceived to be a suitable investment based on fundamental analysis, or was it to leave financial resources to benefit the heirs?" Heirs who affirm the latter conclusion are receptive to considering alternative asset allocations.

An effective way to address endowment bias for purchased securities, when an estimated "sell price" is far higher than any reasonable FMP's estimate of a "buy price" is to ask, "Would you buy this security today at the current price?" A similar question is, "Why are you not buying more of this security today?" Answering these questions can turn the focus away from the past to the present, toward considering the upside from the current price.

Regret-Aversion Bias

Regret-aversion bias is an emotional bias in which people tend to avoid making decisions out of fear that the decision will turn out poorly. Regret-aversion bias has two dimensions: actions that people take and actions that people *could have* taken. Regret is more intense when the unfavorable outcomes are the result of an action taken versus the result of an action not taken. Thus, no action becomes the default decision.

Consequences of Regret-Aversion Bias

As a result of regret-aversion bias, FMPs may do the following:

- Be too conservative in their investment choices as a result of poor outcomes on risky investments in the past. FMPs may wish to avoid the regret of making another bad investment and decide that low-risk instruments are better. This behavior can lead to long-term underperformance and failure to reach investment goals.
- Engage in herding behavior. FMPs may feel safer in popular investments in order to limit potential future regret. It seems safe to be with the crowd, and a reduction in potential emotional pain is perceived. Regret aversion may lead to preference for stocks of well-known companies even in the face of equal risk and return expectations. Choosing the stocks of less-familiar companies is perceived as riskier and involves more personal responsibility and greater potential for regret. As John Maynard Keynes (1936) wrote, "Worldly wisdom teaches that it is better for reputation to fail conventionally than to succeed unconventionally."

Detection of and Guidelines for Overcoming Regret-Aversion Bias

FMPs should quantify the risk-reducing and return-enhancing advantages of diversification and proper asset allocation. Regret aversion can cause some FMPs to invest too conservatively or too riskily depending on the current trends. With proper diversification, FMPs will accept the appropriate level of risk in their portfolios depending, of course, on return objectives. To prevent investments from being too conservative, FMPs must recognize that losses happen to everyone and keep in mind the long-term benefits of including risky assets in portfolios. Recognizing that bubbles happen and keeping in mind long-term objectives will prevent a client from making investments that are too risky.

EXAMPLE 14

Tiffany Jordan is a hedge fund manager with a history of outstanding performance. For the past 10 years, Jordan's fund has used an equity market–neutral strategy (a long–short strategy that strives to eliminate market risk—i.e., beta should be zero), which has proved effective as a result of Jordan's hard work. An equity market–neutral strategy normally generates large daily trading volume and shifts in individual security positions. Jordan's reputation has grown over the years as her fund has consistently beaten its benchmark. Employee turnover on her team has been high; Jordan tends to be quick to blame and rarely gives credit to team members for success. During the past 12 months, her fund has been significantly underperforming its benchmark.

One of Jordan's junior analysts, Jeremy Tang, is concerned about the underperformance and notes the following:

Observation 1: Certain positions are significantly underwater, have very high risk profiles, and have been held for much longer than normal.

Observation 2: The fund's trading volume has decreased by more than 40% during the past year.

Observation 3: The portfolio is more concentrated in a few sectors than in the past.

Worried that the portfolio may be in violation of the fund's investment policy statement (IPS), Tang brings this concern to Jordan's attention during a regular weekly team meeting. Jordan dismisses Tang's analysis and tells the team not to worry because she knows what she is doing. Jordan indicates that because she believes the pricing misalignment will correct itself, the portfolio would be unable to take advantage of the reversion to the mean if she were to sell certain losing positions. She reassures the team that this strategy has performed well in the past and that the markets will revert, bringing the fund's returns back to normal levels.

Tang tactfully suggests that the team review the fund's IPS together, and Jordan interrupts him and reminds the team that she has memorized the IPS by heart. Tang contemplates his next step. He is concerned that Jordan is displaying behavioral biases that are affecting the fund's performance.

1. By taking credit for successes but assigning blame for failures, Jordan is *most likely* demonstrating:

   A. loss-aversion bias.

   B. self-attribution bias.

   C. illusion of control bias.

   Solution:

   B is correct. In self-attribution bias, people take credit for successes and assign responsibilities for failure. Jordan claims successful decisions for herself while attributing poor decisions to the team. Her self-esteem affects how she looks at success and failure. Self-attribution and illusion of knowledge biases contribute to overconfidence bias, which Jordan clearly demonstrates later when she tells the team that she knows what she is doing.

2. Which of Tang's observations is *least likely* to be the consequence of Jordan demonstrating loss-aversion bias?

   A. Observation 1

   B. Observation 2

C. Observation 3

Solution:

C is correct. Loss aversion by itself may cause a sector concentration; however, a market-neutral strategy tends to focus on individual stocks without regard to sector. The sector exposure would be mitigated with the balancing of the individual long and short positions.

3. Which of Jordan's actions *least* supports that she may be affected by the illusion of control bias?

A. Her dismissal of Tang's analysis

B. Her routine of holding weekly team meetings

C. Her comment on market turnaround and current holdings

Solution:

B is correct. Holding weekly team meetings, which indicates a willingness to listen to feedback from others, is not representative of the illusion of control bias. In the illusion of control bias, people believe they can control outcomes to a greater extent than is possible. Individuals exhibiting this bias display great certainty in their predictions of outcomes of chance events and ignore others' viewpoints. Jordan is sure that the market will turn around even though it is out of her control. She chooses not to listen to Tang, who is questioning her viewpoint.

4. How does Jordan *most likely* demonstrate loss-aversion bias?

A. Telling the team not to worry

B. Reducing the portfolio turnover this year

C. Deciding to hold the losing positions until they turn around

Solution:

C is correct. Jordan's behavior is a classic example of loss aversion: When a loss occurs, she holds on to these positions longer than warranted. By doing so, Jordan has accepted more risk in the portfolio. In loss-aversion bias, people exhibit a strong preference to avoid losses versus achieving gains. One of the consequences of loss aversion bias is that the financial management professional (in this case, Jordan) may hold losing investments in the hope that they will return to breakeven or better.

5. Which of the following emotional biases has Jordan *most likely* exhibited?

A. Endowment

B. Regret aversion

C. Overconfidence

Solution:

C is correct. Jordan exhibits overconfidence in several ways. She ignores the analysis done by Tang. This may be because Jordan believes she is smarter and more informed than her team members, which is typical of an individual with an illusion of knowledge bias. The certainty she demonstrates that the market will revert is evidence of overconfidence. Her overconfidence is intensified by her self-attribution bias, which is demonstrated through her dealings with her team when she blames them for losses while taking credit for gains. Finally, her portfolio's underperformance against the benchmark is a consequence of overconfidence bias.

6. Which of the following biases did Jordan *not* demonstrate?

   A. Self-attribution

   B. Representativeness

   C. Illusion of knowledge

   Solution:

   B is correct. Nowhere in the scenario did it mention that Jordan classified certain information into a personalized category. Representativeness bias is a cognitive bias in which people tend to classify new information based on past experiences and classifications. Jordan is not relating her certainty about the future or her decision to hold losing positions back to anything she has done or experienced in the past.

7. Which of Tang's findings is *not* a typical consequence of self-control bias?

   A. Failure to explore other portfolio opportunities

   B. Asset allocation imbalance problems in the portfolio

   C. A higher risk profile in the portfolio resulting from pursuit of higher returns

   Solution:

   A is correct. Failing to explore other opportunities is a demonstration of status quo bias, not self-control. Self-control bias occurs when individuals deviate from their long-term goals—in this case, the IPS—because of a lack of self-discipline. Jordan is not adhering to the strategy that has succeeded in the past. The consequences of self-control bias include accepting too much risk in the portfolio (C) and asset allocation imbalance problems (B) as Jordan attempts to generate higher returns.

5 BEHAVIORAL FINANCE AND MARKET BEHAVIOR

☐ describe how behavioral biases of investors can lead to market characteristics that may not be explained by traditional finance

Some persistent market patterns run counter to market efficiency. This section focuses on the contributions of behavioral finance to understanding these exceptions to market efficiency, such as momentum, value, bubbles, and crashes, by explaining them as functions of behavioral biases.

Defining Market Anomalies

Anomalies are apparent deviations from the efficient market hypothesis, identified by persistent abnormal returns that differ from zero and are predictable in direction. Not every deviation is anomalous. Misclassifications tend to stem from three sources: choice of asset pricing model, statistical issues, and temporary disequilibria.

Classifying returns as "abnormal" presupposes a definition of "normal returns," which generally depends on the asset pricing model used. If a reasonable change in the method of estimating normal returns causes an anomaly to disappear, then it is reasonable to suggest that the anomaly is an illusion. Fama (1998) includes in this category apparently low returns following initial public offerings (called the "IPO puzzle") and the positive abnormal returns apparent in the 12 months after a stock split. Similarly, when high returns persist on a particular class of securities, or relative to a specific factor in valuation, it might simply be compensation for excess risk rather than an anomaly.

Other apparent anomalies may be explained by the small samples involved, a statistical bias in selection or survivorship, or data mining that overanalyzes data for patterns and treats spurious correlations as relevant. The magnitude of any over- or underperformance also depends critically on the choice of benchmark, which can make it hard to interpret results.

Finally, from time to time, markets can present *temporary disequilibrium behavior*, unusual features that may survive for a period of years but ultimately disappear. Publication of the anomaly, which draws attention to the pattern, usually starts the arbitrage that removes the behavior. For example, the small company January effect, part of the turn-of-the-year effect, does not appear persistent once appropriate adjustment for risk is made. The weekend effect, involving lower stock market returns on Mondays, appears to have diminished in the United States and United Kingdom.

The anomalies discussed in this section reflect behavior that has been identified and analyzed in a number of markets around the world and during different periods. The patterns have been documented in many academic studies, with broadly similar conclusions. Behavioral finance can help provide good explanations by identifying underlying behavioral biases.

Momentum

Studies have documented, in a range of markets globally, *momentum* or *trending effects* in which future price behavior correlates with that of the recent past (Jegadeesh and Titman 1993; Dimson, Marsh, and Staunton 2008). The positive correlation typically lasts for up to two years before showing a reversal or reversion to the mean, evident in two- to five-year return periods.

EXAMPLE 15

The Momentum Effect: London Business School Study

The study involves buying the top 20% of a performance-ranked list of stocks and selling short the bottom 20%. In the 52 years to 2007 in the UK market, the stocks that had outperformed the market most in the previous 12 months went on to generate an annualized return of 18.3%, whereas the market's worst underperformers rose by 6.8% on average. During that period, the market as a whole rose by 13.5% a year. In a subsequent study using data from 2000 to 2007, the momentum effect was also evident in each of the 16 other international markets researched.

The authors noted, "The momentum effect, both in the United Kingdom and globally, has been pervasive and persistent. Though costly to implement on a standalone basis, all investors need to be acutely aware of momentum. Even if they do not set out to exploit it, momentum is likely to be an important determinant of their investment performance."

Source: Dimson, Marsh, and Staunton (2008).

Momentum can be partly explained by availability, hindsight, and loss aversion biases.

Studies have identified faulty learning models within traders, in which reasoning is based on their recent experience. Behaviorally, this is *availability bias*. In this context, availability bias is also called the *recency effect*, which is the tendency to recall recent events more vividly and give them undue weight. In such models, if the price of an asset rises for a period of time, investors may simply extrapolate this rise to the future. Research points to a tendency for individual private investors to extrapolate trends and to suffer more from recency bias, whereas many investment professionals expect reversion to the mean.

Regret is the feeling that an opportunity has been missed and is typically an expression of *hindsight bias*, which reflects the human tendency to see past events as having been predictable. Regret can be particularly acute when the market is volatile and investors feel they could have predicted the significant market moves, thereby increasing profit or reducing loss. Faced with regret from not owning a mutual fund or stock when it performed well in the previous year, investors may be driven emotionally to remedy this regret. These behavioral factors can explain short-term year-on-year trending and contribute to overtrading.

Bubbles and Crashes

Although bubbles and crashes have been documented for a long time (Mackay's *Extraordinary Popular Delusions and the Madness of Crowds* was published in 1841), their existence presents a challenge to the concept of market efficiency. Historical examples include the technology bubble of 1999–2000 and the residential property boom of 2005–2007, evident in a range of economies globally including the United States, the United Kingdom, and Australia. Exhibit 2 illustrates the residential property boom in the United Kingdom.

Exhibit 2: UK House Price Average Multiple of Average Family Income

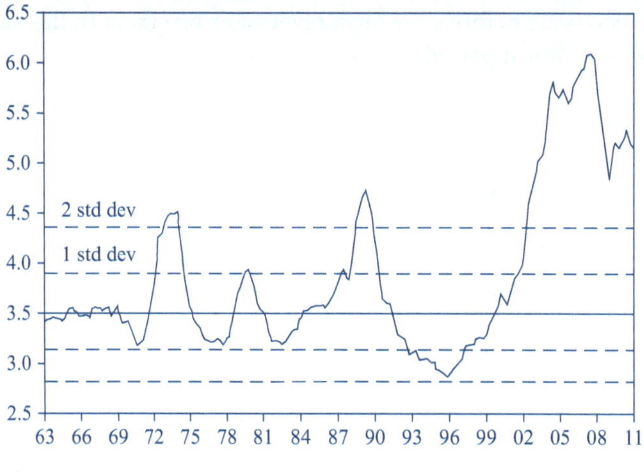

Source: Datastream.

First, note that some bubbles may have rational explanations. Rational investors may expect a future crash but not know its exact timing. For periods of time, there may not be effective arbitrage because of the cost of selling short, unwillingness of investors to bear extended losses, or simply unavailability of suitable instruments. These factors were considerations in past technology and real estate bubbles. Investment managers incentivized on, or accountable for, short-term performance may even rationalize their participation in the bubble in terms of commercial or career risk.

Investors' behaviors and incentives during bubbles are illustrated in Exhibit 16. The manager of Fund A believed he could exit a bubble profitably by selling near the top. The manager of Fund B correctly avoided the bubble, but clients held the manager accountable for short-run performance, which resulted in the fund's closure.

EXAMPLE 16

Investor Behavior in Bubbles

Consider the differing behavior of two managers of major hedge funds during the technology stock bubble of 1998–2000:

The manager of Hedge Fund A was asked why he did not get out of internet stocks earlier even though he knew by December 1999 that technology stocks were overvalued. He replied, "We thought it was the eighth inning, and it was the ninth. I did not think the NASDAQ composite would go down 33% in 15 days." Faced with losses, and despite his previous strong 12-year record, he resigned as Hedge Fund A's manager in April 2000.

The manager of Hedge Fund B refused to invest in technology stocks in 1998 and 1999 because he thought they were overvalued. After strong performance over 17 years, Hedge Fund B was dissolved in 2000 because its returns could not keep up with the returns generated by technology stocks.

Behavioral finance does not yet provide a full explanation for bubbles and crashes, but a number of specific cognitive biases and emotional biases prevalent during such periods can be identified.

In bubbles, investors often exhibit symptoms of *overconfidence*; overtrading, underestimation of risks, failure to diversify, and rejection of contradictory information. With overconfidence, investors are more active and trading volume increases, thus lowering their expected profits. For overconfident investors (active traders), studies have shown that returns are less than returns to either less active traders or the market while risk is higher. At the market level, volatility also often increases in a market with overconfident traders.

The overconfidence and excessive trading that contribute to a bubble are linked to *confirmation bias* and *self-attribution bias*. In a rising market, sales of stocks from a portfolio will typically be profitable, even if winners are being sold too soon. Investors can have faulty learning models that bias their understanding of this profit to take personal credit for success, a form of *hindsight bias*. Selling for a gain appears to validate a good decision in an original purchase and may confer a sense of pride in locking in the profit. This dynamic fuels overconfidence that can lead to poor decisions. Regret aversion can also encourage investors to participate in a bubble, believing they are "missing out" on profit opportunities as stocks appreciate.

As a bubble unwinds, markets may underreact because of anchoring when investors do not sufficiently update their beliefs. The early stages of unwinding a bubble can involve investors in cognitive dissonance, who ignore losses and attempt to rationalize flawed decisions. Eventually, investors capitulate, which accelerates price declines.

Value

Value stocks are typically characterized by low price-to-earnings ratios, high book-to-market equity, and low price-to-dividend ratios. Growth stock characteristics are generally the opposite of value stock characteristics. For example, growth stocks are characterized by low book-to-market equity, high price-to-earnings ratios, and high price-to-dividend ratios. A number of studies have identified outperformance of value stocks relative to growth stocks over long periods. Fama and French (1998) found that value stocks (high book-to-market equity) outperformed growth stocks (low book-to-market equity) in 12 of 13 major markets during the 1975–1995 period.

Fama and French have also found, however, that the value stock anomaly disappears in a three-factor asset pricing model. This result suggests that size and book-to-market factors are not mispricing but instead represent compensation for risk exposures, such as the greater potential of companies with these characteristics to suffer distress during economic downturns.

A number of other studies have offered behavioral explanations for value anomalies, presenting the anomalies as mispricing rather than compensation for increased risk. These studies recognize the emotional factors involved in appraising stocks. The **halo effect**, for example, extends a favorable evaluation of some characteristics to other characteristics. A company with a good growth record and good previous share price performance might be seen as a good investment, with higher expected returns than its risk characteristics merit. This view is a form of representativeness that can lead investors to extrapolate recent past performance into expected returns. Overconfidence can also be involved in predicting growth rates, potentially leading growth stocks to be overvalued.

Studies have also identified that emotions play a role in estimating risk and expected return of stocks. The impact of emotional biases may be greater with less sophisticated or retail investors, but it has also been identified as a bias in analysts and professional investors. The emotional attraction of a stock can be enhanced by personal experience of products, the value of the brand, marketing expenditures, and the proximity of the headquarters to the analyst or investor. This last issue reflects the **home bias** anomaly, by which portfolios exhibit a strong bias in favor of domestic securities in the context of global portfolios. The effect has also been noted within geographical boundaries, favoring companies headquartered nearer the investor. Home bias may reflect a perceived relative informational advantage, a greater feeling of comfort with the access to company executives that proximity brings (either personal or local brokerage), or a psychological desire to invest in a local community.

To the extent to which less sophisticated investors are influenced by emotions, they may value growth companies more highly. Stock returns of funds that are rated as popular in a *Fortune* magazine survey are found to be subsequently low. A more positive emotional rating in a company leads investors to perceive the company's stock as less risky. Although the capital asset pricing model assumes risk and expected return are positively correlated, many investors behave as if the correlation is negative, expecting higher returns with lower risk.

SUMMARY

Behavioral biases potentially affect the behaviors and decisions of financial market participants. By understanding these biases, financial market participants may be able to moderate or adapt to them and, as a result, improve upon economic outcomes. Behavioral biases may be categorized as either cognitive errors or emotional biases. The type of bias influences whether its impact may be moderated or adapted to.

Among the points made in this reading are the following:

- Individuals do not necessarily act rationally and consider all available information in the decision-making process because they may be influenced by behavioral biases.
- Biases may lead to suboptimal decisions.

- Behavioral biases may be categorized as either cognitive errors or emotional biases. A single bias may have aspects of both, however, with one type of bias dominating.
- Cognitive errors stem from basic statistical, information-processing, or memory errors; cognitive errors typically result from faulty reasoning.
- Emotional biases stem from impulse or intuition and tend to result from reasoning influenced by feelings.
- Cognitive errors are more easily corrected for because they stem from faulty reasoning rather than an emotional predisposition.
- Emotional biases are harder to correct for because they are based on feelings, which can be difficult to change.
- To adapt to a bias is to recognize and accept the bias and to adjust for the bias rather than to attempt to moderate the bias.
- To moderate a bias is to recognize the bias and to attempt to reduce or even eliminate the bias within the individual.
- Cognitive errors can be further classified into two categories: belief perseverance biases and information-processing biases.
- Belief perseverance errors reflect an inclination to maintain beliefs. The belief is maintained by committing statistical, information-processing, or memory errors. Belief perseverance biases are closely related to the psychological concept of cognitive dissonance.
- Belief perseverance biases include conservatism, confirmation, representativeness, illusion of control, and hindsight.
- Information-processing biases result in information being processed and used illogically or irrationally.
- Information-processing biases include anchoring and adjustment, mental accounting, framing, and availability.
- Emotional biases include loss aversion, overconfidence, self-control, status quo, endowment, and regret aversion.
- Understanding and detecting biases is the first step in overcoming the effect of biases on financial decisions. By understanding behavioral biases, financial market participants may be able to moderate or adapt to the biases and, as a result, improve upon economic outcomes.
- Behavioral finance has the potential to explain some apparent deviations from market efficiency (market anomalies).

REFERENCES

Fama, Eugene. 1998. "Market Efficiency, Long-Term Returns, and Behavioral Finance." *Journal of Financial Economics* 49 vol. (3):283–306. doi:10.1016/S0304-405X(98)00026-9

Keynes, John Maynard. 1936. *The General Theory of Employment, Interest, and Money*. New York: Harcourt, Brace.

Statman, Meir. 1999. "Behavioral Finance: Past Battles and Future Engagements." *Financial Analysts Journal* 55 vol. (6):18–27. doi:10.2469/faj.v55.n6.2311

Statman, Meir. 2008. "What Is Behavioral Finance?" In *Handbook of Finance*, ed. Fabozzi, Frank. Hoboken, NJ: John Wiley & Sons.

Thaler, Richard H. 1980. "Toward a Positive Theory of Economic Choice." *Journal of Economic Behavior & Organization* 1 vol. (1):39–60. doi:10.1016/0167-2681(80)90051-7

PRACTICE PROBLEMS

1. Under-diversified portfolios are not a potential implication of which of the following behavioral biases?

   A. Representativeness

   B. Illusion of control

   C. Confirmation

2. The advice "Don't confuse brains with a bull market" is aimed at mitigating which of the following behavioral biases?

   A. Self-control

   B. Conservatism

   C. Overconfidence

3. Status quo bias is least similar to which of the following behavioral biases?

   A. Endowment

   B. Regret aversion

   C. Confirmation

4. Which strategy would best mitigate or prevent endowment bias?

   A. Actively seeking out information that challenges existing beliefs

   B. When new information is presented, asking "How does this information change my forecast?"

   C. Asking "Would you buy this security today at the current price?"

5. Jun Park, CFA, works at a hedge fund. Most of Park's colleagues are also CFA charterholders. At an event with recent university graduates, Park comments, "Most CFA charterholders work at hedge funds." Park's remark exhibits which behavioral bias?

   A. Availability

   B. Conservatism

   C. Framing

6. In the 1980s, Japan was viewed by many FMPs as the model economy. Although its growth began to decelerate sharply by 1990, it was not until the mid to late 1990s that FMPs' GDP forecasts were consistently achieved. By taking several years to adapt their forecasts to the lower growth environment, FMPs exhibited which behavioral bias?

   A. Mental accounting

   B. Overconfidence

   C. Conservatism

The following information relates to questions 7-10

Caitríona Daosri is a portfolio manager for an international bank, where she advises high-net-worth clients. Daosri is meeting with a new client, Estêvão Kai, a 40-year-old surgeon with €4 million across various accounts and a salary of €500,000 per annum. Kai explains to Daosri that he has four accounts at four different banks, each with specific sources and uses of funds, as shown in the following table:

Bank Account	Source of Deposits	Use of Funds
1	Salary	Living expenses
2	Bonus	Charitable gifts
3	Portfolio interest	Savings for retirement
4	Portfolio dividends	Mother's living expenses

7. Based on the description of how Kai manages his finances as outlined in Exhibit 1, Kai most likely exhibits the behavioral bias of:

   A. endowment.

   B. mental accounting.

   C. framing.

8. Which of the following is a likely consequence of Kai's approach to managing his finances?

   A. Concentrated portfolio positions

   B. Forgone opportunities to reduce risk by combining assets with low correlations

   C. Excessive trading

9. Which strategy should Daosri use or recommend to Kai?

   A. Keep written records of investment decisions.

   B. Ask questions such as, "Is the decision the result of focusing on a net gain or net loss position?"

   C. Aggregate all accounts and portfolios into a single spreadsheet.

10. Which of the following individual behavioral biases is most strongly associated with market bubbles?

    A. Overconfidence

    B. Representativeness

    C. Framing

---

11. The halo effect, which may be evident in FMP's assessments of a company with a

history of high revenue growth, is a form of which behavioral bias?

A. Endowment

B. Representativeness

C. Regret aversion

12. All of the following are reasons that an apparent deviation from the efficient market hypothesis might not be anomalous except:

A. The abnormal returns represent compensation for exposure to risk.

B. Changing the asset pricing model makes the deviation to disappear.

C. The deviation is well known or documented.

13. Investment managers incentivized or accountable for short-term performance by current and prospective clients is a potentially rational explanation for which of the following?

A. Home bias

B. Bubbles

C. Value stocks outperforming growth stocks

14. Momentum, can be partly explained by the following behavioral biases except:

A. availability.

B. home bias.

C. regret.

15. All of the following are reasons that the historical outperformance of value stocks versus growth stocks may not be anomalous except:

A. Abnormal returns represent compensation for risk exposures, such as the heightened risk of value stocks to suffer distress during downturns.

B. Companies with strong historical growth rates are viewed as good investments, with higher expected returns than risk characteristics merit.

C. The deviation disappears by incorporating a three-factor asset pricing model.

SOLUTIONS

1. A is correct. Under-diversified portfolios are a consequence of both illusion of control and confirmation biases. Researchers have found that some investors prefer to invest in companies that they feel they have control over, such as the companies they work for, leading them to hold concentrated positions. Confirmation bias may lead to FMPs ignoring negative news, paying attention only to information confirming that a company is a good investment, which may result in large positions. Representativeness bias is not typically associated with under-diversified portfolios.

2. C is correct. This advice is specifically aimed at reducing self-attribution bias, a form of overconfidence bias. This bias may result in FMPs taking credit for investment success, as well as assigning responsibility to others for investment failures, when in reality the investment results reflect exogenous market forces.

3. C is correct. Both endowment bias and regret-aversion bias often result in indecision or inertia—a typical outcome of status quo bias, in which people prefer to not make changes even when changes are warranted.

4. C is correct. Endowment bias refers to people attributing additional, unwarranted value to things they possess versus things they do not. This bias is evident in FMPs that systematically and materially overvalue securities in their portfolio versus securities not in their portfolio. The question "Would you buy this security today at the current price?" turns the investor's attention to assessing the reasonableness of the current price as a buy price rather than solely as a selling price.

5. A is correct. Park is extrapolating his observation based on a narrow range of experience (working at a hedge fund that employs many CFA charterholders) to the entire population of CFA charterholders. Using a narrow range of experience is a form of availability bias.

6. C is correct. Conservatism bias results in maintain or only slowly updating views and forecasts despite the presence of new information. FMPs in the 1990s were reluctant to update forecasts, despite materially different new information for several years.

7. B is correct. Kai has segregated money into four different accounts based on the sources and uses of his funds. Although intuitively appealing, this approach is irrational because money is fungible across the four accounts. Nothing is stopping Kai from collapsing them into a single "account" with a holistic portfolio strategy.

8. B is correct. The most common consequence of mental accounting is neglecting opportunities to reduce risk by combining assets with low correlations, because each account's asset allocation is examined discretely. Offsetting positions across accounts, or an overall inefficient allocation with respect to risk, can lead to suboptimal aggregate performance.

9. C is correct. Aggregating mental accounts is a logical strategy to combat mental accounting. It is the opposite of disaggregating money into separate accounts.

10. A is correct. The overconfidence and excessive trading that contribute to a bubble are linked to self-attribution bias, a form of overconfidence. In a rising market, sales of stocks from a portfolio will typically be profitable, even if winners are being sold too soon, and FMPs will attribute profits and strong performance to

their investment acumen and subsequently underestimate risks.

11. B is correct. Representativeness refers to the tendency to adopt a view or forecast based on individual information or a small sample, as well to use simple classifications. The halo effect is an example of representativeness, because FMPs extend an overall favorable evaluation to an investment (e.g., a "good company") based on one or few characteristics (e.g., a "visionary CEO").

12. C is correct. Bubbles and crashes are well-known and well-documented phenomena yet represent market anomalies.

13. B is correct. Investment managers' incentives—or perhaps more accurately, their perception of their incentives—for short-term performance were named as considerations in the technology and real estate bubbles. Not participating in the bubble presented certain FMPs with commercial or career risk.

14. B is correct. Home bias refers to FMPs preferentially investing in domestic securities, likely reflecting perceived relative informational advantages, a greater feeling of comfort with the access to company executives that proximity brings (either personal or through a local brokerage), or a psychological desire to invest in a local community. Momentum, on the other hand, has been documented in a range of markets around the world, in a time-dependent manner, and reflects some FMPs' availability bias, manifested as a belief that stocks will continue to rise because recently they have only risen, as well as regret aversion by those who invest in past winners because they regret not investing in them in the past.

15. B is correct. This choice describes the halo effect, which does offer a behavioral explanation for the poor performance of growth stocks versus value stocks. Growth stocks are mispriced relative to their risk characteristics, because FMPs focusing on just a few properties, such as a high historical revenue growth rate, while neglecting other characteristics.

LEARNING MODULE

6

Introduction to Risk Management

by Don M. Chance, PhD, CFA, and Michael E. Edleson, PhD, CFA.

Don M. Chance, PhD, CFA, is at Louisiana State University (USA). Michael E. Edleson, PhD, CFA, is at the University of Chicago (USA).

LEARNING OUTCOMES

Mastery	The candidate should be able to:
☐	define risk management
☐	describe features of a risk management framework
☐	define risk governance and describe elements of effective risk governance
☐	explain how risk tolerance affects risk management
☐	describe risk budgeting and its role in risk governance
☐	identify financial and non-financial sources of risk and describe how they may interact
☐	describe methods for measuring and modifying risk exposures and factors to consider in choosing among the methods

INTRODUCTION

1

Risk—and risk management—is an inescapable part of economic activity. People generally manage their affairs to be as happy and secure as their environment and resources will allow. But regardless of how carefully these affairs are managed, there is risk because the outcome, whether good or bad, is seldom predictable with complete certainty. There is risk inherent in nearly everything we do, but this reading will focus on economic and financial risk, particularly as it relates to investment management.

All businesses and investors manage risk, whether consciously or not, in the choices they make. At its core, business and investing are about allocating resources and capital to chosen risks. In their decision process, within an environment of uncertainty, these organizations may take steps to avoid some risks, pursue the risks that provide the highest rewards, and measure and mitigate their exposure to these risks as necessary. Risk management processes and tools make difficult business and financial problems easier to address in an uncertain world. Risk is not just a matter of fate; it is something that organizations can actively manage with their decisions, within a risk management framework. Risk is an integral part of the business or investment process. Even in the earliest models of modern portfolio theory, such as mean–variance portfolio optimization and the capital asset pricing model, investment return is linked directly to risk but requires that risk be managed optimally. Proper identification and measurement of risk, and keeping risks aligned with the goals of the enterprise, are key factors in managing businesses and investments. Good risk management results in a higher chance of a preferred outcome—more value for the company or portfolio or more utility for the individual.

Portfolio managers need to be familiar with risk management not only to improve the portfolio's risk–return outcome, but also because of two other ways in which they use risk management at an enterprise level. First, they help to manage their own companies that have their own enterprise risk issues. Second, many portfolio assets are claims on companies that have risks. Portfolio managers need to evaluate the companies' risks and how those companies are addressing them.

This reading takes a broad approach that addresses both the risk management of enterprises in general and portfolio risk management. The principles underlying portfolio risk management are generally applicable to the risk management of financial and non-financial institutions as well.

The concept of risk management is also relevant to individuals. Although many large organizations formally practice risk management, most individuals practice it more informally and some practice it haphazardly, oftentimes responding to risk events after they occur. Although many individuals do take reasonable precautions against unwanted risks, these precautions are often against obvious risks. The more subtle risks are often ignored. Unfortunately, many individuals do not view risk management as a formal, systematic process that would help them achieve not only their financial goals but also the ultimate goal, or maximum utility as economists like to call it, but they should.

Although the primary focus of this reading is on institutions, we will also cover risk management as it applies to individuals. We will show that many common themes underlie risk management—themes that are applicable to both organizations and individuals.

Although often viewed as defensive, risk management is a valuable offensive weapon in the manager's arsenal. In the quest for preferred outcomes, such as higher profit, returns, or share price, management does not usually get to choose the outcomes but does choose the risks it takes in pursuit of those outcomes. The choice of which risks to undertake through the allocation of its scarce resources is the key tool available to management. An organization with a comprehensive risk management culture in place, in which risk is integral to every key strategy and decision, should perform better in the long-term, in good times and bad, as a result of better decision making.

The fact that all businesses and investors engage in risky activities (i.e., activities with uncertain outcomes) raises a number of important questions. The questions that this reading will address include the following:

- What is risk management, and why is it important?
- What risks does an organization (or individual) face in pursuing its objectives?
- How are an organization's goals affected by risk, and how does it make risk management decisions to produce better results?
- How does risk governance guide the risk management process and risk budgeting to integrate an organization's goals with its activities?
- How does an organization measure and evaluate the risks it faces, and what tools does it have to address these risks?

The answers to these questions collectively help to define the process of risk management. This reading is organized along the lines of these questions. Sections 2 and 3 describe the risk management process, and Sections 4–6 discuss risk governance and risk tolerance. Sections 7 and 8 cover the identification of various risks, and Sections 9–11 addresses the measurement and management of risks.

RISK MANAGEMENT PROCESS 2

☐ define risk management

Risk, broadly speaking, is exposure to uncertainty. Risk is also the concept used to describe all of the uncertain environmental variables that lead to variation in and unpredictability of outcomes. More colloquially, risk is about the chance of a loss or adverse outcome as a result of an action, inaction, or external event.

This last view may make it sound as if risk is something to be avoided. But that is not at all the case. Risk is a key ingredient in the recipe for business or investment success; return without risk is generally a false hope and usually a prescription for falling short of one's goals. Risks taken must be carefully chosen, understood, and well-managed to have a chance at adding value through decisions. Risk and return are the interconnected forces of the financial universe. Many decision makers focus on return, which is not something that is easily controlled, as opposed to risk, or exposure to risk, which may actually be managed or controlled.

Risk exposure is the extent to which the underlying environmental or market risks result in actual risk borne by a business or investor who has assets or liabilities that are sensitive to those risks. It is the state of being exposed or vulnerable to a risk. Risk exposure results from the decisions of an organization or investor to take on risk-sensitive assets and liabilities.

Suppose there is an important announcement in Japan that will result in the yen either appreciating or depreciating by 1%. The range of possible outcomes in real situations is clearly not as simple as the up-or-down 1% case used here, but we will use a simplified example to make an important point. The risk is the uncertain outcome of this event, and the currency risk to a non-Japanese business is the uncertain return or variation in return in domestic currency terms that results from the event. The risk can be described as the range of resulting outcomes and is often thought of in terms of a probability distribution of future returns. Suppose that the underlying amount is ¥1,000,000. The risk exposure of a business may be zero or it could be sizable, depending on whether the business has assets or liabilities tied to this risk—in this case, exposure to that currency. One million yen would, in this example, result in ¥10,000 of risk exposure (1% of ¥1,000,000). Risk management would include, among other things, quantifying and understanding this risk exposure, deciding how and why to have the exposure and how much risk the participant can bear, and possibly mitigating this risk by tailoring the exposure in several ways. The risk management process would inform the decision of whether to operate or invest in this risky currency.

The word "risk" can be confusing because it is used by different people at different times to mean so many different things. Even when used properly, the term has three related but different meanings, which this example illustrates well. Risk can mean, in turn, the underlying uncertainty, the extent of the risky action taken, or the resulting range of risky outcomes to the organization. In this example, the first meaning is the uncertain +1% or −1% movement of the currency. The second meaning is the ¥1,000,000 worth of risky currency, the position taken by the business. The third meaning is the +¥10,000 or −¥10,000 risky outcome that might accrue to the business for having engaged in this risky activity. A common way of more precisely distinguishing among these three "risks" in usage is: *risk driver* for the underlying risk, *risk position* to describe or quantify the risky action taken, and *risk exposure* for the potential valuation change that may result. In the oversimplified example above, the risk exposure is simply the risk position multiplied by the risk driver. In practice the term "risk" is used interchangeably for all three meanings.

> ***Risk management*** *is the process by which an organization or individual defines the level of risk to be taken, measures the level of risk being taken, and adjusts the latter toward the former, with the goal of maximizing the company's or portfolio's value or the individual's overall satisfaction, or utility.*

Said differently, risk management comprises all the decisions and actions needed to *best* achieve organizational or personal objectives while bearing a tolerable level of risk. Risk management is *not* about minimizing risk; it is about actively understanding and embracing those risks that best balance the achievement of goals with an acceptable chance of failure, quantifying the exposure, and continually monitoring and modifying it. A company that shied away from all risk would find that it could not operate. In trying to create wealth, all organizations will find themselves "in the risk business." Risk management is not about avoiding risks any more than a practical diet is about avoiding calories. Risk management is not even about predicting risks. "The Doctrine of No Surprises" is a key mantra among many risk managers, but it does not mean they are expected to predict what will happen. Instead, it means that if an unpredictable event, either positive or negative, happens in an uncertain world, the *impact* of that event on the organization or portfolio would not be a surprise and would have been quantified and considered in advance.

For example, a risk manager of a bank would not have been expected to know that a real estate crisis was going to occur and cause significant defaults on the bank's real estate securities. But a good risk manager would help the bank's management decide how much exposure it should have in these securities by quantifying the potential financial impact of such a crisis destroying, say, 60% of the bank's capital. A good risk management process would include a deep discussion at the governance level about the balance between the likely returns and the unlikely—but sizable—losses and whether such losses are tolerable. Management would ensure that the risk analysis and discussion actively affects their investment decisions, that the potential loss is continuously quantified and communicated, and that it will take actions to mitigate or transfer any portion of the risk exposure that cannot be tolerated.[1] The only surprise here should be the market shock itself; the risk manager should have prepared the organization through stress-testing and scenario analysis, continuously reporting in advance on the potential impact of this sizable risk exposure.

A poor risk management process would have ignored the possibility, though small, of such a significant market event and not quantified the potential loss from exposure to a real estate crisis. As such, the bank's management would have had no idea that more than half of the bank's capital could be at risk, not addressed this risk in any governance/risk appetite discussion, ignored these risks in its investment decisions, and not taken any action to mitigate this risk. In a good risk management process,

1 For example, hedges may be used to limit loss of capital to 20%.

most of the work is done before an adverse event happens; in a poor risk management process, perhaps just as much work gets done, but it all comes after the event, which is after the damage has been done.

Good risk management does not prevent losses, but provides a full top-to-bottom framework that rigorously informs the decision-making process—before, during, and after a risk event. Because risks and exposures are dynamic, risk management is a continuous process that is always being reevaluated and revised. If this process is done well, it provides management and staff with the knowledge to navigate as efficiently as possible toward the goals set by the governing body. In turn, this effort increases *ex ante* the value of the business or investment decisions undertaken. Good risk management may allow managers to more quickly or effectively act in the face of a crisis. But *ex post*, even the best risk management may not stop a portfolio from losing money in a market crash nor prevent a business from reduced profits in an economic downturn.

RISK MANAGEMENT FRAMEWORK 3

- ☐ describe features of a risk management framework
- ☐ define risk governance and describe elements of effective risk governance

A **risk management framework** flows logically from the definition of risk management that was previously given: It is the infrastructure, process, and analytics needed to support effective risk management in an organization. This process should fully integrate the "risk" and "return" aspects of the enterprise into decisions in support of best achieving its goals within its tolerance for risk. Risk management is not a "one size fits all" solution; it is integral to the enterprise's goals and needs. Thus, it is best achieved through a custom solution. Despite customization, every risk management system or framework should address the following key factors:

- Risk governance
- Risk identification and measurement
- Risk infrastructure
- Defined policies and processes
- Risk monitoring, mitigation, and management
- Communications
- Strategic analysis or integration

Not surprisingly, these factors often overlap in practice. They are defined and discussed here.

Governance is the top-level system of structures, rights, and obligations by which organizations are directed and controlled. Normally performed at the board level, governance is how goals are defined, authority is granted, and top-level decisions are made. The foundation for risk management in the organization is set at the board level as well. **Risk governance** is the top-down process and guidance that directs risk management activities to align with and support the overall enterprise and is addressed in more detail in Sections 4–6. Good governance should include defining an organization's risk tolerance and providing risk oversight. Governance is often driven by regulatory concerns, as well as by the fiduciary role of the governing body.

A risk management committee is another facet of governance; it provides top decision makers with a forum for regularly considering risk management issues. To achieve the best results for an organization, risk governance should take an enterprise-wide view. **Enterprise risk management** is an overarching governance approach applied throughout the organization and consistent with its strategy, guiding the risk management framework to focus risk activities on the objectives, health, and value of the *entire* organization.

Risk identification and measurement is the main quantitative core of risk management; but more than that, it must include the qualitative assessment and evaluation of all potential sources of risk and the organization's risk exposures. This ongoing work involves analyzing the environment for relevant risk drivers, which is the common term used for any fundamental underlying factor that results in a risk that is relevant or important to an organization, analyzing the business or portfolio to ascertain risk exposures, tracking changes in those risk exposures, and calculating risk metrics to size these risks under various scenarios and stresses.

Risks are not limited to what is going on in the financial markets. There are many types of risk that can potentially impact a business, portfolio, or individual.

The power of technology has allowed for risk management to be more quantitative and timely. Management can measure and monitor risk, run scenarios, conduct statistical analysis, work with more complex models, and examine more dimensions and risk drivers as well as do it faster. This use of technology needs to be balanced with and supplement—not supplant—experienced business judgment. Technology has made risk infrastructure even more important and beneficial in managing risks.

Risk infrastructure refers to the people and systems required to track risk exposures and perform most of the quantitative risk analysis to allow an assessment of the organization's risk profile. Infrastructure would include risk capture (the important operational process by which a risk exposure gets populated into a risk system), a database and data model, analytic models and systems, a stress or scenario engine, and an ability to generate reports, as well as some amount of skilled and empowered personnel resources dedicated to building and executing the risk framework. With increased reliance on technology, more time and effort must be allotted to test data, models, and results in order to avoid the ironic outcome of the risk of errors coming from within risk systems.

Obviously, the scope of risk infrastructure will be related to the resources, or potential losses, of the organization. Individuals and smaller businesses may rely heavily on an external partner or provider for much of their risk infrastructure and analysis.

Policies and processes are the extension of risk governance into both the day-to-day operation and decision-making processes of the organization. There may be limits, requirements, constraints, and guidelines—some quantitative, some procedural—to ensure risky activities are in line with the organization's predetermined risk tolerance and regulatory requirements. Much of this is just common-sense business practice: updating and protecting data, controlling cash flows, conducting due diligence on investments, handling exceptions and escalations, and making checklists to support important decisions. In a good risk framework, processes would naturally evolve to consider risk at all key decision points, such as investment decisions and asset allocation. Risk management should become an integrated part of the business and not just a policing or regulatory function.

The process of *risk monitoring, mitigation, and management* is the most obvious facet of a risk framework, but also one of the most difficult. Actively monitoring and managing risk requires pulling together risk governance, identification and measurement, infrastructure, and policies and processes and continually reviewing and reevaluating in the face of changing risk exposures and risk drivers. It requires recognizing when risk exposure is not aligned with risk tolerance and then taking action to bring them back into alignment.[2]

Communication of critical risk issues must happen continually and across all levels of the organization. Governance parameters, such as risk tolerances and associated constraints, must be clearly communicated to, and understood by, managers. Risk metrics must be reported in a clear and timely manner. Risk issues must be reviewed and discussed as a standard part of decision making. Changes in exposure must be discussed so that action can be taken as appropriate. There should also be a feedback loop with the governance body so that top-level risk guidance can be validated or updated and communicated back to the rest of the organization.

Strategic analysis and integration help turn risk management into an offensive weapon to improve performance. Good risk management is a key to increasing the value of the overall business or portfolio. A risk management framework should provide the tools to better understand the how and why of performance and help sort out which activities are adding value, and which are not. In investing, rigorous analysis can support better investment decisions and improve strategy and risk-adjusted returns.

Exhibit 1: The Risk Management Framework in an Enterprise Context

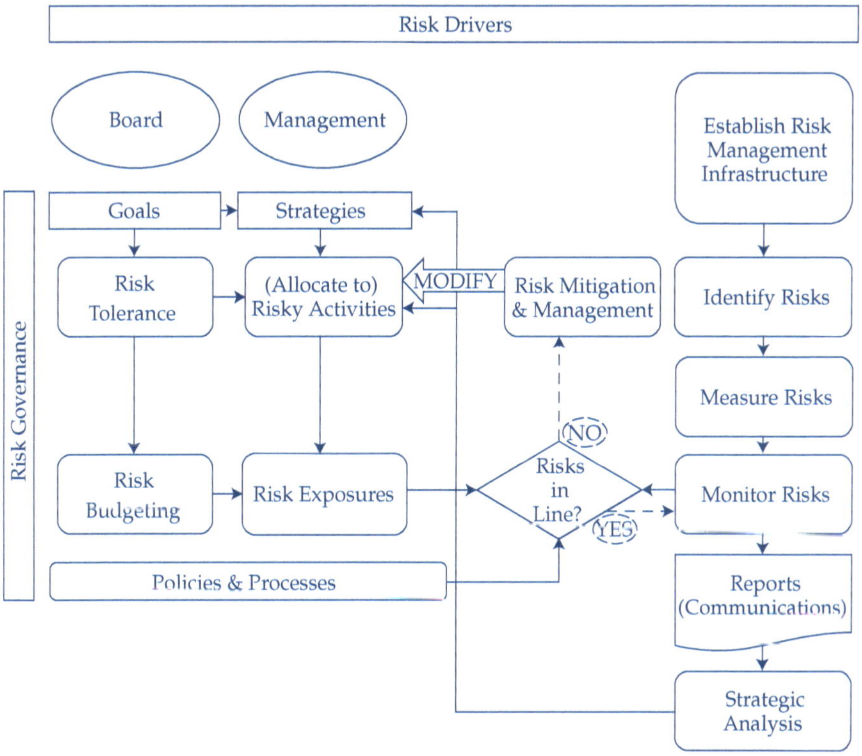

Exhibit 1 illustrates the process of risk management for an enterprise, pulling all the described elements of the risk framework together. Although there are a very high number of risks faced by every organization, most organizations are primarily affected by a small number of key risk drivers, or primary underlying factors that create risk. Along the left side is risk governance, which represents board-level decisions and encompasses and affects the boxes immediately to its right. The governance body,

2 Risk mitigation and management is discussed in more detail in Sections 9–11.

often called a board, defines the goals of the organization and, in turn, decides on its risk tolerance. It may additionally provide guidance on how or where that risk is taken (risk budgeting). The board is also involved in setting high-level policies that will affect most risk management processes. These risk governance activities are a crucial keystone of the risk framework and will be discussed in detail in the next section. When the rest of the risk framework hinges off of these top-down governance elements and is focused on the goals of the entire enterprise (as shown here), the end result is effective enterprise risk management.

The role of management, shown in the middle column, is to plan and execute value-maximizing strategies consistent with their governance guidance. Each management activity in the framework flows not only from management (shown with the arrows) but also from the governance activities on the left. Thus, not only are management's strategies designed to achieve the board's goals, but management also allocates capital to risky activities (its business or investing choices) to execute its strategies consistent with the defined risk tolerance. The risk exposures that result from management's choice of activities should also be aligned with the governing body's risk budget. In addition, management participates actively in setting or implementing policies and establishing procedures that relate to when, how, how much, and by whom each of the other elements of the risk framework are performed.[3]

The rest of the risk management framework comprises a number of important risk activities to help the business achieve all of its strategic and governance goals and mandates. These other elements to implement risk management are shown in the far right column of the illustration. Driven by its need to establish a risk management program to support the enterprise's goals, management would provide the requisite resources for risk management activities by establishing a risk management infrastructure. With risk processes defined and risk infrastructure in place, risks are then identified and measured, which is a regular and continual process of translating risk exposures (produced by the risky activities) into meaningful and generally quantitative risk metrics.

The next major steps—risk monitoring, mitigation, and management—are where much of a firm's day-to-day risk management activity is focused. These activities are split across three boxes in the illustration. Risk levels are continuously monitored, having just been measured.[4] There is a major decision at the monitoring stage: Management must check that all the risks are in line and not outside the limits of the defined risk tolerance or budget.[5] This process involves evaluating the actual risk exposures compared with the organization's risk policies and procedures to ensure that everything is in compliance. If the answer is "no," then risk mitigation and management actions need to be taken to modify risk levels and to bring them back into compliance. There are a variety of methods to accomplish this task, which are addressed in Sections 9–11. Whatever the method, management's allocation of the risk budget to risky activities will be altered by this modification, which includes changing the organization's risk exposures, starting the circle again through the steps on the right, and re-checking to see if risk levels are now consistent with risk policies.

3 In essence, there could be an arrow from policies and processes to every other box to the right, but these rather obvious relationships are intentionally omitted in the diagram to avoid clutter. Likewise, risk exposures inform nearly all the boxes to the right. Risk management is innately quite interrelated.

4 Continuous usually does not mean real-time; the frequency of monitoring is based on the resources available, the level of systems support, and the need for risk information in the decision process. At large financial firms, this monitoring will generally be daily; for small businesses and individuals it might be quarterly.

5 This task is generally delegated to a risk manager; but whatever the title, someone must be accountable for this important check.

When risks *are* in line with limits, policies, tolerances, mandates, and so on, then the process moves back to continuous monitoring followed by communicating risk levels.[6] This communication, at a minimum, includes reporting key risk metrics on a regular and timely basis across the organization to assist management in its decision-making process and the board in fulfilling its governance duties. Finally, strategic analysis is supported by the risk measurement, reporting, and other steps of the enterprise risk management process. By analyzing all of the enterprise's strategies and risky activities via the risk measurement lens, management can improve its decision-making process and ascertain where to invest its limited capital and risk budget most fruitfully. This step is generally underappreciated and is an inexpensive and beneficial by-product of having built a risk framework. The last two boxes or steps (reports and strategic analysis) represent important feedback loops to inform and improve both governance and the portfolio of risky activities that make up the business.

There are many feedback loops in properly executed risk management. In practice, most of these steps overlap most of the time and are being performed simultaneously. Good risk management ties together all these steps from the highest governance decisions to lower-level specifics, such as models, reports, and operational checklists.

The risk environment is dynamic, and many of our notions of probabilities and likely risk outcomes change in ways we probably could not predict. The risk management framework should be robust enough to anticipate this dynamism—to expect the unexpected. It should be evolutionary—flexible enough to grow with a company or individual and its new challenges.

The complexity of the risk management framework depends on the complexity of an organization's risk exposures and their resources. But that does not mean that smaller organizations or individuals should skip the risk management process; they may simply be able to do less, or have to work with external partners to assist with large portions of the framework, or be less formal about the process. Ultimately, the key principles just covered are still important even to the smallest organization, even if the specific components do not get assembled as described.

THE RISK MANAGEMENT PROCESS FOR AN INDIVIDUAL

Although an individual has neither the resources nor the organizational overhead of a large business, the importance of risk management is not diminished and the risk management framework still applies, albeit most likely in a scaled-down form. Though nearly all of the essential elements of the process illustrated in Exhibit 1 are still useful, the individual can reduce the recipe to six essential ingredients, consistent with the reduced scope of the individual's risk exposures.

The first step for an individual is much like that shown in Exhibit 1 for the most complex organization: the determination of goals or objectives. This step would include most of the elements associated with risk governance, just without all the organizational complexity.

The next functional step involves choosing investments (or other assets) and identifying their risks. Lacking any risk infrastructure, the individual may at this stage already require the services of an investment professional or financial adviser. This step and subsequent steps will probably be executed by the adviser, although the individual principal still needs to stay knowledgeable and involved. In the context of the illustration in Exhibit 1, the individual is effectively their own governance body and the adviser serves the role of management.

6 While not obvious in the illustration, communication and reporting should happen whether or not risk levels are in compliance; such communications are even more important when risk levels are out of alignment with tolerances.

The next steps for the individual are equivalent to the heart of the risk management process: risk monitoring and risk mitigation and management. The individual would first evaluate their risk exposure (like the diamond or decision step in the illustration), then consider various alternative approaches to modify the risk if necessary, followed by implementing the risk management solution (insuring, hedging, trading, etc.).

The final functional step for an individual's risk management process would be evaluation and review. This step is parallel to the back-end of the risk management illustration, the boxes at the bottom right. This process may occur with much less frequency for an individual—but it is no less important.

Each individual should simplify the risk management process as required so that they do not end up considering it "too esoteric and complicated to worry about" and thus ignoring risk management altogether. The potential costs of avoiding risk management are essentially the same for an individual as for a large corporation or a hedge fund, although perhaps with less money involved.

At its core, business and investing are about allocating resources and capital to chosen risks. Understanding which risks drive better outcomes should be one of the goals of risk management, and it makes good *risk* management inextricably linked with good management generally. When effective risk management is truly integrated at all levels of the decision-making process and the overall management process, the organization has developed an effective *risk culture*. This culture generally produces better results than just considering risk issues as a separate afterthought, and, in turn, it produces *much* better results than ignoring risk issues altogether in the decision-making process. For individuals, the adoption of a risk culture should result in a personal awareness of the many types of risks, their rewards, the costs, the relationships between them, and the methods of aligning the risks borne with the risks and outcomes desired. This awareness should lead to better investment return and/or smaller losses for the risk taken, resulting in higher satisfaction.

There are a number of other benefits from establishing good risk management: (1) Most obvious is less frequent surprises and a better notion of what the damage would be in the event of a surprise; (2) more decision discipline leading to better consideration of trade-offs and better risk–return relationships; (3) better response and risk mitigation stemming from more awareness and active monitoring, which should trim some of the worst losses; (4) better efficiency and fewer operational errors from policies and procedures, transparency, and risk awareness; (5) better relations, with more trust, between the governing body and management, which generally results in more effective delegation; (6) a better image or reputation because analysts and investors perceive a company as prudent and value-focused. Together, all these benefits should lead to higher value for the enterprise.

EXAMPLE 1

Risk Management and Risk Management Framework

1. Which of the following is *not* a goal of risk management?

   A. Measuring risk exposures

   B. Minimizing exposure to risk

   C. Defining the level of risk appetite

Solution

B is correct. The definition of risk management includes both defining the level of risk desired and measuring the level of risk taken. Risk management means taking risks actively and in the best, most value-added way possible and is not about minimizing risks.

2. Which element of a risk management framework sets the overall context for risk management in an organization?

   A. Governance

   B. Risk infrastructure

   C. Policies and processes

   Solution

   A is correct. Governance is the element of the risk management framework that is the top-level foundation for risk management. Although policies, procedures, and infrastructure are necessary to implement a risk management framework, it is governance that provides the overall context for an organization's risk management.

3. Which element of risk management makes up the analytical component of the process?

   A. Communication

   B. Risk governance

   C. Risk identification and measurement

   Solution

   C is correct. Risk identification and measurement is the quantitative part of the process. It involves identifying the risks and summarizing their potential quantitative impact. Communication and risk governance are largely qualitative.

4. Which element of risk management involves action when risk exposures are found to be out of line with risk tolerance?

   A. Risk governance

   B. Risk identification and measurement

   C. Risk monitoring, mitigation, and management

   Solution

   C is correct. Risk monitoring, mitigation, and management require recognizing and taking action when these (risk exposure and risk tolerance) are not in line, as shown in the middle of Exhibit 1. Risk governance involves setting the risk tolerance. Risk identification and measurement involves identifying and measuring the risk exposures.

4 RISK GOVERNANCE - AN ENTERPRISE VIEW

☐ define risk governance and describe elements of effective risk governance

Risk governance is the foundation for risk management. As defined earlier, it is the top-down process and guidance that directs risk management activities to align with and support the goals of the overall enterprise. It typically emanates from a board of directors with fiduciary obligations and risk oversight and who prescribe goals and authorities. Referring back to the definition of risk management, note that risk management is keenly focused on the risk and value of the overall enterprise.

An Enterprise View of Risk Governance

In addition to the responsibility for risk oversight, there are two other important areas in which the governing body drives the risk framework. First, it determines the organization's goals, direction, and priorities, which combined serve as a key foundation for enterprise risk management. Recall that enterprise risk management is an overarching governance approach applied across the organization that focuses risk activities on the objectives, health, and value of the whole organization. Second, it spells out the risk appetite or tolerance, meaning which risks are acceptable, which risks are to be mitigated and to what extent, and which risks are unacceptable. Risk governance should also provide a sense of the worst losses that could be tolerated in various scenarios, and management should manage risk accordingly. These considerations should flow naturally into decisions about risk budgeting to guide implementation of an optimal program that is consistent with that risk tolerance.

Risk governance is the impact of the governing body of an organization on the risk management framework. It provides context for and clarity on an organization's value drivers and risk appetite, specifies clear authority to management to execute risk management, and ensures risk oversight to continually determine whether risk management is functioning well and consistent with the organization's value maximization. It is the governing body's job to tie the organizational goals and risk framework together; thus, risk governance happens within an enterprise context. Risk governance and risk oversight also entail compliance with regulatory requirements. Risk governance is a difficult and demanding discipline, and if it is going to flourish in an organization, it needs visible commitment from the top.

Providing clear guidance with sufficient leeway to execute strategy is often a difficult balance. Even more challenging is providing for advance discussion and a clear decision and statement of organizational risk appetite. There is usually substantial discussion about this risk appetite *after* a crisis, but too often there is very little discussion during periods of normalcy, when it would be much more beneficial. Because risk is one of the main strategic tools that management can regulate, it is especially important for governing bodies to openly discuss risk, consider scenarios, understand the impact of negative outcomes on the organization, and make it clear where they are not willing to venture. Much like an automobile that comes with a red zone on some dials to establish boundaries for safe operation, risk governance bodies should likewise establish hypothetical red zones to ensure the safe operation of their enterprise.

Enterprise risk management (focusing risk activities on the objectives, health, and value of the *whole* organization) requires that the entire economic balance sheet of the business be considered, not just the assets or one part of the business in isolation. A narrower view of risk management is unlikely to meet the goal of maximizing the value of the entire enterprise.

Pension fund management provides a classic example of the importance of considering enterprise risk management: "Funds" are the assets and "pension" is the liability. But a true enterprise view requires an even broader outlook. A corporate pension fund's manager might try to maximize only the fund's assets, but this would generally do a disservice to the corporation. The assets and liabilities of a pension fund are both sensitive to market variables, so ignoring the liabilities would be ignoring half the risk. With liabilities that are quite bond-like, a pension fund manager using all equities for maximum growth would potentially make the overall fund insolvent in a market collapse with declining interest rates because, in such a situation, the liabilities would increase substantially in value while the assets fell. Risk tolerance for the assets in isolation would be far different from the risk tolerance of the entire enterprise. One should look beyond just the pension liabilities, which are likely to be a small part of the overall enterprise. Broader still, a true enterprise risk view in this case would *also* consider the parent corporation's business risk profile and not just the pension assets and liabilities. In a market collapse, the overall business might be in a recessionary phase, rendering increasing contributions from the corporation to its pension fund quite painful. Factoring the corporate risk profile into the pension fund investment strategy may cause the risk tolerance to be lower in this case.

Risk governance that focuses on the entire enterprise will result in risk management that is much less likely to be at odds with the goals of the organization and more likely to enhance long-run value. Likewise, consideration of a full spectrum of risks, and not just the most obvious quantitative risks, will result in better risk governance.

The enterprise view of risk management is equally applicable and important to an individual, even if the term "enterprise" is not often used in an individual context.[7] The appropriate set of risks for an individual must be viewed not in isolation, but in consideration of the goals and characteristics of the individual in a holistic view. For example, an adviser may be designing an investment portfolio to maximize a client's wealth and optimize the risk–return trade-off at some perceived comfortable level of risk.[8] But the client, whose wealth consists not only of financial assets but also of valuable **human capital**, might prefer that risk allocation decisions be made in view of both forms of capital, optimizing her total wealth. For example, a client with a career in real estate would most likely benefit if her financial portfolio is invested in a way that considers her earnings exposure to real estate related risks. Holdings of real estate securities above a certain level, even if optimal from an isolated portfolio perspective, might make this individual less than optimally diversified from a total wealth perspective. In another example, Investor X, who has substantial inflation-adjusted pension benefits, is different from Investor Y, who has a fixed pension benefit, and different still from Investor Z, who has no pension benefit and retires with solely his own investment portfolio. These three investors will require remarkably different investment solutions, not only to deal with inflation but also to deal with the uncertainty surrounding lifespans. Individuals with different goals and characteristics will need differing investment and risk solutions that are best suited to their individual situations. In fact, because of the extremely variable life cycle of an individual and the discrete nature of many individuals' goals, the enterprise view is even more important to risk management for individuals than it is for institutions.

Risk governance extends into management to include ways to ensure that the risk framework of an organization stays consistent with top-level guidance. One useful approach is to provide a regular forum to discuss the risk framework and key risk issues at the management level. In other words, a risk management committee would be a key element of good risk governance. Its activities could parallel the governance body's risk deliberations, but at an operational level as opposed to high-level oversight. In this forum, governance overlaps with many of the other aspects of the organization's risk framework as discussed in Sections 2–3. In fact, if done well, it integrates all of them.

In the same vein, another element of good risk governance is the formal appointment of a responsible executive as chief risk officer (CRO). This officer should be responsible for building and implementing the risk framework for the enterprise and

7 Enterprise risk management is an easier concept for an individual; compared with an organization in which deciding, coordinating, and communicating goals can be a big challenge, the scope of risk management efforts for an individual is smaller and more manageable.

8 Here, the individual is the governing body, setting individual goals and risk appetite; the financial professional or wealth manager is the "management team" executing much of the rest of the risk framework.

managing the many activities therein. In the same manner that risks are inextricably linked with the core business activities, the CRO is likewise a key participant in the strategic decisions of the enterprise—this position is not solely a policing role. Although the chief executive is responsible for risk as well as all other aspects of an enterprise, it makes no more sense for the CEO to perform the role of the CRO than it would be for the CEO to perform the role of the CFO. Many financial firms now have a CRO in executive management,[9] which had become best practice even in the years prior to the 2008 crisis.

5 RISK TOLERANCE

☐ explain how risk tolerance affects risk management

Perhaps the most important element of good risk governance is the **risk tolerance** discussion and decision within the governing body. Business and investment strategy centers on selecting a portfolio of acceptable risk activities that will maximize value and produce the highest returns possible for the given risk level. At the governance level, the duty is generally not to select these activities—a job that usually falls to management—but to establish the organization's risk appetite. Certain risks or levels of risks may be deemed acceptable, other risks deemed unacceptable, and in the middle are risks that may be pursued in a risk-limited fashion. Said differently, risk tolerance identifies the extent to which the organization is willing to experience losses or opportunity costs and to fail in meeting its objectives.

> The risk tolerance decision *for an individual* is similar, but not identical, to that of a business enterprise. In traditional finance theory, the individual focuses on maximizing unobservable utility, whereas the business maximizes a generally observable value—the market value or equity price of the company. Although individuals are facing life and certain death on an uncertain timetable, most businesses tend to be relatively short-lived organizations, but with an expectation of immortality. The decisions about risk tolerance from those two very different viewpoints can be expected to differ—for example, risk tolerance in organizations often treats its continued existence as a major consideration. In many ways, the individual's risk tolerance decision is the harder one.

The enterprise risk management perspective is the right lens through which to view the risk appetite question. The risk tolerance decision begins with two different analyses that must be integrated—an "inside" view and an "outside" view. First, what shortfalls within an organization would cause it to fail, or at least fail to achieve some critical goals? Second, what uncertain forces is the organization exposed to? That is, what are its risk drivers? With the answers to these two difficult questions in hand, a board could begin defining dimensions and levels of risk that it finds too uncomfortable to take on. This risk tolerance should be formally chosen and communicated *before* a crisis, and will serve as the high-level guidance for management in its strategic selection

9 Although this is common for financial firms or other large organizations, many less-complex companies will forgo a formal risk structure. The board still maintains its risk governance responsibilities; and it is up to them to work out with management as to how, and to what extent, to meet these responsibilities.

of risks. Many organizations will do this *after* a crisis, which is better than not doing it at all but is much like buying insurance after the loss occurs. It is best to take care of it when there seems to be no particularly pressing reason to do so. Similarly, some individuals may not give much thought to their own risk tolerance until after a crisis occurs, when they belatedly decide that the risk was not worth taking.

For example, suppose a Spanish construction equipment manufacturing company's board is determining its risk tolerance. From the inside perspective, it has two main concerns: revenue and liquidity. It determines that it can tolerate a 5%–10% drop in revenue, but that a 20% drop would trigger its debt covenants and put the launch of its new flagship product at risk. Related to this strategy, it needs €40 million of cash flow annually for the next three years for critical capital expenditures and can leave almost none of this cash flow at risk. From the outside perspective, it realizes that there are three main uncertainties or risk drivers over which it has no control: changes in the value of the US dollar, interest rate changes, and market returns on industrial sector equities. Both its business results and its own stock price are strongly correlated with these three risks and could be adversely affected by any of them.

Rather than taking a passive approach as a risk observer, the board in this example uses a top-level analysis to formulate its risk tolerance. In this case, it may decide to limit maximum cash flow variation to €10 million annually and revenue exposure to –10% in a global recession. In addition, it may specify other stated limits, such as the maximum exposure to currency or other risks. This guidance may affect the riskiness of other product strategies that management may pursue. The company may require more expensive financing options to reduce cash flow uncertainty. The governance restrictions may drive risk mitigation programs, such as a hedging strategy, especially for the primary risk drivers that are stated areas of concern.

Governance guidance is important in helping an enterprise target where it should actively pursue risk and where it should mitigate or modify risk. Strategic goals centered on core competencies should be pursued, which leads the company into taking risks that best position the enterprise for success and value creation. Companies sometimes take risks in areas where they have no expertise, which puts their core value creation and their entire organization at peril. A well-functioning risk program would limit or hedge those non-core risks in areas where they have no comparative advantage. Modifying risk is covered in detail in Sections 9–11.

How does a company determine its risk tolerance? There is certainly no formula. Most importantly, a company's goals, its expertise in certain areas, and its strategies will help a board determine which risks the company may pursue and with how much intensity. The ability of a company to respond dynamically to adverse events may allow for a higher risk tolerance. The amount of loss a company can sustain without impairing its status as a going concern should factor into its risk tolerance; some companies are more fragile than others. The competitive landscape matters because both the board's and investors' expectations are usually developed in the context of how a company is positioned in its industry. The government and regulatory landscape is important too, both in their *ex ante* demands on how companies approach risk and in the likely *ex post* reaction in the event of disasters. Quantitative analyses such as scenario analysis, economic models, and sensitivities to macro risk drivers might be used to assess where a board's zone of comfort is bounded. There are other factors that should *not* determine risk tolerance, but in many cases they do. Personal motivations, beliefs, and agendas of board members (the agency problem); company size; whether the market environment seems stable; short-term pressures; and management compensation often affect risk tolerance in ways that might not be in line with the owners' best interests.

Once risk tolerance is determined, the overall risk framework should be geared toward measuring, managing, and communicating compliance with this risk tolerance—getting the risk exposure in line with the enterprise's risk appetite.

This sort of governance exercise not only helps ensure that the organization survives through the worst of times, but also helps ensure a strategic trade-off between risk and return in the decision process, which, in turn, improves potential returns for the given level of risk and value. It is quite easy to find business strategies and investment approaches that produce apparently outsized returns, but they might be at the cost of putting the organization at extreme risk. A somewhat extreme example would be a company selling put options on its own equity, which could produce higher short-term profits but would dramatically increase the chance of the company failing in a steep market decline. Excessive leverage is another risky strategy for boosting short-term profits that may decrease value or lead to failure in the long run. A formal risk governance process with a stated risk tolerance would naturally result in avoidance of many easier, less well-reasoned strategies that entail excessive risk compared with the firm's risk tolerance. Instead, it would lead the strategic discussion into alternative strategies that are more likely to add value while taking reasonable risk within the enterprise's risk tolerance and not simply trade ruin for return. Sincere, good risk governance and risk culture can avoid excessively risky strategies that might put the long-term enterprise value at risk. This approach should produce enhanced value for the enterprise.

6 RISK BUDGETING

☐ describe risk budgeting and its role in risk governance

Risk budgeting picks up where risk tolerance leaves off. Whereas risk tolerance focuses on the appetite for risk and what is and is not acceptable, risk budgeting has a more specific focus on how that risk is taken. Risk budgeting quantifies and allocates the tolerable risk by specific metrics; it extends and guides implementation of the risk tolerance decision.

Risk budgeting applies to both business management and portfolio management. Its foundation is the perspective that business or portfolio management involves assembling a number of risk activities or securities, which can be collated into an assemblage of various risk characteristics. For example, a traditional view of a portfolio might be that it is allocated 20% to hedge funds, 30% to private equity, and the remaining 50% is split between stocks and bonds. An alternative risk view of the same portfolio might be 70% driven by global equity returns, 20% by domestic equity returns, with the remaining 10% driven by interest rates. The equity component might be allocated 65% to value and 35% to growth. The portfolio might also have 45% illiquid securities and the remainder liquid. Other allocations can be stated in terms of exposures to inflation, long-term interest rates, currencies, and so on. These multiple dimensions for viewing the allocation of a portfolio are not mutually exclusive: they co-exist. If one is evaluating the risk exposure of a portfolio and trying to keep it in line with a stated risk tolerance, one would be far more concerned with the risk characteristics of the investment assets and portfolio rather than their common classifications of stocks, hedge funds, real estate, private equity, and so on. These terms tell us a little about risk but not enough. Equity is traditionally riskier than hedge funds, but some equities are of quite low risk and some hedge funds are of quite high risk. The risk view may be more meaningful and useful in understanding the portfolio risk than the traditional asset allocation view.

Risk budgeting is any means of allocating a portfolio based on some risk characteristics of the investments. In the purest sense, the term "budget" implies that there is a total risk limit for the organization. Although this approach is not formally required,[10] it would certainly be good practice to have a risk budget that is consistent with the organization's risk tolerance. A risk budget provides a means of implementing the risk tolerance at a strategic level, or in other words, a means of bridging from the high-level governance risk decision to the many management decisions, large and small, that result in the actual risk exposures.

A risk budget can be complex and multi-dimensional, or it can be a simple, one-dimensional risk measure. Even the simplest measure can provide significant benefits in developing an effective risk culture. Four well-known single-dimension measures that are often used are standard deviation, beta, value at risk (VaR), and scenario loss, but there are many others. It is common for some hedge funds to budget risk using standard deviation, managing to a fixed-risk fund target, and evaluating individual investments based on their returns and risks as they affect the *ex ante* standard deviation.

More complex forms of risk budgeting use multiple dimensions of risk. One popular approach evaluates risks by their underlying risk classes, such as equity, fixed income, commodity risk, and so on, and then allocates investments by their risk class. Also common are risk factor approaches to risk budgeting, in which exposure to various factors is used to attempt to capture associated risk premiums. An example would be to budget an allocation to give greater emphasis to value stocks based on the belief that they may provide a higher risk-adjusted return than growth stocks. This tactic might be layered over a strategic budget with a certain "beta" as the overall equity risk, supplemented with value and additional factor tilts specified up to some level.

Risk budgeting, although a desirable element of risk governance, cuts across the entire risk management framework, providing a focal point for each of the facets of risk management described in Sections 2 and 3. And although it is true that in practice many organizations operate without a risk budget, it is generally because there has been no specific declaration of their risk tolerance. If a board has a clear understanding of its risk appetite, both the board and management will want some means of implementing a strategic allocation that is consistent with it. Thus, the risk budget becomes a critical overarching construct for the organization's risk framework.

Some individuals may, often through the assistance of a financial planner, engage in some form of risk budgeting, but many do not execute it well or carry it far enough. A classic example of this failure is the tendency of many individuals to invest their financial portfolios in their employers. The risk budget for their total wealth—financial and human capital—is extremely concentrated in one firm and/or one industry. Not surprisingly, such risk budgets typically occur not through formal planning because most formal plans would recognize the problem, but through inaction or inattention.

One major benefit of even the most basic risk budgeting is that it forces risk trade-offs and supports a culture in which risk is considered as a part of all key decisions. Suppose that all the activities a business wants to pursue are in excess of the risk budget. The budgeting of risk should result in an approach, whether explicit or not, of choosing to invest where the return per unit of risk is the highest. Better still, it should also result in a market-benchmarked choice of risk intensity, between possibly doing less of each risky investment or doing more, but with a risk-mitigating hedge. This benefit is extremely important. By choosing between a market hedge or less of a risky investment, one ends up evaluating the investment directly against the market risk–return benchmark. Thus, one is not only comparing risk–return relationships among one's investment choices, but also comparing active versus passive strategies; that is, evaluating investment choices as a whole against the "market return" on a risk-equivalent basis. In other words, one ends up attempting to add active value in each of one's decisions while still staying within the confines of the organization's risk tolerance. The result is even more powerful than merely ensuring that the business

10 One could do risk budgeting even if there were no other risk governance guidance.

is compensated well for the risks they decide to accept. Just having a risk budget in place, forces decision makers to try to add value to the enterprise in every risky decision they make. The risk-budgeting framework makes this consideration innate to the decision process.

EXAMPLE 2

Risk Governance

1. Which of the following approaches is *most* consistent with an enterprise view of risk governance?

   A. Separate strategic planning processes for each part of the enterprise

   B. Considering an organization's risk tolerance when developing its asset allocation

   C. Trying to achieve the highest possible risk-adjusted return on a company's pension fund's assets

   Solution

   B is correct. The enterprise view is characterized by a focus on the organization as a whole—its goals, value, and risk tolerance. It is not about strategies or risks at the individual business line level.

2. Which of the following statements about risk tolerance is *most* accurate?

   A. Risk tolerance is best discussed after a crisis, when awareness of risk is heightened.

   B. The risk tolerance discussion is about the actions management will take to minimize losses.

   C. The organization's risk tolerance describes the extent to which the organization is willing to experience losses.

   Solution

   C is correct. Risk tolerance identifies the extent to which the organization is willing to experience losses or opportunity costs and fail in meeting its objectives. It is best discussed before a crisis and is primarily a risk governance or oversight issue at the board level, not a management or tactical one.

3. Which of the following is *not* consistent with a risk-budgeting approach to portfolio management?

   A. Limiting the beta of the portfolio to 0.75

   B. Allocating investments by their amount of underlying risk sources or factors

   C. Limiting the amount of money available to be spent on hedging strategies by each portfolio manager

   Solution

   C is correct. Risk budgeting is any means of allocating a portfolio by some risk characteristics of the investments. This approach could be a strict limit on beta or some other risk measure or an approach that uses risk classes or factors to allocate investments. Risk budgeting does not require nor prohibit hedging, although hedging is available as an implementation tool to support risk budgeting and overall risk governance.

4. Who would be the *least* appropriate for controlling the risk management function in a large organization?

   A. Chief risk officer

   B. Chief financial officer

   C. Risk management committee

Solution

B is correct. A chief risk officer or a risk management committee is an individual or group that specializes in risk management. A chief financial officer may have considerable knowledge of risk management, may supervise a CRO, and would likely have some involvement in a risk management committee, but a CFO has broader responsibilities and cannot provide the specialization and attention to risk management that is necessary in a large organization.

IDENTIFICATION OF RISK - FINANCIAL VS. NON-FINANCIAL RISK

7

☐ identify financial and non-financial sources of risk and describe how they may interact

Having laid the framework for understanding the concept of risk management and risk governance, we now move into the implementation of the process. One of the first important parts of the process is the identification of risks. In this reading, we identify two general categorizations of risks. The first is the set of risks that originate from the financial markets. Accordingly, we refer to this type of risk as **financial risks**. The second group of risks includes those that emanate from outside the financial markets. As such, we refer to these as **non-financial risks**. Although most risks ultimately have monetary consequences, we reserve the term "financial risks" to refer to the risks that arise from events occurring in the financial markets, such as changes in prices or interest rates.[11] In this reading, we will consider the types of financial and non-financial risks faced by organizations and individuals.

Financial Risks

The risk management industry has come to classify three types of risks as primarily financial in nature. The three primary types of financial risks are market risk, credit risk, and liquidity risk. **Market risk** is the risk that arises from movements in interest rates, stock prices, exchange rates, and commodity prices. This categorization is not to say that these four main factors are the underlying drivers of market risks. Market risks typically arise from certain fundamental economic conditions or events in the economy or industry or developments in specific companies. These are the underlying risk drivers, which we will cover later.

11 We use the term "financial markets" in a very broad sense. A company may also be exposed to commodity price risk, which we would include as a financial risk.

Market risks are among the most obvious and visible risks faced by most organizations and many individuals. The financial markets receive considerable attention in the media, and information on financial market activity is abundant. Institutional investors and many corporations devote considerable resources to processing this information with the objective of optimizing performance. Many individuals also devote considerable attention to market risk, and financial publications and television and radio shows are widely followed in the general population. The state of knowledge in risk management is probably greatest in the area of market risk.

The second primary financial risk is credit risk. **Credit risk** is the risk of loss if one party fails to pay an amount owed on an obligation, such as a bond, loan, or derivative, to another party. In a loan, only one party owes money to the other. In some types of derivatives, only one party owes money to the other, and in other types of derivatives, either party can owe the other. This type of risk is also sometimes called default risk and sometimes counterparty risk. As with market risk, the root source of the risk can arise from fundamental conditions in the economy, industry, or weakness in the market for a company's products. Ultimately, default is an asset-specific risk. Bond and derivatives investors must consider credit risk as one of their primary decision tools.[12] Similar to market risk, credit risk is also a highly visible risk with considerable attention paid to defaults, bankruptcies, and the stresses arising from inadequate cash flow in relation to leverage. Credit risk is a particularly significant risk in that although market prices can go down and bounce back up, defaults and bankruptcies have extremely long-term implications for borrowers.

Although market and credit risk are extremely common risks to institutions, they are also assumed by individuals in their personal investments. One other financial risk, however, is much more common to institutions, although it can be faced by individuals, often unknowingly. This third risk is **liquidity risk**, which is the risk of a significant downward valuation adjustment when selling a financial asset. In order to sell an asset, a party may need to reduce the price to a level that is less than the marked value or the seller's assessment of the asset's true value based on the fundamentals of the asset. In certain market conditions, the seller must make a significant price concession. Having to make price concessions is not necessarily unusual and does not imply a poorly functioning market. Indeed, given no shift in demand, a rightward shift of a supply curve in order to sell a larger quantity is entirely consistent with the notion that a seller must lower the price to sell a greater quantity.

All assets have transaction costs in the market, such as the bid–ask spread. The existence of a sell price that is less than a buy price, however, is not a risk but simply a cost. It is the *uncertainty* of that valuation spread that creates this type of risk. Thus, liquidity risk could also be called "transaction cost risk." The liquidity risk of a \$10 stock purchased for \$10 is not the risk that one would receive the "bid" price of only \$9.99 right after one bought it. That \$0.01 spread is a known cost when the stock is purchased, so it is not a risk. The risk is that this spread cost might increase dramatically as a result of either changing market conditions or attempting to maintain a position significantly larger than the normal trading volume for the stock. This problem becomes a serious issue for risk management when the liquidation price falls to less than the seller's estimate of the fundamental value of the asset. Although this risk is often associated with illiquid assets,[13] it really stems from a couple of sources. First, market liquidity varies over time and the market for specific assets may become less

12 With certain derivatives (swaps and forwards), either party could be forced to pay off to the other, so each party is concerned about whether its counterparty will pay off, meaning that for some products, credit risk is bilateral.

13 The illiquid nature of an asset is not itself the risk because that is a direct cost borne immediately upon purchase. Still, uncertainty around the valuation of illiquid assets is a pervasive issue, so it is natural to associate liquidity risk with liquidity characteristics. More importantly, though, the term *liquidity risk* also commonly refers to a much broader set of risks for the organization, which are addressed in the next section.

liquid; second, as the size of a position increases, the cost and uncertainty associated with liquidating it will increase. In some extreme cases, there may be no price above zero at which the seller can sell the asset.

Of course, one might argue that the cost of illiquidity, and liquidity risk, should thus be part of the investor's assessment of fundamental value, and indeed it is for many analysts. If not, liquidity risk can sometimes be confused with a form of valuation denial in which investors believe that they paid an appropriate price and that the market has not converged to its true value. But less liquidity means a thin market and a lack of investor interest, which may be fertile ground for investment opportunities. Although lack of liquidity can offer benefits, such as the opportunity to buy an asset well before everyone else sees that it is an attractive investment, liquidity risk is generally considered to be a negative factor with which risk managers and indeed all investors must contend.

Non-Financial Risks

Recall that we refer to financial risks as those arising primarily from events occurring in the financial markets. Although most risks have monetary consequences, there are a number of risks that are typically classified as non-financial in nature. These risks arise from a variety of sources, such as from actions within the organization or from external origins, such as the environment as well as from the relationship between the organization and counterparties, regulators, governments, suppliers, and customers.

One important risk of this type is closely related to default risk but deals more with the settling of payments that occur just before a default. This risk is called settlement risk. As an example, suppose Party A enters into a forward contract to purchase ¥200 million of Japanese government bonds from Party B. At expiration if all goes well, Party A would wire the money and Party B would transfer the bonds. Each party fulfills its obligation expecting that the other will do so as well. However, suppose Party A wires the money but Party B does not send the bonds because it has declared bankruptcy. At this point, Party A cannot get the money back, except possibly much later through the potentially slow and cumbersome bankruptcy process.[14] Although the financial consequences are very high, the root source of this risk is the timing of the payment process itself.

Organizations face two types of risks related to the law, and as such, this risk is referred to as legal risk. One risk is simply the risk of being sued over a transaction or for that matter, anything an organization does or fails to do. In financial risk management, however, the major legal concern is that the terms of a contract will not be upheld by the legal system. For example, suppose Bank E enters into a derivatives contract with Party F. Assume that as the underlying changes in price, Party F incurs a loss, whereas there is a corresponding gain to Bank E. But suppose that Party F then identifies a legal issue that it interprets as giving it the right to refuse to pay. If the court upholds Party F's position, Bank E could incur a loss. Litigation always involves uncertainty because even a seemingly weak case can prevail in court.

The following three non-financial risks are related: regulatory risk, accounting risk, and tax risk. They could even be collectively referred to as compliance risk because they all deal with the matter of conforming to policies, laws, rules, and regulations as set forth by governments and authoritative bodies, such as accounting governing boards. Obviously the regulatory, accounting, and tax environment is always subject to change, but the rapid expansion of financial products and strategies in relation to the relatively slow manner in which government and private regulators are able to

14 This type of risk often arises because of significant time zone differences. Settlement risk is also called Herstatt risk; Herstatt was the name of a German bank that failed in 1974 after receiving "overnight" payments and then defaulting.

respond means that laws and regulations are nearly always catching up with the financial world. When these laws and regulations are updated, it can result in significant unexpected costs, back taxes, financial restatements, and penalties.

Another type of non-financial risk is model risk, which is the risk of a valuation error from improperly using a model. This risk arises when an organization uses the wrong model or uses the right model incorrectly. A simple example applicable to both a portfolio manager and a corporate analyst is the assumption of constant dividend growth in the dividend discount model when, in fact, growth is not constant.

Closely related to model risk is tail risk—more events in the tail of the distribution than would be expected by probability models. This risk is a facet of market risk, but it also infects valuations and models when it is ignored or mishandled. Tail risk is known to be especially severe for the normal distribution, which tends to be overused in modeling. As an example, consider the monthly returns on the S&P 500 Index from January 1950 to October 2018. The monthly average return was 0.70%, and the monthly standard deviation was 4.10%. If we rank the monthly returns, we would find that the largest negative return was –21.76%, which occurred in the well-known market crash of October 1987. With a normal distribution, we would find that a return that low would occur only once every 2,199,935 years.[15] The second and third worst monthly returns of –16.94% (October 2008) and –14.58% (August 1998) would occur only once every 6,916 and 654 years respectively. If the normal distribution is a realistic descriptor of returns, results of these magnitudes should *never* have occurred in recorded market history, and yet we have seen three such instances. Interestingly, according to the normal distribution, the largest positive return of 16.30% in October 1974 would occur only once every 888 years. Technically, one could argue that if we go another 2,199,935 years and do not observe a monthly return as low as –21.76%, then the assumption of a normal distribution might seem reasonable, but it seems safe to reject the normal distribution for at least another two million years. Similar comments can apply to the second and third worst returns albeit over shorter periods.

Many quantitative models (e.g., option models) and decision models (e.g., portfolio construction and asset allocation, relying on variances and covariances in analysis and decisions) ignore the existence of fat tails in returns; as a result, market risk is often considered and dealt with in an oversimplified fashion. Tail risk, as the term is used in practice, is important and is discussed separately because financial professionals realize the implicit failure of modeling market risk. More plainly, ignoring tail risk is a form of model risk. And although tail risk might seem more of a financial risk than a non-financial risk, the mistake occurs internally, arising from poor choices made in modeling.

Most of the internal risks faced by an organization are often grouped together and referred to as operational risk. **Operational risk** is the risk that arises from inadequate or failed people, systems, and internal policies, procedures, and processes, as well as from external events that are beyond the control of the organization but that affect its operations. Although the factors that give rise to such risks can arise externally, the risks themselves are largely internal to an organization because it would be expected to have its people, systems and internal policies, procedures, and processes functioning effectively regardless of pressures placed on it by external forces.

Employees themselves are major sources of potential internal risks. Banks are keenly aware of the vulnerability to employee theft, given the ease with which so many employees have access to accounts and systems for making entries. But even perfectly honest employees make mistakes, and some can be quite costly. The employee who credits someone's account $100,000 for a $100 deposit may have made an honest mistake, but it is a mistake that could quickly lead to the rapid disappearance of

15 This calculation and those that follow are based on determining the probability of the given return or less.

money. In the past, employees up to senior management have been guilty of perpetrating accounting fraud, not necessarily for their own direct benefit but to make the company look better.

In banks and other companies that trade in the financial markets, there is the risk that a trader or portfolio manager will fail to follow laws, rules, or guidelines and put the company at great financial risk. This individual is commonly described as a "rogue trader." Personified by Nick Leeson of Barings Bank, who in 1995 destroyed the 200-year old company by engaging in a series of highly speculative trades to cover up losses, the rogue trader has become a standard concern of risk managers. Although it was never clear if Leeson's trades were truly unauthorized, his legacy left the fear that institutions bear the risk that one trader can imperil the entire organization by making large and highly speculative trades that put the bank's entire capital base at risk. In essence, a rogue trader is a trader who engages in risky transactions without regard for the organization's limits or conforming to its controls.

Organizations are also threatened by business interruptions, such as those caused by extreme weather and natural disasters. Events such as floods, earthquakes, or hurricanes can cause significant damage and temporarily shut down an organization. Although extreme weather and natural disasters are external forces that are completely out of the control of an organization, it does not excuse the organization from having the appropriate internal procedures for managing problems caused by their external environment. Simple and fairly low-cost actions, such as having generators, backup facilities, or providing employees the option to work remotely, can go a long way toward keeping employees working during extreme weather events and when natural disasters strike. Yet, some organization have not heeded inclement weather forecasts. Failing to react to warnings can result in considerable loss.

In a world that is increasingly digital, cyber risk is a major operational risk that spares no organization and that can have significant consequences. Organizations are expected to understand and manage the risk associated with the disruption of or failure related to their information technology (IT) systems. For example, a hacker breaking into a company's IT system and stealing customer or client data is an external threat. Hacking, however, is not simply a random act of mischief. Companies are aware of the threat of hackers, and hackers can break in to a system only if that system is vulnerable. An organization is responsible for ensuring cyber security and establishing sufficiently robust IT safeguards, such as data encryption, to deter hackers from breaking in and either stealing or causing disruption. Cyber-attacks and data breaches can have serious reputational and compliance consequences. For example, all organizations targeting European citizens must comply with the General Data Protection Regulation (GDPR) and notify regulators and data subjects of any data breaches regarding sensitive personal information within 72 hours. Failure to do so can lead to fines of several million euros, including for organizations based outside the European Union. In addition to the threats posed by hackers and viruses, even secure IT systems themselves are a particular source of risk. Programming errors and bugs can create the possibility of costly mistakes.

Terrorism is another form of operational risks that poses a threat to organizations and individuals. The 1993 attacks on the World Trade Center led many companies to recognize that the New York City financial district was a major terrorist target and that, as such, their operations could be shut down by these acts of violence. When the more destructive attacks of 11 September 2001 occurred, many organizations had already established backup facilities sufficiently far away from that area. Of course, such risk is not confined to major financial centers, and indeed, organizations worldwide have begun to take security measures that address this operational risk.

Some of these operational risks are insurable, at least to a modest extent. We will briefly discuss insurance later, but most companies would much prefer to take proactive steps toward prevention than to incur the inconvenience of losses and then have an outside organization compensate them for their losses.

Solvency risk is the risk that the organization does not survive or succeed because it runs out of cash, even though it might otherwise be solvent.[16] This was probably the most underappreciated component of risk prior to the financial crisis of 2008.[17] The collapse of Lehman Brothers was often associated with an excess of leverage, which was certainly a key factor in its failure. But it was solvency risk that forced the company into bankruptcy. Almost overnight, Lehman's liquidity disappeared because most funding sources would no longer willingly bear Lehman's counterparty risk. Even if it had experienced large market gains on the day it went under, it had already been destroyed by solvency risk. Across the entire financial industry, from hedge funds to pension funds, painful but valuable lessons were learned about the critical importance of funds availability and solvency risk, even if all other risks were well-aligned. Solvency risk is now viewed as one of the key factors in running a successful hedge fund because investors are extremely sensitive to not recovering their investment in the event of a "run on the fund."

Solvency, in the personal or institutional sense, is the availability of funding to continue to operate without liquidating—or at a less extreme level, to be able to make good on liabilities and meet one's cash flow requirements. Solvency risk is the ultimate example of the importance of taking an enterprise view of risk management. For example, a university's investment officer might have a perfectly well-balanced set of risks in the endowment portfolio when viewed in isolation. But as a part of a university, the portfolio may be affected by a deep recession because the university's professional degree revenue, grant money, and donations will fall at the same time as the portfolio's investment value and cash distributions are in decline. Although the endowment and university may survive, it might be necessary for the endowment to take many emergency actions that impair its value, simply attributable to the overall solvency risk and the ultimate need of the enterprise to not run out of cash.

Solvency risk is easily mitigated, though never eliminated, by a large number of possible safeguards, none of which is free. Many businesses produce short-term higher returns by essentially ignoring solvency risk, but in doing so, they are not managing risk very well. Since the 2008 crisis, most businesses are keenly aware of the consequences of bad solvency management, and have taken such steps as using less leverage, securing more stable sources of financing, investing in models to provide more transparency on solvency risk, incorporating solvency risk at an enterprise level in risk governance, and holding more cash equivalents and assets with less liquidity risk.

Individuals can also face a number of risks of an operational nature. These include hackers breaking into one's computer and the threat of burglary and robbery. One of the most commonly cited risks for individuals is identity theft. For individuals, however, we consider their primary non-financial risks to be related to their life and health as well as other life-changing events.

Obviously, the health of an individual is an extremely important risk. Poor health can result from poor choices in life, but it can also arise from factors that are outside the control of the individual. These risks can result in direct health care expenses, reduced income because of disability, and reduced lifespan or quality of life. People vary widely in the risk management strategies they undertake to control their health,

16 Solvency risk is often referred to as liquidity risk by industry professionals, even though the expression *liquidity risk* was used earlier to refer to the risk of valuation shock when selling a security. Although the term "liquidity risk" is used in practice in both contexts, in this reading we will refer to the risk relating to the cash position of an organization as "solvency risk."

17 Bank runs are perhaps the simplest example of solvency risk. An otherwise solvent bank can easily be ruined by a bank run that wipes out its ability to make good on short-term liabilities.

such as in their choices in diet, exercise, preventive health care, and avoidance of undue health risks. Some individuals address only their financial exposure to health risks, and still others do not take proactive steps to address this risk at all.

Closely related to health risk is mortality risk—the risk of dying relatively young—and longevity risk—the risk of outliving one's financial resources. Not only are these risks a primary determinant of the quality of life, they are also critical factors in investment planning. Although it is probably desirable not to know when one will die, financial planning for one's years in retirement is heavily dependent on one's mortality assumption. Insurance companies, defined benefit pension plans, and vendors of retirement annuities need only know the group average mortality. Mortality tables are reasonably accurate, so these institutions have relatively precise estimates of death rates for groups as a whole. Individuals themselves, however, clearly do not know how long they will live. People who use defined contribution plans must therefore build portfolios and control retirement distributions so that their assets outlive them, which is difficult to do when they do not know when they will die. No one wants to outlive their money, but with an increasingly aging population and good health care, this problem is becoming a greater concern.

There are a number of other major non-financial risks that individuals face, which are generally involved with some sort of life-changing disaster. The largest ones—fire, natural disaster, or massive liability stemming from harming others, such as in a car accident—are generally considered "property and casualty" risks and are insured as such.

INTERACTIONS BETWEEN RISKS 8

☐ identify financial and non-financial sources of risk and describe how they may interact

In some cases, a risk classified into one category could easily have been classified into another. Indeed, the interactions between risks are numerous. It has been said that market risk begets credit risk, which begets operational risk. That is, given unexpected market moves, one party then owes the other party money. Given the debtor–creditor nature of the relationship, the two parties must have internal operations that process the transactions and pay or collect the money. Thus, whenever there is credit risk, there is settlement risk. If there were no market risk, the other risks in the chain would likely be relatively minor. Legal risk often arises from market or credit risk. Large market moves create losses for one party. There is a long history of parties searching for loopholes in contracts and suing to avoid incurring the loss.

One simple example of an adverse risk interaction is counterparty risk. When trading a derivative contract, it is important to consider the cost of counterparty risk. Suppose Party A buys an out-of-the-money put option with a strike price of ¥1000—a contract theoretically worth ¥100 entitling him to as much as ¥1000 from Counterparty C if an underlying equity index is down. But there is a 2% chance that C could default; and assume that the possibility of default is considered independent of the performance of the equity market. This transaction, with payoffs adjusted for the possibility of default, might price at, say, ¥98 to A. But in reality, the credit risk of C's default is likely dependent on the equity market return. If the probability distribution of default risk overlaps substantially with that of the market being down, which is a likely scenario, then the risks interact, and the cost of risk is higher. In this example, perhaps the probability of C defaulting is 10% or more when the put option is in the money. So, A's expected payoff is lower as a result of facing a credit risk that is compounded by market risk. In fact, it is quite likely that in the extreme event—a deep decline in the equity market when A would presumably receive ¥1000—Party A will in all likelihood get nothing. Thus, the investor bears much more risk than initially thought as a result of the failure to consider the interaction of the two risks. And in doing so, Party A overpaid for the contract. This sort of risk interaction is so common in markets that practitioners have given it a very fitting term—"wrong-way risk." In fact, it was extremely common in the financial crisis of 2008, when holders of many securities based on mortgage credit believed that the risks were well-diversified when in truth, the risks were quite systematic.

Another example of interacting risks was experienced by many banks, funds, and private investment partnerships in 2008, as well as the hedge fund Long-Term Capital Management in 1998. Leverage, which manifested itself in higher market risk, interacted in an extremely toxic manner with liquidity risk and solvency risk and impaired or shuttered many investment firms.[18]

In most adverse financial risk interactions, the whole is much worse than the sum of its parts; the combined risk compounds the individual risks in a non-linear manner. For this example, a 2× levered organization might produce a 2% loss when its unlevered twin or baseline risk bears a 1% loss. If liquidity is a serious issue for the organization, then at a 10% baseline loss, the organization might face some moderate distress from liquidity or funding problems that it ends up losing 25% instead of 20%. It would not be surprising if this organization failed at a 30% baseline loss because of the toxic interplay between levered risk and liquidity problems. This resulting non-linear reaction to risk drivers exists across many risk interactions in many markets, making up-front scenario planning even more valuable to the risk process, a point we will return to later.

Earlier, we briefly described a common example of interacting risks for individuals. Suppose an individual works for a publicly traded company and, through an incentive program, receives shares of the company in her company retirement portfolio or for her personal holdings. Company policies may require that employees hold on to these shares for a number of years. When that time has elapsed, however, many individuals fail to recognize the incredibly concentrated risk they are assuming, so they hold on to their shares. An employee's reasoning for not selling the shares is often that the company she works for has been a solid performing company for many years, so she feels no reason to worry. Moreover, the team spirit often imbued in employees generates pride that can make employees believe that there is no better place in which to work and to invest their money. But if something goes wrong in the company or the industry, the employee may lose her job *and* her savings—an incredibly adverse interaction between market risk and human capital risk. The 2003 collapse of Enron remains a powerful historical example, with many loyal and honest employees losing virtually all of their retirement savings by failing to recognize this risk.

In sum, it is important to recognize that risks do not usually arise independently, but generally interact with one another, a problem that is even more critical in stressed market conditions. The resulting combined risk is practically always non-linear in that the total risk faced is worse than the sum of the risks of the separate components. Most risk models and systems do not directly account for risk interactions, which makes the consequences of the risk interaction even worse. Governance bodies, company management, and financial analysts should be keenly aware of the potential risk and damage of risks in combination, and be aware of the dangers of treating risks as separate and unrelated.

18 This example illustrates yet another risk, systemic risk, that is a significant concern to regulators and governments. Stresses and failures in one sector transmit to stresses and failures in other sectors, which can ultimately impact an entire economy. Systemic risk is the ultimate example of interactions among risks.

EXAMPLE 3

Financial and Non-Financial Sources of Risk

1. Which of the following is *not* a financial risk?

   A. Credit risk

   B. Market risk

   C. Operational risk

   Solution

   C is correct. Operational risk is the only risk listed that is considered non-financial, even though it may have financial consequences. Credit and market risks derive from the possibility of default and market movements, respectively, and along with liquidity risk, are considered financial risks.

2. Which of the following *best* describes an example of interactions among risks?

   A. A stock in Russia declines at the same time as a stock in Japan declines.

   B. Political events cause a decline in economic conditions and an increase in credit spreads.

   C. A market decline makes a derivative counterparty less creditworthy while causing it to owe more money on that derivative contract.

   Solution

   C is correct. Although most risks are likely to be interconnected in some way, in some cases the risks an organization is exposed to will *interact* in such a way that a loss (or gain) in one exposure will lead directly to a loss in a different exposure as well, such as with many counterparty contracts. Conditions in A and B are much more directly linked in that market participants fully expect what follows—for example, in B, an outbreak of war in one region of the world could well cause widespread uncertainty; a flight to quality, such as to government-backed securities; and a widening in spreads for credit-risky securities. In C, in contrast, the reduction in creditworthiness following the market decline may be expected, but owing more money on an already existing contract as a result comes from the interaction of risks.

3. Which of the following *best* describes a financial risk?

   A. The risk of an increase in interest rates.

   B. The risk that regulations will make a transaction illegal.

   C. The risk of an individual trading without limits or controls.

   Solution

   A is correct because this risk arises from the financial markets.

4. Which of the following is *not* an example of model risk?

   A. Assuming the tails of a returns distribution are thin when they are, in fact, fat.

   B. Using standard deviation to measure risk when the returns distribution is asymmetric.

C. Using the one-year risk-free rate to discount the face value of a one-year government bond.

Solution

C is correct. The risk-free rate is generally the appropriate rate to use in discounting government bonds. Although government bonds are generally default free, their returns are certainly risky. Assuming a returns distribution has thin tails when it does not and assuming symmetry in an asymmetric distribution are both forms of model risk.

5. Which of the following is the risk that arises when it becomes difficult to sell a security in a highly stressed market?

A. Liquidity risk

B. Systemic risk

C. Wrong-way risk

Solution

A is correct. Securities vary highly in how liquid they are. Those with low liquidity are those for which either the number of agents willing to invest or the amount of capital these agents are willing to invest is limited. When markets are stressed, these limited number of investors or small amount of capital dry up, leading to the inability to sell the security at any price the seller feels is reasonable. Systemic risk is the risk of failure of the entire financial system and a much broader risk than liquidity risk. Wrong-way risk is the extent to which one's exposure to a counterparty is positively related to the counterparty's credit risk.

6. The risks that individuals face based on mortality create which of the following problems?

A. The risk of loss of income to their families.

B. Covariance risk associated with their human capital and their investment portfolios.

C. The interacting effects of solvency risk and the risk of being taken advantage of by an unscrupulous financial adviser.

Solution

A is correct. The uncertainty about death creates two risks: mortality risk and longevity risk. The mortality risk (risk of dying relatively young) is manifested by a termination of the income stream generated by the person. In contrast, longevity risk is the risk of outliving one's financial resources.

9 MEASURING AND MODIFYING RISK: DRIVERS AND METRICS

☐ describe methods for measuring and modifying risk exposures and factors to consider in choosing among the methods

The core element of risk management is the measurement and modification of risk. One cannot modify risk without measuring it. The primary purpose of measuring risk is to determine whether the risk being taken, or being considered, is consistent with the pre-defined risk tolerance. To understand how risk is measured, it is important to understand the basic elements that drive risk.

Drivers

This section illustrates the origins of risk. Risk is a part of life itself. None of us knows from one day to the next everything that will happen to us in the next 24 hours, let alone over a longer period. We may get a phone call that a relative is extremely sick, or we may be contacted by a head-hunter about an attractive job possibility. We may learn that we are going to be given an award from a prestigious organization, or we may find that our identity has been stolen. All of us can almost surely name something that happened the previous day that was not anticipated. Most of these happenings are minor and often quickly forgotten. Others are serious. Some are good. Some are bad. Some are unpredictable outcomes of known events, such as whether we get an offer following a job interview or whether a medical test reveals that we are healthy or ill. Some events are completely unanticipated, such as getting a phone call from an old friend we have not talked to in many years or having a flat tire on the drive home. Fortunately, the vast majority of risks in life are minor. The ones that are not minor, however, have the potential to be highly unpredictable and financially, and sometimes physically and emotionally, quite costly.

In a conceptual sense, financial risks are no different from the other risks we face in life. All risks arise from the fact that the future is unknown. Financial risks largely emanate from economic risks, and economic risks emanate from the uncertainties of life.

Financial markets generate prices that fluctuate as investors absorb information about the global and domestic state of the economy, the company's industry, and the idiosyncratic characteristics of the company itself. Global and domestic macroeconomies are driven by the companies that operate within them, but much of the tone as well as the ground rules are set by governments and quasi-governmental agencies, such as central banks. Taxes, regulations, laws, and monetary and fiscal policy establish a legal and economic environment and a set of ground rules that greatly affect the degree and quality of economic activity that takes place. Attempts by governments and central banks of different countries to coordinate economic policies can lead to some degrees of success if harmonized, but if not, they can create an environment in which companies engage in practices designed to seek favorable treatment in some countries and avoid unfavorable treatment in others.[19]

All economies, in turn, are composed of industries. Government policies also affect industries, in some cases encouraging economic activity in some industries while discouraging it in others. Some industries are stable, weathering macroeconomic storms quite well, whereas others are highly cyclical.

The uncertainties of global and domestic macroeconomic and central bank policies create risks for economies and industries that we often treat as systematic. Seemingly minor events, such as filling the position of central bank chairperson, are often viewed by investors as major events, signaling possibly a change in policy that can greatly affect the macroeconomy and possibly certain industries.

19 This practice is sometimes called regulatory arbitrage. The policies of certain countries can be more conducive to establishing operations. Examples are the flow of money into countries whose banking laws are less restrictive and more conducive to secrecy and incorporation in or moving a company to a country with lighter regulations or more favorable tax treatment.

Moving down to a more fundamental level, investors face the unsystematic or idiosyncratic risks of individual companies. Modern investment analysis prescribes that diversified portfolios bear no unsystematic risk. We are then led to believe that unsystematic risk does not matter in a well-diversified portfolio. But unsystematic risk does matter to the management of a company. It also matters to poorly diversified investors. And it certainly matters to the financial analysts who cover specific companies. And what would appear to be unsystematic risk can oftentimes actually be systematic. For example, poor credit risk management by a major bank can turn into a global financial crisis if that bank is "too big to fail."

In sum, the basic drivers of risk arise from global and domestic macroeconomies, industries, and individual companies. Risk management can control some of this risk, but it cannot control all of it. For example, the risk manager of a company may be able to reduce the likelihood that his company will default, but he cannot control movements in interest rates. For the latter risk, he must accept that interest rate volatility is a given and that he can only position the company to be able to ensure that its risk exposure is aligned with its objective and risk tolerance. In order to do so, he must first be able to measure the risk.

Metrics

The notion of metrics in the context of risk refers to the quantitative measures of risk exposure. The most basic metric associated with risk is probability. Probability is a measure of the relative frequency with which one would expect an outcome, series of outcomes, or range of outcomes to occur. One can speak about the probability of rolling a six in one roll of a die as 1/6, the chance of rain in the next 24 hours as 20%, or the odds of a central bank taking actions to increase interest rates of 50%. These are all probabilities, differing in concept by the fact that the die roll is associated with an objective probability measure, whereas the other two examples are subjective probabilities. It is important to note that probability, in and of itself, is not a sufficient metric of risk. A chance of financial loss of 25% does not tell us everything we need to know. There are other measures of risk that incorporate probability but give us more information.

The standard deviation is a measure of the dispersion in a probability distribution. Although there is a formal mathematical definition of standard deviation, at this point we need only understand the conceptual definition. Standard deviation measures a range over which a certain percentage of the outcomes would be expected to occur. For example, in a normal distribution, about 68% of the time the outcomes will lie within plus or minus one standard deviation of the expected value. Two standard deviations in both directions would cover about 95% of the outcomes, whereas three would encompass 99% of the outcomes. Although standard deviation, or volatility, is widely used in the financial world, it does have significant limitations. In particular, standard deviation may not be an appropriate measure of risk for non-normal distributions. Standard deviation may not exist for return distributions with fat tails.

Moreover, according to modern portfolio theory, the risk captured by an asset's standard deviation overstates the risk of that asset's returns in the context of a diversified portfolio. Investors can easily diversify their holdings, thereby eliminating a portion of the risk in their portfolios by diversifying away the security-specific risk. As a result, most financial valuation theories assert that the ability of investors to eliminate security-specific risk, or non-systematic risk, means that investors should not expect to earn a premium to compensate them for the assumption of this risk. As a consequence, the risk of a security may be better measured by its **beta**, a measure of the sensitivity of a security's returns to the returns on the market portfolio. Beta measures relative risk, meaning how much market risk an asset contributes to a well-diversified portfolio.[20]

Beta describes risk well for a portfolio of equities, but other sources of risk may require other descriptive risk metrics. The risk associated with derivatives is one example of this. Although derivatives are widely used to manage risk, they do so by assuming other risks. Even if the derivative is being used to establish a hedge of an existing exposure to risk, it would still result in the assumption of additional risk because the assumed risk is being used to offset an existing risk. For example, if one purchases a call option denominated in euros to buy Russian rubles, one would be assuming the risk of the ruble/euro exchange rate. Because most derivatives exposures are highly leveraged, it is critical that the risk of derivatives be properly measured. There are several specialized measures of derivatives risk.

The sensitivity of the derivative price to a small change in the value of the underlying asset is called the **delta**. It is perhaps the most important measure of derivatives risk. Yet delta is limited to capturing only small changes in the value of the underlying. Large changes are captured by the concept of **gamma**. Whereas delta is a first-order risk, gamma is considered a second-order risk because it reflects the risk of changes in delta.[21] Some derivatives, such as options, are also sensitive to changes in the volatility of the underlying. This risk is captured by a concept called **vega**, which is a first-order measure of the change in the derivative price for a change in the volatility of the underlying. Derivatives are also sensitive to changes in interest rates, which are reflected in a measure called **rho**. Most options have relatively low sensitivity to interest rates.[22] These, and other mathematically derived derivatives metrics, are collectively referred to as "the Greeks."

Other asset classes may have their own special metrics to describe risk. One well-known example, **duration**, is a measure of the interest rate sensitivity of a fixed-income instrument. Analogous to delta, it is a first-order risk. The wide variety of financial instrument types and asset classes leads to a proliferation of terminology and risk measures, with most of them having no meaning outside their asset class. As financial organizations and asset risk modeling became more sophisticated and computer power increased, an approach was needed to measure and describe financial risk across the broad spectrum of asset classes. Spurred by the onset of global bank capital regulation, this led to the development of value at risk.

Value at risk or **VaR** is a measure of the size of the tail of the distribution of profits on a portfolio or for an organization. A VaR measure contains three elements: an amount stated in units of currency, a time period, and a probability. For example, assume a London bank determines that its VaR is £3 million at 5% for one day. This statement means that the bank expects to lose a minimum of £3 million in one day 5% of the time. A critical, and often overlooked word, is *minimum*. In this example, the bank expects that its losses will be at least £3 million in one day with 5% probability. In a VaR measure, there is no ultimate maximum that one can state. VaR is thus a minimum extreme loss metric. With a probability of 5% and a measurement period of one day, we can interpret the bank's VaR as expecting a minimum loss of £3

---

20 Earlier, we discussed the fact that unsystematic risk matters to some parties. Here we seem to be saying that it should not matter to anyone. Capital market models almost always assume that investors can diversify quite easily and, as a result, they should not expect to earn a premium for bearing diversifiable risk. This assumption does not mean that everyone's wealth is well-diversified. Investors who do not diversify probably cannot expect to earn a return for bearing diversifiable risk, but it does not mean that these investors should not care about measuring the risk they choose to assume by not diversifying.

21 The notion of a first-order risk versus a second-order risk can be seen by considering the following. Suppose A affects B and B, in turn, affects C. A does not affect C directly but does so only indirectly. A is a first-order risk for B and a second-order risk for C.

22 Options on interest rates, however, have a high sensitivity to interest rates, but only because interest rates are the underlying, and thus, the source of market risk.

million once every 20 business days. VaR can also be used to measure credit losses, although the construction of the measure is considerably more difficult given the extreme asymmetry of the risk.

VaR is a simple but controversial measure. There are several ways to estimate VaR, each of which has its own advantages and disadvantages. The different measures can lead to highly diverse estimates. Moreover, VaR is subject to the same model risk as derivative pricing models. VaR is based on a particular assumption about the probability distribution of returns or profits. If that assumption is incorrect, the VaR estimate will be incorrect. VaR also requires certain inputs. If those inputs are incorrect, the VaR estimate will be incorrect. Many critics of VaR have argued that naive users of VaR can be lulled into a false sense of security. A presumably tolerable VaR can give the illusion that the risk is under control, when in fact, it is not. Yet, VaR is accepted as a risk measure by most banking regulators and is approved for disclosure purposes in typical accounting standards. As with any risk measure, one should supplement it with other measures.

As emphasized earlier, VaR does not tell the maximum loss. The maximum loss is the entire equity of an organization or the entire value of a portfolio, but the statistics used to estimate VaR can be used to gauge average extreme losses. Conditional VaR or **CVaR** is a common tail loss measure, defined as the weighted average of all loss outcomes in the statistical distribution that exceed the VaR loss. Another tail risk metric in the credit risk space that is analogous to CVaR is expected loss given default, which answers the question for a debt security, "If the underlying company or asset defaults, how much do we lose on average?"

VaR focuses on the left tail of the distribution and purports to tell us the expected frequency of extreme negative returns, but it can understate the actual risk. For example, the normal distribution gives us a well-defined measure of extreme negative returns, which are balanced by extreme positive returns. Yet, actual historical return distributions have shown that there are more extreme negative returns than would be expected under the normal distribution. We previously described this concern in the form of tail risk. In response to this concern, statisticians have developed a branch of study that focuses primarily on extreme outcomes, which is called **extreme value theory**, and leads to measures of the statistical characteristics of outcomes that occur in the tails of the distribution. There are mathematical rules that define the statistical properties of such large outcomes, and these rules have been widely used for years in the insurance business. In the past 20 years or so, risk managers have taken to using them to help gauge the likelihood of outcomes that exceed those that would normally be expected.

Two measures in particular that are often used to complement VaR are **scenario analysis** and **stress testing**. These are common sense approaches that ask "If this happens, then how are we affected?" Scenario analysis can be thought of as a package of stress tests, usually with some common underlying theme. A scenario defines a set of conditions or market movements that could occur and would put some pressure on a portfolio. An example might be a sharp increase in interest rates coupled with a significant decline in the value of a currency. The portfolio is then evaluated to determine its expected loss under these scenarios. A different means of posing a scenario analysis is stress testing, which is done by proposing specific asset price moves generally involving extremely large and high pressure scenarios that would occur only rarely but would have the potential for destabilizing the entire organization. The US Federal Reserve and other central banks have begun requiring major banks to stress test their portfolios. Although scenario analysis and stress testing can provide some information, they are, as noted previously for other measures, subject to model risk.

Of course, the measures just mentioned focus primarily on market risk. Credit risk, which is covered in more detail in readings on fixed-income analysis, has long relied heavily on the credit ratings provided by private companies, such as Moody's

Analytics, Standard & Poor's, and Fitch Ratings. In effect, a large part of credit analysis for many lenders has been outsourced since the early part of the 20th century. Most lenders, however, do not rely exclusively on these rating companies. They do their own analysis, which focuses on the creditor's liquidity, profitability, and leverage. Liquidity measures, such as the current ratio, may indicate how well a borrower can cover short-term obligations. Solvency ratios, such as cash flow coverage or interest coverage, may reveal whether a borrower generates enough cash or earnings to make its promised interest payments. Profitability measures, such as return on assets, estimate whether a company is sufficiently profitable so that it can easily accommodate debt. Leverage measures, such as the ratio of debt to total assets, reflect whether a company has sufficient equity capital in relation to its debt to absorb losses and negative cash flows without defaulting. Credit analysis also examines the strength and cyclicality of the macroeconomy and the company's industry. Other widely used measures of credit risk include credit VaR, probability of default, expected loss given default, and the probability of a credit rating change.

One of the problems of credit risk measurement is that credit events, such as a ratings downgrade or a default, are relatively rare for a particular organization. Certainly, in the aggregate there are many credit losses, but very few companies that default have a history of defaulting. Without a history to go by, estimating the likelihood of an event that has never actually occurred is extremely difficult. Imagine the challenge of assigning a default probability to Lehman Brothers in 2007. It had been in operation since 1850 and had never defaulted. Yet in 2008, Lehman Brothers, one of the most successful financial companies of all time, filed for bankruptcy. Because of the infrequency of default, risk managers normally attempt to assess default probability by aggregating companies with similar characteristics.[23]

Another useful source of information for risk managers about these rare events is the *ex ante* risk cost that is implied by the market pricing of derivatives. A **credit default swap (CDS)** on an issuing company has an observable price that acts as a signal to a bondholder of the risk cost of a default. Put options, exotic options, insurance contracts, and other financial instruments may contain valuable signals of the cost of rare adverse events, or at least the price of hedging them.

Operational risk is one of the most difficult risks to measure. Consider the operational risk event reported in 2014 in which hackers broke into Home Depot's credit card data base. Assessing the likelihood of such an event and estimating the potential losses would be almost impossible. The threat of litigation alone for years afterward is difficult to quantify. As with credit risk, significant operational risk events are rare but usually quite costly if they do occur. Hence, attempts to quantify the risk usually involve a third party aggregating operational risk events across numerous companies and publishing the statistics.

As mentioned, there are numerous other risks that would likewise be difficult to measure. For example, there is always the possibility of changes in accounting rules, laws, tax rates, and regulatory requirements that can result in significant costs as companies adapt their policies and actions from one regulatory environment to a new one. How would one measure such risks? Moreover, the time period spanned by these risks is extremely long, and in fact, theoretically infinite. Changes in these rules and laws are often motivated by politics. How does one quantify such risks when there are no real numeric measures? Analysis invariably reverts to subjective evaluation of the likelihood of such threats and their potential losses.

23 In some sense, aggregating companies with similar characteristics is what credit ratings do. Companies rated BAA/Baa+ can be quite diverse but all are considered similar with respect to their ability to pay their debts.

As we have described, many risks are measurable, at least on an *ex post* basis. Market-related risks are blessed with large quantities of data, so they are relatively measurable. Credit, operational, and other risks are somewhat rare events. Although it is probably a good thing that such events are indeed rare, their infrequency makes measurement more difficult. Nonetheless, virtually any risk manager will attempt to obtain at least a subjective sense of the expected frequency, likelihood, and cost of these events. With either objective or subjective measurements in mind, risk managers can then proceed to modify these risks accordingly.

10 RISK MODIFICATION: PREVENTION, AVOIDANCE, AND ACCEPTANCE

☐ describe methods for measuring and modifying risk exposures and factors to consider in choosing among the methods

The notion of risk modification presumes that an analysis has been conducted in the risk governance stage that defines how much risk is acceptable. Coupled with measurements of the actual risk, as discussed in the previous section, the risk manager then proceeds to align the actual risk with the acceptable risk.

It is important to understand, however, that risk modification is not strictly risk reduction. For example, a portfolio with the strategic objective of maintaining a 50/50 split between equity and cash will naturally find that in a market in which cash outperforms equity, the split between equity and cash will tilt toward cash. Thus, the portfolio becomes less risky. Beyond a certain point, the risk of the portfolio is unacceptably low given the return target. Thus, risk modification would take the form of rebalancing by increasing the risk. For the most part, however, risk management focuses more on reducing the risk. Risk reduction is commonly referred to as hedging. A hedge is a transaction put in place to reduce risk. Some hedges are designed to lead to the ultimate in risk reduction—the complete elimination of risk. Others are simply designed to lower the risk to an acceptable level.[24] For some companies, risk management is primarily concerned with keeping the organization solvent. Regardless of the focus, much of what is done to manage risk is the same. In this section, we will examine four broad categories of risk modification: risk prevention and avoidance, risk acceptance, risk transfer, and risk shifting.

Risk Prevention and Avoidance

One method of managing risk is taking steps to avoid it altogether; however, avoiding risk may not be as simple as it appears. It is difficult to completely avoid risk, but more importantly, it is unclear that every risk should be completely avoided particularly if there are high costs associated with eliminating the risk. Instead we choose a trade-off between cost and benefits. The actual trade-off may be subject to debate because risk assessment and risk management are subject to variation from one person to another.

We could nearly eliminate the risk of being injured or killed in an automobile accident if we choose to never drive or ride in a car. Like any risk-avoidance strategy, however, there would more than likely be a trade-off in terms of the loss of the benefits

24 For example, in the case of the portfolio with a strategic target of 50/50 equity and cash, if equity outperforms cash, the portfolio will tilt toward equity. At some point, a risk-reducing strategy would then be in order. This type of hedge would reduce the risk but not eliminate it.

provided by the activity. We could try to protect our children from all harm, but that may come at the expense of preparing them poorly for adult life. We could invest our entire retirement savings in cash, but would most likely give up protection against inflation and lose out on the opportunity to benefit from long-term economic growth and the performance of investable assets that benefit from that growth.

Insurance companies rely heavily on the techniques of risk prevention and avoidance. An automobile insurance company would prefer that their policyholders never drive their cars. Although it cannot prohibit them from doing so, it can reward them with lower premiums if they drive less and have safe driving records. A life insurance company would prefer that their policyholders do not smoke, and it can reward non-smokers with lower rates.

Nearly every risk we take has an upside, at least as perceived by the person taking the risk. Some counterexamples might seem to belie this point, but not if viewed from the point of view of the risk taker. One could argue that there are no benefits from smoking, but people who smoke may have the opinion that the pleasure they receive exceeds the costs. Casino gambling incurs the risk of significant financial loss and addiction, but it is risk that is acceptable to the consumers who incur it relative to the perceived benefits they receive. The risks of extreme sports, such as skydiving, would seem to be exceeded by the benefits obtained by participants, and yet participants engage in them with apparently much enjoyment. People undertake all types of risky behaviors because they obtain commensurate benefits. These examples are simply cases in which the decision maker chooses to bear a certain degree of risk. They are conceptually the same as an investor who chooses to accept a relatively high degree of risk. Likewise, those who live their lives engaging in very few risky activities are conceptually the same as the investor who keeps only a modest exposure to risky assets.

In organizations, the decision to avoid risk is generally made at the governance level as a part of setting the risk tolerance. Boards will often decide that there are some business or investment activities simply not worth pursuing based on either the goals of the organization or the perceived risk–return trade-off. These are strategic decisions. Boards may exclude some areas or activities to allow management to focus on choosing risks in other areas where they presumably have a better chance of adding value.

We recap this section by noting that risk prevention and avoidance is simply an element of the decision of how much risk to accept, given the trade-off between the risk of loss and the benefit of gain. This could be a direct benefit or an indirect benefit of avoiding or eliminating a risk. Most decisions in life involve a trade-off between benefits and costs, neither of which is necessarily easy to measure. Thus, risk management is an ongoing process of fine-tuning exposure to achieve the level of risk that is desired in relation to the benefits.

If the risk measurement process shows that the risk exceeds the acceptable level, there are three approaches to managing the risk: self-insuring, risk transfer, and risk shifting.

Risk Acceptance: Self-Insurance and Diversification

In many cases, from both a risk tolerance and a strategic standpoint, it makes sense to keep a risk exposure—but to do so in the most efficient manner possible. Self-insurance is the notion of bearing a risk that is considered undesirable but too costly to eliminate by external means. In some cases, self-insuring means simply to bear the risk. In other cases, it may involve the establishment of a reserve to cover losses. Choosing to not have health insurance can be an optimal choice for some young, healthy adults without responsibility for children. Setting aside some money to cover potential health costs completes the picture of an individual who completely self-insures. Similarly, a young healthy individual who does not buy life insurance but engages in a systematic, well-conceived savings and investment plan is engaging in self-insurance.

One must be careful with this approach, however, because there is a fine line between self-insurance and denial. To the extent that self-insurance results in risks that are completely in line with the enterprise's risk tolerance, it would be an example of good governance. But if there is a risk that is outside the enterprise's risk tolerance, and management decides to bear that risk anyway, saying it is self-insuring, management is basically ignoring that risk, disregarding and violating its risk tolerance, and practicing bad risk governance. For example, an investment management firm, via its risk tolerance decision, may decide that it cannot bear any investment loss exceeding €1 billion and may apply a variety of risk management tools to limit its market and credit risk accordingly. But suppose that the firm makes no move to limit or insure its risks from fraud or a rogue trader on the grounds that it is "self-insuring" this risk, which could result in a loss as high as €3 billion. By leaving itself open to a loss that far exceeds its stated risk tolerance, management is violating the firm's risk governance.

From the perspective of a business organization, self-insurance is obtained by setting aside sufficient capital to cover losses. The banking industry is a classic example of self-insurance. Although in many countries government insurance may protect depositors, banks self-insure to some extent by maintaining capital and loan loss reserves.

Another form of accepting risk, but doing so in the most efficient manner possible, is diversification. Technically, it is a risk-mitigation technique. But diversification and "the efficient frontier" are so central to modern portfolio analysis that capturing the full benefits of diversification seems the obvious thing for all organizations to pursue—a starting point at which other risk modification could be appended. Although diversification is one form of risk management, it is usually not effective if used in isolation.

In the next two subsections, we discuss how undesired risk can be modified or eliminated by selling the risk to another party. We make two subtle classifications of these methods: risk transfer and risk shifting.

11 RISK MODIFICATION: TRANSFERRING, SHIFTING, AND HOW TO CHOOSE

☐ describe methods for measuring and modifying risk exposures and factors to consider in choosing among the methods

Risk transfer is the process of passing on a risk to another party, often, but not always, in the form of an insurance policy. Insurance is a legal contract in which one party, the insurer, agrees to cover some percentage of a loss incurred by another party, the insured, from a specific event in return for the payment of a premium by the insured. Insurance as a method of risk modification has been in existence for very long time, and in fact, is even mentioned in the Code of Hammurabi almost 4,000 years ago. Insurance has been widely used in the commercial shipping and farming industries going back hundreds of years. Insurance is almost as old as commerce itself.[25]

From the point of view of the insurer, insurance almost always works on the basis of diversification or pooling of risks. An insurer attempts to sell many policies with risks that have low correlations. The insurer assesses the pooled risks and charges a premium that covers the expected aggregate losses and the insurer's operating costs

25 It is worth noting that the insurance industry has for a long time referred to itself using the term "risk management." A department of risk management in a large organization is often the group that manages the organization's insurance policies. But since around 1990 or so, the term "risk management" has increasingly come to refer to far more than insurance.

as well as leaves a profit. Insurers need accurate statistics on aggregate risks, but these are often not difficult to obtain. These actuarial data are widely available on accidents, illnesses, property and casualty damage, and death. In principle, a well-diversified insurer does not care if a single insured party has significantly larger-than-average claims as long as there is no reason to believe that the claims are correlated. There will be other parties that have smaller-than-average claims.

Insurers do have to manage their risks carefully. Some risks can be correlated. In the US Gulf Coast region, property insurance, which includes coverage for loss by hurricanes, is typically more expensive than property insurance in other regions. Even with a higher premium, an insurer has to avoid providing too much property coverage in an area where a systemic event, such as a hurricane, can occur in order to diversify its risk exposure.

Although insurers carefully assess their risk and charge premiums that they believe accurately reflect expected losses, they nonetheless remain responsible for potentially large claims. Insurers also manage their risk by avoiding writing too many policies with similar and potentially correlated risks and by selling some of the risk to another insurer, a practice known as reinsurance. A company that primarily insures property in the US Midwest, which is highly subject to tornado risk, might be willing to accept some Gulf Coast hurricane risk for a reasonable premium. Insurers often write provisions into contracts to exclude coverage of special cases. For example, a war might nullify insurance coverage in an area. Most insurance policies also contain provisions to guard against moral hazards, such as suicide or destroying one's own property. In the last 20 years or so, some insurance companies have issued bonds that permit them to legally avoid paying principal and/or interest if insurance claims exceed a certain amount. These instruments, known as catastrophe bonds, essentially pass some of the insurance risk on to the investors who buy the bonds.

Most insurance policies do not cover *all* of the risk that is insured. It is common for policies to contain a provision known as a deductible. A deductible is a monetary amount of the loss that will be covered by the insured before any claims are paid. Thus, both the insured and the insurer bear some of the risk, although the insurer usually bears the greater amount. Deductibles serve several purposes. Because insurers incur fixed costs for each claim, deductibles reduce the number of small claims. Deductibles also encourage good risk management by the insured parties. Finally, deductibles offer the insured the opportunity to combine risk transfer with self-insurance and thereby achieve a potentially better trade-off of risk and reward.

As noted, the concept of insurance relies on the diversification or pooling of risks. In a few cases, however, the risks are not easy to pool. For example, suppose a volatile but extremely successful actor is signed to star in a movie. The production company knows that it runs the risk that the actor will engage in behavior that damages the ability of the company to finish the movie. The number of volatile and extremely successful actors for whom policies could be written at the same time is somewhat limited. Thus, an insurer would have to bear that risk without the benefit of diversification.

For example, suppose a television network plans to cover the Olympics but is concerned about a possible cancellation or boycott. It might want an insurance policy to cover it against loss. Specialized coverage is possible through such companies as Lloyd's of London. The approximately 350-year old Lloyd's is famous for covering unusual risks. It does so by organizing groups of investors who are willing to bear a risk for a premium. These groups, called syndicates, are subject to the full extent of losses. In many cases, investors in these syndicates have been required to pay substantial amounts of money to cover losses.[26] These examples illustrate how syndicates work.

26 NBC insured the 1980 Summer Olympics in Moscow through Lloyd's of London to the extent that if a US boycott occurred, Lloyd's would pay NBC for losses that it incurred by prepaying the Soviet Union for broadcasting rights. The United States did boycott the Olympics and NBC collected on its policy.

Although there is only one Olympics to insure, there may also be only one actor to insure. Because the two risks are uncorrelated, a company could write policies on both risks and would achieve some diversification. Moreover, there are other unusual risks that can be covered such that the aggregate pool would represent a highly diverse set of risks that have low correlations.

A very slight variation of insurance is a surety bond. With a surety bond, an insurer promises to pay an insured a certain amount of money if a third party fails to fulfill its obligation. For example, if a party engages the services of another party, the first party is covered if the party obligated to provide the service fails to perform to a satisfactory degree. Surety bonds are widely used in commercial activity when one party bears the risk of the potentially high cost of non-performance by another party. A slight variation of a surety bond is a fidelity bond, which is often used to cover against losses that result from employee dishonesty. Bonds of this type work very similarly to insurance and rely on the pooling of uncorrelated risks.[27] Other similar arrangements include indemnity clauses and hold harmless arrangements, such as when two parties sign a contract and one party agrees to hold the other harmless and/or indemnify the other in the event of loss.

The use of insurance by so many as a risk management tool suggests that the cost of risk exceeds the actuarial cost to many individuals and enterprises. *Ex ante* consideration of the cost of a risk in terms of the organization's value or utility ties risk mitigation back to the risk tolerance decision and the most fundamental governance decisions on which value-added strategies to pursue. As an alternative to *ignoring* the cost of risk, the impact on enterprise value should be quite positive.

Risk Shifting

Whereas risk transfer refers to actions taken that pass the risk on to other parties, **risk shifting** refers to actions that change the distribution of risk outcomes. Risk transfer is often associated with insurance, whereas risk shifting generally involves derivatives as the risk modification vehicle. Although insurance is a form of risk management based on the pooling or diversification of risks, risk shifting diverts some portion of the risk distribution to another market participant who either bears the risk or intermediates that risk by moving it to yet another party. The organization may want to adjust its probability distribution of returns, essentially adjusting the payoff diagram of its risk exposures. An example is a company that is willing to make slightly less profit than it otherwise would if the stock market is up to prevent it from losing too much money if the stock market is down, for example, more than 20% next year. It is adjusting its potential economic outcomes by shifting the probability distribution of its profits conditional on market performance. Risk shifting represents the bulk of hedging and is the most common form of risk modification for financial organizations.

The principal device through which risk shifting is performed is a derivative. We briefly mentioned derivatives earlier in this reading. By definition, a derivative is a financial instrument that derives its price from the price of an underlying asset or rate. Because the price of the underlying and the price of the derivative are so closely related, derivatives can provide essentially the same exposure as the underlying but can do so at lower cost and capital requirements. As such, derivatives permit the efficient shifting of risk across the probability distribution and from one party to another. One can hold the underlying and take an offsetting position in the derivative or vice versa. Whereas insurance can be designed to perform similarly, insurance functions

27 In the context of surety and fidelity bonds, the word "bond" does not mean a debt obligation issued by one party, the borrower, and bought by another, the lender. In this context, the word refers to assuring one party that it bears no risk for the actions of a specific other party.

primarily through the pooling of diverse risks. With derivatives, risks are shifted across probability distributions or payoffs and across parties, to leave specific outcomes of the conditional probability distribution with the parties most willing to bear the risk.

There are several types of derivatives, and the manner in which they provide risk shifting varies by type. Derivatives are classified into two categories: forward commitments or contingent claims. Forward commitments are agreements that obligate two parties to undertake a transaction at a future date at a price or rate agreed on when the commitment is made. Forward commitments include such instruments as forward contracts, futures contracts, and swaps. Forward commitments can be used to lock in a future interest rate for a borrower or lender, the purchase or sale price of an asset, or an exchange rate for a currency. Parties who engage in forward commitments do not pay any money at the initiation of the contract. In lieu of any up-front payment from one party to the other, the two parties agree on the terms of the transaction that will be consummated at the end of the contract. Depending on movements in the price or rate of the underlying, one party will ultimately gain from the transaction while the other will lose or, in the less likely case, both parties could breakeven. For example, a corporate treasurer can use a forward contract to lock in the rate at which a foreign cash flow will be converted into the company's domestic currency. Regardless of movements in the exchange rate during the life of the contract, the foreign cash flow will convert to the domestic currency at a rate that is locked in when the contract is initiated. On the opposite side of the transaction, the party can be a speculator who simply bears the risk, or it can be a dealer who intermediates the risk between the hedger and the speculator. We will discuss dealers in more detail in a few paragraphs.

EXAMPLE 4

Risk Shifting: Foreign Exchange Risk and Forward Commitments

You are a UK investor, investing 60% in a UK index fund tracking the FTSE 100, the leading index of the UK equity market, and 40% in US Treasuries. You expect returns in US dollars on the US Treasuries of 1.6%, and because you expect 0% return on the USD/GBP exchange rate, this return expectation equals your return expectation in sterling. You expect a return of 5.5% on the FTSE 100. Hence, the expected return on your portfolio is 3.9%.

$$R_P = w_1 \times R_1 + (1 - w_1) \times [(1 + R_{lc}) \times (1 + R_{FX}) - 1].$$

$$R_P = 0.6 \times 0.055 + 0.4 \times [(1 + .015) \times (1 + 0.0) - 1] = 0.039 = 3.9\%.$$

Risk (standard deviation of returns) for the FTSE 100 is 13.2%, and the risk on US Treasuries in sterling is 11.0%. Correlations between US Treasuries, the FTSE 100, and the USD/GBP exchange rate are shown in the following correlation matrix.

	FTSE 100	US Treasuries	USD/GBP
FTSE 100	1.00	–0.32	–0.06
US Treasuries	–0.32	1.00	0.33
USD/GBP	–0.06	0.33	1.00

Using the information provided above, we can calculate the risk of the portfolio with UK large-capitalization equities and US Treasuries as follows:

$$\sigma_p = \sqrt{w_1^2\sigma_1^2 + w_2^2\sigma_2^2 + w_3^2\sigma_3^2 + 2\rho_{1,2}w_1w_2\sigma_1\sigma_2 + 2\rho_{1,3}w_1w_3\sigma_1\sigma_3 + 2\rho_{1,3}w_1w_3\sigma_1\sigma_3}.$$

$\sigma_p = (0.6^2 \times 0.132^2 + 0.4^2 \times 0.040^2 + 0.4^2 \times 0.090^2 + 2 \times -0.32 \times 0.6 \times 0.4 \times 0.132 \times 0.040 + 2 \times -0.06 \times 0.6 \times 0.4 \times 0.132 \times 0.090 + 2 \times 0.33 \times 0.4 \times 0.4 \times 0.040 \times 0.090)^{1/2}$

$\sigma_p = 0.0841 \approx 8.4\%$.

The risk of this portfolio is 8.4%.

As an investor, you would like to examine possibilities to reduce the risk to this portfolio without giving up too much return, and you suspect that the volatility of the USD/GBP exchange rate contributes to risk while not adding to return. You want to know the impact of hedging the currency exposure of the US Treasury investment by means of entering into a forward contract selling USD into GBP in one year's time. You want to hedge 100% of the currency risk of the US Treasury investment.

You have been told that the forward price of a currency expressed in another currency is equal to the current spot price, corrected for the difference between the deposit rates of the countries involved over the time period ("tenor") of the forward contract. The current spot price of USD in sterling is GBP0.7040. The one-year forward price is 0.7038, as 12-month deposit rates in the United Kingdom and the United States are very close to one another.

1. What would be the impact on the risk of the portfolio if you hedge 100% of your US Treasury investment's value using this one-year forward contract?

   Solution

   In a perfect hedge, the impact is the same as ignoring the currency exposure in the US Treasury investment altogether. Filling out the standard deviations and correlations as above in the following formula gives

   $$\sigma_p = \sqrt{w_1^2\sigma_1^2 + w_2^2\sigma_2^2 + 2w_1w_2\rho_{12}\sigma_1\sigma_2}.$$

   $$\sigma_p = \sqrt{(0.6^2 \times 0.132^2) + (0.4^2 \times 0.040^2) + 2 \times 0.6 \times 0.4 \times (-0.32) \times 0.132 \times 0.040}.$$

   $\sigma_p = 0.0757 \approx 7.6\%$.

   This compares to 8.4% risk in the unhedged portfolio, a substantial reduction of risk.

2. Does the decision to 100% hedge the foreign exchange exposure have any consequences for the expected return on the hedged portfolio relative to the unhedged portfolio?

   Solution

   The forward price of the currency will play a role in the return expected on the hedged portfolio. The forward price of USD in GBP is 0.7038, which is 0.03% lower than the spot price today. Because you hedge 40% of current portfolio value, the impact on your expected return is 40% × –0.03%, reducing the hedged portfolio return to 3.87% = 3.9% – 0.03%.

3. Will the proposed transaction eliminate all currency risk associated with the US Treasury investment?

   Solution

   No, unfortunately not. As time progresses, the US Treasury investment will fluctuate in value and by the end of the tenor of the forward contract will be worth less or more in USD than the amount of USD you have sold. You have ended up under- or overhedged. In fact, because you expect the value of your investment to increase with your expected return (minus cash distributions), it is logical to expect to be underhedged. The amount to which you are under- or overhedged is subject to currency risk. The risk of being under- or overhedged can be managed by comparing, at regular intervals, the notional value of the forward position with the value of the investment and correct the hedge as required. The decision on how often to evaluate this is a trade-off between costs (monitoring costs, transaction costs) and risk.

The other type of derivative is a contingent claim, which is commonly known as an option. An option is a contract between two parties that gives one party the right to buy or sell an underlying asset or to pay or receive a known underlying rate. An option takes the form of either a call option, which provides the right to buy the underlying or to pay a known rate, or a put option, which provides the right to sell the underlying or to receive a known rate.

With a forward commitment, both parties are mutually obligated to each other. Because an option grants the right, but not the obligation, to one party, that party has an advantage over the other. Consequently, that party, the buyer of the option, must pay cash, called the premium, to the seller of the option at the start of the contract. Once the premium is paid, the option buyer has no further obligation. He can either exercise the option or he can let the option expire unexercised. In the latter case, the option buyer incurs a loss equal to the premium. If the option is a call and it is exercised, the buyer pays the fixed price or rate and receives the underlying. If the option is a put and it is exercised, the buyer receives the fixed price or rate and delivers the underlying.[28] If the buyer of the option does exercise it, he may achieve a gain that exceeds the premium paid but the gain could also be less than the premium paid, thereby resulting in a net overall loss. An option buyer could be using the option to speculate on an upward move in the underlying if a call or downward move if a put. Alternatively, the option buyer could be hedging. In the example used earlier for forward commitments, the corporate treasurer anticipating an inflow of cash in a foreign currency could buy a put option to sell that currency, thereby converting it into his domestic cash flow at a known fixed rate. The option gives the treasurer the flexibility to not exercise it if the underlying currency rises in value. This flexibility comes at the cost of having to pay a premium at the start of the transaction, thus shifting the financial outcome across the entire probability distribution of that uncertain currency rate. In contrast, with the forward contract, the treasurer does not have to pay cash at the start but is obligated to convert at the agreed-upon rate.

Derivatives can be created in public forums, such as on derivatives exchanges, or privately between two parties. On derivatives exchanges, there are a large number of individual and institutional traders that make markets in derivatives. For private derivatives transactions, there is an extensive market of large bank and non-bank dealers willing to buy and sell derivatives. In both types of markets, these dealers assume the risk of being transferred from parties who originate the transactions. These dealers almost always restructure and transfer some portion, if not all, of the risk by finding

28 Instead of one party delivering the underlying, some options call for settlement in cash of an equivalent amount. Some forward commitments also settle in cash.

other parties that are willing to take on that risk. Ultimately, the risk is assumed by some party willing to accept the risk, producing an economically efficient outcome for all parties.

How to Choose Which Method for Modifying Risk

Choosing which risk mitigation method to use—risk prevention and avoidance, self-insuring, risk transfer, or risk shifting—is a critical part of the risk management process. Fortunately, the methods are not mutually exclusive, and many organizations use all methods to some extent. No single method provides a clear-cut advantage over the others. As with all decisions, the trade-off is one of costs versus benefits that are weighed in light of the risk tolerance of the organization or individual.

For example, many companies that have extensive foreign operations and are, therefore, highly exposed to exchange rate risk, hedge that risk using derivatives. Some companies prefer forwards, some prefer swaps, some prefer options, and some use multiple instruments. Some companies attempt to hedge currency risk by setting up operations in foreign countries rather than manufacturing domestically and shipping the goods to foreign countries.[29] Some companies manage their currency risk by attempting to balance currency assets and liabilities. Some airlines hedge the risk of oil price changes and others do not. Some airlines that do hedge this risk do so to a far greater degree than others. Additionally, some prefer the certainty of forwards and swaps, whereas others prefer the flexibility of options, even with the up-front cost that options require. Most insurance companies rely on their actuarial knowledge but supplement it with proactive measures, such as selling risk to other parties.

To the extent possible, most organizations should avoid risks that provide few benefits and potentially extreme costs. Reasonable, low-cost precautions against risks with few benefits should always be taken. Thus, risk prevention and risk avoidance are probably the first choice of measures, especially for risks that lie outside the core competencies of the organization and have little reasonable expectation of adding value. Nonetheless, avoidance may not be the best value for its cost. Moreover, avoiding risk may mean avoiding opportunity. Thus, an organization often cannot simply decide not to take a risk, at least not for all undesirable risks.

Organizations that have large amounts of free cash flow may choose to self-insure some risks, but few organizations have so much cash that they can afford to self-insure all risks. Some risks can potentially imperil the entire capital base. Most companies would, however, prefer to self-insure to the extent possible because self-insurance reduces the costs associated with external monitoring and gives the organization the greatest flexibility. Self-insurance and avoidance should generally be clearly addressed at the governance level and be consistent with stated risk tolerance.

Risk transfer, or the use of insurance, is a widely used risk management tactic, but it may not be suitable for many types of risks. Some risks simply are not insurable, at least not in a cost-effective way. Insurance works best when risks can be pooled, and that is not the case for many types of risks, particularly those that can affect a large number of parties at the same time. The use of risk shifting tools, such as derivatives, may not be available for all types of risks, thus limiting their use in risk mitigation. For financial risks that exceed risk appetite, risk shifting is a very common choice.

The various risk management methods are not equal in terms of the risk reduction and the risk profile that remains. For example, contingent claims, such as insurance, provide the flexibility in the form of offering opportunity to profit in one direction

29 Here is another example of the interactions of risks. A decision to manufacture products in a foreign country involves trade-offs between exchange rate risk, political risk, and a variety of other risks germane to that country's economy, not to mention a potentially different degree of operational risk, in the pursuit of higher profits.

and have a loss reduced in the other, but they require payment of cash up front. In contrast, forward commitments lock in an outcome. In other words, they provide little flexibility, but they require no cash payment up front. The risk profile that exists when a contingent claim hedge is put in place differs significantly from the risk profile that exists when a forward commitment hedge is placed. This process requires significant understanding and discussion at all levels of the organization.

To recap, risk takers should identify risks that offer few rewards in light of potential costs and avoid those risks when possible. They should self-insure where it makes sense and diversify to the extent possible. They should consider insurance when risks can be pooled effectively if the cost of the insurance is less than the expected benefit. If derivatives are used, they must consider the trade-off of locking in outcomes with forward commitments versus the flexibility relative to cash cost of contingent claims, which can tailor the desired outcomes or payoffs by shifting the risk. Ultimately, the decision is always one of balancing costs against benefits while producing a risk profile that is consistent with the risk management objectives of the organization.

EXAMPLE 5

Measuring and Modifying Risk

1. From the perspective of an organization, which of the following *best* describes risk drivers?

   A. The probabilities of adverse events

   B. The statistical methods that measure risk

   C. Factors that influence macroeconomies and industries

   Solution

   C is correct. Risks (and risk drivers) arise from fundamental factors in macroeconomies and industries.

2. Which of the following concepts directly measures the risk of derivatives?

   A. Probability

   B. Delta and gamma

   C. Beta and standard deviation

   Solution

   B is correct. Delta and gamma are measures of the movement in an option price, given a movement in the underlying. The other answers can reflect some elements of derivatives risk, but they are not direct measures of the risk.

3. The *best* definition of value at risk is:

   A. the expected loss if a counterparty defaults.

   B. the maximum loss an organization would expect to incur over a holding period.

   C. the minimum loss expected over a holding period a certain percentage of the time.

   Solution

   C is correct. VaR measures a minimum loss expected over a holding period a certain percentage of the time. It is not an expected loss, nor does it reflect the maximum possible loss, which is the entire equity of the organization.

4. Which of the following are methods commonly used to supplement VaR to measure the risk of extreme events?

   A. Standard deviation

   B. Loss given default

   C. Scenario analysis and stress testing

   Solution

   C is correct. Scenario analysis and stress testing both examine the performance of a portfolio subject to extreme events. The other two answers are metrics used in portfolio analysis but are not typically associated with extreme events.

5. Which of the following is a true statement about insurable risks?

   A. Insurable risks are less costly.

   B. Insurable risks have smaller loss limits.

   C. Insurable risks are typically diversifiable by the insurer.

   Solution

   C is correct. Insurance works by pooling risks. It is not necessarily less costly than derivatives nor does it have lower loss limits.

SUMMARY

Success in business and investing requires the skillful selection and management of risks. A well-developed risk management process ties together an organization's goals, strategic competencies, and tools to create value to help it both thrive and survive. Good risk management results in better decision making and a keener assessment of the many important trade-offs in business and investing, helping managers maximize value.

- Risk and risk management are critical to good business and investing. Risk management is *not* only about avoiding risk.
- Taking risk is an active choice by boards and management, investment managers, and individuals. Risks must be understood and carefully chosen and managed.
- Risk exposure is the extent to which an organization's value may be affected through sensitivity to underlying risks.
- Risk management is a process that defines risk tolerance and measures, monitors, and modifies risks to be in line with that tolerance.
- A risk management framework is the infrastructure, processes, and analytics needed to support effective risk management; it includes risk governance, risk identification and measurement, risk infrastructure, risk policies and processes, risk mitigation and management, communication, and strategic risk analysis and integration.
- Risk governance is the top-level foundation for risk management, including risk oversight and setting risk tolerance for the organization.
- Risk identification and measurement is the quantitative and qualitative assessment of all potential sources of risk and the organization's risk exposures.

- Risk infrastructure comprises the resources and systems required to track and assess the organization's risk profile.
- Risk policies and processes are management's complement to risk governance at the operating level.
- Risk mitigation and management is the active monitoring and adjusting of risk exposures, integrating all the other factors of the risk management framework.
- Communication includes risk reporting and active feedback loops so that the risk process improves decision making.
- Strategic risk analysis and integration involves using these risk tools to rigorously sort out the factors that are and are not adding value as well as incorporating this analysis into the management decision process, with the intent of improving outcomes.
- Employing a risk management committee, along with a chief risk officer (CRO), are hallmarks of a strong risk governance framework.
- Governance and the entire risk process should take an enterprise risk management perspective to ensure that the value of the entire enterprise is maximized.
- Risk tolerance, a key element of good risk governance, delineates which risks are acceptable, which are unacceptable, and how much risk the overall organization can be exposed to.
- Risk budgeting is any means of allocating investments or assets by their risk characteristics.
- Financial risks are those that arise from activity in the financial markets.
- Non-financial risks arise from actions within an organization or from external origins, such as the environment, the community, regulators, politicians, suppliers, and customers.
- Financial risks consist of market risk, credit risk, and liquidity risk.
- Market risk arises from movements in stock prices, interest rates, exchange rates, and commodity prices.
- Credit risk is the risk that a counterparty will not pay an amount owed.
- Liquidity risk is the risk that, as a result of degradation in market conditions or the lack of market participants, one will be unable to sell an asset without lowering the price to less than the fundamental value.
- Non-financial risks consist of a variety of risks, including settlement risk, legal risk, regulatory risk, accounting risk, tax risk, model risk, tail risk, and operational risk.
- Operational risk is the risk that arises either from within the operations of an organization or from external events that are beyond the control of the organization but affect its operations. Operational risk can be caused by employees, the weather and natural disasters, vulnerabilities of IT systems, or terrorism.
- Solvency risk is the risk that the organization does not survive or succeed because it runs out of cash to meet its financial obligations.
- Individuals face many of the same organizational risks outlined here but also face health risk, mortality or longevity risk, and property and casualty risk.
- Risks are not necessarily independent because many risks arise as a result of other risks; risk interactions can be extremely non-linear and harmful.

- Risk drivers are the fundamental global and domestic macroeconomic and industry factors that create risk.
- Common measures of risk include standard deviation or volatility; asset-specific measures, such as beta or duration; derivative measures, such as delta, gamma, vega, and rho; and tail measures such as value at risk, CVaR and expected loss given default.
- Risk can be modified by prevention and avoidance, risk transfer (insurance), or risk shifting (derivatives).
- Risk can be mitigated internally through self-insurance or diversification.
- The primary determinants of which method is best for modifying risk are the benefits weighed against the costs, with consideration for the overall final risk profile and adherence to risk governance objectives.

PRACTICE PROBLEMS

1. Risk management in the case of individuals is *best* described as concerned with:
   A. hedging risk exposures.
   B. maximizing utility while bearing a tolerable level of risk.
   C. maximizing utility while avoiding exposure to undesirable risks.

2. Which of the following may be controlled by an investor?
   A. Risk
   B. Raw returns
   C. Risk-adjusted returns

3. The process of risk management includes:
   A. minimizing risk.
   B. maximizing returns.
   C. defining and measuring risks being taken.

4. The factors a risk management framework should address include all of the following *except*:
   A. communications.
   B. policies and processes.
   C. names of responsible individuals.

5. Which of the following *best* describes activities that are supported by a risk management infrastructure?
   A. Risk tolerance, budgeting, and reporting
   B. Risk tolerance, measurement, and monitoring
   C. Risk identification, measurement, and monitoring

6. Risk governance:
   A. aligns risk management activities with the goals of the overall enterprise.
   B. defines the qualitative assessment and evaluation of potential sources of risk in an organization.
   C. delegates responsibility for risk management to all levels of the organization's hierarchy.

7. Effective risk governance in an enterprise provides guidance on all of the following *except*:
   A. unacceptable risks.

B. worst losses that may be tolerated.

C. specific methods to mitigate risk for each subsidiary in the enterprise.

8. A firm's risk management committee would be expected to do all of the following *except*:

   A. approving the governing body's proposed risk policies.

   B. deliberating the governing body's risk policies at the operational level.

   C. providing top decision-makers with a forum for considering risk management issues.

9. Once an enterprise's risk tolerance is determined, the role of risk management is to:

   A. analyze risk drivers.

   B. align risk exposures with risk appetite.

   C. identify the extent to which the enterprise is willing to fail in meeting its objectives.

10. Which factor should *most* affect a company's ability to tolerate risk?

    A. A stable market environment

    B. The beliefs of the individual board members

    C. The ability to dynamically respond to adverse events

11. Which of the following is the correct sequence of events for risk governance and management that focuses on the entire enterprise? Establishing:

    A. risk tolerance, then risk budgeting, and then risk exposures.

    B. risk exposures, then risk tolerance, and then risk budgeting.

    C. risk budgeting, then risk exposures, and then risk tolerance.

12. Risk budgeting includes all of the following *except*:

    A. determining the target return.

    B. quantifying tolerable risk by specific metrics.

    C. allocating a portfolio by some risk characteristics of the investments.

13. A benefit of risk budgeting is that it:

    A. considers risk tradeoffs.

    B. establishes a firm's risk tolerance.

    C. reduces uncertainty facing the firm.

14. Which of the following risks is *best* described as a financial risk?

    A. Credit

B. Solvency

C. Operational

15. Liquidity risk is *most* associated with:

A. the probability of default.

B. a widening bid–ask spread.

C. a poorly functioning market.

16. An example of a non-financial risk is:

A. market risk.

B. liquidity risk.

C. settlement risk.

17. If a company has a one-day 5% Value at Risk of $1 million, this means:

A. 5% of the time the firm is expected to lose at least $1 million in one day.

B. 95% of the time the firm is expected to lose at least $1 million in one day.

C. 5% of the time the firm is expected to lose no more than $1 million in one day.

18. An organization choosing to accept a risk exposure may:

A. buy insurance.

B. enter into a derivative contract.

C. establish a reserve fund to cover losses.

19. The choice of risk-modification method is based on:

A. minimizing risk at the lowest cost.

B. maximizing returns at the lowest cost.

C. weighing costs versus benefits in light of the organization's risk tolerance.

SOLUTIONS

1. B is correct. For individuals, risk management concerns maximizing utility while taking risk consistent with individual's level of risk tolerance.

2. A is correct. Many decision makers focus on return, which is not something that is easily controlled, as opposed to risk, or exposure to risk, which may actually be managed or controlled

3. C is correct. Risks need to be defined and measured so as to be consistent with the organization's chosen level of risk tolerance and target for returns or other outcomes.

4. C is correct. While risk infrastructure, which a risk management framework must address, refers to the people and systems required to track risk exposures, there is no requirement to actually name the responsible individuals.

5. C is correct. *Risk infrastructure* refers to the people and systems required to track risk exposures and perform most of the quantitative risk analysis to allow an assessment of the organization's risk profile. The risk management infrastructure identifies, measures, and monitors risks (among other things).

6. A is correct. Risk governance is the top-down process that defines risk tolerance, provides risk oversight and guidance to align risk with enterprise goals.

7. C is correct. Risk governance is not about specifying methods to mitigate risk at the business line level. Rather, it is about establishing an appropriate level of risk for the entire enterprise. Specifics of dealing with risk fall under risk management and the risk infrastructure framework.

8. A is correct. The risk management committee is a part of the risk governance structure at the operational level—as such, it does not approve the governing body's policies.

9. B is correct. When risk tolerance has been determined, the risk framework should be geared toward measuring, managing, and complying with the risk tolerance, or aligning risk exposure with risk tolerance. The risk tolerance decision begins by looking at what shortfalls within an organization would cause it to fail to achieve some critical goals and what are the organization's risk drivers.

10. C is correct. If a company has the ability to adapt quickly to adverse events may allow for a higher risk tolerance. There are other factors, such as beliefs of board members and a stable market environment, which may but should not affect risk tolerance.

11. A is correct. In establishing a risk management system, determining risk tolerance must happen before specific risks can be accepted or reduced. Risk tolerance defines the appetite for risk. Risk budgeting determine how or where the risk is taken and quantifies the tolerable risk by specific metrics. Risk exposures can then be measured and compared against the acceptable risk.

12. A is correct. Risk budgeting does not include determining the target return. Risk budgeting quantifies and allocates the tolerable risk by specific metrics.

13. A is correct. The process of risk budgeting forces the firm to consider risk tradeoffs. As a result, the firm should choose to invest where the return per unit

of risk is the highest.

14. A is correct. A financial risk originates from the financial markets. Credit risk is one of three financial risks identified in the reading: Credit risk is the chance of loss due to an outside party defaulting on an obligation. Solvency risk depends at least in part on factors internal to the organization and operational risk is an *internal* risk arising from the people and processes within the organization.

15. B is correct. Liquidity risk is also called transaction cost risk. When the bid–ask spread widens, purchase and sale transactions become increasingly costly. The risk arises from the uncertainty of the spread.

16. C is correct. Settlement risk is related to default risk but deals with the timing of payments rather than the risk of default.

17. A is correct. The VaR measure indicates the probability of a loss of at least a certain level in a time period.

18. C is correct. Risk acceptance is similar to self-insurance. An organization choosing to self-insure may set up a reserve fund to cover losses. Buying insurance is a form of risk transfer and using derivatives is a form of risk-shifting, not risk acceptance.

19. C is correct. Among the risk-modification methods of risk avoidance, risk acceptance, risk transfer, and risk shifting none has a clear advantage. One must weigh benefits and costs in light of the firm's risk tolerance when choosing the method to use.

Glossary

Abandonment option The option to terminate an investment at some future time if the financial results are disappointing.

Abnormal return The amount by which a security's actual return differs from its expected return, given the security's risk and the market's return.

Absolute dispersion The amount of variability present without comparison to any reference point or benchmark.

Accelerated book build An offering of securities by an investment bank acting as principal that is accomplished in only one or two days.

Accounting profit Income as reported on the income statement, in accordance with prevailing accounting standards, before the provisions for income tax expense. Also called *income before taxes* or *pretax income*.

Accredited investors Investors that meet certain minimum regulatory net worth or other requirements in order to invest in certain types of alternative assets.

Accrued interest The amount of interest in currency or par value terms of a fixed-income instrument that accumulates from the last coupon payment until the trade settlement date. The amount is paid by the buyer to the seller.

Action lag Delay from policy decisions to implementation.

Active investment An approach to investing in which the investor seeks to outperform a given benchmark.

Active return The return on a portfolio minus the return on the portfolio's benchmark.

Activist Short for "activist shareholder." Managers secure sufficient equity holdings to allow them to seek a position in a company's board and influence corporate policies or direction.

Activity ratios Ratios that measure how well a company is managing key current assets and working capital over time.

Ad hoc committee A small group of lenders or bondholders who negotiate with an issuer on debt restructuring and refinancing before the issuer submits a final proposal to the wider group of all lenders and bondholders.

Add-on pricing A pricing approach based on high-margin optional features, customizations, and additional content.

Add-on rate A yield or pricing convention for money market instrument quotations. It is the interest earned on an instrument, derived from the difference between the price and face value, expressed as a percentage of the price and multiplied by the periodicity of the annual rate.

Agency costs Direct and indirect costs borne by the principal in a principal-agent relationship owing primarily to information asymmetries. Agency costs include the costs of monitoring and assessing the agent as well as missed opportunities.

Agency RMBS Securities created by the pooling of residential mortgage-backed securities in the United States by either the Federal National Mortgage Association (Fannie Mae) or the Federal Home Loan Mortgage Corporation (Freddie Mac). These RMBS carry the full faith and credit of the government, essentially a guarantee with respect to timely payment of interest and repayment of principal.

All-or-nothing (AON) orders An order that includes the instruction to trade only if the trade fills the entire quantity (size) specified.

Allocationally efficient A characteristic of a market, a financial system, or an economy that promotes the allocation of resources to their highest value uses.

Altcoin A cryptocurrency other than Bitcoin.

Alternative data Data that are generated from non-traditional sources, such as social media and sensor networks.

Alternative hypothesis The hypothesis that is accepted if the null hypothesis is rejected.

Alternative investment markets Market for investments other than traditional securities investments (i.e., traditional common and preferred shares and traditional fixed income instruments). The term usually encompasses direct and indirect investment in real estate (including timberland and farmland) and commodities (including precious metals); hedge funds, private equity, and other investments requiring specialized due diligence.

Alternative trading systems Trading venues that function like exchanges but that do not exercise regulatory authority over their subscribers except with respect to the conduct of the subscribers' trading in their trading systems. Also called *electronic communications networks* or *multilateral trading facilities*.

American depository receipt A US dollar-denominated security that trades like a common share on US exchanges.

American depository share The underlying shares on which American depository receipts are based. They trade in the issuing company's domestic market.

American options Options that may be exercised at any time from contract inception until maturity.

American-style Type of option contract that can be exercised at any time up to the option's expiration date.

Amortization The process of allocating the cost of intangible long-term assets having a finite useful life to accounting periods; the allocation of the amount of a bond premium or discount to the periods remaining until bond maturity.

Amortizing debt A loan or bond with a payment schedule that calls for the complete repayment of principal over the instrument's time to maturity.

Analysis of variance (ANOVA) A table that presents the sums of squares, degrees of freedom, mean squares, and F-statistic for a regression model.

Analytical duration Estimates of duration using mathematical formulas. Estimates of the impact of yield changes on bond prices using analytical duration implicitly assume that benchmark yields and spreads are independent variables and are uncorrelated.

Anchoring and adjustment bias An information-processing bias in which the use of a psychological heuristic influences the way people estimate probabilities.

Annual general meeting (AGM) A yearly meeting of the corporate board of directors and shareholders, typically held in person and digitally, during which votes on directors, compensation plans, shareholder resolutions, and any other matters properly brought forward at the meeting are held. Issuer management may also make presentations and hold events.

Anomalies Apparent deviations from market efficiency.

Antidilutive With reference to a transaction or a security, one that would increase earnings per share (EPS) or result in EPS higher than the company's basic EPS—antidilutive securities are not included in the calculation of diluted EPS.

Arbitrage (1) The simultaneous purchase of an undervalued asset or portfolio and sale of an overvalued but equivalent asset or portfolio in order to obtain a riskless profit on the price differential. Taking advantage of a market inefficiency in a risk-free manner. (2) The condition in a financial market in which equivalent assets or combinations of assets sell for two different prices, creating an opportunity to profit at no risk with no commitment of money. In a well-functioning financial market, few arbitrage opportunities are possible. (3) A risk-free operation that earns an expected positive net profit but requires no net investment of money.

Arbitrageurs Traders who engage in arbitrage. See *arbitrage*.

Arithmetic mean The sum of the observations divided by the number of observations.

Artificial intelligence (AI) Computer systems that are capable of performing tasks that previously required human intelligence. AI methods are sometimes better suited to identify complex, non-linear relationships than are traditional quantitative and statistical methods.

Ask The price at which a dealer or trader is willing to sell an asset, typically qualified by a maximum quantity (ask size). See *offer*.

Ask size The maximum quantity of an asset that pertains to a specific ask price from a trader. For example, if the ask for a share issue is $30 for a size of 1,000 shares, the trader is offering to sell at $30 up to 1,000 shares.

Asset allocation The process of determining how investment funds should be distributed among asset classes.

Asset class A group of assets that have similar characteristics, attributes, and risk–return relationships.

Asset utilization ratios Ratios that measure how efficiently a company performs day-to-day tasks, such as the collection of receivables and management of inventory.

Asset-backed commercial paper Secured form of commercial paper issuance. Loans or receivables are sold to a special purpose entity that issues the ABCP and makes interest and principal payments to investors from asset cash flows.

Asset-backed securities (ABS) A type of bond issued by a legal entity called a special purpose entity created solely to own assets such as loans, receivables, and mortgages and to distribute cash flows to ABS investors. Generally, ABS backed by mortgages are known as mortgage-backed securities (MBS) while ABS refer to non-mortgage ABS.

Asset-backed token A token that represents the ownership of a physical asset that does not exist on the blockchain and whose value is based on the underlying asset.

Asset-based valuation models Valuation based on estimates of the market value of a company's assets.

Asymmetric information Also known as *information asymmetry*; the differential of information between corporate insiders and outsiders regarding the company's performance and prospects. Managers typically have more information about the company's performance and prospects than owners and creditors.

At-the-money Describes a unique situation in which the price of the underlying is equal to an option's exercise price. Like an out-of-the-money option, the intrinsic value is zero.

Auction/reverse auction models Pricing models that establish prices through bidding (by sellers in the case of reverse auctions).

Autarky Countries seeking political self-sufficiency with little or no external trade or finance. State-owned enterprises control strategic domestic industries.

Automatic stabilizer A countercyclical factor that automatically comes into play as an economy slows and unemployment rises.

Availability bias An information-processing bias in which people take a heuristic approach to estimating the probability of an outcome based on how easily the outcome comes to mind.

Available-for-sale Under US GAAP, debt securities not classified as either held-to-maturity or held-for-trading securities. The investor is willing to sell but not actively planning to sell. In general, available-for-sale debt securities are reported at fair value on the balance sheet, with unrealized gains included as a component of other comprehensive income.

Average revenue (AR) Total revenue divided by quantity sold.

Backfill Bias A problem whereby certain surviving hedge funds may be added to databases and various hedge fund indexes only after they are initially successful and start to report their returns. Also see *survivorship bias*.

Backup line of credit A type of credit enhancement provided by a bank to an issuer of commercial paper to ensure that the issuer will have access to sufficient liquidity to repay maturing commercial paper if issuing new paper is not a viable option.

Backwardation A downward-sloping, or inverted, forward curve in a futures market.

Balance sheet ratios Financial ratios involving balance sheet items only.

Balanced With respect to a government budget, one in which spending and revenues (taxes) are equal.

Balloon payment A large payment required at maturity to retire a bond's outstanding principal amount.

Base rates The reference rate on which a bank bases lending rates to all other customers.

Base-rate neglect A type of representativeness bias in which the base rate or probability of the categorization is not adequately considered.

Basic EPS Net earnings available to common shareholders (i.e., net income minus preferred dividends) divided by the weighted average number of common shares outstanding.

Basis risk The possibility that the expected value of a derivative differs unexpectedly from that of the underlying.

Basket of listed depository receipts (BLDR) An exchange-traded fund (ETF) that represents a portfolio of depository receipts.

Bayes' formula The rule for updating the probability of an event of interest—given a set of prior probabilities for the event, information, and information given the event—if you receive new information.

Bearer bonds Bonds for which ownership is not recorded; only the clearing system knows who the bond owner is.

Behavioral finance A field of finance that examines the psychological variables that affect and often distort the investment decision making of investors, analysts, and portfolio managers.

Behind the market Said of prices specified in orders that are worse than the best current price; e.g., for a limit buy order, a limit price below the best bid.

Benchmark A bond used to compare against another bond to discern attributes, often a government bond with the same or similar time-to-maturity as the bond under analysis.

Benchmark spread The difference in yield-to-maturity between a bond and that of a benchmark bond.

Best bid The highest bid in the market.

Best effort offering An offering of a security using an investment bank in which the investment bank, as agent for the issuer, promises to use its best efforts to sell the offering but does not guarantee that a specific amount will be sold.

Best offer The lowest offer (ask price) in the market.

Best-in-class An ESG implementation approach that seeks to identify the most favorable companies and sectors based on ESG considerations. Also called *positive screening*.

Beta A measure of the sensitivity of a given investment or portfolio to movements in the overall market.

Bid The price at which a dealer or trader is willing to buy an asset, typically qualified by a maximum quantity.

Bid size The maximum quantity of an asset that pertains to a specific bid price from a trader.

Big data The vast amount of information being generated by both traditional sources—for example, stock exchanges, companies, governments—and non-traditional sources—for example, electronic devices, social media, sensor networks, and company exhaust.

Bilateralism The conduct of political, economic, financial, or cultural cooperation between two countries. Countries engaging in bilateralism may have relations with many different countries but in one-at-a-time agreements without multiple partners. Typically, countries exist on a spectrum between bilateralism and multilateralism.

Bimodal A distribution that has two most frequently occurring values.

Bitcoin A cryptocurrency using blockchain technology that was created in 2009.

Bivariate correlation Also known as Pearson correlation. A parametric measure of the relationship between two variables.

Black swan risk An event that is rare and difficult to predict but has an important impact.

Block brokers A broker (agent) that provides brokerage services for large-size trades.

Blockchain A type of digital ledger in which information is recorded sequentially and then linked together and secured using cryptographic methods.

Blue chip Widely held large market capitalization companies that are considered financially sound and are leaders in their respective industry or local stock market.

Board of directors A body or individual selected by a limited company's member(s) or shareholder(s), in a manner determined by the company's charter, that manages the company. Typically, for larger companies, boards of directors appoint and oversee executive management.

Bond equivalent yield A money market interest rate quoted on a 365-day add-on rate basis.

Bond indenture A legal document between a bond issuer and investors that governs each party's rights and responsibilities.

Bond market vigilantes Bond market participants who might reduce their demand for long-term bonds, thus pushing up their yields.

Bondholders Investors in an entity's securitized debt claims, such as commercial paper, notes, and bonds. Common types of bondholders include investment funds and institutional investors.

Bonds Contractual agreements between an issuer and bondholders.

Bonus issue of shares A type of dividend in which a company distributes additional shares of its common stock to shareholders instead of cash.

Book building Investment bankers' process of compiling a "book" or list of indications of interest to buy part of an offering.

Book value Shareholders' equity (total assets minus total liabilities) minus the value of preferred stock; common shareholders' equity.

Boom An expansionary phase characterized by economic growth "testing the limits" of the economy.

Bootstrap A resampling method that repeatedly draws samples with replacement of the selected elements from the original observed sample. Bootstrap is usually conducted by using computer simulation and is often used to find standard error or construct confidence intervals of population parameters.

Bottom-up analysis An investment selection approach that focuses on company-specific circumstances rather than emphasizing economic cycles or industry analysis.

Box and whisker plot A graphic for visualizing the dispersion of data across quartiles. It consists of a box with "whiskers" connected to the box.

Breakeven point Represents the price of the underlying in a derivative contract in which the profit to both counterparties would be zero.

Bridge financing Interim financing that provides funds until permanent financing can be arranged.

Broker An agent who executes orders to buy or sell securities on behalf of a client in exchange for a commission.

Brokered market A market in which brokers arrange trades among their clients.

Broker–dealer A financial intermediary (often a company) that may function as a principal (dealer) or as an agent (broker) depending on the type of trade.

Brownfield investments The third stage of development of an infrastructure asset. Brownfield investments involve expanding existing facilities and may involve privatization of public assets or a sale leaseback of completed greenfield projects. They are characterized by a shorter investment period with immediate cash flows and an operating history.

Budget surplus/deficit The difference between government revenue and expenditure for a stated fixed period of time.

Bullet bond A bond whose principal repayment is made entirely at maturity.

Bundling A pricing approach that refers to combining multiple products or services so that customers are incentivized or required to buy them together.

Business cycles Are recurrent expansions and contractions in economic activity affecting broad segments of the economy.

Business model A concise description of how a business works and makes revenues and profits, including its customers, products or services, channels for reaching customers, and pricing.

Businesses Organization entities formed and managed for the purpose of providing a return or economic benefits to its investors and owners.

Buy-side firm An investment management company or other investor that uses the services of brokers or dealers (i.e., the client of the sell side firms).

Buyback A transaction in which a company buys back its own shares. Unlike stock dividends and stock splits, share repurchases use corporate cash.

Cabotage The right to transport passengers or goods within a country by a foreign firm. Many countries—including those with multilateral trade agreements—impose restrictions on cabotage across transportation subsectors, meaning that shippers, airlines, and truck drivers are not allowed to transport goods and services within another country's borders.

Call market A market in which trades occur only at a particular time and place (i.e., when the market is called).

Call money rate The interest rate that buyers pay for their margin loan.

Call option The right to buy an underlying.

Call period The time during which the issuer of a callable bond can exercise the call option.

Call price The price at which the issuer of a callable bond has the right to purchase the bond from investors.

Call protection period The time during which the issuer of a callable bond is not allowed to exercise the call option.

Call risk The uncertain maturity and limited price appreciation associated with callable bonds.

Callable bond A bond containing an embedded call option that gives the issuer the right to buy the bond back from the investor at specified prices on predetermined dates.

Cannibalization A transfer of sales or market share from one product to another product owned by the same company. It tends to occur when the two products are actual or perceived substitutes.

Capacity The ability of the borrower to make its debt payments on time.

Capital Other company resources available that reduce reliance on debt.

Capital allocation The process that companies use for decision making on capital investments—those projects with a life of one year or longer.

Capital allocation line (CAL) A graph line that describes the combinations of expected return and standard deviation of return available to an investor from combining the optimal portfolio of risky assets with the risk-free asset.

Capital asset pricing model (CAPM) An equation describing the expected return on any asset (or portfolio) as a linear function of its beta relative to the market portfolio.

Capital expenditure Expenditure on physical capital (fixed assets).

Capital investments An expenditure for an asset or resource with a useful life of more than one year.

Capital market expectations (CME) Expectations concerning the risk and return prospects of asset classes.

Capital market line (CML) The line with an intercept point equal to the risk-free rate that is tangent to the efficient frontier of risky assets; represents the efficient frontier when a risk-free asset is available for investment.

Capital market securities Fixed-income securities with original maturities greater than one year.

Capital markets Financial markets that trade securities of longer duration, such as bonds and equities.

Capital restrictions Controls placed on foreigners' ability to own domestic assets and/or domestic residents' ability to own foreign assets.

Capital structure The mix of debt and equity that a company uses to finance its business; a company's specific mix of long-term financing.

Capital-indexed bond A type of index-linked bond for which changes in the index are captured with adjustments to the principal. A common example is Treasury Inflation Protected Securities (TIPS) issued by the United States government.

Capital-intensive businesses Companies or business activities that are characterized by a relatively low fixed asset turnover, a high percentage of capital expenditures to sales, or a high net-working-capital-to-sales ratio.

Capital-light businesses Also known as *asset light businesses*, companies or business activities characterized by relatively high fixed asset turnover, a low percentage of capital expenditures to sales, or a low net-working-capital-to-sales ratio.

Carried interest A performance fee (also referred to as an incentive fee, or carry) that is applied based on excess returns above a hurdle rate.

Carrying Investing and holding an asset for a period of time.

Carrying amount The amount at which an asset or liability is valued according to accounting principles.

Carrying value Of a fixed-income instrument is the purchase price plus (minus) the amortized amount of the discount (premium) if the bond is purchased at a price below (above) par value.

Cartel Participants in collusive agreements that are made openly and formally.

Cash conversion cycle The amount of time between an issuer paying its suppliers in cash and receiving cash from its customers.

Cash flow additivity principle The principle that dollar amounts indexed at the same point in time are additive.

Cash flow from operations A cash profit measure over a period for an issuer's primary business activities. It includes cash from customers as well as interest and dividends received from financial investments, less cash paid to employees and suppliers as well as taxes paid to governments and interest paid to lenders.

Cash flow hedge Refers to a specific **hedge accounting** classification in which a derivative is designated as absorbing the variable cash flow of a floating-rate asset or liability, such as foreign exchange, interest rates, or commodities.

Cash markets Markets in which specific assets are exchanged at current prices. Cash markets are often referred to as **spot markets**.

Cash prices The current prices prevailing in **cash markets**.

Cash ratio A measure of liquidity that is the ratio of cash and marketable securities to current liabilities.

Catch-up clause A clause in an agreement that favors the GP. For a GP who earns a 20% performance fee, a catch-up clause allows the GP to receive 100% of the distributions above the hurdle rate *until* she receives 20% of the profits generated, and then every excess dollar is split 80/20 between the LPs and GP.

CDS credit spread Reflects the credit spread of a credit default swap (CDS) derivative contract. As with cash bonds, CDS credit spreads depend on the probability of default (POD) and the loss given default (LGD).

Central bank digital currencies (CBDCs) A tokenized version of the currency issued by the central bank, such as a digital bank note or coin, and a digital liability of the central bank.

Central bank funds market The market in which deposit-taking banks that have an excess reserve with their national central bank can lend money to banks that need funds for maturities ranging from overnight to one year. Called the federal or fed funds market in the United States.

Central bank funds rate The interest rate at which central bank funds are bought (borrowed) and sold (lent) for maturities ranging from overnight to one year. Called federal or fed funds rate in the United States.

Central clearing mandate A requirement instituted by global regulatory authorities following the 2008 global financial crisis that most **over-the-counter (OTC)** derivatives be **cleared** by a **central counterparty (CCP)**.

Central counterparty (CCP) An economic entity that assumes the **counterparty credit risk** between derivative **counterparties**, one of which is typically a financial intermediary. CCPs provide **clearing** and **settlement** for most **derivative contracts**.

Central limit theorem The theorem that states the sum (and the mean) of a set of independent, identically distributed random variables with finite variances is normally distributed, whatever distribution the random variables follow.

Certificate of deposit (CD) An instrument that represents a specified amount of funds on deposit with a bank for a specified maturity and interest rate. CDs are issued in various denominations and can be negotiable or non-negotiable.

Channels Venues where a company markets and/or delivers its products and services.

Character The quality of a debt issuer's management.

Checking accounts Bank deposits with no stated maturity available for transactional purposes that pay little or no interest. Also known as a *demand deposit*.

Circuit breaker A pause in intraday trading for a brief period if a price limit is reached.

Classical cycle Refers to fluctuations in the level of economic activity when measured by GDP in volume terms.

Clawback A requirement that the general partner return any funds distributed as incentive fees until the limited partners have received their initial investment and a percentage of the total profit.

Clearing An exchange's process of verifying the execution of a transaction, exchange of payments, and recording of participants.

Clearing instructions Instructions that indicate how to arrange the final settlement ("clearing") of a trade.

Clearinghouse An entity associated with a futures market that acts as middleman between the contracting parties and guarantees to each party the performance of the other.

Closed-end fund A mutual fund in which no new investment money is accepted. New investors invest by buying existing shares, and investors in the fund liquidate by selling their shares to other investors.

Cluster sampling A procedure that divides a population into subpopulation groups (clusters) representative of the population and then randomly draws certain clusters to form a sample.

Co-investing In co-investing, the investor invests in assets *indirectly* through the fund but also possesses rights (known as co-investment rights) to invest *directly* in the same assets. Through co-investing, an investor is able to make an investment *alongside* a fund when the fund identifies deals.

Code of ethics An established guide that communicates an organization's values and overall expectations regarding member behavior. A code of ethics serves as a general guide for how community members should act.

Coefficient of determination (R^2) The percentage of the variation of the dependent variable that is explained by the independent variable. It is a measure of goodness of fit of a regression model.

Coefficient of variation The ratio of a set of observations' standard deviation to the observations' mean value.

Cognitive cost The effort involved in processing new information and updating beliefs.

Cognitive dissonance The mental discomfort that occurs when new information conflicts with previously held beliefs or cognitions.

Cognitive errors Behavioral biases resulting from faulty reasoning; cognitive errors stem from basic statistical, information-processing, or memory errors.

Coincident economic indicators Turning points that are usually close to those of the overall economy; they are believed to have value for identifying the economy's present state.

Collateral Assets or financial guarantees underlying a debt obligation that are above and beyond the issuer's promise to pay.

Collateral manager Buys and sells debt obligations for and from the CDO's collateral pool to generate sufficient cash flows to meet the obligations to the CDO bondholders.

Collateralized bond obligations (CBOs) CDOs backed by high-yield corporate and emerging market bonds.

Collateralized debt obligations (CDOs) Securities backed by a diversified pool of one or more debt obligations. CDOs can be backed by a broad range of debt.

Collateralized loan obligations (CLOs) Investment vehicle with exposure to a portfolio of leveraged loans separated into tranches with different cash flow claims and exposure to losses based on a waterfall.

Collateralized mortgage obligations Securitize mortgage pass-through securities or multiple pools of loans. CMOs are structured to redistribute the cash flows to different bond classes or tranches and create securities that have different exposures to prepayment risk.

Commercial paper (CP) Short-term, negotiable, unsecured promissory note that represents a debt obligation of the issuer.

Committed (regular) lines of credit Bank commitments to extend credit; the commitment is considered a short-term liability and is usually in effect for 364 days (one day short of a full year).

Committed capital The amount that the limited partners have agreed to provide to the private equity fund.

Commodities A product or service from a firm that is indistinguishable from products or services of competing firms, usually conforming to a common standard or grade imposed by convention or regulation.

Commoditization A process by which competing products become less differentiated over time and become interchangeable "commodities" in the eyes of customers. This process is typically associated with declining profitability for the selling firms.

Commodity producers A firm that makes and/or sells commodities.

Commodity swap A type of swap involving the exchange of payments over multiple dates as determined by specified reference prices or indexes relating to commodities.

Common market Level of economic integration that incorporates all aspects of the customs union and extends it by allowing free movement of factors of production among members.

Common shares A type of security that represents an ownership interest in a company. Also called *common stock*.

Common stock A type of security that represents an ownership interest in a company. Also called *common shares*.

Common-size analysis The restatement of financial statement items using a common denominator or reference item that allows one to identify trends and major differences; an example is an income statement in which all items are expressed as a percent of revenue.

Companies Organization entities formed and managed for the purpose of providing a return or economic benefits to its investors and owners.

Company research report A document that presents an analyst's investment recommendation on an issuer and its securities, supported by financial modeling, industry overviews and competitive analyses, valuation scenarios, ESG considerations, and investment risks.

Complete markets Informally, markets in which the variety of distinct securities traded is so broad that any desired payoff in a future state-of-the-world is achievable.

Concession agreement A contractual arrangement under which an entity (also known as a grantor) establishes terms and conditions with a developer or operator (referred to as a concessionaire) to plan, build, operate, finance, and maintain an infrastructure asset for a specific period.

Conditional expected value The expected value of a stated event given that another event has occurred.

Conditional pass-through covered bonds Convert to pass-through securities after the original maturity date if all bond payments have not yet been made.

Conditional variances The variance of one variable, given the outcome of another.

Conditions The general economic, competitive, and business environment faced by all borrowers that may affect their ability to service or refinance debt.

Confidence level The complement of the level of significance.

Confirmation bias A type of cognitive bias that makes individuals view information that confirms beliefs they already hold as more salient.

Consensus protocol A set of rules governing how blocks can join the blockchain that is designed to resist attempts at malicious manipulation up to a certain level of security; it can be either a proof of work or a proof of stake.

Conservatism bias A belief perseverance bias in which people maintain their prior views or forecasts by inadequately incorporating new information.

Constant yield-price trajectory A graphical depiction of the relationship between time to maturity and a bond price, assuming no default, that shows that a bond price approaches par as time passes.

Constituent securities With respect to an index, the individual securities within an index.

Contango Refers to spot price below forward price in a futures market.

Contingency provision Clause in a legal document that allows for some action if a specific event or circumstance occurs.

Contingency table A table of the frequency distribution of observations classified on the basis of two discrete variables.

Contingent claim A type of derivative in which one of the *counterparties* determines whether and when the trade will settle. An *option* is a common type of contingent claim.

Contingent convertible bonds Bonds that automatically convert to equity if a specific event or circumstance occurs, such as the issuer's equity capital falling below the minimum requirement set by regulators.

Continuous trading market A market in which trades can be arranged and executed any time the market is open.

Continuously compounded return The natural logarithm of 1 plus the holding period return, or equivalently, the natural logarithm of the ending price over the beginning price.

Contract manufacturers Companies that make products for other companies that meet specific terms and specifications.

Contract size Amount(s) used for calculation to price and value the derivative. The contract size is often referred to as "notional amount or notional principal."

Contraction The period of a business cycle after the peak and before the trough; often called a *recession* or, if exceptionally severe, called a *depression*.

Contraction risk The risk of earlier repayment of a mortgage-backed security than expected.

Contractionary Tending to cause the real economy to contract.

Contractionary fiscal policy A fiscal policy that has the objective to make the real economy contract.

Contribution margin A profitability measure using variable costs: unit price less unit variable cost. It can also be expressed as a percentage of price or sales.

Controlling shareholder An individual or entity that owns a majority of the voting rights in a corporation.

Convenience sampling A procedure of selecting an element from a population on the basis of whether or not it is accessible to a researcher or how easy it is for a researcher to access the element.

Convenience yield A non-cash benefit of holding a physical commodity versus a derivative.

Conversion price Predetermined share price at which convertible debt may be fully exchanged for common shares during the conversion period.

Conversion ratio The number of common shares a convertible bond or noteholder may receive in exchange for a specific bond par value.

Conversion value The current contingency feature value derived by comparing a convertible bond's price with its value if a bondholder were to exchange bonds for shares.

Convertible bond A bond that gives the bondholder the right to exchange the bond for a specified number of common shares in the issuing company.

Convertible debt A fixed-income instrument which combines the features of debt with equity via a contingent feature, allowing debtholders to exchange their claim for common shares at a predetermined fixed price in the future.

Convertible preference shares A type of equity security that entitles shareholders to convert their shares into a specified number of common shares.

Convexity The second order, usually a positive change in the price of a bond for a given change in yield, which can be negative for a callable bond such as a high-yield bond.

Convexity adjustment A measure that is used to complement modified duration to capture the second-order effect of yield changes on a bond's price. It is equal to the annual convexity statistic times one-half times the given change in the yield-to-maturity squared.

Convexity bias Refers to the difference in price changes for a given change in yield between interest rate futures and interest rate forward contracts. That is, interest rate forwards exhibit a non-linear or convex relationship between price and yield, while the price–yield relationship is linear for interest rate futures.

Cooperation The process by which countries work together toward some shared goal or purpose. These goals may, and often do, vary widely—from strategic or military concerns, to economic influence, to cultural preferences.

Cooperative country A country that engages and reciprocates in rules standardization; harmonization of tariffs; international agreements on trade, immigration, or regulation; and allowing the free flow of information, including technology transfer.

Core real estate strategies Strategies with exposure to well-leased, high-quality commercial and residential real estate in the best markets, generally offered by open-end funds. Investors expect core real estate to deliver stable returns, primarily from income from the property.

Core-plus real estate strategies Value-add investments that require modest redevelopment or upgrades to lease any vacant space together with possible alternative use of the underlying properties. Compared to core real estate strategies, these may be appealing for investors seeking higher returns and willing to accept additional risks from development, redevelopment, repositioning, and leasing.

Corporate issuers Limited companies or corporations that seek financing in financial markets by, for example, issuing debt or equity securities.

Corporations Another term for limited companies, though often used to refer to public limited companies. See *limited company*, *private limited company*, and *public limited company*.

Correlation A measure of the linear relationship between two random variables.

Correlation coefficient A number between −1 and +1 that measures the consistency or tendency for two investments to act in a similar way. It is used to determine the effect on portfolio risk when two assets are combined.

Cost averaging The periodic investment of a fixed amount of money.

Cost of capital The cost of financing for a company; the rate of return that suppliers of capital require as compensation for their contribution of capital (also called *opportunity cost of funds*).

Cost of carry The net of the costs and benefits related to owning an underlying asset for a specific period.

Cost of debt The required return on debt financing for a company, such as when it issues a bond, takes out a bank loan, or leases an asset through a finance lease.

Cost of equity The return required by equity investors to compensate for both the time value of money and the risk. Also referred to as the required rate of return on common stock or the required return on equity.

Counterparty Legal entities entering a **derivative contract**.

Counterparty credit risk The likelihood that a **counterparty** is unable to meet its financial obligations under the contract.

Counterparty risk The risk that the other party to a contract will fail to honor the terms of the contract.

Country The geopolitical environment as well as the legal and political system faced by all issuers in a jurisdiction that may affect debt payment.

Coupon Periodic interest payments paid by a bond issuer to investors, typically expressed as a percentage of par on an annual basis.

Cournot assumption Assumption in which each firm determines its profit-maximizing production level assuming that the other firms' output will not change.

Covariance A measure of the co-movement (linear association) between two random variables.

Covenants The terms and conditions of lending agreements that the issuer must comply with; they specify the actions that an issuer is obligated to perform (affirmative covenant) or prohibited from performing (negative covenant).

Credit default swap (CDS) A type of credit derivative in which one party, the credit protection buyer who is seeking credit protection against a third party, makes a series of regularly scheduled payments to the other party, the credit protection seller. The seller makes no payments until a credit event occurs.

Credit enhancements Provisions or methods that allow a borrower improve their creditworthiness in a structured transaction.

Credit event An occurrence that triggers the settlement of a CDS contract, including failure to make a debt payment, debt restructuring, or a bankruptcy filing.

Credit facilities Loan agreements with pre-specified terms and limits but with fluctuating balances based on borrower-specific needs at different points in time, analogous to a credit card.

Credit migration risk The risk that a bond issuer's creditworthiness deteriorates, or migrates lower, leading investors to believe the risk of default is higher. Also called **downgrade risk**.

Credit rating Letter-grade, qualitative measures of an issuer's ability to meet its debt obligations based on both the probability of default and the expected loss under a default scenario.

Credit rating agencies Institutions that issue and maintain credit ratings. The three largest are Standard & Poor's, Moody's, and Fitch Ratings.

Credit risk The expected economic loss under a potential borrower default over the life of the contract.

Credit spread The compensation for the risk of default in a debt security, typically measured by the yield-to-maturity difference between a bond and a comparable government benchmark security.

Credit spread risk The risk of greater expected loss due to changes in credit conditions as a result of macroeconomic, market, and/or issuer-related factors.

Credit tranching Internal credit enhancement where cash flows into a senior/subordinate structure.

Credit-linked notes Bonds whose coupon changes when the bonds' credit rating changes.

Critical values Values of the test statistic at which the decision changes from fail to reject the null hypothesis to reject the null hypothesis.

Cross-default clause Covenant or contract clause that specifies borrowers are considered in default if they default on another debt obligation.

Cross-sectional analysis Analysis over a group as of a given time.

Crossing networks Trading systems that match buyers and sellers who are willing to trade at prices obtained from other markets.

Crowdsourcing A business model that enables users to contribute directly to a product, service, or online content.

Cryptocurrency An electronic medium of exchange that lacks physical form.

Cryptocurrency wallet A storage unit for public and/or private keys for cryptocurrency transactions. These wallets may be a physical device, program, or service.

Cryptography An algorithmic process to encrypt data, making the data unusable if received by unauthorized parties.

Cumulative preference shares Preference shares for which any dividends that are not paid accrue and must be paid in full before dividends on common shares can be paid.

Cumulative voting A voting process whereby shareholders can accumulate and vote all their shares for a single candidate in an election, as opposed to having to allocate their voting rights evenly among all candidates.

Currencies Monies issued by national monetary authorities.

Currency Money issued by national monetary authorities.

Currency swap A swap in which each party makes interest payments to the other in different currencies.

Current government spending With respect to government expenditures, spending on goods and services that are provided on a regular, recurring basis including health, education, and defense.

Current ratio A measure of liquidity that is the ratio of current assets to current liabilities.

Current yield The sum of the coupon payments received over the year divided by the flat price. Also called the income, interest yield, or running yield.

Customs union Extends the free trade area (FTA) by not only allowing free movement of goods and services among members, but also creating a common trade policy against nonmembers.

CVaR Conditional VaR, a tail loss measure. The weighted average of all loss outcomes in the statistical distribution that exceed the VaR loss.

Daily settlement A specific process of *mark-to-market* by a central clearing party in which the profits and losses of all counterparties to derivatives contracts are determined using settlement prices for each contract.

Dark pools Alternative trading systems that do not display the orders that their clients send to them.

Data mining The practice of determining a model by extensive searching through a dataset for statistically significant patterns. Also called *data snooping*.

Data science An interdisciplinary field that harnesses advances in computer science, statistics, and other disciplines for the purpose of extracting information from big data (or data in general).

Data snooping The subconscious or conscious manipulation of data in a way that produces a statistically significant result (i.e., the p-value is sufficiently small or the t-statistic sufficiently large to indicate statistical significance), such as by running multiple simulations and naively accepting the best result. Also known as p-hacking.

Day order An order that is good for the day on which it is submitted. If it has not been filled by the close of business, the order expires unfilled.

Days of inventory on hand (DOH) The average number of days it would take to sell the amount of inventory on hand. It is calculated as either the ending or average balance of inventories divided by (cost of goods sold/days in the period).

Days payable outstanding (DPO) The average number of days it takes a company to pay its suppliers. It is calculated as either the ending or average balance of accounts payable divided by (cost of goods sold/days in the period).

Days sales outstanding (DSO) The average number of days it takes for a company to receive payment from customers who purchase goods or services on credit. It is calculated as either the ending or average balance of accounts receivable divided by (revenues/days in the period).

Dealers Financial intermediaries, such as commercial banks or investment banks, who transact as **counterparties** with derivative end users.

Debt A claim against an entity to receive cash, stock, or other assets at a future date. From the perspective of the debtor or borrower, an obligation to pay cash, stock, or other assets at a future date. Generally, debt claims are unconditional and are senior to equity claims.

Debt service coverage ratio A key indicator of credit performance equal to the ratio of net operating income to debt service.

Debt tax shield The tax benefit from interest paid on debt being tax deductible from income, equal to the marginal tax rate multiplied by the value of the debt.

Debt-to-assets ratio A solvency ratio calculated as total debt divided by total assets.

Debt-to-capital ratio A solvency ratio calculated as total debt divided by total debt plus total shareholders' equity.

Debt-to-equity ratio A solvency ratio calculated as total debt divided by total shareholders' equity.

Debt-to-income ratio (DTI) Residential lending metric that compares an individual's monthly debt payments to their monthly pre-tax, gross income.

Debut issuer An issuer approaching the bond market for the first time.

Deciles Values that divide a distribution ranked smallest to largest into 10 equal parts.

Declaration date The day that the corporation issues a statement declaring a specific dividend.

Decreasing returns to scale When a production process leads to increases in output that are proportionately smaller than the increase in inputs.

Deductible temporary differences Temporary differences that result in a reduction of or deduction from taxable income in a future period when the balance sheet item is recovered or settled.

Deep learning An area of artificial intelligence in which a system uses neural networks to perform multistage, non-linear data processing to identify patterns. Also called *deep learning nets*.

Deep learning nets See *Deep learning*.

Deep-in-the-money option An option that is highly likely to be exercised.

Deep-out-of-the-money option An option that is highly unlikely to be exercised.

Default When a borrower on a mortgage loan fails to meet the obligations of the loan.

Default risk premium An extra return that compensates investors for the possibility that the borrower will fail to make a promised payment at the contracted time and in the contracted amount.

Defeasance Mechanism that allows prepayment on mortgage, but the borrower must purchase a portfolio of government securities that fully replicates the cash flows of the remaining scheduled principal and interest payments, including the balloon loan balance, on the loan.

Defensive interval ratio A liquidity ratio that estimates the number of days that an entity could meet cash needs from liquid assets; calculated as (cash + short-term marketable investments + receivables) divided by daily cash expenditures.

Deferred coupon bonds Bonds that pay no coupons for their first few years but then pay a higher coupon than they otherwise normally would for the remainder of their life. Also called *split coupon bonds*.

Deferred tax assets A balance sheet asset that arises when an excess amount is paid for income taxes relative to accounting profit. The taxable income is higher than accounting profit and income tax payable exceeds tax expense. The company expects to recover the difference during the course of future operations when tax expense exceeds income tax payable.

Deferred tax liabilities A balance sheet liability that arises when a deficit amount is paid for income taxes relative to accounting profit. The taxable income is less than the accounting profit and income tax payable is less than tax expense. The company expects to eliminate the liability over the course of future operations when income tax payable exceeds tax expense.

Defined benefit pension plans (DB plans) Plans in which the company promises to pay a certain annual amount (defined benefit) to the employee after retirement. The company bears the investment risk of the plan assets.

Defined contribution pension plans Individual accounts to which an employee and typically the employer makes contributions during their working years and expect to draw on the accumulated funds at retirement. The employee bears the investment and inflation risk of the plan assets.

Deflation Negative inflation.

Degree of financial leverage The ratio of percentage change in net income to percentage change in operating income over a period. It is a measure of how sensitive net income is to changes in operating income, driven by the firm's use of debt in its capital structure.

Degree of operating leverage The ratio of percentage change in operating income to percentage change in sales over a period. It is a measure of how sensitive operating income is to changes in sales, driven by the fixed and variable cost composition of operating expenses.

Delta The sensitivity of the derivative price to a small change in the value of the underlying asset.

Demand shock A typically unexpected disturbance to demand, such as an unexpected interruption in trade or transportation.

Dependent variable The variable that is explained by a regression model.

Depository bank A bank that raises funds from depositors and other investors and lends it to borrowers.

Depository institutions Commercial banks, savings and loan banks, credit unions, and similar institutions that raise funds from depositors and other investors and lend it to borrowers.

Depository receipt A security that trades like an ordinary share on a local exchange and represents an economic interest in a foreign company.

Depreciation The process of systematically allocating the cost of long-lived (tangible) assets to the periods during which the assets are expected to provide economic benefits.

Derivative A financial instrument that derives its value from the performance of an underlying asset or factor (e.g., stock price, interest rate, or exchange rate).

Derivative contract A legal agreement between counterparties with a specific **maturity**, or length of time, until the closing of the transaction, or **settlement**.

Derivative pricing rule A pricing rule used by crossing networks in which a price is taken (derived) from the price that is current in the asset's primary market.

Differentiated products A product or service from a firm that is distinguishable or distinct from those of competing firms. It is customers who determine and value whether a product is differentiated.

Diffuse prior The assumption of equal prior probabilities.

Diffusion index Reflects the proportion of the index's components that are moving in a pattern consistent with the overall index.

Digital assets The umbrella term covering assets that can be created, stored, and transmitted electronically and have associated ownership or use rights. Digital assets include a variety of assets, such as cryptocurrencies, tokens (security and utility), and digital collectables.

Diluted EPS The EPS that would result if all dilutive securities were converted into common shares.

Dilution An increase in the number of shares outstanding from share issuance that decreases the percentage of shares owned by existing shareholders.

Direct investing Occurs when an investor makes a direct investment in an asset without the use of an intermediary.

Direct lending Providing capital directly from private debt investors.

Direct listing Where the equity of a security is floated on the public markets directly, without underwriters, reducing the complexity and cost of the transaction.

Direct sales Marketing and/or delivering products and services to customers without an intermediary or third party between the customer and seller.

Direct taxes Taxes levied directly on income, wealth, and corporate profits.

Discount factor The price equivalent of a zero rate. Also may be stated as the present value of a currency unit on a future date.

Discount rate A yield or pricing convention for money market instrument quotations. It is the interest earned on an instrument, derived from the difference between the price and face value, expressed as a percentage of the face value and multiplied by the periodicity of the annual rate.

Discounted cash flow models Valuation models that estimate the intrinsic value of a security as the present value of the future benefits expected to be received from the security.

Discriminatory pricing rule A pricing rule used in continuous markets in which the limit price of the order or quote that first arrived determines the trade price.

Diseconomies of scale Increase in cost per unit resulting from increased production.

Dispersion The variability of a population or sample of observations around the central tendency.

Display size The size of an order displayed to public view.

Disposition effect A type of cognitive bias that makes individuals unwilling to sell their possessions at a loss.

Distressed debt Debt of mature companies in financial difficulty, in bankruptcy, or likely to default on debt.

Distressed/restructuring These strategies focus on securities of companies either in or perceived to be near bankruptcy. In one approach, hedge funds simply purchase fixed-income securities trading at a significant discount to par but that are still senior enough to be backed by sufficient corporate assets.

Distributed ledger A type of database that can be shared among entities in a network.

Distributed ledger technology (DLT) Technology based on a distributed ledger.

Diversification ratio The ratio of the standard deviation of an equally weighted portfolio to the standard deviation of a randomly selected security.

Dividend discount model (DDM) The model of the value of stock that is the present value of all future dividends, discounted at the required return on equity.

Dividend payout ratio The ratio of cash dividends paid to earnings for a period.

Dividends Distributions of profits and/or net assets from a corporation to its shareholders. While often in cash, dividends can be also be paid in stock or assets, such as property.

Divisor A number (denominator) used to determine the value of a price return index. It is initially chosen at the inception of an index and subsequently adjusted by the index provider, as necessary, to avoid changes in the index value that are unrelated to changes in the prices of its constituent securities.

Domestic bonds A type of bond for which the issuer's domicile and jurisdiction of issuance are the same.

Domestic content provisions Stipulate that some percentage of the value added or components used in production should be of domestic origin.

Double taxation Income is taxed twice.

Downside risk The potential for loss.

Drag on liquidity An action or event that reduces available funds or delays cash inflows.

Drivers Causative factors that explain the level of and changes in an output variable.

DSC ratio A property's annual net operating income (NOI) divided by the debt service.

Dual-class structure A capital structure that includes at least two classes of equity shares with unequal voting rights.

Dupont analysis An approach to decomposing return on investment, e.g., return on equity, as the product of other financial ratios.

Duration The first-order, linear change in a bond's price for a given yield change in yield, which is a negative or inverse relationship.

Duration gap the difference between a bond's Macaulay duration and its investor's investment horizon.

Dynamic pricing A pricing approach that charges different prices at different times. Specific examples include off-peak pricing, "surge" pricing, and "congestion" pricing.

Early repayment option May entitle the borrower to prepay all or part of the outstanding mortgage principal prior to maturity. This creates a risk from the lender's or investor's viewpoint because the cash flow amounts and timing cannot be known with certainty.

Earnings surprise The difference between reported EPS and expected EPS. Also referred to as *unexpected earnings*.

Economic indicators Economic statistics provided by government and established private organizations that contain information on an economy's recent past activity or its current or future position in the business cycle.

Economic infrastructure investments A category of infrastructure investments that support economic activity through transportation assets, information and communication technology assets, and utility and energy assets.

Economic stabilization Reduction of the magnitude of economic fluctuations.

Economic union Incorporates all aspects of a common market and in addition requires common economic institutions and coordination of economic policies among members.

Economies of scale A decline in costs per unit as output grows, generally resulting from having fixed costs in the cost structure that are spread over more units of output.

Economies of scope A decline in costs per unit as the number of product or business lines increases, generally resulting from having shared costs between the product lines.

Effective annual rate An interest rate with a periodicity of one.

Effective convexity An interest rate risk statistic that measures the non-linear/second-order effect of changes in the benchmark yield curve on a bond's price.

Effective duration The sensitivity of the bond's price to an instantaneous parallel shift in a benchmark yield curve—for example, the government par curve.

Efficient market A market in which asset prices reflect new information quickly and rationally. See also, *informationally efficient market.*

Either/or fee A custom fee arrangement whereby major investors are offered a structure where managers agree to charge *either* a lower management fee *or* a higher incentive fee, whichever is greater.

Electronic communications networks (ECNs) See *alternative trading systems* and *multilateral trading facilities.*

Embedded derivative A derivative within an underlying, such as a callable, putable, or convertible bond.

Embedded options Contingency provisions found in a bond's indenture representing rights that enable their holders to take advantage of interest rate movements. They can be exercised by the issuer, by the bondholder, or automatically depending on the course of interest rates.

Emotional biases Behavioral biases resulting from reasoning influenced by feelings; emotional biases stem from impulse or intuition.

Empirical duration Estimation of the price–yield relationship using historical bond market data in statistical models.

Employee stock ownership plan (ESOP) A type of employee benefit plan in which a company sets up a trust fund to receive contributions of newly issued shares or cash to buy existing shares. Contributions are tax deductible up to certain limits. Shares in the trust fund are allocated to individual employees based on relative pay or a formula.

Endowment bias An emotional bias in which people value an asset more when they hold rights to it than when they do not.

Enterprise risk management An overall assessment of a company's risk position. A centralized approach to risk management sometimes called firmwide risk management.

Enterprise value A measure of a company's total market value from which the value of cash and short-term investments have been subtracted.

Equal weighting An index weighting method in which an equal weight is assigned to each constituent security at inception.

Equity Ownership interest in an entity. A residual claim on the assets of an entity after more senior claims, such as debt, have been satisfied. Also known as *net assets*.

Equity swap A swap transaction in which at least one cash flow is tied to the return to an equity portfolio position, often an equity index.

Error term Represents the difference between the observed value of the independent variable and that expected from the true underlying population relation between the dependent and independent variable.

Estimated parameters In a simple linear regression, the estimated parameters are the intercept and slope of the fitted line.

Ether A programmable cryptocurrency created on the Ethereum blockchain in 2015 that allows for the execution of smart contracts.

Ethical principles Beliefs regarding what is good, acceptable, or obligatory behavior and what is bad, unacceptable, or forbidden behavior.

Ethics The study of moral principles or of making good choices. Ethics encompasses a set of moral principles and rules of conduct that provide guidance for our behavior.

Eurobonds A type of bond issued internationally, outside the jurisdiction of the country in whose currency the bond is denominated.

European options Options that may be exercised only at contract maturity.

European-style Said of an option contract that can only be exercised on the option's expiration date.

Event risk Risk that evolves around set dates, such as elections, new legislation, or other date-driven milestones, such as holidays or political anniversaries, known in advance. Example: Brexit referendum.

Ex-dividend date The first date that a share trades without (i.e., "ex") the right to receive the declared dividend for the period.

Excess kurtosis Degree of kurtosis (fatness of tails) relative to the kurtosis of the normal distribution.

Excess spread Surplus difference of yield remaining after payments to bondholders are made after expenses are made and losses are covered.

Exchange A rules-based, open access market venue where financial instruments are traded, with price and volume transparency accessible by issuers, investors, and their intermediaries.

Exchange-traded derivative (ETD) Futures, options, and other financial contracts available on exchanges.

Execution instructions Instructions that indicate how to fill an order.

Exercise The decision to transact the underlying by an option holder.

Exercise date The day that an option is exercised by its holder. For a call option, the day the strike price is paid and underlying is purchased. For a put option, when the strike price is received and the underlying is sold.

Exercise price The pre-agreed execution price specified in an option contract. Sometimes, this price is referred to as the strike price.

Exogenous risk A sudden or unanticipated risk that impacts either a country's cooperative stance, the ability of non-state actors to globalize, or both. Examples include sudden uprisings, invasions, or the aftermath of natural disasters.

Expansion The period of a business cycle after its lowest point and before its highest point.

Expansionary Tending to cause the real economy to grow.

Expansionary fiscal policy Fiscal policy aimed at achieving real economic growth.

Expected exposure (EE) The size of the investor's claim at the time of default.

Expected loss (EL) Default probability times loss severity given default.

Expected return on the portfolio Denoted as ($E(R_p)$). The weighted average of the expected returns (R_1 to R_n) on the component securities using their respective weights (w_1 to w_n).

Expected value of a random variable The probability-weighted average of the possible outcomes of a random variable.

Expert system A type of computer programming, often based on "if–then" rules, that attempts to simulate the knowledge base and analytical abilities of human experts in specific problem-solving contexts.

Export subsidy Paid by the government to the firm when it exports a unit of a good that is being subsidized.

Exposure at default (EAD) The size of the investor's claim at the time of default.

Extension risk The risk of later repayment of a mortgage-backed security than expected.

External credit enhancements Provisions or methods from a third party that allow a borrower improve their creditworthiness in a structured transaction.

External debt Sovereign debt owed to foreign creditors.

Extra dividend A dividend paid by a company that does not pay dividends on a regular schedule, or a dividend that supplements regular cash dividends with an extra payment.

Extraordinary general meetings (EGMs) Meetings besides an AGM of the corporate board and shareholders, typically held to deliberate and vote on urgent matters. Corporate charters and bylaws specify who can call an EGM and under what conditions.

Extreme value theory A branch of statistics that focuses primarily on extreme outcomes.

Face value The amount of principal on a bond, also known as par value.

Factoring arrangement When a company sells its accounts receivable to a lender (known as a factor) that assumes responsibility for the credit-granting and collection process.

Fair value A market-based measure of an investment based on observable or derived assumptions to determine a price that market participants would use to exchange an asset or liability in an orderly transaction at a specific time.

Fair value hedge Refers to a specific **hedge accounting** designation that applies when a derivative is deemed to offset the fluctuation in fair value of an asset or liability.

Fallen angels Formerly investment-grade-rated issuers whose bonds are downgraded to high yield due to credit deterioration.

Fat-Tailed Describes a distribution that has fatter tails than a normal distribution (also called leptokurtic).

Fed funds rate The US interbank lending rate on overnight borrowings of reserves.

Federal funds rate The US interbank lending rate on overnight borrowings of reserves. Also known as *Fed Funds rate*.

Fiat money Money that is not convertible into any other commodity.

Fiduciary call A combination of a purchased call option and investment in a risk-free bond with face value of the option's exercise price.

Fill or kill See *immediate or cancel order*.

Finance lease A type of lease which is more akin to the purchase or sale of the underlying asset.

Financial leverage The use of debt in the capital structure. Measured using ratios such as operating income to operating income less interest expense, total assets to total equity, or debt to equity.

Financial leverage ratio A measure of financial leverage calculated as average total assets divided by average total equity.

Financial risk The risk arising from a company's capital structure and, specifically, from the level of debt and debt-like obligations.

Fintech Technological innovation in the financial services industry, specifically with the design and delivery of financial services and products. It may also refer more broadly to companies involved in developing the new technologies and their applications, as well as the business sector that includes such companies.

Firm commitment A pre-determined amount (price and quantity) is agreed to be exchanged at settlement. Examples of firm commitments include forward contracts, futures contracts, and swaps.

First lien Also known as a priority lien, this investor protection grants a lender the right to take possession of property from a borrower which fails to repay debt.

First lien debt Debt secured by a pledge of certain assets that could include buildings, but it may also include property and equipment, licenses, patents, brands, etc.

First mortgage debt Debt secured by a pledge of a specific property.

Fiscal multiplier The ratio of a change in national income to a change in government spending.

Fiscal policy The use of taxes and government spending to affect the level of aggregate expenditures.

Fixed charge coverage A solvency ratio measuring the number of times interest and lease payments are covered by operating income, calculated as (EBIT + lease payments) divided by (interest payments + lease payments).

Fixed charge coverage ratio A measure of how well a company's earnings covers its fixed expenses, which may include debt payments, interest expense, and lease costs.

Fixed-income instruments Debt instruments such as loans or bonds.

Fixed-income securities Fixed-income instruments designed to be more easily tradeable than a loan, such as a bond.

Fixed-price call A contingency provision that grants an issuer the right to buy back a bond at a predetermined price in the future.

Fixed-rate payer The counterparty paying fixed cash flows in a swap contract. May also be referred to as the floating-rate receiver.

Flat price The full price of a bond minus accrued interest. Flat prices are usually quoted by bond dealers.

Float-adjusted market-capitalization weighting An index weighting method in which the weight assigned to each constituent security is determined by adjusting its market capitalization for its market float.

Floating-rate notes Notes on which interest payments are not fixed but instead vary from period to period depending on the current level of a reference interest rate. Also known as *floaters*.

Floating-rate payer The counterparty paying the variable cash flows in a swap contract. May also be referred to as the fixed-rate receiver.

Forecast object A variable on or related to an issuer's financial statements that an analyst makes a projection for. Examples include drivers of financial statements, financial statement lines, and summary measures like EBITDA.

Foreclosure Allows a lender to take possession of the property and ultimately sell the property to recover funds toward satisfying the outstanding debt obligation.

Foreign bonds A type of bond for which the issuer's domicile and jurisdiction of issuance are different.

Foreign currency reserves Holding by the central bank of non-domestic currency deposits and non-domestic bonds.

Foreign direct investments (FDI) Long-term investments in the productive capacity of a foreign country.

Foreign exchange gains (or losses) Gains (or losses) that occur when the exchange rate changes between the investor's currency and the currency that foreign securities are denominated in.

Forward contract A **derivative contract** for the future exchange of an **underlying** at a fixed price set at contract signing.

Forward price Represents the price agreed upon in a forward contract to be exchanged at the contract's maturity date, T. This price is shown in equations as $F_0(T)$.

Forward price-to-earnings ratio A P/E calculated on the basis of a forecast of EPS; a stock's current price divided by next year's expected earnings.

Forward rate agreement (FRA) An OTC derivatives contract in which counterparties agree to apply a specific interest rate to a future time period.

Founders class shares A way to entice early participation in startup funds whereby managers offer incentives that entitle investors to a lower fee structure and/or other favorable terms.

Framing bias An information-processing bias in which a person answers a question differently based on the way in which it is asked (framed).

Franchising A situation where an owner of an asset and associated intellectual property divests the asset and licenses intellectual property to a third-party operator (franchisee) in exchange for royalties. Franchisees operate under the constraints of a franchise agreement.

Free cash flow The actual cash that would be available to the company's investors after making all investments necessary to maintain the company as an ongoing enterprise (also referred to as free cash flow to the firm); the internally generated funds that can be distributed to the company's investors (e.g., shareholders and bondholders) without impairing the value of the company.

Free cash flow hypothesis The hypothesis that higher debt levels discipline managers by forcing them to make fixed debt service payments and by reducing the company's free cash flow.

Free float The portion of a listed company's equity securities that are not held by insiders, strategic investors, sponsors, founders, and so on, that are more freely available for trading.

Free trade areas One of the most prevalent forms of regional integration, in which all barriers to the flow of goods and services among members have been eliminated.

Free-cash-flow-to-equity models Valuation models based on discounting expected future free cash flow to equity.

Freemium business model A pricing approach that allows customers a certain level of usage or functionality at no charge. Those who wish to use more must pay.

Frequency table A representation of the frequency of occurrence of two discrete variables.

Full price The price of a bond including any accrued interest owed to the seller. It is the flat price plus accrued interest.

Fully amortizing loan A loan or bond with a payment schedule that calls for the complete repayment of principal over the instrument's time to maturity.

Fund investing In fund investing, the investor invests in assets indirectly by contributing capital to a fund as part of a group of investors. Fund investing is available for all major alternative investment types.

Fund of funds Funds that hold a portfolio of hedge funds; also called *funds of hedge funds*.

Fundamental analysis The examination of publicly available information and the formulation of forecasts to estimate the intrinsic value of assets.

Fundamental growth These strategies use fundamental analysis to identify companies expected to exhibit high growth and capital appreciation.

Fundamental long/short In this strategy, the hedge fund takes a long position in companies that are trading at inexpensive levels compared to their potential intrinsic value and shorts those that trade in the other direction, with the intention of reversing this trade to obtain alpha.

Fundamental value These strategies use fundamental analysis to identify undervalued and unloved companies for which there is a possibility that a corporate turnaround, with future revenue and cash flow growth, will result in higher valuations.

Fundamental weighting An index weighting method in which the weight assigned to each constituent security is based on its underlying company's size. It attempts to address the disadvantages of market-capitalization weighting by using measures that are independent of the constituent security's price.

Fungible Freely exchangeable, interchangeable, or substitutable with other things of the same type. Money and commodities are the most common examples.

Futures contract A variation of a forward contract that has essentially the same basic definition but with some additional features, such as a clearinghouse guarantee against credit losses, a daily settlement of gains and losses, and an organized electronic or floor trading facility.

Futures contract basis point value (BPV) The change in price of a futures contract given a 1 basis point (0.01%) change in yield.

Futures margin account An account held by an exchange clearinghouse for each derivatives counterparty. The funds in such an account are used to ensure that counterparties do not default on their contract obligation.

Futures price The pre-agreed price at which a futures contract buyer (seller) agrees to pay (receive) for the underlying at the maturity date of the futures contract.

FX swap The combination of a spot and a forward FX transaction.

G-spread Yield spread in basis points between a bond's yield-to-maturity and that of an actual or interpolated government bond. It represents the return for bearing risks relative to the government bond.

Game theory The set of tools decision makers use to incorporate responses by rival decision makers into their strategies.

Gamma A numerical measure of how sensitive an option's delta (the sensitivity of the derivative's price) is to a change in the value of the underlying.

Gate A provision that when implemented limits or restricts redemptions for a period of time.

General collateral repo Rather than involving a specific security, a repo that instead references a specific group of securities as eligible collateral (such as government bonds of a specific maturity).

General collateral repo rate The interest rate on a general collateral repo.

General obligation (GO) bonds Unsecured bonds issued by a non-sovereign government which are backed by the taxing authority of the issuer.

General obligation bonds Also known as GO bonds. Bonds issued by non-sovereign governments for general purposes and repaid from tax cash flows.

General partners (GPs) Private fund managers responsible for sourcing and deploying capital from limited partner investors over an investment life cycle and distributing returns to those investors over a finite investment holding period.

General partnership A business organizational form owned entirely by general partners.

Geophysical resource endowment Includes such factors as livable geography and climate as well as access to food and water, which are necessary for sustainable growth. Geophysical resource endowment is highly unequal among countries.

Geopolitics The study of how geography affects politics and international relations. These relations matter for investments because they contribute to important drivers of investment performance, including economic growth, business performance, market volatility, and transaction costs.

Gilts Bonds issued by the UK government.

Global depository receipt (GDR) A depository receipt that is issued outside of the company's home country and outside of the United States.

Global minimum-variance portfolio The portfolio on the minimum-variance frontier with the smallest variance of return.

Global registered share (GRS) A common share that is traded on different stock exchanges around the world in different currencies.

Globalization The process of interaction and integration among people, companies, and governments worldwide. It is marked by the spread of products, information, jobs, and culture across borders.

Gold standard With respect to a currency, if a currency is on the gold standard a given amount can be converted into a prespecified amount of gold.

Good-on-close An execution instruction specifying that an order can only be filled at the close of trading. Also called *market-on-close*.

Good-on-open An execution instruction specifying that an order can only be filled at the opening of trading.

Good-till-cancelled order An order specifying that it is valid until the entity placing the order has cancelled it (or, commonly, until some specified amount of time such as 60 days has elapsed, whichever comes sooner).

Goodwill An intangible asset that represents the excess of the purchase price of an acquired company over the value of the net identifiable assets acquired.

Governance tokens In permissionless networks, governance tokens serve as votes to determine how the particular network is run.

Government debt management Government policies that relate to the issuance of debt securities, typically handled by a treasurer or finance ministry.

Government equivalent yield Measures quoted using actual/actual day counts.

Grant date The day that terms of compensation are communicated by an issuer and accepted by an employee recipient.

Green bonds Bonds used to specifically finance environmental-related projects.

Greenfield investments New, "to-be-built" infrastructure projects and assets created to provide a specific essential service or to supply a public good.

Gross profit margin The ratio of gross profit to revenues.

Groupthink A behavioral bias that occurs when a team minimizes conflict and dissent in reaching and maintaining a consensus.

Growth cycle Refers to fluctuations in economic activity around the long-term potential trend growth level, focusing on how much actual economic activity is below or above trend growth in economic activity.

Growth option The option to make additional investments in a project at some future time if the financial results are strong. Also called an *expansion option.*

Growth rate cycle Refers to fluctuations in the growth rate of economic activity.

Haircut The difference between the market value of the security used as collateral and the value of the loan. Also called *repo margin.*

Halo effect An emotional bias that extends a favorable evaluation of some characteristics to other characteristics.

Hard commodities Traded natural resources, such as crude oil and metals, with markets often involving the physical delivery of the underlying upon settlement.

Hard hurdle rate Hurdle ratewhere the manager earns fees on annual returns in excess of the hurdle rate

Hard-bullet covered bonds Type of security where if payments do not occur according to the original schedule of a covered bond, a bond default is triggered and bond payments are accelerated.

Harmonic mean A type of weighted mean computed as the reciprocal of the arithmetic average of the reciprocals.

Hedge The **derivative contract** used in **hedging** an exposure.

Hedge accounting Accounting standard(s) that allow an issuer to offset a hedging instrument (usually a derivative) against a hedged transaction or balance sheet item to reduce financial statement volatility.

Hedge funds Private investment vehicles that may invest in public equities or publicly traded fixed-income assets, private capital, and/or real assets, but they are distinguished by their investment *approach* rather than by the investments themselves.

Hedge ratio The proportion of an underlying that will offset the risk associated with a derivative position.

Hedging The use of a derivative contract to offset or neutralize existing or anticipated exposure to an **underlying**.

Hegemony Countries that are regional or even global leaders and use their political or economic influence of others to control resources.

Held-to-maturity Debt (fixed-income) securities that a company intends to hold to maturity; these are presented at their original cost, updated for any amortisation of discounts or premiums.

Herding Clustered trading that may or may not be based on information.

Herfindahl-Hirschman Index (HHI) A measure of market concentration, calculated as the sum of the squares of competitor market shares. Antitrust regulators in some countries consider markets with an HHI between 1,500 and 2,500 moderately concentrated and consider markets with an HHI over 2,500 highly concentrated.

Heteroskedasticity Non-constant variance across all observations.

Hidden order An order that is exposed not to the public but only to the brokers or exchanges that receive it.

Hidden revenue business model Business models that provide services to users at no charge and generate revenues elsewhere.

High yield Bond issuers and issues rated BB+ (Ba1 on Moody's scale) or lower. Also known as speculative grade and junk.

High-water mark The highest value, net of fees, that a fund has reached in history. It reflects the highest cumulative return used to calculate an incentive fee.

Hindsight bias A type of cognitive bias that makes individuals misremember the past in ways that make them appear to have made better and more well-informed choices.

Holder-of-record date The date that a shareholder listed on the corporation's books will be deemed to have ownership of the shares for purposes of receiving an upcoming dividend.

Holding period return The single-period internal rate of return for a real estate property that includes property income and the change in property value over the period.

Home bias A preference for securities listed on the exchanges of one's home country.

Homogeneity of expectations The assumption that all investors have the same economic expectations and thus have the same expectations of prices, cash flows, and other investment characteristics.

Homoskedasticity Constant variance across all observations.

Horizon yield An investor's total rate of return on a fixed income instrument over their holding period, including reinvested coupon payments. It is an internal rate of return expressed as an annualized rate.

Hostile takeover When a potential acquirer seeks to acquire a company (the target) against the wishes of the target's board of directors. Typically, a tender offer is used to carry out the hostile takeover, against which a board might use a poison pill in its defense.

Household A person or a group of people living in the same residence, taken as a basic unit in economic analysis.

Human capital The present value of an individual's future expected labor income.

Hurdle rate Also called "preferred return." The minimum rate of return on investment that a fund must reach before a GP receives carried interest.

Hypothesis A proposed explanation or theory that can be tested.

Hypothesis testing The process of testing of hypotheses about one or more populations using statistical inference.

I-spread also known as interpolated spread, it is the yield spread for a bond over the standard swap rate in that currency of the same tenor.

Iceberg order An order in which the display size is less than the order's full size.

If-converted method A method for accounting for the effect of convertible securities on earnings per share (EPS) that specifies what EPS would have been if the convertible securities had been converted at the beginning of the period, taking account of the effects of conversion on net income and the weighted average number of shares outstanding.

Illusion of control bias A bias in which people tend to believe that they can control or influence outcomes when, in fact, they cannot.

Immediate or cancel order An order that is valid only upon receipt by the broker or exchange. If such an order cannot be filled in part or in whole upon receipt, it cancels immediately. Also called *fill or kill*.

Impact lag The lag associated with the result of actions affecting the economy with delay.

Implied forward rate An interest rate or yield over a future period implied by the current term structure of interest rates.

Import license Specifies the quantity of a good that can be imported into a country.

In-the-money Describes an option with a positive intrinsic value.

Income tax paid The actual amount paid for income taxes in the period; not a provision, but the actual cash outflow.

Income tax payable The income tax owed by the company on the basis of taxable income.

Increasing returns to scale When a production process leads to increases in output that are proportionately larger than the increase in inputs.

Incurrence test A financial ratio or other measurement taken prior to an action such as debt issuance, usually on a pro forma basis taking the action into account. Satisfaction of the test (e.g., leverage ratio below a certain value) is linked to covenants between the issuer and investors.

Indenture A written contract between a lender and borrower that specifies the terms of the loan, such as interest rate, interest payment schedule, or maturity.

Independent With reference to events, the property that the occurrence of one event does not affect the probability of another event occurring. With reference to two random variables X and Y, they are independent if and only if $P(X,Y) = P(X)P(Y)$.

Independent directors Members of a corporation's board of directors who do not have an employment or familial relationship with the company, nor do they have a relationship that would impair their independence such as an economic interest in a vendor or competitor of the company.

Independent variable An explanatory variable in a regression model.

Independently and Identically distributed With respect to random variables, the property of random variables that are independent of each other but follow the identical probability distribution.

Index-linked bonds A bond whose coupon payments or principal repayment is linked to a specified index.

Indexing An investment strategy in which an investor constructs a portfolio to mirror the performance of a specified index.

Indicator variable A variable that takes on only one of two values, 0 or 1, based on a condition. In simple linear regression, the slope is the difference in the dependent variable for the two conditions. Also referred to as a *dummy variable*.

Indifference curve A curve representing all the combinations of two goods or attributes such that the consumer is entirely indifferent among them.

Indirect taxes Taxes such as taxes on spending, as opposed to direct taxes.

Inflation premium An extra return that compensates investors for expected inflation.

Inflation reports A type of economic publication put out by many central banks.

Inflation-linked bonds Debt instruments that link the principal and interest to inflation.

Information cascade The transmission of information from those participants who act first and whose decisions influence the decisions of others.

Information-motivated traders Traders that trade to profit from information that they believe allows them to predict future prices.

Informationally efficient market A market in which asset prices reflect new information quickly and rationally.

Infrastructure A type of real asset that is intended for public use and provides essential services. These assets are typically long-lived fixed assets, such as bridges and toll roads.

Initial coin offering (ICO) An unregulated process whereby companies raise capital by selling crypto-tokens to investors in exchange for fiat money or another agreed-upon cryptocurrency.

Initial margin The ratio of the price of collateral to the value of cash exchanged in a repo; a value over 1.0 or 100% indicates overcollateralization.

Initial margin requirement The margin requirement on the first day of a transaction as well as on any day in which additional margin funds must be deposited.

Initial public offering (IPO) The first issuance of common shares to the public by a formerly private corporation.

Inside directors Members of a corporation's board of directors who are not independent. Typically, inside directors are employees or founders (and their family) of the company.

Insolvency A situation in which an issuer's total liabilities exceed the market value of its assets.

Institution An established organization or practice in a society or culture. An institution can be a formal structure, such as a university, organization, or process backed by law; or it can be informal, such as a custom or behavioral pattern important to society. Institutions can, but need not be, formed by national governments. Examples of institutions include non-governmental organizations, charities, religious customs, family units, the media, political parties, and educational practice.

Intangible assets Assets without a physical form, such as patents and trademarks.

Interbank market The market of loans and deposits between banks for maturities ranging from overnight to one year.

Intercept The estimated value of the dependent variable when the independent variable is zero.

Interest coverage A solvency ratio calculated as EBIT divided by interest payments.

Interest coverage ratio A measure of an issuer's ability to service its debt, typically the ratio of operating income or EBIT to interest expense.

Interest rate A rate of return that reflects the relationship between differently dated cash flows; a discount rate.

Interest rate swap A swap in which the underlying is an interest rate. Can be viewed as a currency swap in which both currencies are the same and can be created as a combination of currency swaps.

Interest-indexed bond A type of index-linked bond for which changes in the index are captured with adjustments to interest payments.

Internal credit enhancements Provisions or methods a borrower initiates to improve their creditworthiness in a structured transaction, such as overcollateralization or excess spread.

internal rate of return The discount rate that makes net present value equal 0; the discount rate that makes the present value of an investment's costs (outflows) equal to the present value of the investment's benefits (inflows).

Internal rate of return (IRR) The uniform discount rate for a series of cash flows over *n* periods that returns a net present value of zero.

Internet of things The vast array of physical devices, home appliances, smart buildings, vehicles, and other items that are embedded with electronics, sensors, software, and network connections that enable the objects in the system to interact and share information.

Interquartile range The difference between the third and first quartiles of a dataset.

Intrinsic value The amount gained (per unit) by an option buyer if an option is exercised at any given point in time. May be referred to as the exercise value of the option.

Investment banks Financial intermediaries that provide advice to their mostly corporate clients and help them arrange transactions such as initial and seasoned securities offerings.

Investment grade Bond issuers and issues rated BBB- (Baa3 on Moody's scale).

Investment policy statement (IPS) A written planning document that describes a client's investment objectives and risk tolerance over a relevant time horizon, along with constraints that apply to the client's portfolio.

Issue rating A rating which seeks to capture the probability of default or expected loss of the issuer's senior unsecured bonds.

Issuer rating A rating which seeks to capture the credit risk of a specific financial obligation of an issuer which takes such factors as seniority into account.

J-curve effect Net income over a multiyear private investment holding period characterized by negative returns in an initial phase, followed by cash flow and income growth toward the end of the holding period.

Jackknife A resampling method that repeatedly draws samples by taking the original observed data sample and leaving out one observation at a time (without replacement) from the set.

January effect Calendar anomaly that stock market returns in January are significantly higher compared to the rest of the months of the year, with most of the abnormal returns reported during the first five trading days in January. Also called *turn-of-the-year effect.*

Joint probability function A function giving the probability of joint occurrences of values of stated random variables.

Judgmental sampling A procedure of selectively handpicking elements from the population based on a researcher's knowledge and professional judgment.

Junior debt Debt obligation with lower priority of payment than senior debt obligations.

Key rate duration Also known as partial duration, is a measure of a bond's sensitivity to a change in the benchmark yield at a specific maturity.

Keynesians Economists who believe that fiscal policy can have powerful effects on aggregate demand, output, and employment when there is substantial spare capacity in an economy.

Kurtosis The statistical measure that indicates the combined weight of the tails of a distribution relative to the rest of the distribution.

Lagging economic indicators Turning points that take place later than those of the overall economy; they are believed to have value in identifying the economy's past condition.

Law of one price A principle that states that if two investments have the same or equivalent future cash flows regardless of what will happen in the future, then these two investments should have the same current price.

Lead underwriter The lead investment bank in a syndicate of investment banks and broker–dealers involved in a securities underwriting.

Leading economic indicators Turning points that usually precede those of the overall economy; they are believed to have value for predicting the economy's future state, usually near-term.

Legal tender Something that must be accepted when offered in exchange for goods and services.

Lender of last resort An entity willing to lend money when no other entity is ready to do so.

Leptokurtic Describes a distribution that has fatter tails than a normal distribution (also called fat-tailed).

Lessee Tenant or property user that enters a lease with a property owner or lessor.

Lessor Property owner or manager that leases a property to a tenant or property user.

Level of significance The probability of a Type I error in testing a hypothesis.

Leverage A measure for identifying a potentially influential high-leverage point.

Leveraged buyout (LBO) A transaction in which a private acquiror uses equity and a high proportion of debt to acquire a public or private company in order to make changes to increase value over an investment period.

Leveraged loan Where private debt investor firms borrow money to make a direct loan to a borrower.

Leveraged loans Loans made to a borrower or issuer with relatively lower credit quality and/or higher leverage.

Liability-driven investing An investment industry term that generally encompasses asset allocation that is focused on funding an investor's liabilities in institutional contexts.

Licensing arrangements Rights to produce a product or have access to intangible assets using someone else's brand name in return for a royalty (often a percentage of revenues).

Lien A legal right or claim to property by a creditor.

Likelihood The probability of an observation, given a particular set of conditions.

Limit order Instructions to a broker or exchange to obtain the best price immediately available when filling an order, but in no event accept a price higher than a specified (limit) price when buying or accept a price lower than a specified (limit) price when selling.

Limit order book The book or list of limit orders to buy and sell that pertains to a security.

Limited company A business organizational form owned by shareholders or members with limited liability who elect a board of directors to appoint management. Generally, limited companies have indefinite life and easier transfer of ownership interests than limited partnerships.

Limited liability partnership (LLP) A business organizational form available in some jurisdictions owned entirely by limited partners with limited liability.

Limited partners (LPs) Outside investors in a private market fund who own a fractional interest in a limited, closed-end partnership managed by a general partner based on the investment commitment and other terms set out in a limited partner agreement.

Limited partnership Closed-end form of ownership frequently used in private market funds in which private market fund investors, or limited partners, commit capital that is invested, managed, and distributed by a private market fund manager, or general partner, over an investment holding period.

Limited partnership agreement (LPA) A legal document that outlines the rules of the partnership and establishes the framework that ultimately guides the fund's operations throughout its life.

lin-log model A functional form for transforming regression model data in which the dependent variable is linear but the independent variable is logarithmic.

Linear derivatives Firm commitment derivative contracts in which the contract's payoff/profit function is linear with respect to the price of the underlying.

Liquid market Said of a market in which traders can buy or sell with low total transaction costs when they want to trade.

Liquidity The extent to which a company is able to meet its short-term obligations using cash flows and those assets that can be readily transformed into cash.

Liquidity premium The compensation for liquidity risk that increases in proportion to the investment's illiquidity.

Liquidity ratios Financial ratios measuring the company's ability to meet its short-term obligations to creditors as they come due.

Liquidity risk The risk that an investment may not be readily sold at its true value.

Liquidity trap A condition in which the demand for money becomes infinitely elastic (horizontal demand curve) so that injections of money into the economy will not lower interest rates or affect real activity.

Load fund A mutual fund in which, in addition to the annual fee, a percentage fee is charged to invest in the fund and/or for redemptions from the fund.

Loan-to-value ratio (LTV) Ratio of the amount of the mortgage to the property's value. The lower the LTV, the higher the borrower's equity. From the lender's perspective, the higher the borrower's equity, the less likely the borrower is to default.

Loans Debt instruments agreed to between a borrower and lender, typically a bank.

Lockout or revolving period For an ABS with a non-amortizing collateral pool, such as credit card debt, is the period in which the cash proceeds from principal repayments are reinvested in additional loans with a principal equal to the principal repaid. During this period, there is no prepayment risk and potential default risk is generally limited. When the lockout period is over, principal repayments are used to pay off the outstanding principal on the ABS. Lockout period and revolving period are interchangeable.

Lockup period The minimum holding period before investors are allowed to make withdrawals or redeem shares from a fund. Its purpose is to allow the hedge fund manager the required time to implement and potentially realize a strategy's expected results.

log-lin model A functional form for transforming regression model data in which the dependent variable is logarithmic but the independent variable is linear.

log-log model A functional form for transforming regression model data in which both the dependent and independent variables are in logarithmic form.

Long A trading position in a **derivative contract** that gains value as the price of the **underlying** moves higher.

Long position A position in an asset or contract in which one owns the asset or has an exercisable right under the contract.

Long-run average total cost The curve describing average total cost when no costs are considered fixed.

Loss aversion The tendency of people to dislike losses more than they like comparable gains.

Loss given default (LGD) The amount a debtholder fails to recover if a default occurs, usually expressed as a percentage of par value.

Loss severity Portion of a bond's value (including unpaid interest) an investor loses in the event of default.

Loss-aversion bias A bias in which people tend to strongly prefer avoiding losses as opposed to achieving gains.

Low-cost producer A firm with lower production costs than its industry competitors.

M^2 A measure of what a portfolio would have returned if it had taken on the same total risk as the market index.

M^2 alpha Difference between the risk-adjusted performance of the portfolio and the performance of the benchmark.

Macaulay duration the present-value weighted average time to receipt of cash flows for fixed-income instrument, also the holding period needed to balance coupon reinvestment risk and price risk for a one-time instantaneous "parallel" shift in the yield curve once the bond purchase is settled. It is named after Frederick Macaulay, the Canadian economist who introduced the concept in 1938.

Machine learning (ML) Involves computer-based techniques that seek to extract knowledge from large amounts of data without making any assumptions about the data's underlying probability distribution. The goal of ML algorithms is to automate decision-making processes by generalizing, or "learning," from known examples to determine an underlying structure in the data.

Maintenance capital expenditures Investments in assets to keep them in operation or increase their efficiency without extending their useful lives.

Maintenance margin Minimum balance set below the initial margin that each contract buyer and seller must hold in the futures margin account from trade initiation until final settlement at maturity.

Maintenance margin requirement The margin requirement on any day other than the first day of a transaction.

Management buy-in A type of leveraged buyout where the current management team is replaced with the acquiring team involved in managing the company.

Management buyout A private sale to a strategic buyer that includes a company's existing management. The management team commits their own equity capital along with other investors as an incentive to grow the firm's cash flows and value.

Management guidance Management of public companies may publicly provide targets for earnings, revenues, and other measures (e.g., capital expenditures) for the next quarter, year, or longer term. Guidance can be detailed or rather directional and is often updated throughout the year. Initial guidance for next fiscal year might be provided during the fourth-quarter earnings call and updated for completed quarters, and new information provided at the first-, second-, and third-quarter earnings calls. Also known simply as *guidance*.

Margin call Request to a derivatives contract counterparty to immediately deposit funds to return the futures margin account balance to the initial margin.

Margin financing A financing arrangement whereby the prime broker lends shares, bonds, or derivatives and the hedge fund (or investment manager) deposits cash or other collateral into a margin account at the prime broker based on certain fractions of the investment positions.

Margin loan Money borrowed from a broker to purchase securities.

Marginal propensity to consume The proportion of an additional unit of disposable income that is consumed or spent; the change in consumption for a small change in income.

Marginal propensity to save The proportion of an additional unit of disposable income that is saved (not spent).

Mark to market (MTM) The practice in which a central clearing party assigns profits and losses to counterparties to derivative contracts. In exchange-traded markets, this practice takes place daily and is often referred to as daily settlement.

Market anomaly Change in the price or return of a security that cannot directly be linked to current relevant information known in the market or to the release of new information into the market.

Market bid–ask spread The difference between the best bid and the best offer.

Market discount rate The rate of return required by investors given the risk of the bond investment, also known as the required yield or required rate of return.

Market float The number of shares that are available to the investing public.

Market makers **Over-the-counter (OTC) dealers** who typically enter into offsetting bilateral transactions with one another to transfer risk to other parties.

Market model A regression model with the return on a stock as the dependent variable and the returns on a market index as the independent variable.

Market multiple models Valuation models based on share price multiples or enterprise value multiples.

Market neutral These strategies use quantitative, fundamental, and technical analysis to identify under- and overvalued equity securities. The hedge fund takes long positions in undervalued securities and short positions in overvalued securities, while seeking to maintain a market-neutral net position.

Market order Instructions to a broker or exchange to obtain the best price immediately available when filling an order.

Market reference rate (MRR) The interest rate underlying used in interest rate swaps. These rates typically match those of loans or other short-term obligations. Survey-based Libor rates used as reference rates in the past have been replaced by rates based on a daily average of observed market transaction rates. For example, the Secured Overnight Financing Rate (SOFR) is an overnight cash borrowing rate collateralized by US Treasuries. Other MRRs include the euro short-term rate (€STR) and the Sterling Overnight Index Average (SONIA).

Market risk Risk related to market movements, e.g., unexpected changes in share prices, interest rates, currency exchange rates, and commodity prices.

Market share A company's or product's revenue expressed as a percentage of its market size.

Market size Total sales for a good or service, which can be calculated on a global or more regional basis.

Market value The price at which an asset or security can currently be bought or sold in an open market.

Market-capitalization weighting An index weighting method in which the weight assigned to each constituent security is determined by dividing its market capitalization by the total market capitalization (sum of the market capitalization) of all securities in the index. Also called *value weighting*.

Market-on-close An execution instruction specifying that an order can only be filled at the close of trading.

Marketable limit order A buy limit order in which the limit price is placed above the best offer, or a sell limit order in which the limit price is placed below the best bid. Such orders generally will partially or completely fill right away.

Markowitz efficient frontier The graph of the set of portfolios offering the maximum expected return for their level of risk (standard deviation of return).

Master limited partnership (MLP) Has similar features to limited partnerships but is usually a more liquid investment that is often publicly traded.

Master repurchase agreement A legal document governing all repo trades between two parties.

Match funding Financing an asset with a source, such as a loan or bond, that is aligned with certain attributes of the asset, such as duration and the respective streams of income and financing costs.

Material (materiality) Refers to information that is decision-useful for a reasonable investor.

Matrix pricing An estimation process for financial instruments based on the prices of comparable instruments.

Maturity The date of a fixed-income instrument's final payment to investors.

Maturity premium An extra return that compensates investors for the increased sensitivity of the market value of debt to a change in market interest rates as maturity is extended.

Maturity structure of interest rates Also known as the term structure of interest rates, refers to the difference in interest rates or benchmark yields by time-to-maturity.

Mean absolute deviation With reference to a sample, the mean of the absolute values of deviations from the sample mean.

Mean square error (MSE) Calculated as the sum of squares error (SSE) divided by the degrees of freedom, which are the number of observations minus the number of independent variables minus one. Since simple linear regression has just one independent variable, the degrees of freedom calculation is the number of observations minus 2.

Mean square regression (MSR) Calculated as the sum of squares regression (SSR) divided by the number of independent variables in the regression model. In simple linear regression, there is only one independent variable, so MSR equals SSR.

Mean–variance analysis An approach to portfolio analysis using expected means, variances, and covariances of asset returns.

Measure of central tendency A quantitative measure that specifies where data are centered.

Measures of location Quantitative measures that describe the location or distribution of data. They include not only measures of central tendency but also other measures, such as percentiles.

Median The "middlemost" observation; i.e., in a set of observations that has been ranked from highest to lowest, the median will lie in the middle.

Meme coin A type of altcoin that is often inspired by a joke.

Mental accounting bias An information-processing bias in which people treat one sum of money differently from another equal-sized sum based on which mental account the money is assigned to.

Merger arbitrage Special situations investments related to business combinations in which investors seek to capitalize on price discrepancies of securities issued by the target company.

Mesokurtic Describes a distribution with kurtosis equal to that of the normal distribution, namely, kurtosis equal to three.

Mezzanine debt Refers to private credit subordinated to senior secured debt but senior to equity in the borrower's capital structure.

Mezzanine-stage financing Mezzanine venture capital that prepares a company to go public as it continues to expand capacity and enhance its growth trajectory. It represents the bridge financing needed to fund a private firm until it can execute an IPO or be sold.

Miner A validator of transactions on the blockchain that locks blocks of transactions into the blockchain and receives compensation for this process in the form of a digital asset.

Minimum efficient scale The smallest output that a firm can produce such that its long-run average total cost is minimized.

Minimum-variance portfolio The portfolio with the minimum variance for each given level of expected return.

Minority shareholder An individual or entity that owns less than a majority of the voting rights in a corporation.

Mode The most frequently occurring value in a distribution.

Modern portfolio theory (MPT) The analysis of rational portfolio choices based on the efficient use of risk.

Modified duration The first derivative of a bond's price with respect to its yield, this statistic is a measure of interest rate risk used to estimate the percentage price change for a given change in yield-to-maturity.

Monetarists Economists who believe that the rate of growth of the money supply is the primary determinant of the rate of inflation.

Monetary policy Actions taken by a nation's central bank to affect aggregate output and prices through changes in bank reserves, reserve requirements, or its target interest rate.

Monetary transmission mechanism The process whereby a central bank's interest rate gets transmitted through the economy and ultimately affects the rate of increase of prices.

Monetary union An economic union in which the members adopt a common currency.

Money convexity A measure that is used to complement modified duration to capture the second-order effect of yield changes on a bond's price, expressed in currency terms.

Money duration A measure of the price change of a fixed-income instrument in currency units from a change in yield-to-maturity. The money duration can be stated per 100 of par value or in terms of the actual position size. In the United States, money duration is commonly called "dollar duration."

Money market The market for short-term debt instruments (one-year maturity or less).

Money market securities Fixed-income securities with original maturities of one year or less.

Money-weighted return The internal rate of return on a portfolio, taking account of all cash flows.

Moneyness Expresses the relationship between an option's value and its exercise price across the full range of possible underlying prices.

Monopolistic competition Highly competitive form of imperfect competition; the competitive characteristic is a notably large number of firms, while the monopoly aspect is the result of product differentiation.

Monopoly In pure monopoly markets, there are no substitutes for the given product or service. There is a single seller, which exercises considerable power over pricing and output decisions.

Monte Carlo simulation A technique that uses the inverse transformation method for converting a randomly generated uniformly distributed number into a simulated value of a random variable of a desired distribution. Each key decision variable in a Monte Carlo simulation requires an assumed statistical distribution; this assumption facilitates incorporating non-normality, fat tails, and tail dependence as well as solving high-dimensionality problems.

Moral principles Beliefs regarding what is good, acceptable, or obligatory behavior and what is bad, unacceptable, or forbidden behavior.

Mortgage loan Agreement to finance real estate by the collateral of a specified property that obliges the borrower to make a predetermined series of payments to the lender.

Mortgage pass-through security Security created when mortgage lenders pool mortgages together and sell securities to investors. The cash flow from the mortgage pool––monthly payments of principal, interest, and prepayments––are "passed through" to the security holders.

Mortgage-backed securities (MBS) Debt obligations that represent claims to the cash flows from pools of mortgage loans, most commonly on residential property.

Multi-factor model A model that explains a variable in terms of the values of a set of factors.

Multi-market indexes Comprised of indexes from different countries, designed to represent multiple security markets.

Multilateral trading facilities See *alternative trading systems.*

Multilateralism The conduct of countries who participate in mutually beneficial trade relationships and extensive rules harmonization. Private firms are fully integrated into global supply chains with multiple trade partners. Examples of multilateral countries include Germany and Singapore.

Multiple of invested capital (MOIC) Also referred to as the multiple of money or total value to paid-in, this private market performance measure incorporates both the cumulative distributions received and the net asset value of a fund as a proportion of invested capital.

Multiple-price auction A debt securities auction in which bidders receive distinct prices based on their bids.

Multiplier models Valuation models based on share price multiples or enterprise value multiples.

Mutual fund A comingled investment pool in which investors in the fund each have a pro-rata claim on the income and value of the fund.

Nash equilibrium When two or more participants in a non-coop-erative game have no incentive to deviate from their respective equilibrium strategies given their opponent's strategies.

Nationalism The promotion of a country's own economic interests to the exclusion or detriment of the interests of other nations. Nationalism is marked by limited economic and financial cooperation. These actors may focus on national production and sales, limited cross-border investment and capital flows, and restricted currency exchange.

Natural language processing (NLP) A field of research within the field of text analytics and at the intersection of computer science, AI, and linguistics that focuses on developing computer programs to analyze and interpret human language.

Natural resources These include commodities (hard and soft), agricultural land (farmland), and timberland.

Negative externalities A cost to a third party because of the production or consumption of a good or service.

Negative pledge clause Limitations on investments, the disposal of assets, or issuance of debt senior to existing obligations. Negative covenants seek to ensure that an issuer maintains the ability to make interest and principal payments.

Net cash An issuer's total debt less cash and marketable securities. When the balance is negative it is referred to as net cash.

Net debt An issuer's total debt less cash and marketable securities. When the balance is positive it is referred to as net debt.

Net investment hedge Refers to a specific **hedge accounting** designation that applies when either a foreign currency bond or a derivative, such as an FX swap or forward, is used to offset the exchange rate risk of the equity of a foreign operation.

Net present value (NPV) The present value of an investment's cash inflows (benefits) minus the present value of its cash outflows (costs).

Net profit margin An indicator of profitability, calculated as net income divided by revenue; indicates how much of each dollar of revenues is left after all costs and expenses. Also called *profit margin* or *return on sales*.

Net tax rate The tax rate net of transfer payments.

Net working capital Working capital excluding short-term items unrelated to business operations, such as cash, marketable securities, and short-term debt.

Network effects A business model that enables users to contribute directly to a product, service, or online content.

Neural networks A type of computer program design based on how the human brain learns and processes information.

Neutral rate of interest The rate of interest that neither spurs on nor slows down the underlying economy.

No-load fund A mutual fund in which there is no fee for investing in the fund or for redeeming fund shares, although there is an annual fee based on a percentage of the fund's net asset value.

Node Each value on a binomial tree from which successive moves or outcomes branch.

Non-agency RMBS MBS backed by residential mortgages that are issued by private entities and not guaranteed by a federal agency or a GSE.

Non-amortizing loans Type of debt where there are no scheduled principal repayments.

Non-cooperative country A country with inconsistent and even arbitrary rules; restricted movement of goods, services, people, and capital across borders; retaliation; and limited technology exchange.

Non-cumulative preference shares Preference shares for which dividends that are not paid in the current or subsequent periods are forfeited permanently (instead of being accrued and paid at a later date).

Non-financial risks Risks that arise from sources other than changes in the external financial markets, such as changes in accounting rules, legal environment, or tax rates.

Non-fungible token (NFT) A unique cryptographic token on the blockchain that cannot be replicated and is used to represent ownership of physical assets, such as artwork, real estate, or other assets.

Non-linear derivatives Derivatives, such as options or other contingent claims, with payoff/profit profiles that are non-linear (asymmetric) with respect to the price of the underlying.

Non-participating preference shares Preference shares that do not entitle shareholders to share in the profits of the company. Instead, shareholders are only entitled to receive a fixed dividend payment and the par value of the shares in the event of liquidation.

Non-probability sampling A sampling plan dependent on factors other than probability considerations, such as a sampler's judgment or the convenience to access data.

Non-recourse loan Loan in which the lender does not have a claim against the borrower and thus can look only to the property to recover the outstanding mortgage balance.

Non-state actors Those that participate in global political, economic, or financial affairs but do not directly control national security or country resources. Examples of non-state actors are non-governmental organizations (NGOs), multinational companies, charities, and even influential individuals, such as business leaders or cultural icons.

Nonparametric test A test that is not concerned with a parameter or that makes minimal assumptions about the population from which a sample comes.

Nonsystematic risk Unique risk that is local or limited to a particular asset or industry that need not affect assets outside of that asset class.

Normal distribution A continuous, symmetric probability distribution that is completely described by its mean and its variance.

Normalized earnings The expected level of mid-cycle earnings for a company in the absence of any unusual or temporary factors that affect profitability (either positively or negatively).

Notching Ratings adjustment methodology where specific issues from the same borrower may be assigned different credit ratings.

Notice period The length of time (typically 30–90 days) in advance that investors may be required to notify a fund of their intent to redeem some or all of their investment. This allows a fund manager to liquidate a position in an orderly fashion without magnifying losses.

Novation process A process that substitutes the initial **swap execution facility (SEF)** contract with identical trades facing the **central counterparty (CCP)**. The CCP serves as **counterparty** for both financial intermediaries, eliminating bilateral **counterparty credit risk** and providing **clearing** and **settlement** services.

Null hypothesis The hypothesis that is tested.

Off-the-run Seasoned government bonds that are often less liquid.

Off-the-run securities Sovereign debt securities outstanding other than on-the-sun securities. Off-the-run securities are less liquid than on-the-run securities.

Offer The price at which a dealer or trader is willing to sell an asset, typically qualified by a maximum quantity (ask size).

Official interest rate An interest rate that a central bank sets and announces publicly; normally the rate at which it is willing to lend money to the commercial banks. Also called *official policy rate* or *policy rate.*

Official policy rate An interest rate that a central bank sets and announces publicly; normally the rate at which it is willing to lend money to the commercial banks.

Oligopoly Market structure with a relatively small number of firms supplying the market.

Omnichannel Refers to a company selling its products or services in multiple channels, such as in store and online.

On-the-run Most recently issued, and liquid, government bonds.

On-the-run securities The most recently issued and liquid sovereign debt securities.

Open interest The number of outstanding contracts.

Open market operations The purchase or sale of bonds by the national central bank to implement monetary policy. The bonds traded are usually sovereign bonds issued by the national government.

Open-end fund A mutual fund that accepts new investment money and issues additional shares at a value equal to the net asset value of the fund at the time of investment.

Operating cycle The length of time between a company's acquisition of goods or raw materials and the collection of cash from sales to customers.

Operating efficiency ratios Ratios that measure how efficiently a company performs day-to-day tasks, such as the collection of receivables and management of inventory.

Operating leases A type of lease which is more akin to the rental of the underlying asset.

Operating leverage The sensitivity of a firm's operating profit to a change in revenues, determined by the composition of fixed and variable operating costs.

Operating profit margin A profitability ratio calculated as operating income (i.e., income before interest and taxes) divided by revenue. Also called *operating margin.*

Operational deposits Bank deposits generated by clearing, custody, and cash management activities.

Operational independence A bank's ability to execute monetary policy and set interest rates in the way it thought would best meet the inflation target.

Operational risk The risk that arises from inadequate or failed people, systems, and internal policies, procedures, and processes, as well as from external events that are beyond the control of the organization but that affect its operations.

Operationally efficient Said of a market, a financial system, or an economy that has relatively low transaction costs.

Opportunistic real estate strategies Include major redevelopment, repurposing of assets, taking on large vacancies, or speculating on significant improvement in market conditions. These may be appealing for investors seeking higher returns and willing to accept additional risks from development, redevelopment, repositioning, and leasing.

Opportunity cost Reflects the foregone opportunity of investing in a different asset. It is typically denoted by the risk-free rate of interest, *r*.

Optimal capital structure The capital structure at which the value of the company is maximized.

Option A primary example of a **contingent claim**. A **derivative contract** that provides the buyer the right, but not the obligation, to buy or sell an **underlying**.

Option contract See *option.*

Option premium An amount that is paid upfront from the option buyer to the option seller. Reflects the value of the option buyer's right to exercise in the future.

Option-adjusted price The sum of a bond's flat price and value of an embedded option.

Option-adjusted spread or OAS for a bond is its Z-spread adjusted for the value of an embedded option.

Option-adjusted yield A yield measure for a bond adjusted for embedded options.

Order A specification of what instrument to trade, how much to trade, and whether to buy or sell.

Order precedence hierarchy With respect to the execution of orders to trade, a set of rules that determines which orders execute before other orders.

Order-driven markets A market (generally an auction market) that uses rules to arrange trades based on the orders that traders submit; in their pure form, such markets do not make use of dealers.

Ordinary shares Equity shares that are subordinate to all other types of equity (e.g., preferred equity). Also called *common stock* or *common shares.*

Organizational form A legal and tax classification of a business, specific to a jurisdiction, that determines the organization's legal identity, owner–manager relationship, owner liability, taxation, and access to financing.

Out-of-the-money Describes an option with zero intrinsic value because the option buyer would not rationally exercise the option. An example of such would be the case in which the price of the underlying is less than the option's exercise price for a call option.

Over-the-counter (OTC) Refers to derivative markets in which **derivative contracts** are created and traded between derivatives end users and **dealers**, or financial intermediaries, such as commercial banks or investment banks.

Overcollateralization Credit enhancement technique where collateral underlying the transaction exceeds the face value of the issued bonds.

Overconfidence bias A bias in which people demonstrate unwarranted faith in their own intuitive reasoning, judgments, and/or cognitive abilities.

Overfitting When a machine learning model learns the input and target dataset too precisely, making the system more likely to discover false relationships or unsubstantiated patterns that will lead to prediction errors.

P-value The smallest level of significance at which the null hypothesis can be rejected.

Par rate A yield-to-maturity that makes the present value of a bond's cash flows equal to par.

Par swap rate The fixed swap rate that equates the present value of all future expected floating cash flows to the present value of fixed cash flows.

Par value The amount of principal on a bond, also known as face value.

Parallel shift When all maturities along a yield curve increase or decrease in yield in the same direction by the same magnitude. A parallel shift in the yield curve is implicitly assumed in analytical duration and convexity.

Parameter A descriptive measure computed from or used to describe a population of data, conventionally represented by Greek letters.

Parametric test Any test (or procedure) concerned with parameters or whose validity depends on assumptions concerning the population generating the sample.

Pari passu clause A covenant or contract clause that ensures a debt obligation is treated the same as the borrower's other senior debt instruments and is not subordinated to similar obligations.

Partially amortizing bond A loan or bond with a payment schedule that calls for partial repayment of principle over the life of the bond, with the remaining principal paid at maturity.

Participating preference shares Preference shares that entitle shareholders to receive the standard preferred dividend plus the opportunity to receive an additional dividend if the company's profits exceed a pre-specified level.

Pass-through businesses Businesses that, by virtue of their organizational form and/or other legal and regulatory attributes, do not pay entity-level taxes on income or loss; income or loss is passed through to owners, who pay personal taxes.

Pass-through rate The coupon rate of a mortgage pass-through security that is received by the investor after administrative charges. It is lower than the weighted average mortgage rate earned on the underlying pool of mortgages because of administrative charges. The pass-through rate that the investor receives is said to be "net interest" or "net coupon."

Passive investment A buy-and-hold approach in which an investor does not make portfolio changes based on short-term expectations of changing market or security performance.

Payable date The day that the company actually mails out (or electronically transfers) a dividend payment.

Payment date The day that the company actually mails out (or electronically transfers) a dividend payment.

Payment-in-kind A bond feature whereby coupon payments can be fully or partially paid in the form of additional issuance or added to the principal amount.

Payments system The system for the transfer of money.

Pearson correlation A parametric measure of the relationship between two variables.

Pecking order theory The theory that managers consider how their actions might be interpreted by outsiders and thereby order their preferences for various forms of corporate financing. Forms of financing that are least visible to outsiders (e.g., internally generated funds) are most preferable to managers, and those that are most visible (e.g., equity issuance) are least preferable.

Penetration pricing A discount pricing approach used when a firm willingly sacrifices margins in order to build scale and market share.

Percentiles Values that divide a distribution into 100 equal parts.

Perfect competition A market structure in which the individual firm has virtually no impact on market price, because it is assumed to be a very small seller among a very large number of firms selling essentially identical products.

Performance evaluation The measurement and assessment of the outcomes of investment management decisions.

Performance fee Fee paid to the general partner from the limited partner(s) based on realized net profits.

Period costs Costs (e.g., executives' salaries) that cannot be directly matched with the timing of revenues and which are thus expensed immediately.

Periodicity Number of periods in a year, used for compound interest. The periodicity of a fixed-income instrument usually matches the frequency of its coupon payments.

Permanent differences Differences between tax and financial reporting of revenue (expenses) that will not be reversed at some future date. These result in a difference between the company's effective tax rate and statutory tax rate and do not result in a deferred tax item.

Permissioned networks Networks that are fully open only to select participants on a DLT network.

Permissionless networks Networks that are fully open to any user on a DLT network.

Perpetual bonds Bonds with no stated maturity date.

Perpetuity A perpetual annuity, or a set of never-ending level sequential cash flows, with the first cash flow occurring one period from now.

PESTLE analysis A framework for analyzing factors that influence an industry's economic outcomes.

Pet projects A capital investment that is pursued by management but is not economically justifiable by a disinterested party. Motivations for pet projects include self-dealing and vanity.

Physical risks Economic and financial losses from the increase in the severity and frequency of extreme weather due to climate change—for example, the loss of coastal real estate from a storm.

PIPE (private investment in public equity) A private offering to select investors with fewer disclosures and lower transaction costs that allows the issuer to raise capital more quickly and cost effectively.

Platykurtic Describes a distribution that has relatively less weight in the tails than the normal distribution (also called thin-tailed).

Pledge A legal right or claim to property by a creditor. Also called a lien.

Poison pill Officially known as a shareholder rights plan, a poison pill is a hostile-takeover defense adopted by boards of directors according to rules specified in the corporate charter. There are several types of poison pills. Generally, they allow shareholders, *excluding* the shareholder making the hostile bid and their affiliates, to buy newly issued shares at a discounted price. The share issuance would dilute the bidder's ownership percentage, rendering it impossible for the bidder to attain control.

Policy rate An interest rate that a central bank sets and announces publicly; normally the rate at which it is willing to lend money to the commercial banks.

Portfolio companies The individual companies owned by a private equity firm.

Portfolio investment flows Short-term investments in foreign assets, such as stocks or bonds.

Portfolio planning The process of creating a plan for building a portfolio that is expected to satisfy a client's investment objectives.

Position The quantity of an asset that an entity owns or owes.

Posterior probability An updated probability that reflects or comes after new information.

Power of a test The probability of correctly rejecting the null—that is, rejecting the null hypothesis when it is false.

Pre-funding period Allows the trust to acquire during a certain period of time after the close of the transaction.

Preference shares A type of equity interest which ranks above common shares with respect to the payment of dividends and the distribution of the company's net assets upon liquidation. They have characteristics of both debt and equity securities. Also called *preferred stock*.

Preferred stock See *preference shares*.

Premium In the case of bonds, premium refers to the amount by which a bond is priced above its face (par) value. In the case of an option, the amount paid for the option contract.

Prepayment option May entitle the borrower to prepay all or part of the outstanding mortgage principal prior to maturity. This creates a risk from the lender's or investor's viewpoint because the cash flow amounts and timing cannot be known with certainty.

Prepayment risk The risk that the some or all of a mortgage-backed security's principal is repaid at a different speed than expected, either in the form of contraction risk (or earlier repayment than expected) or extension risk (later repayment).

Present value models Valuation models that estimate the intrinsic value of a security as the present value of the future benefits expected to be received from the security. Also called *discounted cash flow models.*

Pretax margin A profitability ratio calculated as earnings before taxes divided by revenue.

Price discrimination A pricing approach that charges different prices to different customers based on their willingness to pay.

Price index Represents the average prices of a basket of goods and services.

Price limits Establish a band relative to the previous day's settlement price within which all trades must occur.

Price multiple A ratio that compares the share price with some sort of monetary flow or value to allow evaluation of the relative worth of a company's stock.

Price priority The principle that the highest priced buy orders and the lowest priced sell orders execute first.

Price return Measures *only* the price appreciation or percentage change in price of the securities in an index or portfolio.

Price return index An index that reflects *only* the price appreciation or percentage change in price of the constituent securities. Also called *price index.*

Price stability In economics, refers to an inflation rate that is low on average and not subject to wide fluctuation.

Price takers Producers that must accept whatever price the market dictates.

Price value of a basis point (PVBP) An estimate of the change in the full price of a bond given a 1 bp change in its yield-to-maturity. The PVBP is also called the "PV01," standing for the "price value of an 01" or "present value of an 01," where "01" means 1 bp. In the United States, it is commonly called the "DV01" for the "dollar value" of 1 bp.

Price weighting An index weighting method in which the weight assigned to each constituent security is determined by dividing its price by the sum of all the prices of the constituent securities.

Price-setting option The option to adjust prices when demand or supply varies from what is forecast.

Price-to-earnings ratio (P/E) The ratio of share price to earnings per share.

Pricing power A company's ability to set prices and other economic terms with customers without affecting its sales volumes.

Primary bond markets Fixed-income markets comprised of issuers issuing bonds to investors to raise capital, often intermediated by a third-party such as an investment bank.

Primary capital markets (primary markets) The market where securities are first sold and the issuers receive the proceeds.

Primary dealer Financial institution that is authorized to deal in new issues of sovereign bonds and that serves primarily as a trading counterparty of the office responsible for issuing sovereign bonds.

Primary market The market where securities are first sold and the issuers receive the proceeds.

Prime broker A broker that provides services that commonly include custody, administration, lending, short borrowing, and trading.

Prime loans Lending made to borrowers of high credit quality with strong employment and credit histories, a low DTI, substantial equity in the underlying property, and a first lien on the mortgaged property serving as the collateral for the loan.

Principal The amount that an issuer agrees to repay the debtholders on the maturity date.

Principal-agent relationship An arrangement in which one party (the agent) has authority to act for or on behalf of another party (the principal). Such an arrangement imposes a duty on the agent to act in the principal's best interest.

Prior probabilities Probabilities reflecting beliefs prior to the arrival of new information.

Priority of claims Priority of payment, with the most senior or highest ranking debt having the first claim on the cash flows and assets of the issuer.

Private capital Funding provided to companies that is not sourced from the public markets.

Private company A company, typically a limited company, that does not list its equity securities on an exchange.

Private debt Capital extended to companies through a loan or other form of debt.

Private debtholders Investors in an entity's non-securitized debt claims, such as a loan or lease. The most common type of private debtholder is a bank.

Private equity Equity investment capital raised from sources other than public markets and traditional institutions.

Private equity fund A hedge fund that seeks to buy, optimize, and ultimately sell portfolio companies to generate profits. See *venture capital fund.*

Private equity securities Securities that are not listed on public exchanges and have no active secondary market. They are issued primarily to institutional investors via non-public offerings, such as private placements.

Private investment in public equity (PIPE) An investment in the equity of a publicly traded firm that is made at a discount to the market value of the firm's shares.

Private limited company A type of limited company in many jurisdictions with pass-through taxation but restrictions on the number of shareholders or members and on the transfer of ownership interest.

Private placement A sale of debt or equity securities to a small group of investors on an unregulated basis. The terms of the offering are negotiated by the issuer and investors.

Probability of default (POD) The likelihood that a borrower fails to make full and timely payments of principal and interest according to debt terms, usually expressed in annual percentage terms.

Probability sampling A sampling plan that allows every member of the population to have an equal chance of being selected.

Probability tree diagram A diagram with branches emanating from nodes representing either mutually exclusive chance events or mutually exclusive decisions.

Production flexibility option The option to alter production when demand varies from what is forecast.

Profession An occupational group that has specific education, expert knowledge, and a framework of practice and behavior that underpins community trust, respect, and recognition.

Profit margin An indicator of profitability, calculated as net income divided by revenue; indicates how much of each dollar of revenues is left after all costs and expenses.

Profitability ratios Ratios that measure a company's ability to generate profitable sales from its resources (assets).

Prospectus Legal document in securitization that describes the structure of the transaction, including the priority and amount of payments to be made to the servicer, administrators, and the ABS holders, as well as the credit enhancements used in the securitization.

Protective put A strategy of purchasing an underlying asset and purchasing a put on the same asset.

Proxy contest When a shareholder or group of shareholders campaigns for certain matters they have submitted to a shareholder vote, often a slate of directors who oppose the incumbent board and management. The incumbent board and management simultaneously campaign for their side.

Proxy voting A form of casting a ballot in an election in which a voter authorizes a representative to vote on their behalf according to instructions. In corporate elections, proxy ballots are cast by shareholders that direct a representative, typically the corporate secretary, to enter their votes as instructed.

Public (listed) company A company with its equity securities traded on an exchange.

Public limited companies A type of limited company in many jurisdictions with entity-level taxation but no restrictions on the number of shareholders or transferability of ownership interest; the most suitable organizational form for a company that seeks to go public.

Public–private partnership A long-term contractual relationship between the public and private sectors for the purpose of having the private sector deliver a project or service traditionally provided by the public sector. Infrastructure is increasingly being financed privately through public–private partnerships by local, regional, and national governments.

Public–private partnership (PPP) An agreement between the public sector and the private sector to finance, build, and operate public infrastructure, such as hospitals and toll roads.

Pull on liquidity An action or event that accelerates cash outflows.

Purchase agreement Legal document in a securitization transaction that outlines the representations and warranties that the seller makes about the assets sold.

Pure discount bonds Bonds that do not pay interest during their life. They are issued at a discount to par value and redeemed at par. Also called zero-coupon bonds.

Put An option that gives the holder the right to sell an underlying asset to another party at a fixed price over a specific period of time.

Put option The right to sell an underlying.

Putable bonds Bonds that give the bondholder the right to sell the bond back to the issuer at a predetermined price on specified dates.

Put–call forward parity Describes the no-arbitrage condition in which at $t = 0$ the present value of the price of a long forward commitment plus the price of the long put must equal the price of the long call plus the price of the risk-free asset (with face value of the exercise price of both the call and the put).

Put–call parity Describes the no-arbitrage condition in which at $t = 0$ the price of the long underlying asset plus the price of the long put must equal the price of the long call plus the price of the risk-free asset (with face value of the exercise price of both the call and the put).

Quantile A value at or below which a stated fraction of the data lies. Also referred to as a fractile.

Quantitative easing An expansionary monetary policy based on aggressive open market purchase operations.

Quartiles Quantiles that divide a distribution into four equal parts.

Quick ratio A measure of liquidity that is the ratio of cash, marketable securities, and receivables to current liabilities.

Quintiles Quantiles that divide a distribution into five equal parts.

Quota rents Profits that foreign producers can earn by raising the price of their goods higher than they would without a quota.

Quotas Government policies that restrict the quantity of a good that can be imported into a country, generally for a specified period of time.

Quote-driven market A market in which dealers acting as principals facilitate trading.

Quoted margin Specified spread of a floating rate instrument over a market reference rate or benchmark.

Range The difference between the maximum and minimum values in a dataset.

Rapid amortization provisions Provisions in receivable ABS that may require early principal amortization if specific events occur. Such provisions are referred to as early amortization and are included to safeguard the credit quality of the issue, particularly during the revolving period.

Razor, razorblade pricing A pricing approach that combines a low price on a piece of equipment and high-margin pricing on repeat-purchase consumables.

Real assets Generally, these are tangible physical assets, such as real estate, infrastructure, and natural resources, but they also include such intangibles as patents, intellectual property, and goodwill. Real assets generate current or expected future cash flows and/or are considered a store of value.

Real estate Includes borrowed or ownership capital in buildings or land. Developed land includes commercial and industrial real estate, residential real estate, and infrastructure.

Real option A right, but not an obligation, for management to make a decision with respect to a capital investment that alters future cash flows from the original forecasted scenario.

Real risk-free interest rate The single-period interest rate for a completely risk-free security if no inflation were expected.

Rebalancing Adjusting the weights of the constituent securities in an index.

Rebalancing policy The set of rules that guide the process of restoring a portfolio's asset class weights to those specified in the strategic asset allocation.

Recapitalization Recapitalization via private equity describes the steps a firm takes to increase or introduce leverage to its portfolio company and pay itself a dividend out of the new capital structure.

Recognition lag The lag in government response to an economic problem resulting from the delay in confirming a change in the state of the economy.

Recourse loan Loan in which the lender has a claim against the borrower for the shortfall (deficiency) between the amount of the outstanding mortgage balance and the proceeds received from the sale of the property.

Recovery rate (RR) The percentage of an outstanding debt claim recovered when an issuer defaults

Redemption fee A fee charged to discourage redemptions and to offset the transaction costs for remaining investors in the fund.

Refinancing rate A type of central bank policy rate.

Regionalism In between the two extremes of bilateralism and multilateralism. In regionalism, a group of countries cooperate with one another. Both bilateralism and regionalism can be conducted at the exclusion of other groups. For example, regional blocs may agree to provide trade benefits to one another and increase barriers for those outside of that group.

Registered bonds Bonds for which ownership is recorded by either name or serial number.

Regression analysis Allows us to test hypotheses about the relationship between two variables, by quantifying the strength of the relationship between the two variables, and to use one variable to make predictions about the other variable.

Regression coefficients The collective term for the intercept and slope coefficients in the regression model.

Regret The feeling that an opportunity has been missed; typically, an expression of *hindsight bias*.

Regret-aversion bias An emotional bias in which people tend to avoid making decisions that will result in action out of fear that the decision will turn out poorly.

Relative dispersion The amount of dispersion relative to a reference value or benchmark.

Reopening Issuing bonds by increasing the size of an existing bond issue with a price significantly different from par.

Replication A strategy in which a derivative's cash flow stream may be recreated using a combination of long or short positions in an underlying asset and borrowing or lending cash.

Repo rate The interest rate on a repurchase agreement.

Representativeness bias A belief perseverance bias in which people tend to classify new information based on past experiences and classifications.

Repurchase agreement (Repo) A form of collateralized loan involving the sale of a security with a simultaneous agreement by the seller to buy back the same security from the purchaser at an agreed-on price and future date. The party who sells the security at the inception of the repurchase agreement and buys it back at maturity is borrowing money from the other party, and the security sold and subsequently repurchased represents the collateral.

Repurchase date The date when the party who sold the security at the inception of a repurchase agreement buys back the security from the cash lending counterparty.

Repurchase price The price at which the party who sold the security at the inception of the repurchase agreement buys back the security from the cash lending counterparty.

Required margin Also known as discount margin. The market-determined yield spread over or under the market reference rate such that a floating-rate loan is priced at par on a rate reset date following issuance.

Required rate of return The rate of return required by investors given the risk of the bond investment, also known as the market discount rate or required yield.

Required yield The rate of return required by investors given the risk of the bond investment, also known as the market discount rate of required rate of return.

Required yield spread The difference in yield-to-maturity between a bond and that of a government benchmark bond with the same or similar time-to-maturity.

Resampling A statistical method that repeatedly draws samples from the original observed data sample for the statistical inference of population parameters.

Reserve currency A currency held by global central banks in significant quantities and widely used to conduct international trade and financial transactions.

Reserve requirement The requirement for banks to hold reserves in proportion to the size of deposits.

Residual The amount of deviation of an observed value of the dependent variable from its estimated value based on the fitted regression line.

Restricted domestic currency A currency with limited convertibility into other currencies due to illiquidity.

Return on assets (ROA) A profitability ratio calculated as net income divided by average total assets; indicates a company's net profit generated per dollar invested in total assets.

Return on equity (ROE) A profitability ratio calculated as net income divided by average shareholders' equity.

Return on invested capital (ROIC) A measure of the profitability of a company relative to the amount of capital invested by the equityholders and debtholders.

Return on sales An indicator of profitability, calculated as net income divided by revenue; indicates how much of each dollar of revenues is left after all costs and expenses. Also referred to as *net profit margin*.

Return-generating model A model that can provide an estimate of the expected return of a security given certain parameters and estimates of the values of the independent variables in the model.

Revenue bonds Bonds issued by non-sovereign governments related to a government sponsored project expected to generate future cash flow as a primary source of repayment.

Reverse repurchase agreement A repurchase agreement viewed from the perspective of the cash lending counterparty.

Reverse stock split A reduction in the number of shares outstanding with a corresponding increase in share price but no change to the company's underlying fundamentals.

Revolving credit agreements The most reliable form of short-term bank borrowing facilities; they are in effect for multiple years (e.g., three to five years) and can have optional medium-term loan features. Also known as *revolvers*.

Rho The change in a given derivative instrument for a given small change in the risk-free interest rate, holding everything else constant. Rho measures the sensitivity of the option to the risk-free interest rate.

Ricardian equivalence An economic theory that implies that it makes no difference whether a government finances a deficit by increasing taxes or issuing debt.

Risk Exposure to uncertainty. The chance of a loss or adverse outcome as a result of an action, inaction, or external event.

Risk averse The assumption that an investor will choose the least risky alternative.

Risk aversion The dislike for risk such that compensation is required in terms of higher expected returns for assuming higher risk.

Risk budgeting The establishment of objectives for individuals, groups, or divisions of an organization that takes into account the allocation of an acceptable level of risk.

Risk exposure The state of being exposed or vulnerable to a risk. The extent to which an organization is sensitive to underlying risks.

Risk governance The top-down process and guidance that directs risk management activities to align with and support the overall enterprise.

Risk management The process of identifying the level of risk an organization wants, measuring the level of risk the organization currently has, taking actions that bring the actual level of risk to the desired level of risk, and monitoring the new actual level of risk so that it continues to be aligned with the desired level of risk.

Risk management framework The infrastructure, process, and analytics needed to support effective risk management in an organization.

Risk premium An extra return expected by investors for bearing some specified risk.

Risk shifting Actions to change the distribution of risk outcomes.

Risk tolerance The level of risk an investor is willing and able to bear.

Risk transfer Strategies implemented to mitigate the impact of specific risks by transferring them to an insurance company.

Risk-neutral pricing A no-arbitrage derivative value established separately from investor views on risk that uses underlying asset volatility and the risk-free rate to calculate the present value of future cash flows.

Risk-neutral probability The computed probability used in binomial option pricing by which the discounted weighted sum of expected values of the underlying equal the current option price. Specifically, this probability is computed using the risk-free rate and assumed up gross return and down gross return of the underlying.

Rollover risk The likelihood that a property owner will lose an existing tenant and forgo income until a new one is found.

Safety-first rules Rules for portfolio selection that focus on the risk that portfolio value or portfolio return will fall below some minimum acceptable level over some time horizon.

Sample correlation coefficient A standardized measure of how two variables in a sample move together. It is the ratio of the sample covariance to the product of the two variables' standard deviations.

Sample covariance A measure of how two variables in a sample move together.

Sample excess kurtosis A sample measure of the degree of a distribution's kurtosis in excess of the normal distribution's kurtosis.

Sample mean The sum of the sample observations divided by the sample size.

Sample skewness A sample measure of the degree of asymmetry of a distribution.

Sample standard deviation The positive square root of the sample variance.

Sample variance The sum of squared deviations around the mean divided by the degrees of freedom.

Sample-size neglect A type of representativeness bias in which financial market participants incorrectly assume that small sample sizes are representative of populations (or "real" data).

Sampling distribution The distribution of all distinct possible values that a statistic can assume when computed from samples of the same size randomly drawn from the same population.

Sampling error The difference between the observed value of a statistic and the estimate resulting from using subsets of the population.

Sampling plan The set of rules used to select a sample.

Saving deposits Bank deposits typically held for non-transactional purposes that often have a stated term.

Scatter plot A two-dimensional graphical plot of paired observations of values for the independent and dependent variables in a simple linear regression.

Scenario analysis A variation of the valuation process combining a base case with alternative outcomes, allowing the incorporation of more favorable or adverse scenarios in the valuation process.

Scraping An automated, large-scale, algorithm-driven approach that retrieves otherwise unstructured data available on websites and creates data in a more structured format.

Seasoned offering An offering in which an issuer sells additional units of a previously issued security.

Secondary bond markets Fixed-income markets comprised of investors trading existing bonds amongst themselves.

Secondary market The market where securities are traded among investors.

Secondary precedence rules Rules that determine how to rank orders placed at the same time.

Secondary sale Sale of a private company stake to another private equity firm or group of financial buyers.

Secondary-stage investments The second stage of development of an infrastructure asset. Secondary-stage investments involve existing infrastructure facilities or fully operational assets that do not require further investment or development over the investment horizon. These assets generate immediate cash flow and returns expected over the investment period.

Sector indexes Indexes that represent and track different economic sectors—such as consumer goods, energy, finance, health care, and technology—on either a national, regional, or global basis.

Secured With collateral; secured debt is backed by the cash flows of the issuer and the collateral as a secondary source of repayment.

Secured loans Loans collateralized by an asset of the borrower.

Security Evidence of equity or debt interest or in an entity or a related right, such as a derivative. Often standardized to conform to security exchange requirements.

Security characteristic line A plot of the excess return of a security on the excess return of the market.

Security market index A portfolio of securities representing a given security market, market segment, or asset class.

Security market line The graphical representation of the CAPM formula, showing the relationship between expected return and beta.

Security selection The process of selecting individual securities; typically, security selection has the objective of generating superior risk-adjusted returns relative to a portfolio's benchmark.

Security tokens Digitizes the ownership rights associated with publicly traded securities.

Segmenting A process of identifying and grouping customers by decision-useful attributes.

Self-attribution bias A bias in which people take too much credit for successes (*self-enhancing*) and assign responsibility to others for failures (*self-protecting*).

Self-control bias A bias in which people fail to act in pursuit of their long-term, overarching goals because of a lack of self-discipline.

Self-investment limits With respect to investment limitations applying to pension plans, restrictions on the percentage of assets that can be invested in securities issued by the pension plan sponsor.

Sell-side firm A broker/dealer that sells securities and provides independent investment research and recommendations to their clients (i.e., buy-side firms).

Semi-strong-form efficient market A market in which security prices reflect all publicly known and available information.

Semiannual bond basis yield Also known as a semiannual bond equivalent yield, it is an annualized interest rate with a periodicity of two.

Semiannual bond equivalent yield Also known as a semiannual bond basis yield, it is an annualized interest rate with a periodicity of two.

Senior debt A debt obligation with higher priority of payment than junior debt obligations.

Senior unsecured debt The highest-ranked debt in an issuer's capital structure which is a general obligation of the borrower.

Seniority Priority of payment of various debt obligations.

Sensitivity analysis A form of analysis used to determine the impact of a change in one or more key variables affecting investment returns or valuation.

Separately managed account (SMA) An investment portfolio managed exclusively for the benefit of an individual or institution.

Service period The time between the grant and vesting dates for an employee share-based award, usually measured in years.

Settlement The closing date at which the counterparties of a derivative contract exchange payment for the underlying as required by the contract.

Settlement price The price determined by an exchange's clearinghouse in the daily settlement of the mark-to-market process. The price reflects an average of the final futures trades of the day.

Share class Types of equity securities that have different voting rights—for example, an issuer may issue Class A shares that carry one vote per share and Class B shares that carry ten votes per share.

Share repurchase A transaction in which a company buys back its own shares. Unlike stock dividends and stock splits, share repurchases use corporate cash.

Shareholder activism A range of actions by a corporation's shareholders that are intended to result in some change in the corporation, typically a change in the board of directors, management, or business strategy.

Shareholder derivative lawsuit A legal action by a shareholder on behalf of a company, not the shareholder personally, against a third party. Often, the third party is a director or manager who the shareholder believes has harmed the company.

Shareholder engagement Shareholder engagement reflects active ownership by investors in which the investor seeks to influence a corporation's decisions on ESG matters, either through dialogue with corporate officers or votes at a shareholder assembly (in the case of equity).

Shareholder theory of corporate governance Espoused by Milton Friedman in his famous 1970 essay, the shareholder theory holds that the objective of a business is to increase profits and shareholder value.

Shareholders Hold a direct equity position in a firm, and both individual persons and financial institutions can be shareholders. The term comes from the individual or investment firm literally having a share of the company. It is most commonly used when talking about the rights and responsibilities that come with being an "owner" of a company, such as stewardship, voting, and engagement. This differentiates it from a situation where an individual or an investment firm lends money or invests in a bond (in other words, they are not an equityholder of a company). Because bond investors do not have a share and are not owners of a company, they cannot vote. Nonetheless, expectations around engagement are increasing for those who invest in loans and bonds as well, making the difference between the two terms more subtle.

Shares Units of ownership interest in a limited company.

Sharpe ratio The ratio of mean excess return to standard deviation (excess return).

Shelf registration A type of public offering that allows the issuer to file a single, all-encompassing offering circular that covers a series of bond issues.

Short A trading position in a **derivative contract** that gains value as the price of the **underlying** moves lower.

Short biased These strategies use quantitative, technical, and fundamental analysis to short overvalued equity securities with limited or no long-side exposures.

Short position A position in an asset or contract in which one has sold an asset one does not own, or in which a right under a contract can be exercised against oneself.

Short selling A transaction in which borrowed securities are sold with the intention to repurchase them at a lower price at a later date and return them to the lender.

Short-run average total cost The curve describing average total cost when some costs are considered fixed.

Shortfall risk The risk that portfolio value or portfolio return will fall below some minimum acceptable level over some time horizon.

Shutdown point The point at which average revenue is equal to the firm's average variable cost.

Side letter A side agreement created between the GP and specific LPs. These agreements exist *outside* the LPA. These agreements provide additional terms and conditions related to the investment agreement.

Signpost An indicator, market level, data piece, or event that signals a risk is becoming more or less likely. An analyst can think of signposts like a traffic light.

Simple linear regression (SLR) An approach for estimating the linear relationship between a dependent variable and a single independent variable by minimizing the sum of the squared deviations between the fitted line and the observed values.

Simple random sample A subset of a larger population created in such a way that each element of the population has an equal probability of being selected to the subset.

Simple random sampling The procedure of drawing a sample to satisfy the definition of a simple random sample.

Simple yield The sum of the coupon payments plus the straight-line amortized share of the gain or loss divided by the bond's flat price. Simple yields are used mostly to quote JGBs.

Simulation A technique for exploring how a target variable (e.g. portfolio returns) would perform in a hypothetical environment specified by the user, rather than a historical setting.

Simulation trial A complete pass through the steps of a simulation.

Single-price auction A debt securities auction in which all bidders pay the same price.

Sinking fund Provisions that reduce the credit risk of a bond issue by requiring the issuer to retire a portion of the bond's principal outstanding each year.

Situational influences External factors, such as environmental or cultural elements, that shape our behavior.

Skewed Not symmetrical.

Skewness A quantitative measure of skew (lack of symmetry); a synonym of skew. It is computed as the average cubed deviation from the mean standardized by dividing by the standard deviation cubed.

Slope coefficient The change in the estimated value of the dependent variable for a one-unit change in the value of the independent variable.

Small country A country that is a price taker in the world market for a product and cannot influence the world market price.

Smart beta Involves the use of simple, transparent, rules-based strategies as a basis for investment decisions.

Smart contracts Computer programs that are designed to self-execute on the basis of pre-specified terms and conditions agreed to by parties to a contract.

Social infrastructure investments A category of infrastructure investments that are directed toward human activities and include such assets as educational, health care, social housing, and correctional facilities, with the focus on providing, operating, and maintaining the asset infrastructure.

Soft commodities Standardized agricultural products, such as cattle and corn, with markets often involving the physical delivery of the underlying upon settlement.

Soft hurdle rate Hurdle rate where the fee is calculated on the entire return when the hurdle is exceeded. With a soft hurdle, GPs are able to catch up performance fees once the hurdle threshold is exceeded.

Soft power A means of influencing another country's decisions without force or coercion. Soft power can be built over time through actions, such as cultural programs, advertisement, travel grants, and university exchange.

Soft-bullet covered bonds Delay the bond default and payment acceleration of bond cash flows until a new final maturity date, which is usually up to a year after the original maturity date.

Solvency Refers to the condition in which firm value exceeds the face value of debt used to finance the firm's assets.

Solvency ratios Ratios that measure a company's ability to meet its long-term obligations.

Solvency risk The risk that an organization does not survive or succeed because it runs out of cash, even though it might otherwise be solvent.

Sophisticated investors Individuals or entities that are permitted in a jurisdiction to trade unregistered or, generally, less regulated securities, including shares of privately held companies; also called *accredited investors*.

Sovereign immunity A principle that limits legal recourse of lenders from forcing a sovereign borrower to declare bankruptcy or liquidate its assets to settle debt claims.

Spearman rank correlation coefficient A measure of correlation applied to ranked data.

Special dividend A dividend paid by a company that does not pay dividends on a regular schedule, or a dividend that supplements regular cash dividends with an extra payment.

Special purpose acquisition company A "blank check" company that exists solely for the purpose of acquiring an unspecified private company within a predetermined period or return capital to investors.

Special purpose entity (SPE) Also referred to as a special purpose vehicle (SPV), this legal entity is created for a specific economic purpose. In the case of a project SPV, the entity's sole purpose is to facilitate the construction, operation, and financing of an infrastructure asset over its contractual life.

Special purpose vehicle See *special purpose entity*.

Special situations An area of private capital investment which targets return by investing in stressed, distressed, or event-driven opportunities.

Split ratings Complex risks viewed very differently by rating agencies

Sponsored A type of depository receipt in which the foreign company whose shares are held by the depository has a direct involvement in the issuance of the receipts.

Spot curve Yields-to-maturity on a series of default-risk-free zero-coupon bonds.

Spot markets Markets in which specific assets are exchanged at current prices. Spot markets are often referred to as **cash markets**.

Spot prices The current prices prevailing in **spot markets**.

Spot rates Yields-to-maturity on default-risk-free zero-coupon bonds.

Spread The difference in yield-to-maturity between a bond and that of a another bond.

Spread risk Bond price risk arising from changes in the yield spread on credit-risky bonds; reflects changes in the market's assessment and/or pricing of credit migration (or downgrade) risk and market liquidity risk.

Spurious correlation Refers to: 1) correlation between two variables that reflects chance relationships in a particular dataset; 2) correlation induced by a calculation that mixes each of two variables with a third variable; and 3) correlation between two variables arising not from a direct relation between them but from their relation to a third variable.

Stablecoin A cryptocurrency that aims to maintain a stable value relative to a specified asset or to a pool or basket of assets.

Stackelberg model A prominent model of strategic decision making in which firms are assumed to make their decisions sequentially.

Staggered board A structure of board elections in which only part of the board is elected simultaneously—for example, only one-third of the board may be up for election each year, so the board can be replaced over three years, not in one year if all seats were elected annually. This structure fosters greater continuity of board members but is an obstacle for shareholders seeking to effect change.

Stakeholder theory of corporate governance An expansion of the shareholder theory of corporate governance under which the objective of a business is to maximize value for, and balance the interests of, a broad group of stakeholders, including shareholders, employees, society, and the non-human environment.

Stakeholders Any party with an interest, financial or non-financial, in an entity or its actions.

Standard deviation The positive square root of the variance; a measure of dispersion in the same units as the original data.

Standard error of the estimate A measure of the distance between the observed values of the dependent variable and those predicted from the estimated regression. The smaller this value, the better the fit of the model. Also known as the standard error of the regression and the root mean square error.

Standard error of the forecast Used to provide an interval estimate around the estimated regression line. It is necessary because the regression line does not describe the relationship between the dependent and independent variables perfectly.

Standard error of the slope coefficient Calculated for simple linear regression by dividing the standard error of the estimate by the square root of the variation of the independent variable.

Standardization The process of creating protocols for the production, sale, transport, or use of a product or service. Standardization occurs when relevant parties agree to follow these protocols together. It helps support expanded economic and financial activities, such as trade and capital flows that support higher economic growth and standards of living, across borders.

Standards of conduct Behaviors required by a group; established benchmarks that clarify or enhance a group's code of ethics.

Standing limit orders A limit order at a price below market and which therefore is waiting to trade.

State actors Typically national governments, political organizations, or country leaders that exert authority over a country's national security and resources. The South African President, Sultan of Brunei, Malaysia's Parliament, and the British Prime Minister are all examples of state actors.

Statement of cash flows A financial statement that details the movement of cash over a period. The statement is classified into operating, investing, and financing activities.

Static trade-off theory of capital structure A theory pertaining to a company's optimal capital structure; the optimal level of debt is found at the point where additional debt would cause the costs of financial distress to increase by a greater amount than the benefit of the additional tax shield.

Statistically significant A result indicating that the null hypothesis can be rejected; with reference to an estimated regression coefficient, frequently understood to mean a result indicating that the corresponding population regression coefficient is different from zero.

Status quo bias An emotional bias in which people do nothing (i.e., maintain the status quo) instead of making a change.

Statutory voting A common method of voting where each share represents one vote.

Step-up bonds Bonds for which the coupon, be it fixed or floating, increases by specified margins at specified dates.

Stock dividend A type of dividend in which a company distributes additional shares of its common stock to shareholders instead of cash.

Stock exchange An exchange in which equity securities are traded. See *exchanges*.

Stock split An increase in the number of shares outstanding with a consequent decrease in share price, but no change to the company's underlying fundamentals.

Stockholder overhang The downward pressure on the share price of stock as large blocks of shares are being sold on the open market.

Stop order An order in which a trader has specified a stop price condition. Also called *stop-loss order*.

Stop-loss order See *stop order*.

Stranded assets A resource that is no longer economically valuable owing to changes in demand, regulations, or availability of substitutes—for example, a newly discovered oil well that will not be brought into production.

Strategic asset allocation A long-term strategy that establishes target allocations for various asset classes and aims to optimize the balance between risk and reward by diversifying investments.

Stratified random sampling A procedure that first divides a population into subpopulations (strata) based on classification criteria and then randomly draws samples from each stratum in sizes proportional to that of each stratum in the population.

Street convention For yield measures on fixed-income instruments that assume payments are made on scheduled dates and ignore weekends and holidays.

Stress testing A specific type of scenario analysis that estimates losses in rare and extremely unfavorable combinations of events or scenarios.

Strong-form efficient market A market in which security prices reflect all public and private information.

Structural budget deficit Also known as the cyclically adjusted budget deficit. The deficit that would exist if the economy was at full employment (or full potential output).

Structural subordination Refers to the positioning of debt, which is issued by a legal entity, typically a holding company, which is separate and therefore one step removed from an operating company, which holds assets pledged under a security agreement to senior secured debtholders.

Structured notes A broad category of securities that incorporate the features of debt instruments and one or more embedded derivatives designed to achieve a particular issuer or investor objective.

Subordinated debt A class of unsecured debt that ranks below a firm's senior unsecured obligations.

Subordination A form of internal credit enhancement that relies on creating more than one bond tranche and ordering the claim priorities for ownership or interest in an asset between the tranches. The ordering of the claim priorities is called a senior/subordinated structure, where the tranches of highest seniority are called senior, followed by subordinated or junior tranches. Also called **credit tranching**.

Subprime loans Lending to borrowers with lower credit quality, high DTI, and/or are loans with higher LTV, and include loans that are secured by second liens otherwise subordinated to other loans.

Sum of squares error (SSE) A measure of the total deviation between observed and estimated values of the dependent variable. It is calculated by subtracting each estimated value $\hat{Y}_i$ from its corresponding observed value Y_i, squaring each of these differences, and then summing all of these squared differences.

Sum of squares regression (SSR) A measure of the explained variation in the dependent variable, calculated as the sum of the squared differences between the predicted value of the dependent variable, Yˆ_i, based on the estimated regression line, and the mean of the dependent variable, Y¯.

Sum of squares total (SST) A measure of the total variation in the dependent variable in a simple linear regression. It is calculated by subtracting the mean of the observed values $\bar{Y}$ from each of the observed values Y_i, squaring each of these differences, and then summing all of these squared differences.

Sunk costs A cost that has already been incurred.

Supervised learning A type of machine learning in which the system attempts to learn to model relationships based on labeled training data.

Supervisory board In some jurisdictions, a corporation's board of directors is formally composed of a supervisory board and a management board. The supervisory board appoints and oversees the management board and often includes representatives of employees and other non-shareholder stakeholders.

Supply chain The sequence of processes involved in the creation and delivery of a physical product to the end customer, both within and external to a firm, regardless of whether those steps are performed by a single firm.

Supply shock A typically unexpected disturbance to supply.

Survivorship bias Relates to the inclusion of only current investment funds in a database. As such, the returns of funds that are no longer available in the marketplace (have been liquidated) are excluded from the database. Also see *backfill bias*.

Swap A firm commitment involving a periodic exchange of cash flows.

Swap contract An agreement between two parties to exchange a series of future cash flows.

Swap execution facility (SEF) A swap trading platform accessed by multiple **dealers**.

Swap rate The fixed rate to be paid by the fixed-rate payer specified in a swap contract.

Syndicate A group of lenders, typically made up of banks.

Synthetic protective put The combination of a synthetic long underlying position (i.e., a long forward and risk-free borrowing) and a purchased put on the underlying.

Systematic risk Risk that affects the entire market or economy; it cannot be avoided and is inherent in the overall market. Systematic risk is also known as *non-diversifiable* or *market risk*.

Systematic sampling A procedure of selecting every *k*th member until reaching a sample of the desired size. The sample that results from this procedure should be approximately random.

Systemic risk Refers to risks supervisory authorities believe are likely to have broad impact across the financial market infrastructure and affect a wide swath of market participants.

Tactical asset allocation A proactive strategy that adjusts asset class allocations within a portfolio based on short-term market trends, economic conditions, or valuation changes to capitalize on temporary market inefficiencies or opportunities to improve returns or manage risk more effectively.

Target capital structure Management's desired proportions of debt and equity financing, usually stated on a book value basis or indirectly using a financial leverage metric, such as net or gross debt to EBITDA or credit rating.

Target independent A bank's ability to determine the definition of inflation that they target, the rate of inflation that they target, and the horizon over which the target is to be achieved.

Target semideviation A measure of downside risk, calculated as the square root of the average of the squared deviations of observations below the target (also called *target downside deviation*).

Tariffs Taxes that a government levies on imported goods.

Tax base The amount at which an asset or liability is valued for tax purposes.

Tax expense An aggregate of an entity's income tax payable (or recoverable in the case of a tax benefit) and any changes in deferred tax assets and liabilities. It is essentially the income tax payable or recoverable if these had been determined based on accounting profit rather than taxable income.

Taxable income The portion of an entity's income that is subject to income taxes under the tax laws of its jurisdiction.

Taxable temporary differences Temporary differences that result in a taxable amount in a future period when determining the taxable profit as the balance sheet item is recovered or settled.

Technical analysis A form of security analysis that uses price and volume data, often displayed graphically, in decision making.

Tender offer A solicitation by a current or prospective shareholder to other shareholders to acquire a substantial percentage, including 100%, of shares at a specified price. This action is usually undertaken by a potential acquirer whose bid was rejected by the issuer's board of directors, prompting the potential acquirer to appeal directly to shareholders.

Tenor Remaining time-to-maturity for a fixed-income instrument.

Term repos Repos with a maturity longer than one day.

Term structure of interest rates Also known as the maturity structure of interest rates, refers to the difference in interest rates or benchmark yields by time-to-maturity.

Terminal stock value The expected value of a share at the end of the investment horizon—in effect, the expected selling price. Also called *terminal value*.

Terminal value The expected value of a share at the end of the investment horizon—in effect, the expected selling price.

Test of the mean of the differences A statistical test for differences based on paired observations drawn from samples that are dependent on each other.

Text analytics Involves the use of computer programs to analyze and derive meaning typically from large, unstructured text- or voice-based datasets, such as company filings, written reports, quarterly earnings calls, social media, email, internet postings, and surveys.

Thematic risks Known risks that evolve and expand over a period of time. Climate change, pattern migration, the rise of populist forces, and the ongoing threat of terrorism fall into this category.

Thin-tailed Describes a distribution that has relatively less weight in the tails than the normal distribution (also called platykurtic).

Tiered pricing A pricing approach that charges different prices to different buyers, commonly based on volume purchased.

Timberland investment management organizations Entities that support institutional investors by managing their investments in timberland by analyzing and acquiring suitable timberland holdings.

Time tranching Structure of a securitization that allows for the redistribution of "prepayment risk" among bond classes by creating bond classes of different expected maturities.

Time value The difference between an option's premium and its intrinsic value.

Time value decay The process by which the time value of an option declines toward zero as the option's expiration date is approached.

Time-weighted rate of return The compound rate of growth of one unit of currency invested in a portfolio during a stated measurement period; a measure of investment performance that is not sensitive to the timing and amount of withdrawals or additions to the portfolio.

Tokenization The process of representing ownership rights to physical assets on a blockchain or distributed ledger.

Top-down analysis An investment selection approach that begins with consideration of macroeconomic conditions and then evaluates markets and industries based upon such conditions.

Total probability rule for expected value A rule explaining the expected value of a random variable in terms of expected values of the random variable conditional on mutually exclusive and exhaustive scenarios.

Total return Measures the price appreciation, or percentage change in price of the securities in an index or portfolio, plus any income received over the period.

Total return index An index that reflects the price appreciation or percentage change in price of the constituent securities plus any income received since inception.

Total working capital The difference between current assets and current liabilities.

Tracking error The standard deviation of the differences between a portfolio's returns and its benchmark's returns; a synonym of active risk.

Tracking risk The standard deviation of the differences between a portfolio's returns and its benchmarks returns. Also called *tracking error*.

Trade creation When regional integration results in the replacement of higher cost domestic production by lower cost imports from other members.

Trade diversion When regional integration results in lower-cost imports from non-member countries being replaced with higher-cost imports from members.

Trade sale A portion or division of a private company sold via either direct sale or auction to a strategic buyer interested in increasing the scale and scope of an existing business.

Trade settlement date The date when the buyer and seller transfer consideration and securities.

Traditional investment markets Markets for traditional investments, which include all publicly traded debts and equities and shares in pooled investment vehicles that hold publicly traded debts and/or equities.

Tranches A grouping of securities within an issue with characteristics that vary from other tranches, such as different credit quality and seniority.

Transfer payments Welfare payments made through the social security system that exist to provide a basic minimum level of income for low-income households.

Transition risks Economic and financial losses from the transition to a lower-carbon economy in response to climate change—for example, the abandonment of an oil well that is no longer economical.

Treasury Inflation-Protected Securities (TIPS) US Treasury bonds with a principal that is adjusted for changes in the Consumer Price Index. TIPS are issued in 5-, 10-, and 30-year maturities.

Treynor ratio A measure of risk-adjusted performance that relates a portfolio's returns in excess of the risk-free rate to a portfolio's beta.

Trimmed mean A mean computed after excluding a stated small percentage of the lowest and highest observations.

Triparty repo A repurchase agreement in which the transacting parties agree to use a third-party agent that provides access to a larger collateral pool and multiple counterparties, as well as valuation and safekeeping of assets.

True yield Measures on fixed-income instruments use actual payment dates, accounting for weekends and holidays. The true yield on an instrument is always lower than the street convention yield.

Turn-of-the-year effect Calendar anomaly that stock market returns in January are significantly higher compared to the rest of the months of the year, with most of the abnormal returns reported during the first five trading days in January.

Two-fund separation theorem The theory that all investors regardless of taste, risk preferences, and initial wealth will hold a combination of two portfolios or funds: a risk-free asset and an optimal portfolio of risky assets.

Two-way table A table of the frequency distribution of observations classified on the basis of two discrete variables. Also known as *Contingency table.*

Two-week repo rate The interest rate on a two-week repurchase agreement; may be used as a policy rate by a central bank.

Type I error The error of rejecting a true null hypothesis; a false positive.

Type II error The error of not rejecting a false null hypothesis; false negative.

Uncommitted lines of credit Sources of bank credit that a bank can refuse to honor. Uncommitted credit lines are made up to a certain principal amount for a pre-determined maximum maturity, charging a market reference rate plus an issuer-specific spread on only the principal outstanding for the period of use.

Underfitted When a machine learning model treats true parameters as if they are noise and is unable to recognize relationships in the training data, making the model more likely to fail to fully discover patterns that underlie the data.

Underlying The asset referred to in a **derivative contract**.

Underwritten offering A type of securities issue mechanism in which the investment bank guarantees the sale of the securities at an offering price that is negotiated with the issuer. Also known as *firm commitment offering*.

Unearned revenue A liability account for money that has been collected for goods or services that have not yet been delivered; payment received in advance of providing a good or service. Also called *deferred revenue* or *deferred income.*

Unimodal A distribution with a single value that is most frequently occurring.

Unit economics The expression of revenues and costs on a per-unit basis.

Unitranche debt A hybrid or blended loan structure combining different tranches of secured and unsecured debt into a single loan with a single, blended interest rate.

Unsecured Without collateral; unsecured debt is backed only by cash flows of the issuer.

Unsponsored A type of depository receipt in which the foreign company whose shares are held by the depository has no involvement in the issuance of the receipts.

Unsupervised learning A type of machine learning in which the system tries to learn the structure of unlabeled data.

Utility tokens Tokens that provide services within a network, such as paying for services and network fees.

Validity instructions Instructions which indicate when the order may be filled.

Value added resellers Businesses that distribute a product and also handle more complex aspects of product installation, customization, service, or support.

Value at risk A money measure of the minimum value of losses expected during a specified time period at a given level of probability.

Value chain The systems and processes in a firm that create value for its customers.

Value proposition The product or service attributes valued by a firm's target customer that lead those customers to prefer that firm's offering.

Value-add real estate strategies Strategies that involve larger-scale redevelopment and repositioning of existing assets and that may allow the investor to earn a higher return compared with core-plus real estate strategies.

Value-based pricing Pricing set primarily by reference to the value of the product or service to customers.

VaR See *value at risk.*

Variance The expected value (the probability-weighted average) of squared deviations from a random variable's expected value.

Variance of a random variable The expected value (the probability-weighted average) of squared deviations from a random variable's expected value.

Variation margin The difference between current margin required and the current collateral price in a repurchase agreement.

Vega A measure of the sensitivity of an option's price to changes in the underlying's volatility.

Velocity The pace at which geopolitical risk impacts an investor portfolio.

Venture capital Private equity investment in a startup or early-stage company involving high risk and a high rate of failure.

Venture capital fund A hedge fund that seeks to buy, optimize, and ultimately sell portfolio companies to generate profits. See *private equity fund.*

Venture debt Private debt funding that provides venture capital backing to start-up or early-stage companies that may be generating little or negative cash flow.

Vest To become unconditionally entitled to.

Vesting date The day that an employee becomes unconditionally entitled to compensation.

Vintage year The year in which a private capital fund makes its first investment.

Volatility The standard deviation of the continuously compounded returns on the underlying asset.

Vote by proxy A mechanism that allows a designated party—such as another shareholder, a shareholder representative, or management—to vote on the shareholder's behalf.

Voting rights The power of shareholders to cast votes in corporate elections for directors and other matters submitted to a shareholder vote.

Warrant Debt feature or security granting the right to purchase additional common equity shares issued by the company at a predetermined price for a given period.

Waterfall structures These represent the distribution order for cash flows and risk to different tranches in a financing structure.

Weak-form efficient market hypothesis The belief that security prices fully reflect all past market data, which refers to all historical price and volume trading information.

Weighted average coupon rate (WAC) Rate calculated for a mortgage pass-through security by weighting the mortgage rate of each mortgage in the pool by the percentage of the outstanding mortgage balance relative to the outstanding amount of all the mortgages in the pool.

Weighted average maturity (WAM) Calculated for a mortgage pass-through security by weighting the remaining number of months to maturity of each mortgage in the pool by the outstanding mortgage balance relative to the outstanding amount of all the mortgages in the pool.

Weighted-average cost of capital (WACC) A weighted average of the after-tax required rates of return on a company's equity, debt, preferred stock, and other long-term financing sources, where the weights are the fraction of each source of financing in the company's current market value or management's target capital structure.

Winsorized mean A mean computed after assigning a stated percentage of the lowest values equal to one specified low value and a stated percentage of the highest values equal to one specified high value.

Write-off/liquidation Refers to a transaction that has not gone well, and the investment is likely to lose value. The private equity firm revises the value of its investment downward or liquidates the portfolio company.

Yield curve A graphical depiction of yields-to-maturity of bonds from the same issuer across maturities.

Yield spread The difference in yield-to-maturity between a bond and that of a another bond.

Yield-to-call An internal rate of return on a fixed-income instrument's cash flows assuming cash flows are received on scheduled dates and the bond is called at a certain call price and date.

Yield-to-maturity Internal rate of return on a fixed-income instrument's cash flows assuming all cash flows are received on their scheduled dates.

Yield-to-worst The lowest among a fixed-income instrument's yields-to-call and yield-to-maturity. A commonly cited yield measure for fixed-rate callable bonds.

Z-spread or zero-volatility spread is a constant yield spread for a bond over a government or swap curve.

Zero-coupon bonds Bonds that do not pay interest during their life. They are issued at a discount to par value and redeemed at par. Also called pure discount bond.